Studies in Modern Chemistry

Advanced courses in chemistry are changing
rapidly in both structure and content. The changes
have led to a demand for up-to-date books that
present recent developments clearly and concisely.
This series is meant to provide advanced students
with books that will bridge the gap between the
standard textbook and the research paper. The
books should also be useful to a chemist who
requires a survey of current work outside his own
field of research. Mathematical treatment has been
kept as simple as is consistent with clear
understanding of the subject.
Careful selection of authors actively engaged in
research in each field, together with the guidance of
four experienced editors, has ensured that
each book ideally suits the needs of persons
seeking a comprehensible and modern treatment
of rapidly developing areas of chemistry.

William C. Agosta, The Rockefeller University
R. S. Nyholm, FRS, University College London

Consulting Editors

Academic editor for this volume

Lord Tedder, FRSE, University of St. Andrews

Studies in Modern Chemistry

Colour Chemistry

R. L. M. Allen

Imperial Chemical Industries Limited

Nelson

Thomas Nelson and Sons Ltd
36 Park Street London W1Y 4DE
P.O. Box 18123 Nairobi Kenya

Thomas Nelson (Australia) Ltd
597 Little Collins Street Melbourne 3000

Thomas Nelson and Sons (Canada) Ltd
81 Curlew Drive Don Mills Ontario

Thomas Nelson (Nigeria) Ltd
P.O. Box 336, Apapa, Lagos

Thomas Nelson and Sons (South Africa) (Proprietary) Ltd
51 Commissioner Street Johannesburg

First published in Great Britain 1971
Copyright © R. L. M. Allen 1971

17 761717 9

Printed by photo-lithography and made in Great Britain at the Pitman Press, Bath

Contents

Preface

Students embarking upon a colour chemistry course usually approach it by way of a general introduction and proceed to more detailed treatment of the subject when they have acquired some knowledge of its character and scope. This book has been written with the twofold purpose of serving as a guide to such students during the introductory part of their course and of supplying the needs in this field of others whose main interest is in a related branch of technology or pure chemistry. An attempt has been made to present the main features of the subject in an easily assimilable form. The great amount of published information renders the choice of material for a short book somewhat difficult, and I am keenly conscious of topics that might be thought worthy of more extensive treatment. However, a concise account cannot be comprehensive, and suggestions for further reading are provided at the end of the book.

The chemistry of colouring matters can be regarded as a branch of pure chemistry, but the development of knowledge in this field has followed a course determined chiefly by the applications of dyes and pigments. It has therefore appeared appropriate to treat the subject here as a branch of technology. Probably it is not generally realised that whereas the *Colour Index* includes about 3,250 dyes with published constitutions, the number of new dyes prepared for evaluation by a single member of a manufacturer's research staff in the course of his career may sometimes be comparable with or even greater than this. Commercial colouring matters represent a small selection from a very large number of experimental products, most of which are not described in published literature.

It is assumed that the reader possesses a knowledge of general chemistry corresponding to that normally attained at the outset of the final year of an ordinary degree course, and no attempt is made to cover the subject matter customarily included in such courses. Restriction of space has precluded the allocation of chapters to the chemistry of intermediates, but no difficulty should arise from this, since good accounts of the subject are readily accessible, and even the newer dyes are largely derived from intermediates of well-known classes.

The present work is in no way a history, but it relates to a subject that has developed enormously since the first synthetic dye was manufactured in 1856, and many discoveries of historical interest have been thought worthy of mention even though some of the products concerned are no longer in use. Improvements are still being made, and a few of the dyes quoted as examples in the earlier part of the book have recently been abandoned in favour of better ones.

Since most dyes and pigments were produced to meet the requirements of colour users the chemical structures adopted have been determined in part by the nature of the application processes. Some knowledge of these processes is therefore essential if the chemistry of colouring matters is to be understood, and for this reason textile and other application processes are briefly described.

Each chapter is provided with fairly plentiful literature references (listed at the end of the book), and a Bibliography contains suggestions for further reading. In general, the references to patent specifications, *BIOS* and *FIAT* reports provide details of processes and the other literature quoted gives wider background information. Students who have access to a good library are recommended to make themselves familiar with original literature. The pursuit of a subject by way of indexes (such as those of *Chemical Abstracts*), reviews and references quoted in the publications first consulted is absorbing, and a mature student will find such methods rewarding as a supplement to the study of recommended books.

Chemical nomenclature is a thorny subject, and usages established primarily for efficient storage and retrieval of information may not invariably be ideal for teaching purposes when comprehensibility is a main objective. Any departure in these pages from the recommendations of the International Union of Pure and Applied Chemistry is due to these considerations.

I thank Imperial Chemical Industries Ltd., Dyestuffs Division, for permission to write the book and the provision of excellent library facilities. Valuable advice has been given by many of my colleagues, and special acknowledgment is made of the practical help kindly given by Dr W. F. Beech, Dr A. H. Berrie, Dr G. Booth, Dr N. Corby, Dr W. Costain, Dr D. M. Fawkes, Mr M. St. C. Flett, Dr J. L. Leng, Mr A. Livingston, Dr E. Macdonald, Dr R. Price, Dr A. Parkinson, Dr D. W. Ramsay, Dr C. V. Stead, Mr J. Wardleworth and Dr D. G. Wilkinson. Dr R. R. Davies read the whole of the typescript and made many valuable suggestions; his constant interest is greatly appreciated, as is also that of Prof. Lord Tedder as Editor and the publishers, who have been invariably helpful. These acknowledgments would not be complete without mention of the authors quoted in the list of references and the Bibliography from whose works much information has been drawn.

I am grateful to my daughter, Miss Enid L. Allen, for assistance in proof correction.

R. L. M. Allen

Imperial Chemical Industries Limited
Dyestuffs Division
Hexagon House
Blackley
Manchester
M9 3DA

Note: Following long-established practice, the word 'shade' is used throughout this book as a noun meaning 'a variety of colour'. Recently, however, the Society of Dyers and Colourists decided that this use of the word is to be deprecated because of its lack of precision, and now recommends that where possible words such as 'colour', 'hue' or 'dyeing' be used instead. The use of the word 'shade' as a verb meaning 'to adjust the colour' is accepted.

Abbreviations

Publications

Ann.	Liebigs Annalen der Chemie
Ann. Phys. Chem.	Annalen der Physik und Chemie
Ber.	Berichte der Deutschen Chemischen Gesellschaft *or* Chemische Berichte
BIOS	Reports of British Intelligence Objectives Sub-committee
Bull. Soc. Mulhouse	Bulletin de la Société Industrielle de Mulhouse
C.A.	Chemical Abstracts
Chem. Z.	Chemiker-Zeitung
FIAT	Reports of Field Information Agency, Technical (US Group Control Council for Germany)
J.A.C.S.	Journal of the American Chemical Society
J.C.S.	Journal of the Chemical Society (London)
J.O.C.C.A.	Journal of the Oil and Colour Chemists' Association
J. Soc. Chem. Ind. Japan	Journal of the Society of Chemical Industry, Japan
J.S.D.C.	Journal of the Society of Dyers and Colourists
Rev. Text. Prog.	Review of Textile Progress
Text. Chem. and Colorist	Textile Chemist and Colorist

Abbreviations for the titles of other journals follow the practice of *Chemical Abstracts*

Manufacturers

ACNA	Aziende Colori Nazionali Affini A.C.N.A.
ACY	American Cyanamide Co.
BASF	Badische Anilin & Soda Fabrik A.G.
CAC	Clayton Aniline Co. Ltd, also CIBA Clayton Ltd
Cassella	Cassella Farbwerke Mainkur A.G.
CIBA	CIBA Ltd
DuP	E. I. du Pont de Nemours & Co. Inc.
FBy	Farbenfabriken Bayer A.G.
FH	Farbwerke Hoechst A.G.
Fran	Compagnie Française des Matières Colorantes
G	General Aniline & Film Corporation
Gy	J. R. Geigy S.A.
ICI	Imperial Chemical Industries Ltd
IG	I.G. Farbenindustrie A.G.
LBH	L. B. Holliday & Co. Ltd
MLB	Farbwerke vorm. Meister, Lucius & Brüning

NAC	National Aniline Division, Allied Chemical Corporation
S	Sandoz Ltd
SCI	Society of Chemical Industry, Basle (now CIBA)
YDC	Yorkshire Dyeware & Chemical Co. Ltd

Patents

Anm	Anmeldung
Belg	Belgian
Fr	French
Fr Addn	French Addition
DRP	German
UK	United Kingdom

Substituent Groups

Ac	Acetyl
Et	Ethyl
Me	Methyl
Ph	Phenyl
Pr	Propyl
R, R^1, etc.	A specified or unspecified substituent

Other Abbreviations

CI	Colour Index
SDC	The Society of Dyers and Colourists

Introduction

1-1 The physical basis of colour

Visible light represents a very small part of the electromagnetic spectrum, and corresponds roughly with radiations within the wavelength range 380–780 mμ (1 mμ = 10 Å = 10^{-7} cm). Daylight covers this range and extends into the ultraviolet region (less than 380 mμ), but its composition varies with the season, time of day and climatic conditions. The light from artificial illuminants is nominally white, but varies widely according to the type of lamp. There is a deficiency of blue in the light of tungsten lamps and of red in that of simple discharge lamps. Correction is possible by using filters to absorb the excess of red or blue, but this results in great loss of efficiency. In mercury-vapour lamps the red deficiency can be largely overcome by introducing fluorescent powders within the discharge tube which absorb very short waves and emit light of greater wavelength, so that a good approximation to daylight results. The human visual system is able to assess colours with some allowance for the deficiencies of artificial light, so that a white object is recognised as such even when seen in yellowish light.

The splitting of white light into its coloured components by a transparent prism, and the various ways in which coloured light can be produced by interference are familar phenomena. In systems of the latter type rays of light following slightly different paths are superimposed so that waves of a particular length are sufficiently retarded in the longer route to arrive out of phase with those traversing the shorter route; cancellation therefore occurs, and the remaining light is accordingly of a colour complementary to that eliminated. The colours of feathers and insects are sometimes due to a structure functioning as a diffraction grating, and such colours disappear if the structure is destroyed mechanically. Most coloured materials, however, owe their colour to the presence of substances that absorb light of a wavelength range within the visible portion of the spectrum, and this property is not destroyed by pulverisation.

The absorption of light by coloured substances is due to electronic transitions between different orbitals within the molecule, and the

1

wavelengths absorbed are determined by energy differences between the orbitals. Every dye or pigment therefore exhibits a pattern of absorption arising from its chemical structure, and this may be represented by an *absorption spectrum* consisting of a graph in which the degree of absorption is plotted as ordinate against wavelength (or frequency) as abscissa. This graph is characteristic of the colouring matter, and may be used for identification purposes. Since at a given wavelength the radiation transmitted is the difference between the incident radiation and that absorbed, the curve can be used equally well as a measure of transmission. Absorption spectra are normally determined from samples in solution. Dyed fibres and pigments in paint or other media absorb light in a characteristic pattern, and the unabsorbed light is mainly reflected rather than transmitted; in such cases, however, the physical form of the particles of colouring matter and substrate affect the nature of the reflected light.

The visible spectrum contains regions recognised by the human visual system in terms of colour, and the approximate wavelength ranges corresponding to the colours are shown in Table 1-1. When

Table 1-1   Relationship of colours observed to wavelengths of light absorbed

Light absorbed		Complementary colour seen
Wavelength (mμ)	Colour	
400–435	Violet	Green–Yellow
435–480	Blue	Yellow
480–490	Green–Blue	Orange
490–500	Blue–Green	Red
500–560	Green	Purple
560–580	Yellow–Green	Violet
580–595	Yellow	Blue
595–605	Orange	Green–Blue
605–750	Red	Blue–Green

light of a given colour is absorbed, the complementary colour (or remaining part of the incident light) is transmitted or reflected; thus a dye or pigment absorbing light within the blue range is seen in daylight as yellow. It should be noted that green light has no complementary spectral colour; the optical stimulus known as purple is the result of a mixture of red and violet light from the extremities of the visible spectrum.

The term 'white light' has no precise significance, since there are many pairs of pure spectral colours which when mixed produce a stimulus corresponding to that of white light. Some examples are shown in Table 1-2.

Table 1-2 Mixtures of pure spectral colours giving an optical stimulus corresponding to that of white light

Wavelength (mμ)	Colour	Stimulus produced
656	Red ⎫	White
492	Green–Blue ⎭	
608	Orange ⎫	White
490	Blue ⎭	
585	Orange–Yellow ⎫	White
485	Blue ⎭	
567	Yellow ⎫	White
464·5	Blue ⎭	
564	Green–Yellow ⎫	White
433	Violet ⎭	

The absorption spectrum of a dye may be complex, and the purity of the colour observed depends on the shape of the curve. Bright colours are the result of narrow absorption bands with sharp peaks, and dullness is associated with broader bands lacking such peaks. Non-spectral colours such as brown are associated with absorption spread fairly evenly over a wide wavelength range, and black is the result of absorption throughout the visible spectrum.

Many substances absorb radiation of wavelengths above and below the visible range, and the fact that such absorption does not give rise to a coloured appearance is due to the limited sensitivity of the eye rather than to any difference in principle. It is doubtful whether any significant improvement in vision would result from an extension of this sensitivity since radiations in the infra-red and ultra-violet regions are strongly absorbed by many materials.

In everyday life coloured materials are often described in loose terms, and at this point it will be well to set out the terms used by colour chemists. The characteristics of a coloured surface may be defined in respect of hue, brightness and strength. Its *hue* is determined by the predominant wavelength or wavelengths of the reflected light, described as yellow, red, blue, etc. Within each band the hue varies with wavelength, moving towards that of the next band in each direction; thus a blue becomes greenish as the wavelength is increased or reddish as it is decreased. It is said that about 150 different hues can be distinguished within the spectrum. *Brightness* may be regarded as a negative characteristic inasmuch as it depends on the absence of reflected light other than that of the hue concerned. *Strength* is inversely proportional to the amount of white light reflected by the surface and serving as a diluent. Although the spectral hues move from violet to red as the wavelength rises from 400–750 mμ, colour chemistry is concerned in practice with reflected or transmitted light, and the effective spectral range therefore consists of the complementary hues beginning with yellow and ending with green Hues are said to increase in *depth* as they move from yellow towards green; thus blue is deeper than red, red than orange and orange than yellow. Any change in a dye molecule causing the hue to move towards green is said to produce a *bathochromic* effect, and the reverse a *hypsochromic* effect. The latter is to be distinguished from a *hyperchromic* effect, which is an increase in the intensity of the absorption, that is, in the extinction coefficient of an absorption band; the reverse is a *hypochromic* effect.

Every known hue can be matched by a suitable mixture of monochromatic red, green and blue light; thus yellow light (wavelength 589 mμ) is indistinguishable by the eye from a suitable mixture of red (670·8 mμ) and green (535 mμ) light. Such mixing of coloured light is *additive,* and is brought about by illuminating a white surface by light of the required wavelengths either simultaneously or in rapid alternation. It is important to distinguish mixing of this kind from *subtractive* mixing, which results from using artists' colours in combination. If a yellow pigment (absorbing all except the yellow and green components of white light) is added to a blue pigment (absorbing all except green and blue light) the mixture appears green since this is the only component absorbed by neither constituent of the mixture. The primary colours of artists and colour photographers therefore differ from those of physicists; they are cyan (white less red), magenta (white less green) and yellow (white less blue).

Although spectrophotometry provides a detailed analysis of light reflected or transmitted by coloured material, it is inadequate as a means of defining colour sensation, since substances with quite different absorption curves may appear identical in colour. Colorimeters of various types have been developed, however, whereby a given colour can be defined in terms of three primary components (red, green and blue in an additive system, or cyan, magenta and yellow in a subtractive system). The subject of colorimetry is outside the scope of this book, but many books giving detailed information are available (see Bibliography).

1-2 Colour vision

Colour is an interpretation by the brain of signals received via the optic nerve from the eye in response to light (other than mixtures corresponding to white light) within an approximate wavelength range of 380–780 mμ. The human visual system is extremely complex, and in spite of much investigation it is still not fully understood. Within the eye an image is formed upon the retina, which contains a great number of photosensitive cells. These are of two main types, the *cones*, which require a high level of luminance, and the *rods*, which respond in conditions of low luminance. It has been estimated that the retina contains 6–7 million cones and 110–130 million rods. The cones are present in high concentration at the *fovea* (a small area near the centre of the retina which provides maximum acuity of vision) and are less densely packed in other parts of the retina. On the other hand rods are entirely absent from the fovea, but are present in increasing number as the distance from it becomes greater. The rods are of one kind only and do not distinguish colours, but cones are of several kinds and provide colour vision. In 1801 Young suggested that the retina contains colour receptors of three kinds, sensitive to red, yellow and blue; shortly afterwards he amended his theory in favour of receptors sensitive to red, green and blue, and on this basis the theory was developed further by Helmholtz in 1852. Several other theories have been put forward postulating receptors of six or seven types, but no histological evidence has been adduced. Granit, however, succeeded in detecting the response to light of varying wavelength by placing a minute electrode in contact with a single fibre of the optic nerve, and in experiments with various animals he found evidence of up to seven different types of photo-receptor. He called these receptors *modulators* and others showing a broad response to light of a wide wavelength range *dominators*. It is difficult to reconcile this evidence insofar as it relates to animals such as the cat with their failure to discriminate colours in behaviour tests. It is probable, however, that the human retina contains receptors with a narrow spectral response of at least seven types.

The response to light of receptor cells of the rod type appears to be associated with their content of the pigment *rhodopsin* (or

[1]

visual purple). This is a compound of 11-*cis* retinene [1] with the protein *opsin*. Under the action of light the pigment forms a series of coloured intermediate products and probably ultimately yields all-*trans* retinene (vitamin A aldehyde) and opsin. It has been shown that one of the intermediate products, *visual yellow*, is reconverted into visual purple in darkness. Numerous chemically related retinal pigments have been isolated from animals and fish of many kinds.

It is possible that cones also contain pigments necessary for their response to light, but none has yet been isolated. This may be because the cones are relatively few, or because suitable extraction techniques have not yet been devised. Among animals the ratio of rod and cone cells varies widely, depending largely on the conditions of luminance in which vision is chiefly required.

For an account of the mechanism by which the response of the receptors is conveyed to the brain the special literature of the subject should be consulted.[1]*

1-3   The early history of dye-making

The colouring matters of nature have always attracted man's interest, and in very early times he discovered ways of extracting them for application to his own articles. Mineral pigments have been used in various forms of art for thousands of years. Since most natural dyes have no direct affinity for textile materials they were applied by means of *mordants*, which functioned as fixing agents. The name is derived from the French *mordre*, and is based on an early belief that these agents corroded the fibre, opening the pores so that dye particles might enter; later it was recognised that mordants combined with dye molecules to form insoluble compounds or 'colour lakes'. Usually the mordant not only fixes the dye but is essential for colour formation, and a single vegetable dye may give a range of hues with different mordants. Metallic salts were used in this way in India about the year 2000 BC. At the same period natural indigo was well known in many parts of the world. It was obtained from the leaves of various species of *Indigofera* plants and applied by means of a fermentation vat, This was an early example of fixation by temporary solubilisation, in which the dye becomes soluble on reduction in the vat, is absorbed by the fibre to be dyed and then oxidised in air with re-formation of the insoluble blue dye.

The extraction of natural dyes became a substantial industry which flourished until the latter part of the 19th century when it was gradually superseded by the new synthetic dye industry. Of many hundreds of natural dyes known only a dozen or so now remain in limited use. Most of them are unable to compete commercially with

* References are listed at the end of the book starting on p. 301.

synthetic dyes because the extraction processes are unsuitable for large-scale operation, the products lack uniformity and their fastness properties are inadequate. A few people believe, however, that nature's products are invariably superior to man's, and enthusiasts for this principle still continue to use natural dyes in handicraft work.[2]

The only natural dye that is still in production on a large scale is *Logwood*. It is derived from the wood of the tree *Haematoxylon Campechianum*, which is cultivated, and also grows wild, in central America. When freshly cut the wood contains haematoxylin [2], the

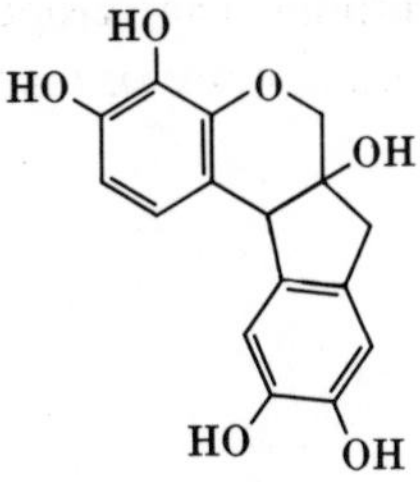

Haematoxylin
[2]

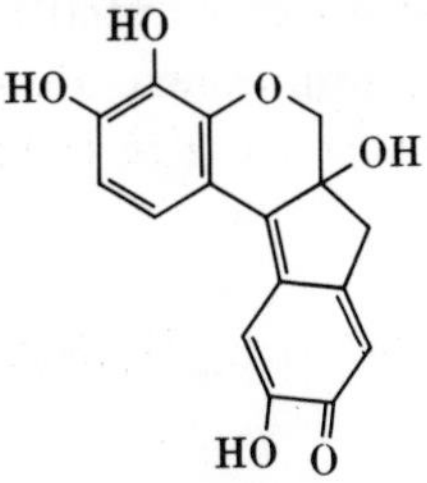

Haematein
[3]

leuco-compound of the colouring matter haematein [3]; oxidation to haematein occurs during ageing or is brought about by deliberate oxidation of the extract. Logwood is still used for dyeing wool, silk, nylon, viscose and acetate fibres, and gives cheap blacks of good fastness properties. The estimated consumption of logwood in the United States in 1964 exceeded 750,000 lb.

Long after most of the natural dyes had been abandoned commercially they retained the interest of chemists, and a great deal of work has been carried out on the determination of their structures. Several excellent books have been devoted to this subject, and there is no necessity for space to be devoted to it here except to describe dyes such as alizarin and indigo of which synthetic equivalents are manufactured; these are dealt with in the appropriate chapters.

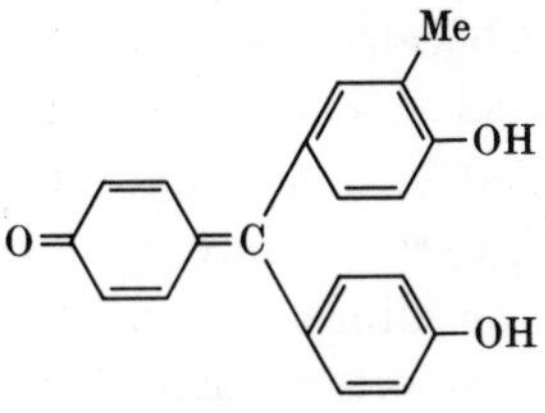

[4]

One of the earliest synthetic dyes was Rosolic acid, prepared by Runge in 1834 by oxidation of crude carbolic acid. This dye, having essentially the structure [4] (with a proportion of a methyl-free analogue), was not manufactured until after 1861, when it was obtained by heating phenol with oxalic acid and sulphuric acid; it was used chiefly in the form of a red lake for wallpaper printing, but is now obsolete. The foundation of the synthetic dye industry was laid in 1856, when William Henry Perkin at the age of 18 discovered the first commercial synthetic dye, *Mauveine*. The story has been told many times, but is worthy of inclusion here.

Not content with his work as Hofmann's assistant at the Royal College of Chemistry, Perkin set up a rough laboratory at his home at Shadwell, and worked there in the evenings and vacations. One of his projects was an attempted synthesis of quinine, the structure of which was then unknown. Perkin tried to obtain it by oxidation of allyltoluidine according to the scheme:

$$2C_{10}H_{13}N + 3O = C_{20}H_{24}N_2O_2 + H_2O$$

In the light of later information it is easy to see that this attempt could not succeed. He obtained only a dirty brownish product, but his curiosity led him to carry out another experiment with the simpler base crude aniline. From this he obtained a black precipitate (later found to be mainly Aniline Black), but by extracting this with alcohol he obtained a mauve dye, originally called *Aniline Purple* or *Tyrian Purple*. This was examined by Messrs Pullar of Perth and, encouraged by their guarded enthusiasm, Perkin determined to manufacture the dye. With the help of his father and brother he established a factory at Greenford Green in 1857, and there the first commercial synthetic dye was produced. Details of its chemistry are discussed in Chapter 8. French chemists were quick to appreciate the importance of Perkin's discovery, and as his French patent was invalid (because of an error in the date of filing) the French were able to manufacture his dye: it was they who gave it the name Mauveine by which it became generally known.

Research on synthetic dyes was pursued in many laboratories, and soon other basic dyes were discovered and manufactured in England, France and Germany. These were mainly triphenylmethanes, but later oxazines, thiazines, acridines and xanthenes were produced. The first commercially important azo dye was *Bismarck Brown*, manufactured in 1865. The history of the establishment of the synthetic dyestuffs industry is recorded in many publications, and these should be consulted for a fuller account than is possible here.

1-4   Classification of dyes

Dyes may be classified according to either their chemical structure or method of application. In many cases a particular chemical class includes dyes of several application classes, and similarly a particular application class may include dyes of varied chemical types. The present book is based on a chemical arrangement as far as possible, but it is convenient to describe vat dyes, pigments and solvent dyes as application classes, and to deal with the very numerous azo dyes partly in accordance with their usage.

The *Colour Index*[3] provides a comprehensive classification of known commercial dyes according to usage in Part 1 and constitution in Part 2. Dyes with published structures therefore appear in both parts, and others only in Part 1.

1-5   Primaries and intermediates

Since some of the earliest synthetic dyes were obtained from aniline, and aniline was known to be a constituent of coal tar, such dyes were loosely called 'aniline dyes' (whether or not they were actually derived from aniline) or 'coal-tar dyes'. The term 'synthetic dyes' is now preferred, since primaries are increasingly obtained from petroleum sources rather than from coal tar. The change is largely due to the replacement of coal gas by natural gas, which has been established in the United States for many years and is now taking place in the United Kingdom. Various processes whereby town gas is produced from oil are also in use.

Whatever their origin, reasonably pure chemical substances used as raw materials for the manufacture of dyes are called *primaries*. The most important of them are benzene, toluene, the xylenes, phenol, the cresols, naphthalene, anthracene and carbazole. Although aromatic compounds are present in petroleum the content is usually so low that they cannot be isolated economically. Borneo petroleum is exceptional in containing as much as 40% of aromatic hydrocarbons. The petroleum industry has developed several processes whereby aromatic compounds are obtained from non-aromatic fractions. The first of these were cracking processes, which were designed to bring about the cleavage of high-boiling components into more volatile fractions but which with the aid of suitable catalysts also enabled naphthenes to be dehydrogenated with formation of aromatic products. The application of these processes was limited by the content of suitable precursors in the natural oil, and they were chiefly of value for the production of fuel of increased octane rating. Later various *re-forming* processes were developed, making use of a wider range of aliphatic compounds and yielding lower-boiling aromatic products. Thus benzene is obtained by dehydrogenation of cycloparaffins (with removal of side-chains where necessary), by dehydrogenation with molecular rearrangement of methylcyclopentane or by dehydrogenation with cyclisation of n-hexane. Toluene is produced by several analogous processes, for example by dehydrogenation of methylcyclohexane in presence of a catalyst (molybdena–alumina, platinum, cobalt molybdate or chrome–alumina).

The Catarole process developed by Petrochemicals Ltd converts paraffinic hydrocarbons at 630°–680°C by means of a copper or copper–iron catalyst into a liquid product (36–54% of feedstock) which is almost entirely aromatic and a gas consisting mainly of ethylene and propylene. The aromatic products are essentially the same as those obtained from coal tar and compounds of lower molecular weight predominate.[4]

The proportions of benzene, toluene and the xylenes in the total production from petroleum are about 10:40:50, but the commercial demand is for a much larger amount of benzene. Several processes have been devised for demethylating toluene and xylene, either of which can be converted into benzene and methane by reaction with hydrogen in presence of a catalyst, such as chromium trioxide on alumina or platinum on alumina. The Thermal Hydro-dealkylation process (Gulf Research and Development Co.) is stated to convert toluene into benzene with at least 95% efficiency without a catalyst.[5]

By means of reactions such as nitration, reduction, halogenation, sulphonation, oxidation, carboxylation, amidation, caustic fusion, hydrolysis or the Friedel–Crafts reaction the primaries are converted into *intermediates*, i.e. colourless substances which by further reactions yield dyes. There may be several stages in the manufacture of a dye, and apart from the primaries all uncoloured substances contributing to the structure of the final dye are classed as intermediates. It is not unusual for a dye (especially an azo dye) to be converted by one or more further reactions into a more complex dye.

A description of the chemistry of primaries and intermediates would require a great deal of space and must therefore be excluded from this book. The great developments in dye chemistry during recent years have not called for a corresponding extension of the chemistry of intermediates, however, and accounts given in older textbooks are sufficient for many purposes even though they are not up-to-date.

Because of their somewhat cumbersome chemical names many intermediates (especially naphthalene derivatives used in manufacture of azo dyes) are commonly known by trivial names. This practice is convenient for those who are familar with it but puzzling to others. The structures of the commoner intermediates having such trivial names and an indication of their main uses are given in the Appendix (p. 300).

1-6 Dyes

Some attention has been given to the physical basis of colour. Coloured substances, however, are not necessarily dyes. A dye is a coloured substance that can be applied in solution or dispersion to a substrate, thus giving it a coloured appearance. Usually the substrate is a textile fibre, but it may be paper, leather, hair, fur, plastic material, wax, a cosmetic base or a foodstuff. In most cases the material to be dyed possesses a natural affinity for appropriate dyes and readily absorbs them from solution or aqueous dispersion under suitable conditions of concentration and temperature; the presence of auxiliary substances may be necessary to control the rate of dyeing, and pH must be suitably adjusted. Dyed fibres usually show some resistance to washing, but fastness properties vary considerably. The forces that give rise to dye–fibre affinity are discussed in Chapter 19.

1-6-1 Water-soluble dyes

Water-solubility is conferred on many dyes by the presence of at least one salt-forming group. The commonest of these is the sulphonic acid group; this is usually introduced into one or more of the intermediate compounds from which the dye is made, but sometimes an insoluble dye is sulphonated. The carboxylic acid group is used similarly, and this is always introduced into the intermediates concerned. Dyes solubilised by either of these groups are generally isolated as their sodium salts. They are described as *anionic* dyes, since it is the anion that is coloured;* this type includes both the Acid and Direct application classes which are used for nitrogenous and cellulosic fibres, respectively. Dyes containing basic groups form water-soluble salts with acids, and these are *cationic* dyes, since the coloured ion is positively charged. Sometimes both acidic and basic groups are present so that an internal salt, or *zwitterion* is formed.

---

* Other anionic systems are described in Chapter 5.

1-6-2 Water-insoluble dyes

There are various systems whereby water-insoluble dyes are applied to textile and other materials, and the dyes concerned may be classified as follows:

Dyes soluble in the substrate. These include *disperse* dyes, which are prepared as finely divided aqueous dispersions for application to synthetic fibres, and also *solvent-soluble* dyes. In this context the term includes organic solvents of all types, and the dyes are applied in media such as spirit and oil stains, varnishes, transparent lacquers, printing inks, waxes, polishes, soaps, cosmetics and petrol.

Temporarily solubilised dyes. These dyes are converted into a water-soluble form by chemical modification, applied to suitable fibres from aqueous solution, then re-converted into the insoluble form within the fibre. The *Vat* and *Sulphur* dyes are applied by means of this principle, both giving alkali-soluble reduction products with affinity for cellulosic fibres. The original insoluble dyes are restored by oxidation in air and the resulting dyeings have high fastness to wet treatments. Systems in which the solubilising groups are eliminated by hydrolysis during or after dyeing have also been used in dyes such as the *Ionamine* (British Dyestuffs Corp.) and *Neocotone* (Society of Chemical Industry, Basle) ranges, but these have now been superseded.

Polycondensation dyes. In recent years several ranges of self-condensing dyes have been developed and various names for the group are in use. The Colour Index Editorial Board is provisionally describing them as *Condense* dyes, and has defined them as 'dyes the molecules of which during or after application react covalently with each other or with molecules of another compound (other than the substrate) to form molecules of much increased size'. The first commercial dyes of this type were the *Inthion* colours (FH), which are said to form polymeric disulphides on the fibre by reaction of thiosulphuric acid groups with sodium sulphide:

$$n\ NaO_3S\text{---}SCH_2\text{---}Dye\text{---}CH_2S\text{---}SO_3Na + n\ Na_2S \rightarrow$$
$$[\text{---}SCH_2\text{---}Dye\text{---}CH_2S\text{---}]n + n\ Na_2SO_3 + n\ Na_2S_2O_3$$

The *Dykolite* dyes (Southern Dyestuff Co.) are of a similar type. Polycondensation dyes are described in Chapter 14.

Dyes formed within the fibre. The Azoic (or Insoluble Azo) dyes are produced by applying coupling and diazo components to cellulosic fibres either in succession or together so that azo pigment particles are formed in cavities within the fibre structure. The particles are caused to aggregate by a subsequent hot soaping, so that they become firmly fixed and are resistant to wet treatments.

Phthalocyanine dyes can be produced on the fibre by applying a precursor such as aminoiminoisoindole with a copper or nickel salt and a reducing agent and then baking or steaming. In an improved process metal complexes of polyisoindolines have been applied similarly, and the *Phthalogen* dyes (FBy) (see Section 15-5) are products of this type.

Mordant dyes of the alizarin type (Section 9-2) and basic dyes applied to cotton mordanted with tannic acid or a synthetic agent (Chapter 8) are properly included in this group since they are converted into insoluble derivatives within the fibre.

Pigments. Pigments differ from dyes in that they have no affinity for fibres or other substrates, and whereas dyes may form aggregates containing a few molecules a typical pigment particle with a diameter of about 1 μ contains a very large number of molecules. Pigments are applied in the form of a suspension in a drying oil or a resinous vehicle in which they are insoluble or in a plastic supporting medium. From some points of view it is convenient to treat dyes and pigments separately, but since pigments are used for colouring synthetic fibres it is necessary to include them in the present classification. Water-insoluble dyes formed upon the fibre (see above) are pigments in specialised applications. Other applications of pigments are dealt with in Chapters 15 and 16.

2 Colour and constitution

When Perkin manufactured the first synthetic dye in 1857 little
was known of the chemistry of dyes, and, in fact, the constitution of
Perkin's Mauveine was not established until many years later. As
more and more dyes were discovered and their chemistry was
studied, working rules emerged whereby colour and dyeing properties could be related with structure. Some of the more important
contributions to the development of the subject are now briefly
discussed.

In 1868 Graebe and Liebermann[1] observed that all organic dyes
then known were decolorised on reduction, and they suggested that
colour is associated with unsaturation. In 1876 Witt[2] extended this
view by pointing out that the colour of organic dyes is associated
with the presence of certain groups of atoms, which he called
chromophores. Examples of these include the nitro, nitroso, azo,
ethylene and carbonyl groups, and it will be seen that all are unsaturated. Witt gave the name *chromogens* to compounds containing
such groups, and showed that although they are coloured, they do
not behave as dyes for the natural fibres unless they are also substituted by basic or weakly acidic groups such as $-NH_2$, $-NH(CH_3)$,
$-N(CH_3)_2$ or $-OH$. The presence of groups of this kind greatly
increases the colour-yielding power of a chromophore, and for this
reason they became known as *auxochromes*.

In 1879 Nietzki[3] pointed out that the colour of dyes is deepened
by addition of substituents, and that the effect is roughly proportional to the increase in molecular weight. Certain groups have a
hypsochromic effect, however, and there are many exceptions to
this rule. The next major development was the quinonoid theory
advanced by H. E. Armstrong[4] in 1888. He showed that most
dyes can be represented in a quinonoid form, and suggested that
this type of structure gives rise to colour, but did not attempt to
explain why.

The view that colour might be due to 'rhythmic vibrations in the
ether' caused by an oscillation of the quinonoid condition between
two benzene rings was put forward by A. Baeyer[5] in 1907. In the

same year Hewitt and Mitchell[6] observed that in azo dyes the
depth of colour increases with the length of a chain of alternating
single and double bonds (called a 'conjugated chain'), and ascribed
this effect to diminution in the frequency of the chief oscillation.
The soundness of this generalisation was confirmed in quantitative
experiments by Watson and Meek.[7] More recently Brooker and his
co-workers[8] found that in a series of methine dyes of general structure

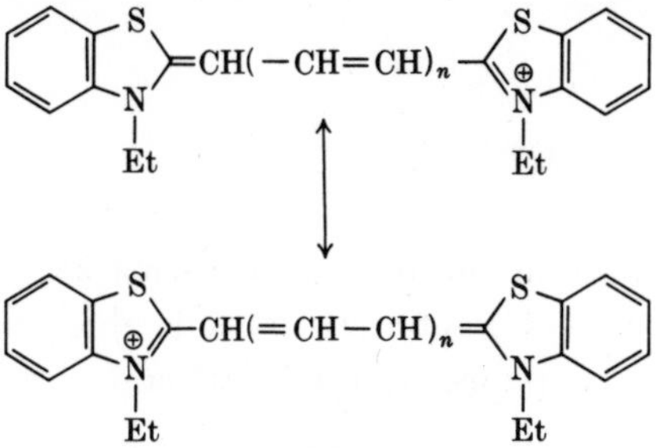

[5]

[5] in which n has values of 0, 1, 2 and 3 the wavelengths of absorption maxima in methanol solution are 423, 557·5, 650 and 758 mμ,
respectively; after the first shift, the increments are thus nearly
uniform.

Watson[9] pointed out that the depth of colour is affected by
other factors besides the length of conjugated chain reversed. If the
dye molecule is weighted without altering the length of conjugated
chain, vibrations become slower and the shade is rendered bluer;
thus on brominating fluorescein, eosine (Section 8-6) is obtained,
with a much deeper hue. The system may be likened to a stretched
string, whose vibrations are slowed by increase in either its length
or weight (keeping tension constant). The presence of an additional
auxochrome (as in polyhydroxyanthraquinones) usually has a
marked deepening influence on hue, and a pronounced effect also
often results from modification of an auxochrome as when an amino
group is alkylated or arylated.

Whereas Baeyer had visualized the oscillation of an atom in the
molecule of Döbner's Violet, Adams and Rosenstein[10] in describing

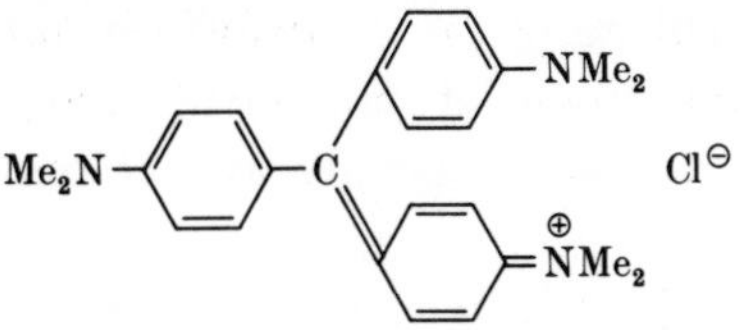

[6]

a study of Crystal Violet [6] commented that the vibration might
involve only an electron. In 1935 Bury[11] pointed out that the

distinction between electrovalent and covalent bonds which had become known since Baeyer's time enabled the oscillation in Döbner's Violet to be regarded as a case of resonance:

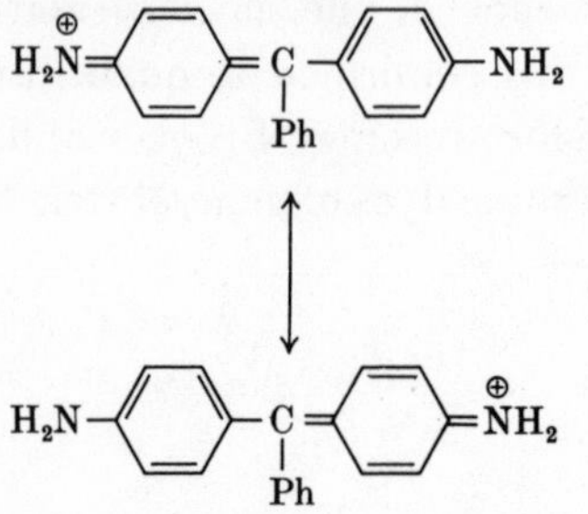

He re-stated Baeyer's hypothesis in more modern terms as: 'The intense absorption of light that characterizes dyes is due to an intimate association of a chromophore and of resonance in the molecule'.

In Döbner's Violet the structures are identical, but this is not so in the case of an unsymmetrical dye, such as Methyl Violet (Section 8-2-3), in which the possibilities of oscillation are more complex. In basic dyes of this kind resonance is associated with the cation, but in dyes such as benzaurine [7] it is in the anion:

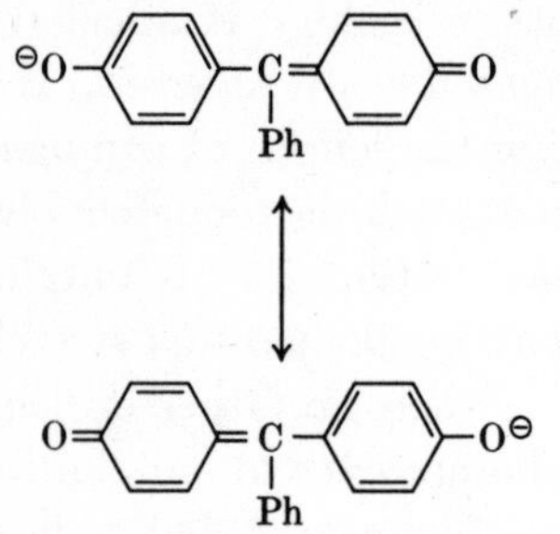

[7]

In either case an auxochrome is required to enable resonance of the type postulated to take place.

An auxochrome may also serve to bring about a shift in the main absorption band from the ultra-violet into the visible part of the spectrum, so that a colourless substance is transformed into a coloured one. Affinity for natural fibres is dependent upon the presence of an auxochrome, but dyeing properties and colour are not directly related.

Although most dyes contain an auxochrome the presence of such a group is not essential. Many vat dyes, for example, which usually contain two or more keto groups as chromophores, have no auxo-chrome. These dyes are insoluble in water, but on reduction phenolic hydroxyl groups are formed from the keto groups so that alkali-soluble derivatives are produced in the vat. At this stage the hydroxyl groups can function as auxochromes and for this reason the vat may be deeply coloured, but after the reduced dye has been adsorbed by the fibre it is reoxidised to its original keto form and the auxochromic groups are thereby eliminated. The resulting water-insoluble dye is usually strongly coloured, but may be lighter in hue in comparison with the reduced form.

It is now usual to regard the molecule of a dye as consisting of a chromophoric system in which the classical chromophore forms part of a conjugated chain of single and double bonds, often terminating in a polar atom or group (the classical auxochrome) which can exist in two adjacent states of covalency. There may be two terminal polar groups, or more in complex dyes. In such systems there are two or more extreme structures, and the transition from one to another takes the form of an electron surge through the conjugated chain (with reversal of the bonds in its links). Pauling[12] pointed out that the passage of an electron is likely to occur in stages, so that there must be a series of intermediate structures. At each stage a carbon atom becomes positively charged, and there is a temporary deficiency in the system of one or two double bonds in relation to the extreme structures. The intermediate stages are higher in energy than the extremes. According to this conception the molecule becomes 'excited' by the absorption of light with increase in electronic energy, and tends to assume intermediate structures. The difference in energy levels determines the wavelength of light absorbed, and the observed colour of the dye corresponds to its complement.

A mathematical analysis of resonance between members of a series of ionic structures in polymethine and other dyes has been carried out by means of the *valence bond* method,[13] and the results of this work are in good agreement with observed absorption characteristics of the dyes concerned.[14] The complexity of this treatment is unfortunately such that it is impracticable to use it for quantitative prediction of absorption maxima.

The problem has been approached with greater success in a different way by the *molecular orbital* method, and the principles concerned are now described.

The energy of a molecule includes components derived from (a) the motions of electrons around their nuclei, (b) vibration of atoms within the molecule, (c) rotation of the molecule and (d) energy transitions within the atomic nuclei. A given molecule possesses a series of energy levels, and can take up or lose energy in steps corresponding to the differences between the various levels. The electronic energy levels are comparatively widely separated and lead to the absorption of ultra-violet and visible light; vibrational levels are closer and transitions between them correspond to absorption in the near infra-red; rotational levels represent subdivisions of the vibrational levels, and their small differences account for absorption in the far infra-red and microwave regions.

According to the principles of quantum mechanics, although electrons behave in some respects as particles they also exhibit the properties of waves. The electron may be assigned a wave-function (a complex function of position and time), defined in simple cases by the solution of Schrödinger's fundamental equation. This means that the energy of the electron can only have certain discrete values. It follows that there is a series of fixed energy levels which may be occupied by an electron, and these are known as orbitals. For each orbital there is a region in space where an electron is likely to be found, and may be represented as a series of three-dimensional figures showing the distribution of ψ. These figures do not define precise limits to electron movement, but for a small volume ψ^2 represents the probability that the electron will be in that volume at any one instant.

A series of orbitals is associated with every atom, and the energy of an electron determines which of them it may occupy. The Pauli Exclusion Principle permits each to be occupied by a maximum of two electrons spinning in opposite directions. A molecular orbital (MO) is formed by the overlapping of outer singly occupied orbitals of two or more atoms, and several types may be distinguished, each having a characteristic shape, size and energy; these are denoted by symbols such as σ, σ^*, π or π^*. Atomic orbitals that are incapable of combination such as those containing inner shell or 'lone-pair' electrons are described as non-bonding (n).

In a homo- or hetero-nuclear diatomic molecule AB the atomic orbitals interact with formation of a molecular orbital MO_{AB} which may be expressed mathematically as a linear combination

$$MO_{AB} = a\psi_A + b\psi_B \tag{2-1}$$

where a and b are weighting coefficients. In a homonuclear molecule in which A = B the ratio a/b is ± 1, but in a heteronuclear molecule two ratios are obtained differing in magnitude as well as in sign. In each case MO_{AB} has two possible values and accordingly there are two orbitals. The wave-function is a measure of amplitude, and the two values correspond to conditions in which the atomic orbitals are in phase (giving a low-energy MO) or out of phase (giving a high-energy MO). When a/b is positive the electron density is at a maximum between the two nuclei, resulting in an attractive state, and the MO is of the bonding type; when a/b is negative electron density between the nuclei is low, leading to repulsion, and the MO is then antibonding.

In the lowest or ground electronic state of most organic molecules all the bonding and non-bonding orbitals are fully occupied and the antibonding orbitals are empty. Absorption of a quantum of energy of a wavelength within the visible spectrum causes a σ or π bonding electron associated with a covalent bond or a non-bonding n electron to be promoted to an empty antibonding level, thus bringing about an electronically excited state. In simple molecules the electronic energy levels may be represented as follows (the use of an asterisk indicating an antibonding orbital):

$$\Delta E \left\{ \begin{array}{ll} \sigma^* \ \underline{\hspace{3cm}} \\ \pi^* \ \underline{\hspace{3cm}} \end{array} \right\} \text{antibonding orbitals} \\ \quad n \ \underline{\hspace{3cm}} \quad \text{non-bonding orbitals} \\ \left. \begin{array}{ll} \pi \ \underline{\hspace{3cm}} \\ \sigma \ \underline{\hspace{3cm}} \end{array} \right\} \text{bonding orbitals}$$

Whereas in the bonding levels π electrons have higher energy than σ electrons the reverse is the case in antibonding levels. Transitions of the type $n \rightarrow \pi^*$ normally give rise to spectral bands at longer wavelengths than those due to transitions $\pi \rightarrow \pi^*$ or $\sigma \rightarrow \sigma^*$ (the latter being usually in the far ultra-violet region). In dye molecules the situation is more complex since there are as many π levels as there are conjugated atoms.

The energy gain (ΔE) is in the first approximation equal to the energy difference between the two molecular orbitals concerned in the transition, and is related to the wavelength (λ) of the light absorbed by the equation:

$$\Delta E = E_{\Psi_A} - E_{\Psi_D} = \frac{hc}{\lambda} \tag{2-2}$$

where ψ_A and ψ_D are acceptor and donor orbitals, respectively, h is Planck's constant and c is the velocity of light.

Since the capacity of coloured substances for storage of the energy derived from the absorption of light is clearly limited, it must be assumed that it is lost by transformation into heat, by luminescence or by degradation of the molecule. Fading on exposure to light varies according to the extent of such degradation.

The treatment outlined, known as the *linear combination of atomic orbitals* (*LCAO*) method, has been applied with considerable success to account qualitatively for the positions and intensities of the absorption bands in many dye molecules.

The *free electron* method provides a somewhat simpler approach by restricting attention to the conjugated π electron systems, which are regarded as mainly responsible for the colour of dyes. Assuming that electrons are free to move within the conjugated system, Kuhn[15] showed that the wavelength of the maximum of the first absorption band (λ_1) can be calculated by means of the expression

$$\lambda_1 = \frac{8mcL^2}{h(n+1)} \tag{2-3}$$

where m is the mass of an electron, c is the velocity of light, L is the length of the conjugated chain, h is Planck's constant and n is the number of π electrons. Calculations by this method have shown good agreement with observed values of λ for several cyanine and triphenylmethane dyes, and it may become of practical value in the study of dyes of other classes.

More comprehensive descriptions of this subject will be found in several recent reviews (see Bibliography).

The chemistry of azo dyes

Azo dyes are characterised by presence in the molecule of one or more azo groups —N = N—, which form bridges between organic residues, of which at least one is usually an aromatic nucleus. Many methods are available for preparing azo compounds, but manufacture of azo dyes is always based on the coupling of diazonium compounds with phenols, naphthols, arylamines, pyrazolones or other suitable components to give hydroxyazo or aminoazo compounds or their tautomeric equivalents. In the resulting dyes the azo group is the chromophore and the hydroxyl or amino group is an auxochrome.

The importance of azo dyes is shown by the fact that they account for over 60% of the total number of dye structures known to be manufactured. A full range of shades is available, but on hydrophilic fibres the blues and greens lack fastness to light unless they are metallised; the metallised derivatives have dull shades. The chemistry of these dyes ranges from simple monoazo compounds to complex polyazo structures with a molecular weight of 1800 or more, and their properties vary accordingly.

Azo chemistry is founded on the work of Peter Griess, who discovered the diazo compounds in 1858,[1] and later prepared many dyes derived from them. One of these was 4-aminoazobenzene, which became the first commercial azo dye, manufactured in England in 1863 and marketed under the name *Aniline Yellow*;[2] its constitution was unknown at the time, but was established by Martius and Griess[3] in 1866. This dye had poor properties, but another dye discovered by Martius and manufactured in the same year under the name *Manchester Brown* and later called *Bismarck Brown* is still in use. It has the structure [8].

The earlier azo dyes were obtained by treating arylamines in acid solution with half of an equivalent amount of nitrous acid, so that part of the base was diazotised and the remainder served as coupling component. A different coupling component was first

$$\text{H}_2\text{N} - \underset{\text{NH}_2}{\bigcirc} - \text{N} = \text{N} - \bigcirc - \text{N} = \text{N} - \underset{\text{H}_2\text{N}}{\bigcirc} - \text{NH}_2$$

[8]

used in 1876 when *Chrysoidine* was manufactured by coupling diazotised aniline with an equivalent proportion of *m*-phenylenediamine. Soon afterwards Roussin introduced a series of orange dyes known as *Oranges I, II, III* and *IV*, obtained by coupling diazotised sulphanilic acid with α-naphthol, β-naphthol, *N,N*-dimethylaniline and diphenylamine, respectively, and the success of these dyes stimulated rapid development of the chemistry of azo dyes and the use of naphthalene derivatives. In 1879 Nietzki obtained the first disazo dye by coupling diazotised 4-aminoazobenzene-3,4'-disulphonic acid with β-naphthol, and it was manufactured by Kalle & Co. under the name *Biebrich Scarlet*. A disazo dye of a different type was prepared two years later by Wallach, who coupled one molecule of diazotised crude xylidine and one molecule of diazotised sulphanilic acid with resorcinol. This dye was called *Resorcin Brown*, and it is still used for application to leather.

The dyes manufactured up to 1884 were applied to wool or silk from weakly acid baths, but cotton could be dyed only after preliminary treatment with a mordant. The fibre was treated in a bath of tannic acid solution, then with a solution of tartar emetic so that antimony tannate was precipitated within the fibre; this compound reacted with basic dyes such as Bismarck Brown or Chrysoidine applied later to form insoluble coloured lakes, and the fibre so dyed showed some resistance to washing. The fastness to both washing and light was quite low, however. In 1884 Griess discovered that disazo dyes obtained by coupling tetrazotised benzidinedisulphonic acid with components such as naphthionic acid could be applied to cotton without a mordant.[4] The affinity of these dyes was low, but about two months later Böttiger discovered the first direct cotton dye of commercial value.[5] This was *Congo Red*, obtained by coupling one molecule of tetrazotised benzidine with two molecules of naphthionic acid, thus differing from Griess's dyes only in a lower content of sulphonic acid groups. The dye is highly sensitive to acids, and is well known as a laboratory indicator; it is also fugitive to light, but remains in restricted used as a cotton dye in spite of these faults.

Many other substantive dyes for cellulosic fibres have been manufactured, not only from benzidine and its derivatives but also from intermediates of other types. An almost complete range of shades has been produced, and at the same time fastness properties have been greatly improved. The introduction of a succession of synthetic fibres has led to a continued demand for new dyes, and azo dyes have been developed in great numbers for these applications.

An account of the chemistry of azo dyes is now given, and this is followed by a description of their main applications in Chapters 4–7.

3-1 Stereoisomerism

The presence of a double bond in azo compounds gives rise to stereoisomerism, and in certain cases there is evidence of the existence of *cis* and *trans* forms. Azobenzene, for example, can be isolated in two well defined forms [9] and [10] having different physical properties.

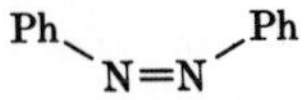

cis-azobenzene
m.p. 71·4°C
[9]

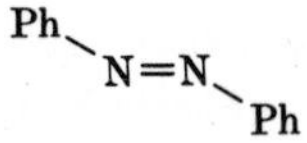

trans-azobenzene
m.p. 68°C
[10]

The *trans* is partially converted into the *cis* form on exposure to strong light, but the change is reversed during storage in darkness. In hydroxyazo dyes, *cis* forms are in general very unstable and have not so far been isolated. *o*-Hydroxyazo and *o*-aminoazo compounds are effectively locked in the *trans* structure by the presence of a hydrogen bond between the hydroxyl or amino group and an azo nitrogen atom [11, 12].

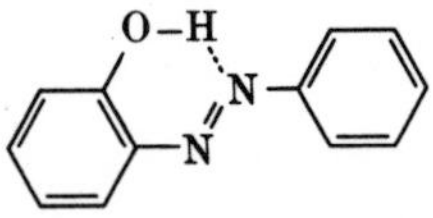

[11]

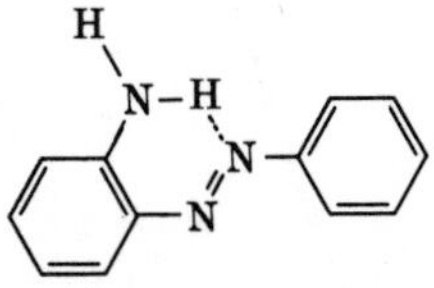

[12]

The stereoisomerism of azo dyes is of practical importance, however, in that it gives rise to the phenomenon of *phototropy*. This is a marked change in the shade of certain dyes (especially yellows and oranges) when applied to non-polar fibres such as cellulose acetate and exposed to strong light; the change is reversed during storage in darkness. It is believed that partial conversion of the *trans* into the *cis* form occurs on exposure, and the reverse occurs when the energising action of light is withdrawn. It is significant that phototropy is shown only on fibres in which dyes dissolve, the *trans-cis* conversion evidently being prevented in dyed fibres of cellulose or protein in which the molecules of dye are held by adsorption.

Atherton and Peters[6] explained the phenomenon of phototropy in azo dyes with the aid of the diagram reproduced in Fig. 3-1 which shows the *cis* and *trans* forms as relatively stable configurations with a difference in energy content. The two forms are separated by an energy barrier representing the work required to twist the molecule through the intermediate strained positions of the azo link. A molecule in the *cis* form requires an amount of energy E_1 to bring about conversion into the *trans* form, and the reverse change requires an amount E_2. E_1 and E_2 are respectively comparable with and much greater than the energy possessed by the dye molecule in solution at room temperature. Therefore molecules in the *cis* form readily acquire enough energy to convert them into the *trans* form, but few *trans* molecules are sufficiently energised to bring about the reverse change unless energy is received from an external source. Exposure to light causes equilibrium to move in favour of the *cis* form.

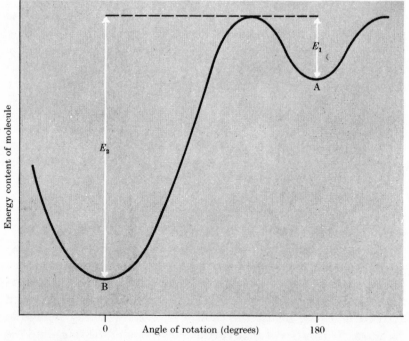

Fig. 3-1. A energy content of *cis*. B energy content of *trans*. E_1 activation energy of *cis* → *trans* conversion. E_2 activation energy of *trans* → *cis* conversion.

3-2   Tautomerism in hydroxyazo and aminoazo compounds

In 1884, Zincke[7] showed that the product of coupling diazobenzene chloride with α-naphthol is indistinguishable from that obtained by condensing 1,4-naphthoquinone with phenylhydrazine. The presence of both hydroxyl and keto groups has been established, and the two forms [13] and [14] are in equilibrium in the products of each reaction. Interconversion is so rapid that reactions characteristic of either form can proceed as though the other were absent. The

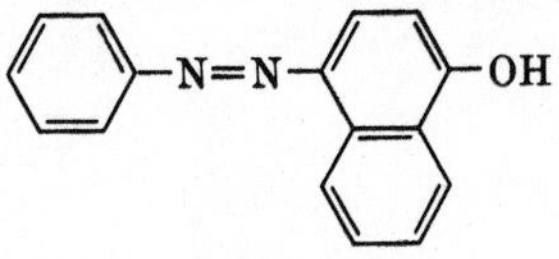

[13]

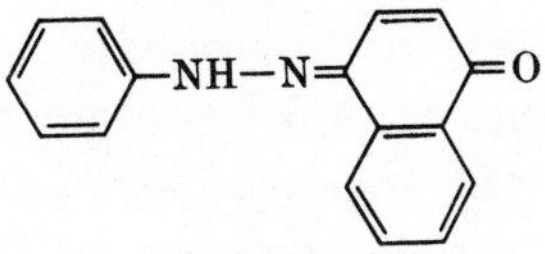

[14]

absorption spectra of the two forms are different, and it has been shown that the state of equilibrium in solution varies according to the solvent.[8]

In hydroxyazo compounds of the benzene series equilibrium strongly favours the azo form, but as a general rule in corresponding polycyclic compounds the proportion of hydrazone form increases with the number of rings. Whereas the coupling of diazotised arylamines with β-naphthol gives 1-arylazo-2-naphthols, condensation of 1,2-naphthoquinone with arylhydrazines yields the isomeric 2-arylazo-1-naphthols. In both the benzene and naphthalene series, p-hydroxyazo compounds behave as acids and are soluble in aqueous sodium hydroxide, but o-hydroxyazo compounds such as 1-phenylazo-2-naphthol are unaffected by alkali under these conditions. The suppression of hydroxylic properties is ascribed to the formation of a hydrogen bond between the hydroxyl group and an azo nitrogen atom; the tautomeric equilibrium may be represented as follows:

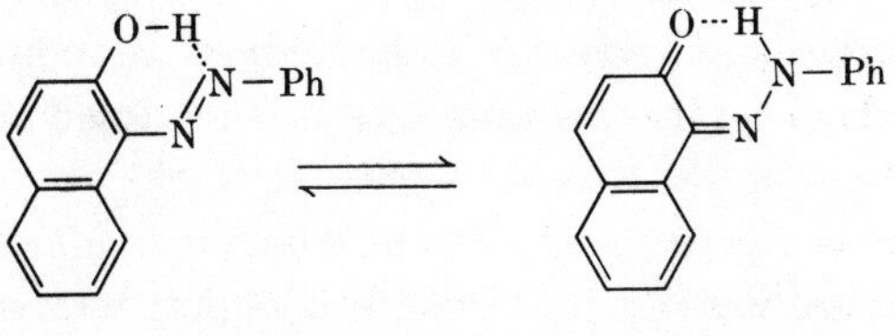

There is a possibility of tautomerism in o- and p-aminoazo compounds, e.g.:

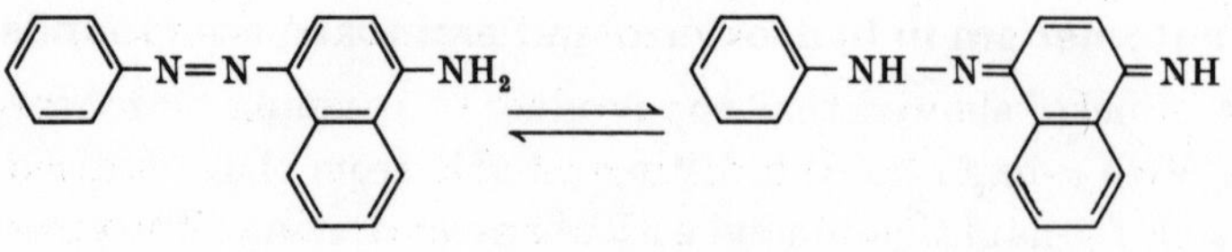

The evidence of absorption spectra shows, however, that such compounds normally exist only in the aminoazo form. In *o*-aminoazo compounds intramolecular hydrogen bonding occurs:

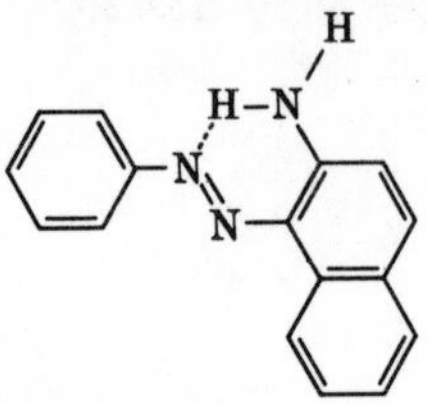

and probably intermolecular bonding occurs in *p*-aminoazo compounds.[9] In the benzene series the hydrogen bond does not prevent diazotisation of *o*-aminoazo compounds, but this reaction cannot be carried out in corresponding naphthalene derivatives; in both series *p*-amino derivatives are readily diazotised. There is a parallel in the *o*-hydroxyazo compounds in that benzenoid derivatives are soluble in aqueous alkali, but naphthalene analogues are not. 4-Benzeneazo-1-naphthol, however, is readily soluble in dilute aqueous caustic soda.

3-3 Principles governing azo coupling

Azo dyes are obtained by coupling a diazotised amine with a coupling component in aqueous solution or suspension. The diazotised amine is usually an aromatic compound, but amino derivatives of heterocyclic compounds are sometimes used. Coupling components are commonly phenols, naphthols, arylamines, aminonaphthols, acetoacetarylamides or pyrazolones. If the dye is to be soluble in water at least one of the components is likely to contain a solubilising group such as a sulphonic or carboxylic acid group, and several such groups may be present in the final molecule. Basic azo dyes, however, form water-soluble salts with suitable acids and do not require additional solubilising substituents.

The chemistry of aromatic and heterocyclic diazonium compound is fully described in standard textbooks, and here it is assumed that the reader is familiar with it or has access to suitable works.

Coupling of diazonium compounds with phenols occurs in alkaline solution; cold conditions are usually preferred, but higher temperatures are sometimes required (see Section 3-5). Benzenediazonium chloride couples with phenol, giving mainly *p*-hydroxyazobenzene with some o-hydroxyazobenzene. A second molecule of the dia-zonium compound will react with formation of 2,4-bis(benzeneazo)-phenol, and it is even possible to obtain 2,4,6-tris(benzeneazo)-phenol by further reaction, but the third coupling is not easily completed. If the position *para* to the hydroxyl group is occupied, as in p-cresol, coupling occurs in an *ortho* position. Coupling activity is promoted by the presence of electronegative substituents in aromatic diazonium compounds, especially in *ortho* or *para* positions with respect to the diazonium group, but the presence of such groups in coupling components tends to inhibit coupling.

In normal conditions diazonium compounds couple with α-naphthol mainly at position 4, or at position 2 if 4 is already occu-pied. If negative substituents are present in positions 3 or 5 coupling usually occurs only at 2. 2,4-Disazo derivatives can be obtained from unsubstituted α-naphthol. Diazonium compounds couple with β-naphthol only at position 1, and a negatively substituted diazonium compound may even displace an existing substituent in that position. Substituents in positions 3–7 usually have no marked effect on the ease of coupling, but a sulphonic acid group in position 8 has a considerable retarding influence.

Coupling with primary aromatic amines occurs in neutral or weakly acid conditions, but the reaction is slower than that with phenols. Diazonium compounds couple with aniline, o-toluidine, 2,4,- or 2,5-dimethylaniline at the amino group with formation of diazo-amino compounds, but by warming with mineral acid these can be converted into p-aminoazo compounds. With amines such as m-toluidine, 2,5-dimethoxyaniline or 2-methoxy-5-methylaniline, on the other hand, nuclear coupling takes place, and the p-aminoazo derivatives are obtained at once; it is possible, however, that even in these cases diazoamino compounds are formed in a transient intermediate stage. Tertiary amines such as N,N-dimethylaniline, which cannot give rise to diazoamino compounds, couple readily to give p-azo derivatives. In such components substituents in positions 2 or 4 tend to inhibit coupling.

p-Azo derivatives of aniline or other amines yielding diazoamino compounds can be obtained by first preparing formaldehyde-bisulphite derivatives, which couple only in the nucleus, and removing the sulphomethyl groups by hydrolysis after coupling.

m-Phenylenediamine couples very easily with diazonium com-pounds to give 4-azo derivatives. A second molecule reacts to yield a mixture of 2,4- and 4,6-disazo derivatives, the former being favoured by acid and the latter by alkaline conditions. Diazo-amino compounds are not formed in the naphthalene series.

α-Naphthylamine couples preferentially at position 4, and a second azo group can be introduced at 2; if there is a substituent at 4 coupling occurs at 2. β-Naphthylamine couples only at position 1. 1-Arylazo-2-naphthylamines are resistant to diazotisation, but 4-arylazo-1-naphthylamines can be diazotised and coupled further to give disazo compounds.

The coupling properties of sulphonated aminonaphthols are of importance because some of these compounds are extensively used as coupling components for azo dyes of various kinds. In acid conditions coupling is directed by the amino group into an *ortho* or *para* position, but in alkaline medium the azo group enters in an *ortho* or *para* position with respect to the hydroxyl group. Sometimes disazo dyes can be obtained by coupling first one molecule of a diazonium compound in acid medium, then a second molecule in alkaline medium. The important intermediates 1-amino-8-naphthol-3,6-disulphonic acid (H acid) and 2-amino-5-naphthol-7-sulphonic acid (J acid) can be coupled in this way to yield disazo dyes, but 3-amino-5-naphthol-7-sulphonic acid (γ acid) and 1-amino-5-naphthol-7-sulphonic acid (M acid) will couple only once, either *ortho* to the amino group in acid medium or *ortho* to the hydroxyl group in alkaline medium. This difference is usually ascribed to hydrogen bond formation in the *ortho* or *peri*-hydroxyazo compounds obtained by coupling diazonium compounds with γ or M acid; the resulting suppression of hydroxylic character does not occur in azo derivatives of H and J acids where the hydroxyl groups are more remote from the azo link. There is some evidence that other factors may be involved, however.[10]

The coupling principles described relate to main reactions but in many cases coupling components contain more than one reactive position, and coupling is then distributed between the various possible sites. The coupling ratios can sometimes be altered within wide limits by variation in conditions. Thus although simple benzenoid diazonium compounds normally attack α-naphthol in the 4 position to the extent of about 99%, Bamberger[11] obtained a 90% yield of 2-(*p*-nitrobenzeneazo)-1-naphthol by coupling in benzene medium. Stamm and Zollinger[12] found that in the coupling of *o*-nitrodiazobenzene with 1-naphthol-3-sulphonic acid, temperature considerably affects the ratio of coupling in the 2 and 4 positions; at pH 4·68 the observed *o/p* ratios were 3·2 at 10°, 4·35 at 20° and 7·55 at 30°C. Substituents in the diazonium compound have a considerable effect; thus whereas positively substituted diazobenzene derivatives couple with 1-naphthol-3-sulphonic acid mainly in the 2 position, 2,4-dinitrodiazobenzene couples with it almost entirely in the 4 position. Diazotised 1-amino-6-nitro-2-naphthol 4-sulphonic acid, however, couples with α-naphthol mainly in the 2 position. The use of a strongly alkaline medium has been found to favour *ortho* coupling in certain cases.[13] Pyridine, which is occasionally used as a catalyst to accelerate slow couplings, usually favours *para* coupling.[14]

The suppression of hydroxylic properties in *o*-hydroxyazo compounds caused by hydrogen bond formation is of great importance in azo dyes and pigments required to be alkali-resistant. For such products intermediates are chosen to ensure that coupling is confined to the *ortho* position with respect to the hydroxyl group; this explains why β-naphthol is much more important than α-naphthol in dye chemistry. Promotion of *ortho* coupling is also essential in dyes that are to be metallised.

The mechanism of diazo coupling is similar to that of other aromatic substitution reactions in which the nucleus is attacked by an electrophilic cation (E):

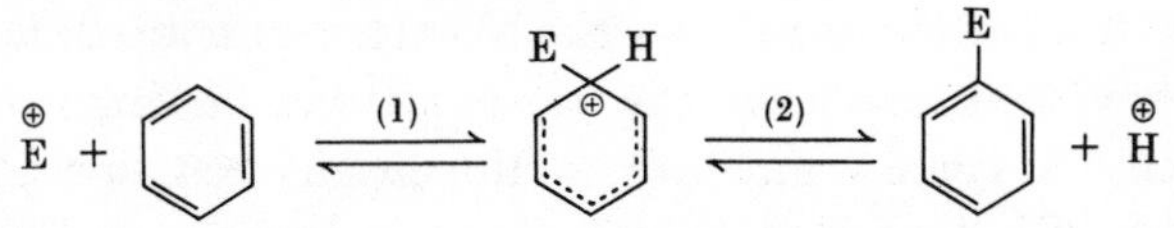

Since diazonium cations are much weaker electrophiles than those concerned in nitrations or sulphonations they are able to attack only highly activated aromatic nuclei such as phenoxide ions or arylamines.[15]

3-4   Nomenclature and classification

Intermediates used in manufacture of azo dyes are of five main types, conveniently designated by code letters as follows:

A   Diazotisable primary amine

D   Tetrazotisable diamine

E   Coupling component (or End component) able to couple with one equivalent of a diazonium compound

M   Primary aromatic amine able to couple with a diazonium compound to give an aminoazo compound which can be diazotised and coupled again

Z   Coupling component able to couple with two or more equivalents of a diazonium compound (or different diazonium compounds)

These code letters are conveniently used with arrows (meaning 'diazotised and coupled with') to distinguish azo dyes of the various types; thus monoazo dyes obtained by diazotising an amine and coupling with an end component are said to be of the type A → E. Individual dyes are represented similarly (e.g., aniline → β-naphthol), and by using trivial names for common intermediates the structure of complex dyes can be shown clearly and concisely. In polyazo dyes the arrows may be numbered to show the order of coupling, and it is useful to indicate whether coupling is carried out in acid or alkaline medium if this affects the coupling position. A typical trisazo dye (CI Direct Black 4; CI 30245) may be represented as follows:

$$\text{Benzidine} \overset{3}{\nearrow} \underset{1}{\searrow} \quad \begin{array}{l} m\text{-tolylenediamine} \\[4pt] (\text{acid}) \text{ H acid (alk)} \overset{2}{\leftarrow} \text{aniline} \end{array}$$

The following chemical classification of azo dyes is based on that used in the Colour Index.

3-4-1   Monoazo dyes

These include all dyes of the type A → E. No attempt is made here to describe subdivisions based on the various types of diazo and end components. A typical example is the bright red dye *Azo Geranine 2G* (ICI) (CI Acid Red 1; CI 18050), which is made by coupling diazotised aniline with *N*-acetyl H acid in alkaline medium. It has the structure:

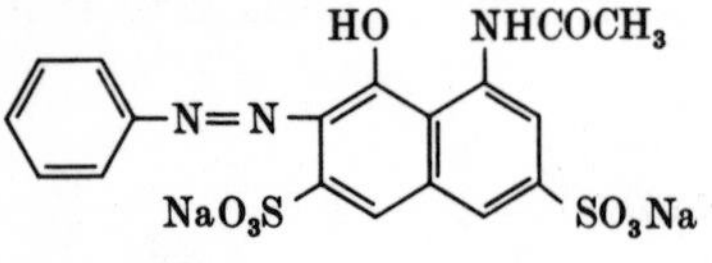

Examples of monoazo pigments are described in Section 16-2.

3-4-2   Disazo dyes

There are three main types of disazo dyes, illustrated by the following examples:

Dyes of the type $A^1 \to Z \leftarrow A^2$.

Example: *Naphthalene Black 12B* (ICI)
(CI Acid Black 1; CI 20470)

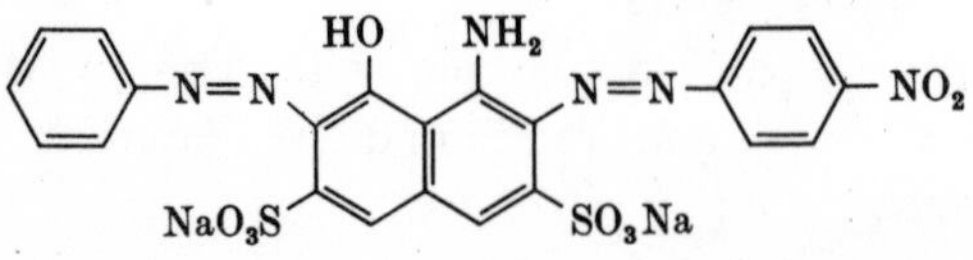

This is obtained by coupling diazotised *p*-nitroaniline with H acid in acid medium, then diazotised aniline with the product in alkaline medium. It is a bluish black acid dye extensively used on wool.

Dyes of the type $D \nearrow^{E^1}_{\searrow E^2}$

Example: *Chlorazol Bordeaux B* (ICI)
(CI Direct Red 13; CI 22155)

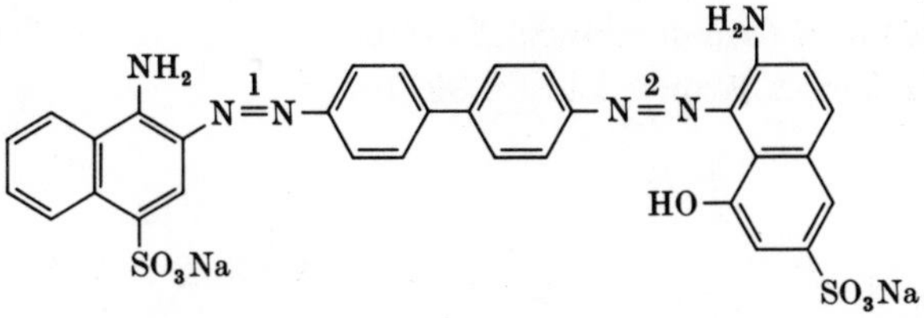

NH₂ ... N$\overset{1}{=}$N ... N$\overset{2}{=}$N ... H₂N, HO, SO₃Na, SO₃Na

This is obtained by coupling tetrazotised benzidine first with naphthionic acid in alkaline medium, then with γ acid in acid medium. In tetrazotised benzidines one diazonium group activates the other, so that the first coupling is more vigorous than the second. If possible the less reactive coupling component is used first. The dye illustrated gives bordeaux (bluish red) shades on cellulosic fibres.

Dyes of the type A → M → E.

Example: *Dispersol Fast Orange B* (ICI)
(CI Disperse Orange 13; CI 26080)

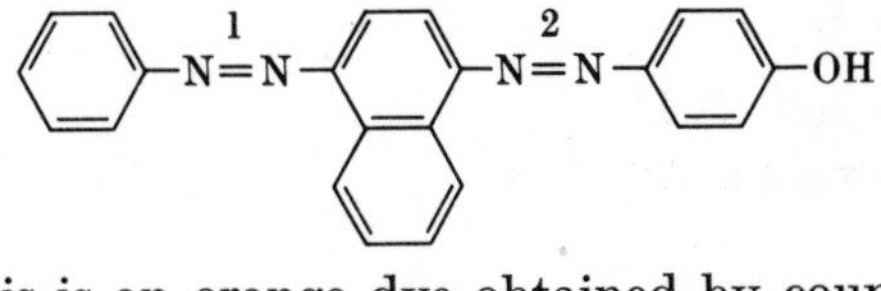

N$\overset{1}{=}$N ... N$\overset{2}{=}$N ... OH

This is an orange dye obtained by coupling diazotised aniline with α-naphthylamine in acid medium, then diazotising the resulting aminoazo compound and coupling with phenol in alkaline medium. It is used in the form of aqueous dispersion for dyeing acetate or nylon fibres.

A fourth type $A^1 \to Z \cdot X \cdot Z \leftarrow A^2$ is distinguished by the Colour Index, in which the bifunctional coupling component Z . X . Z is a compound such as the urea derivative obtained by reaction of two molecules of an aminonaphthol with phosgene. Carbonyl J acid [15] is an example of such an intermediate. This type of dye may be regarded as a subdivision of the first type.

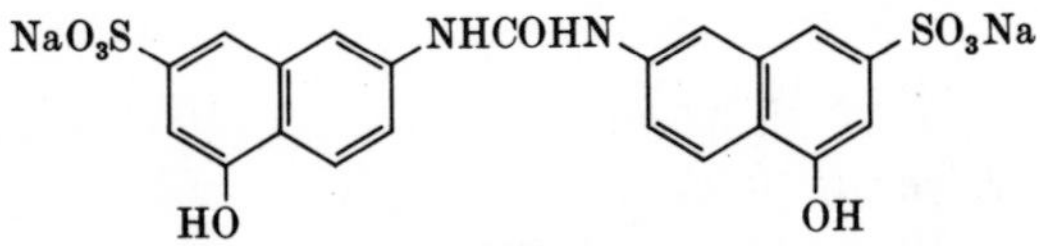

NaO₃S ... NHCOHN ... SO₃Na, HO, OH

[15]

3-4-3 Trisazo dyes

Commercial trisazo dyes are mostly among the following three types:

Dyes of the type $D \begin{matrix} \nearrow E \\ \searrow Z \leftarrow A \end{matrix}$

Example: *Chlorazol Orange Brown X* (ICI)
(CI Direct Brown 1A; CI 30110)

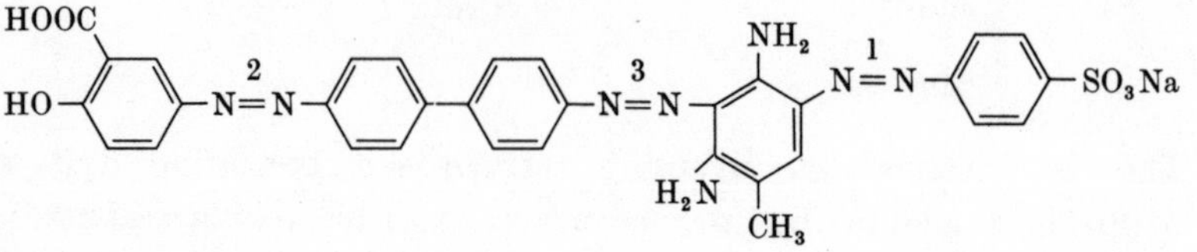

This dye is manufactured by coupling tetrazotised benzidine with one equivalent of salicylic acid in alkaline medium, then with one equivalent of the product of coupling diazotised sulphanilic acid with *m*-tolylenediamine. It is a general-purpose brown dye used chiefly on cellulosic fibres.

Dyes of the type $D \begin{matrix} \nearrow E^1 \\ \searrow M \rightarrow E^2 \end{matrix}$

Example: *Chlorazol Drab RH* (ICI)
(CI Direct Brown 46; CI 31785)

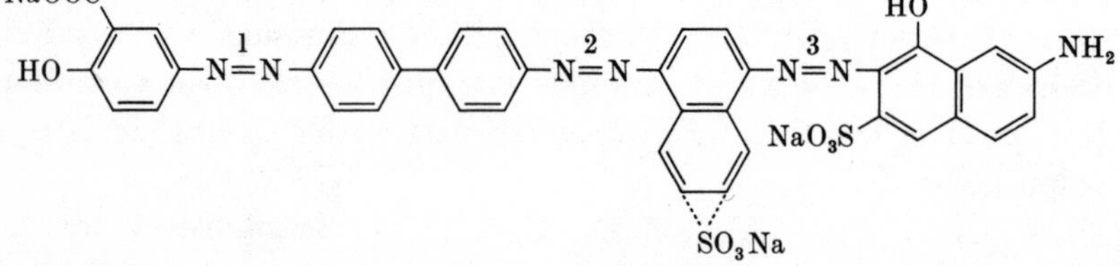

This dye, giving dull brownish olive shades on cellulosic fibres, is obtained by coupling tetrazotised benzidine first with salicylic acid in alkaline medium, then with mixed Cleve's acids (1-naphthylamine-6- + -7-sulphonic acids), diazotising and coupling with γ acid in alkaline medium.

Dyes of the type $A \rightarrow M^1 \rightarrow M^2 \rightarrow E$.

Example: *Durazol Blue 2R* (ICI)
(CI Direct Blue 71; CI 34140)

Manufacture of this dye involves coupling diazotised 3-amino-naphthalene-1,5-disulphonic acid with 1-naphthylamine, diazotising and coupling with 1,7-Cleve's acid (1-naphthylamine-7-sulphonic acid), then diazotising again and coupling with J acid in alkaline medium. The dye is used to give dull blue shades, mainly on cellulosic fibres.

The Colour Index includes a few trisazo dyes of the types

$A^1 \rightarrow M \rightarrow Z \leftarrow A^2$ (5 examples) and $A^1 \rightarrow Z \overset{\nearrow A^2}{\underset{\searrow A^3}{}}$ (3 examples).

3-4-4　Tetrakisazo dyes

As the number of azo groups in a dye molecule is increased it becomes more difficult to obtain the product in a pure condition, partly because coupling tends to take place at more than one position and partly because some diazo decomposition occurs at each stage. Many tetrakisazo dyes are mixtures, and the structures assigned to them indicate the stages of manufacture rather than the constitution of the product. They are used mainly for brown or black shades on cellulosic fibres or leather, but their importance has declined, since as a result of the development of metallised and reactive dyes complex polyazo structures are no longer essential for deep shades and high substantivity.

Tetrakisazo dyes included in the Colour Index (of which many were shown as obsolete at the date of publication, and others have become so since) are of the ten types listed below. The numbers of examples represent the dyes manufactured at the date of compilation of the Supplement and it will be seen that one type was entirely obsolete at that time:

$A^1 \rightarrow Z^1 \leftarrow D \rightarrow Z^2 \leftarrow A^2$　　　(10 examples)

$E^1 \leftarrow D^1 \rightarrow Z \leftarrow D^2 \rightarrow E^2$　　　(3 examples)

$E^1 \leftarrow M^1 \leftarrow D \rightarrow M^2 \rightarrow E^2$　　　(6 examples)

$E^1 \leftarrow D \rightarrow M^1 \rightarrow M^2 \rightarrow E^2$　　　(3 examples)

$A \rightarrow Z \leftarrow D \rightarrow M \rightarrow E$　　　(0 examples)

$A \rightarrow M \rightarrow Z \leftarrow D \rightarrow E$　　　(1 example)

$$E \leftarrow D \rightarrow M \rightarrow Z \leftarrow A \qquad \text{(3 examples)}$$
$$A^1 \rightarrow M^1 \rightarrow Z \leftarrow M^2 \leftarrow A^2 \qquad \text{(5 examples)}$$
$$A^1 \rightarrow M^1 \rightarrow M^2 \rightarrow Z \leftarrow A^2 \qquad \text{(2 examples)}$$
$$A \rightarrow M^1 \rightarrow M^2 \rightarrow M^3 \rightarrow E \qquad \text{(3 examples)}$$

An example of the first type is CI Direct Brown 44 (CI 35005, CI 35010). Several varieties of this dye are manufactured by coupling two molecules of diazotised sulphanilic acid (or naphthionic or another naphthylaminesulphonic acid) with Bismarck Brown (CI Basic Brown 1; CI 21000). The products are mixtures containing a major constituent with a structure such as [16]. This group

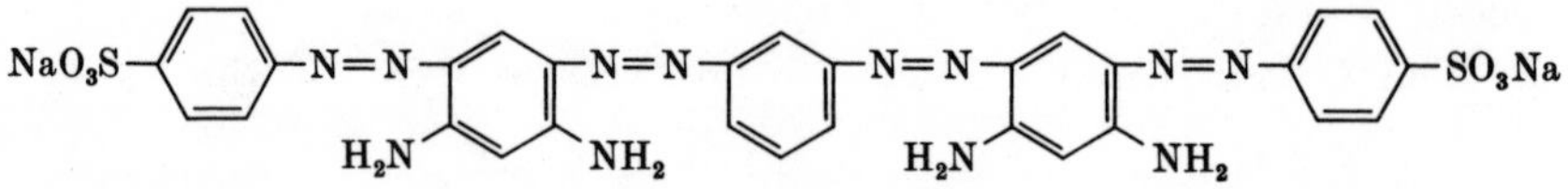

[16]

of dyes represents the simplest tetrakisazo type, which can be obtained in only two reaction stages. They are used for application to cotton, and are often aftertreated with diazotised p-nitroaniline, redder brown shades of slightly improved fastness to washing and light being thereby attained.

3-4-5   Other Polyazo dyes

Seven dyes (manufactured at the date of publication) containing more than four azo groups, and one with as many as eight, are listed in the Colour Index. Since they are complex mixtures of small significance they are not discussed here.

3-4-6   Azo dyes containing another chromophore

There are a few dyes containing a stilbene, thiazole, anthraquinone or phthalocyanine residue in addition to the azo chromophore. An interesting example of an anthraquinone-azo dye is CI Vat Yellow 10 (CI 65430), with the structure [17]. In spite of the presence of the

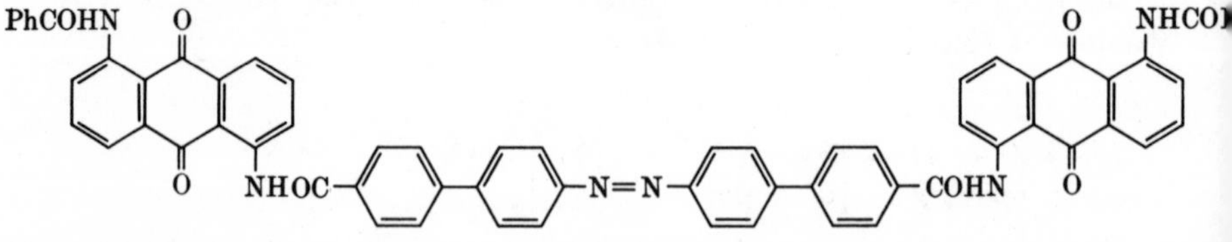

[17]

azo group this dye can be reduced to the alkali-soluble leuco compound as with other vat dyes (see Chapter 10).

3-5 Preparative methods

The preparation of an azo dye by a coupling reaction is at first sight
a simple matter, and when a student adds a diazonium compound
to a naphthol in alkaline solution and observes the immediate
production of a strongly coloured product he is inclined to regard
the reaction as reliable and quantitative. Side reactions usually
occur to some extent, however, and in order to obtain the product in
a pure state and maximum yield conditions must be selected to
suit the combination concerned. The main factors are pH value and
temperature, and these must be arranged to favour coupling rather
than diazo decomposition. The pH value is critical, since if it is too
high non-coupling diazotate ions are formed, but if too low the
coupling component becomes unreactive. For any given combination there is therefore an optimum range which is determined by the
diazo equilibrium constant and the pK value of the coupling component. When there is a possibility of coupling at more than one
position the pH value must be chosen to favour the product desired
in accordance with the principles already described (Section 3-3).
In most cases a temperature below 10°C is to be preferred, but if a
fairly stable diazo compound with low coupling energy is concerned
it may be desirable to operate at a higher temperature, and in such
cases 40°C is not unusual.

Since diazo compounds are usually unstable they are not normally isolated but the screened solution is run directly into the solution
of the coupling component. In acid couplings the rate of addition
is usually not critical, and in some cases the coupling component may
be added to the diazo solution. When coupling in alkaline medium,
however, it is advisable to make the addition in such a way that the
amount of uncoupled diazo compound remains small. Progress is
followed by placing a spot of the reaction mixture on filter paper,
and allowing it to diffuse into adjacent spots of solutions of diazo
and coupling components. Coloration at the intersection with the
former shows the presence of excess coupling component, or at the
intersection with the latter excess diazo component. Colour formation in both zones or in the general outspread shows that coupling
is taking place slowly. For these tests it may be desirable to use
reagents other than those of the coupling, chosen to give rapid
coupling and absence of alkali sensitivity; p-chlorodiazobenzene
chloride and weakly alkaline H acid solutions are often used.

When coupling in acid medium the presence of excess nitrous
acid in the diazo solution is to be avoided since it may cause impurity
by reaction with the coupling component. The excess may be

removed very rapidly by addition of a small amount of sulphamic acid, but excess must be avoided in the case of heavily nitrated diazo compounds which may react with sulphamic acid. Pyridine is sometimes used as a catalyst to accelerate slow coupling in manufacture of polyazo dyes.

Weakly basic amines are often diazotised in concentrated sulphuric acid, and in such cases it may be desirable to isolate the diazo compound in order to eliminate the large excess of acid. This can be done if the diazonium salt is sufficiently stable to be safe to handle and not too readily soluble in water; such conditions are often fulfilled in fairly large molecules.

When coupling has been completed the dyestuff may be largely in suspension or it may have to be salted out. In either case it is often advantageous to warm the suspension in order to bring about crystal growth or aggregation of particles and thus facilitate filtration. It is convenient to examine the product by paper or thin-layer chromatography at this stage, and if unduly contaminated it can be re-dissolved and salted out again.

In manufacture of azo pigments it is necessary to minimise diazo decomposition, since impurities are not readily removed from water-insoluble products. Whenever possible coupling is therefore carried out in weakly acid medium. In these conditions the coupling components are usually insoluble, but if they are reprecipitated from alkaline solution by acidification in presence of a suitable surface-active agent the particle size is small enough to permit coupling with a diazo compound in presence of a buffer such as acetic acid with sodium acetate.

Technical azo dyes for wool, silk and leather

4-1 Dyes for wool

The wool fibre is composed of the protein *keratin*, which consists of long polypeptide chains built from eighteen different amino acids. Most of these acids have the general formula $H_2N . CHR . COOH$, in which R is a side chain of varying character. The chain structure is of the type:

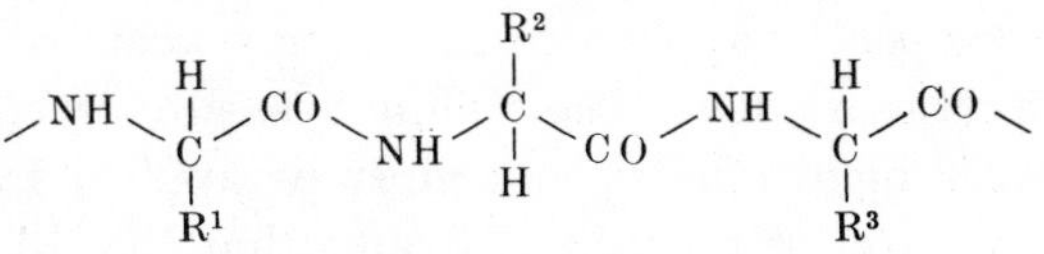

$$\_NH \diagdown \underset{\underset{R^1}{|}}{\overset{\overset{H}{|}}{C}} \diagup CO \diagdown NH \diagdown \underset{\underset{H}{|}}{\overset{\overset{R^2}{|}}{C}} \diagdown CO \diagup NH \diagdown \underset{\underset{R^3}{|}}{\overset{\overset{H}{|}}{C}} \diagup CO \diagdown$$

and at intervals the chains are connected by bridges derived from the amino acid cystine [18]. Some of the side chains end in amino

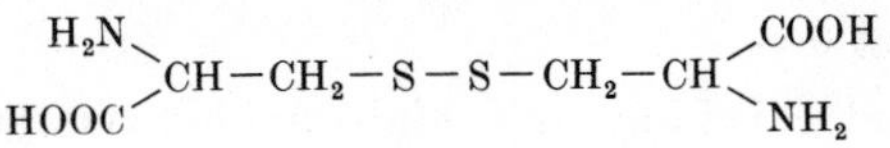

$$\underset{HOOC}{\overset{H_2N}{\diagdown}} CH - CH_2 - S - S - CH_2 - CH \underset{\diagdown NH_2}{\overset{\diagup COOH}{}}$$

[18]

groups and others in carboxyl groups; internal salts are therefore formed and the molecules are bound together by electrovalent linkages. The molecules of keratin are very large, with an average molecular weight estimated at about 60,000.

The wool fibre is readily destroyed by alkali, but withstands acid conditions fairly well; some hydrolysis of peptide linkages occurs on prolonged boiling with acid, however. The carboxylic acid and amino groups in the keratin molecule confer affinity for basic and acid dyes. Basic dyes are now little used on wool since their fugitive properties render them unsuitable for such an expensive and durable fibre. Acid dyes, however, are extensively used, and the general characteristics of this large class and the related mordant and pre-metallised azo dyes are now described.

4-1-1   Acid dyes

Since the bonds between dye anions and amino groups in the wool fibre are easily broken and re-formed, dyes attached in this way are liable to migrate. This property is advantageous, in that level dyeing is readily attained, but it leads to low fastness to wet treatments, and any undyed wool present during washing becomes stained. These characteristics are chiefly apparent in dyes of low molecular weight, and fastness to washing is in general much better in more complex dyes. The larger dye molecules are evidently attached to the fibre by some means other than the ionic bonds mentioned above, and it is believed that they are held by non-polar van der Waals forces exerted between hydrophobic dye anions and hydrophobic regions of the wool fibre, their strength being proportional to the area of contact.

From an application point of view acid dyes are classed as either Levelling or Milling types. The Levelling (sometimes called Equalising) dyes have fairly simple chemical structures, migrate readily on wool, and are easily applied from strongly acid baths; their wet-fastness properties are low. The Milling dyes are structurally more complex, have high affinity, and must be applied from weakly acid baths for control of the rate of dyeing, but they show high fastness to milling and other wet treatments. Milling is a felting process applied to woollen cloth by squeezing or beating, usually in a soap solution. It sometimes follows dyeing, and the dyes used must then have high wet-fastness properties in order to withstand these severe conditions.

The advantages of good levelling and high milling fastness cannot be fully combined in a single dye, but there are general-purpose dyes with intermediate properties. The application classes can be correlated roughly with chemical types, as shown for monoazo and disazo dyes in Table 4-1, which provides a few typical examples. As might be expected from the foregoing generalisations, trisazo and other polyazo dyes are of the milling class, but since shades are usually dull and uneven they are seldom of technical value on wool.

Since fastness to milling is associated with larger molecules it was formerly shown mainly in dyes with the deeper and duller shades. Milling fastness can be conferred on the brighter dyes with simple structures, however, by weighting their molecules with groups that do not form part of the chromophoric system. Many of the *Polar* dyes (Geigy) contain an arysulphonyl group for this purpose, and the *Carbolan* dyes (ICI) contain long hydrocarbon chains. These weighing groups impart a marked improvement in affinity for the fibre without appreciable dulling or deepening of the shade. Examples from these ranges are *Polar Brilliant Red 3B* (Gy) (CI Acid Red 172; CI 18135) and *Carbolan Crimson B* (ICI) (CI Acid Red 138; CI 18073).

Polar Brilliant Red 3B (Gy)

Carbolan Crimson B (ICI)

4-1-2   Mordant dyes

The ancient processes for applying natural dyes without fibre affinity to textile materials by means of mordants have already been mentioned in Section 1-3. It has long been known that the washing fastness of certain acid dyes on wool can be considerably improved by aftertreatment with chromium compounds such as sodium dichromate. The term *Mordant dyes* which was properly applied to most of the old natural dyes now also covers acid dyes metallised in various ways during the application process and the synthetic polyhydroxyanthraquinone dyes discussed in Chapter 9. Clearly all mordant dyes must contain a metallisable structure, but not all dyes of this type are included in the mordant class. The basis of the Colour Index classification is the application process, and only dyes actually applied with a mordant are considered to be mordant dyes. Many acid dyes containing metallisable groups but not metallised in dyehouse or printworks practice are excluded, as are also pre-metallised dyes (Section.4-1-3).

It is pointed out in the Colour Index[1] that the significance of the term *mordant dye* is conventional, but has no logical basis; it does not include basic dyes applied to mordanted cotton nor dyes after-metallised on cotton. Mordant dyes used mainly for wool may have secondary applications on silk, nylon, leather or anodised aluminium. Since the dyes have affinity for wool the function of the metal is not to provide a means of fixation, but to strengthen the attachment already existing. The after-treatment process is known as the *afterchrome method*, and there is an alternative basically similar to the ancient mordanting processes called the *chrome mordant method* in which a dichromate is applied to wool first, either alone or in presence of sulphuric acid or (for dyes sensitive to oxidation) a reducing agent, and the fibre thus mordanted is dyed with a suitable acid dye. In 1900 the Berlin Aniline Company

Table 4-1 Application classes of monoazo and disazo acid dyes

Chemical class	Application classes	Typical hues	Examples
Monoazo Type $A \rightarrow E$	Levelling General purpose	Yellow Orange Red Violet Blue	**Naphthalene Orange G (ICI)** CI Acid Orange 7; CI 15510 (This product is equivalent to Roussin's *Orange II*) Levelling class **Coomassie Blue RL (ICI)** CI Acid Blue 92; CI 13390 General purpose class

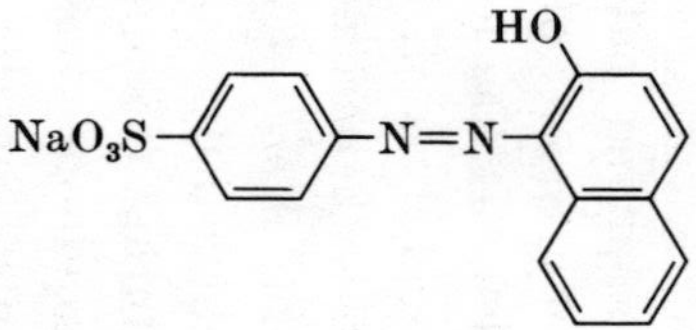

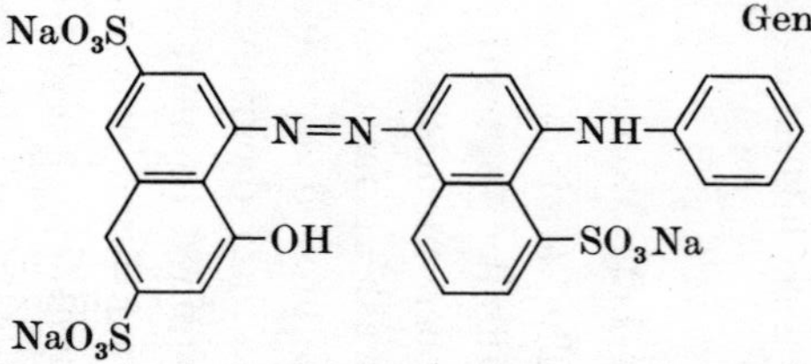

Disazo

Type $A^1 \rightarrow Z \leftarrow A^2$ General purpose

Brown
Dark blue
Dark green
Black

Naphthalene Black 12 B (ICI)
CI Acid Black 1; CI 20470

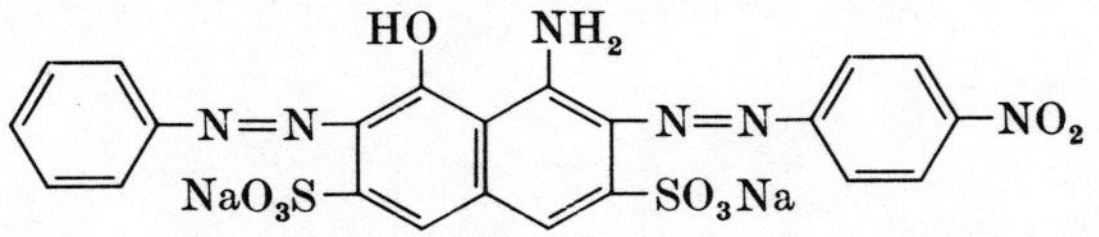

Disazo

Type $D \nearrow^{E^1} \searrow_{E^2}$ Milling

Yellow
Orange
Red

Coomassie Milling Scarlet G (ICI)
CI Acid Red 97; CI 22890

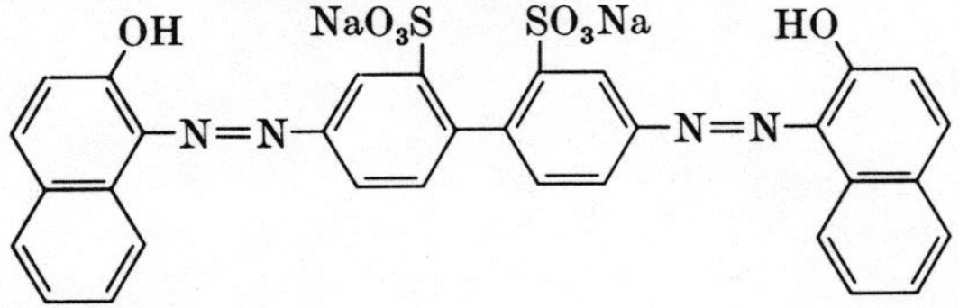

Disazo

Type $A \rightarrow M \rightarrow E$ Milling

Blue
Black

Coomassie Navy Blue 2RN (ICI)
CI Acid Blue 113; CI 26360

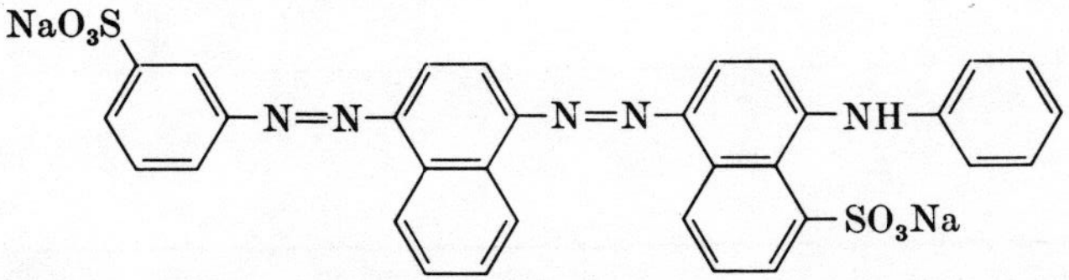

Table 4-2 Examples of azo mordant dyes

Azo class and complexing system	Structure	CI Ref. Nos.	Commercial dyes
Monoazo			
o,o'-Dihydroxyazo		CI Mordant Green 17 CI 17225	Chrome Fast Green G (CIBA)
	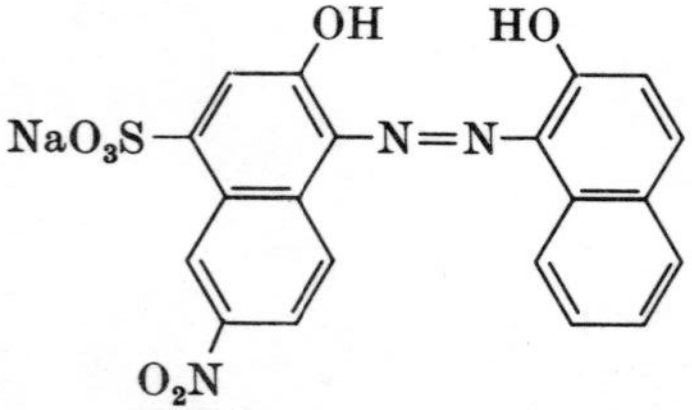	CI Mordant Black 1 CI 15710	Solochrome Black A (ICI)
	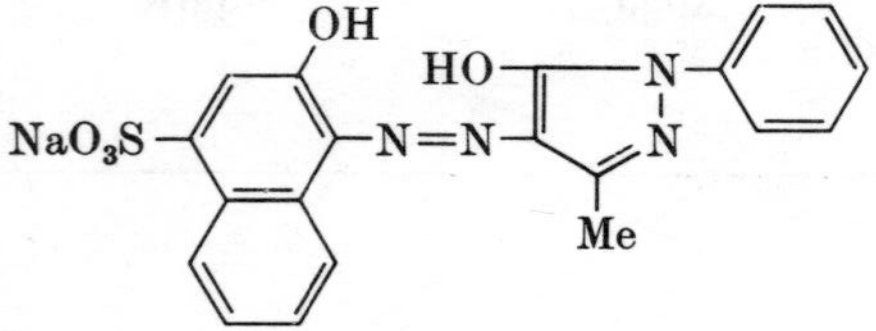	CI Mordant Red 7 CI 18760	Solochrome Red ER (ICI)
o-Carboxy-o'-hydroxyazo	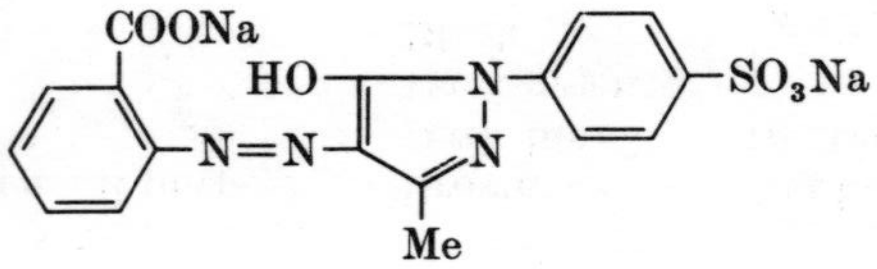	CI Mordant Yellow 8 CI 18821	Solochrome Flavine R (ICI)

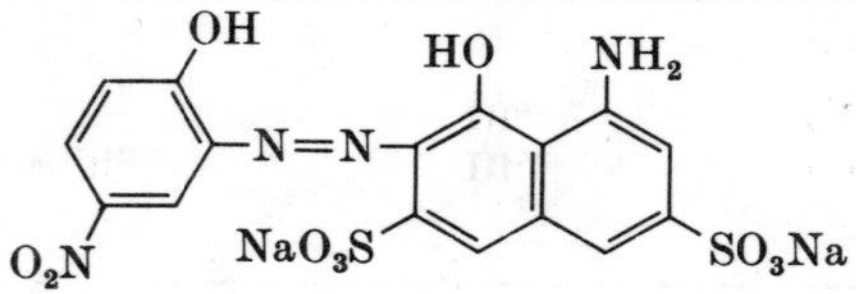

Type	Structure	CI Name / Number	Trade Name
o-Amino-o'-hydroxyazo		CI Mordant Brown 33 CI 13250	Solochrome Brown RH (ICI)
Salicylic acid		CI Mordant Orange 1 CI 14030	Solochrome Orange M (ICI)
8-Hydroxyquinoline		CI Mordant Orange 26 CI 19325	Basolan Chrome Orange GGM (BASF)
Disazo Type $A^1 \rightarrow Z \leftarrow A^2$ o-Amino-o'-hydroxyazo		CI Mordant Brown 1 CI 20110	Solochrome Brown EB (ICI)

Table 4-2 Examples of azo mordant dyes (*contd.*)

Azo class and complexing system	Structure	CI Ref. Nos.	Commercial dyes
Type $D \overset{E^1}{\underset{E^2}{\nwarrow\searrow}}$ Salicylic acid	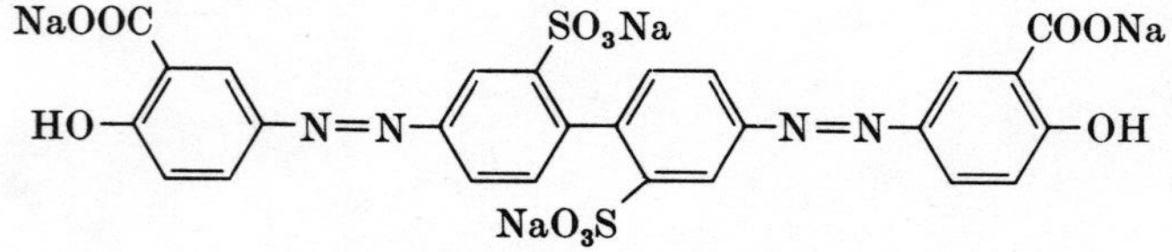	CI Mordant Yellow 26 CI 22880	Eriochrome Flavine R (Gy)
Type $A \to M \to E$ Salicylic acid	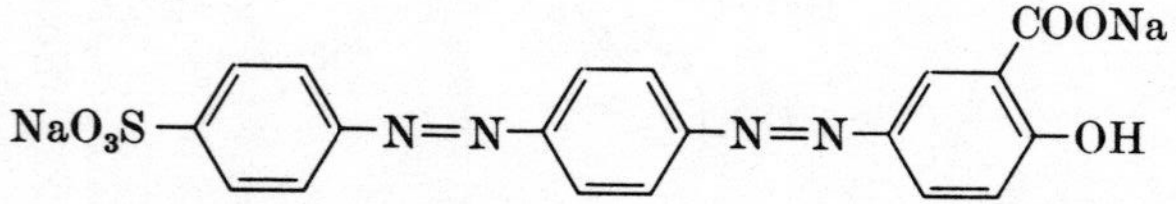	CI Mordant Orange 6 CI 26520	Solochrome Orange GRS (ICI)

devised the *metachrome method* whereby selected dyes can be applied simultaneously with a chroming agent consisting of a mixture of a chromate with ammonium sulphate. The range of suitable dyes has now been greatly extended, and the chroming agent is usually prepared from a dichromate with ammonium sulphate and ammonia. Whereas dichromates usually cause chromium derivatives of dyes to be precipitated in the bath, this does not occur with the chromates formed by the action of ammonia. In the boiling dyebath acid is liberated slowly, so that dichromate is re-formed at a steady rate and the chromium complex is fixed on the fibre. The role of ammonium salts has been studied by Goodall and his collaborators.[2] In all of these processes a deepening and dulling of shade occurs, especially when monoazo dyes are used.

Azo mordant dyes may be regarded as a special class of azo acid dyes. In the anthraquinone class described in Chapter 9, however, mordant dyes are not related to acid dyes in this way since most of them contain no acidic group and are applied by quite different methods.

In the azo series mordant dyes contain a chelating system enabling them to form complexes with chromium or other metals. Hydroxyl, carboxy, amino and substituted amino groups are suitable ligands, and a chelating system results when there are such groups in two ortho positions of aromatic nuclei linked by an azo group. In arylazopyrazolone dyes the enol form provides a hydroxyl group which can form part of a metallisable system. In dyes of these kinds one of the azo nitrogen atoms is linked with the metal atom, but there are other types in which the azo group takes no part in formation of the complex; examples of these are dyes containing a salicylic acid or 8-hydroxyquinoline residue. In the latter types the change of shade on chroming is comparatively small, especially if the chelating system is separated from the chromophoric system by a link such as $-SO_2-$ or $-S-$. In such complexes the metal affords no protection to the azo group, and light fastness is usually lower than that of dyes in which an azo nitrogen is coordinated with chromium.

The structures of complexes with chromium and other metals are discussed in greater detail in the following Section. The processes whereby chromium complexes are formed on the fibre were studied by Rowe, Race and Speakman.[3] They considered the possibility that 1:1 complexes (one atom of chromium associated with one molecule of a monoazo dye) are obtained in which union with the fibre might depend on (1) coordinate valencies of chromium (satisfied *in vitro* by coordinated water molecules), (2) residual cationic valency of chromium and (3) ionic attraction between sulphonic acid groups in the dye and basic groups in wool fibre. Their experiments showed, however, that in at least some dyes a 1:2 complex is formed (one atom of chromium associated with two molecules of a monoazo dye), and they pointed out that in such cases the coordinate valencies of chromium are satisfied within the dye molecule and are therefore not available for combination with the fibre. The larger molecules of 1:2 chromium complexes would result in stronger attachment by van der Waals forces and perhaps also in physical entrapment of dye molecules within the fibre. Studies of the mechanism of mordanting of animal fibres were reviewed in 1944 by Giles.[4]

Mordant dyes of the azo class contain not more than two azo groups. *o,o'*-Dihydroxyazo and salicyclic acid derivatives are numerically predominant. The former are of importance for black and other deep hues, but the latter (in which the azo group is not concerned in complex formation) are used mainly for yellow and orange hues.

Examples of typical azo mordant dyes are given in Table 4-2. In most cases the dyes are marketed by several manufacturers using different names.

4-1-3   Pre-metallised dyes

Disadvantages are associated with each of the three processes for applying mordant dyes discussed above. The chrome mordant and afterchrome processes require two stages, and matching difficulty arises from the change of shade on chroming, especially in the latter, since the depth is determined in the first stage but cannot be assessed until the second has been completed. The afterchrome process is widely used for blacks, however, which are not sensitive to small variations in dyeing conditions. The metachrome process can only be used with certain dyes, and is in general unsuitable for heavy shades.

In 1912 Bohn succeeded in isolating chromium complexes of dyes containing salicylic acid residues, and the *Ergan* dyes of BASF were based on his work. Some seven years later SCI and BASF obtained chromium complexes from sulphonated *o,o'*-dihydroxyazo dyes by treating them with chromium salts in acid medium, and the metallised dyes were marketed as the *Neolan* and *Palatine Fast* dyes, respectively. These ranges, which are still in use, are applied in the same way as are other acid dyes, but require a strongly acid bath. Since the dulling effect of the wool-chromium complex is absent, they give rather brighter shades than the mordant dyes, and there is better provision of the lighter hues. Light fastness is comparable with that of mordant dyes, but there is a slight inferiority in washing fastness. As the dyeing operation is completed in a single stage shades can be matched without difficulty. A typical dye of this type is CI Acid Blue 158 (CI 14880), which has the structure [19].

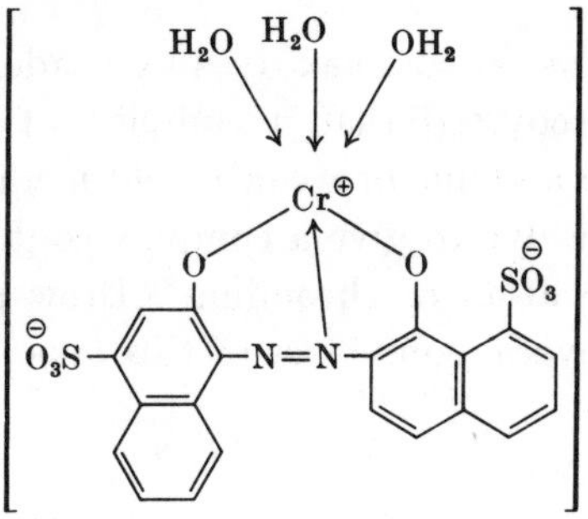

[19]

Since in complexes of this type the dye molecule occupies only three of the six coordination sites of the chromium atom, the remaining sites are occupied by water molecules or hydroxyl ions. It is probable that the ligands are water molecules in acid or neutral media, but their place is taken by hydroxyl ions in alkaline conditions.[5] On the fibre the coordinated water molecules may be at least partly replaced by carboxy, amino or amide groups of the wool molecule, so that a dye–fibre–chromium complex is formed.

Study of molecular models shows that in complex compounds of *trans o,o'*-dihydroxyazo structures the metal atoms (M) can be linked to only one of the nitrogen atoms, but in unsymmetrical compounds two isomers are possible, which may be represented thus:

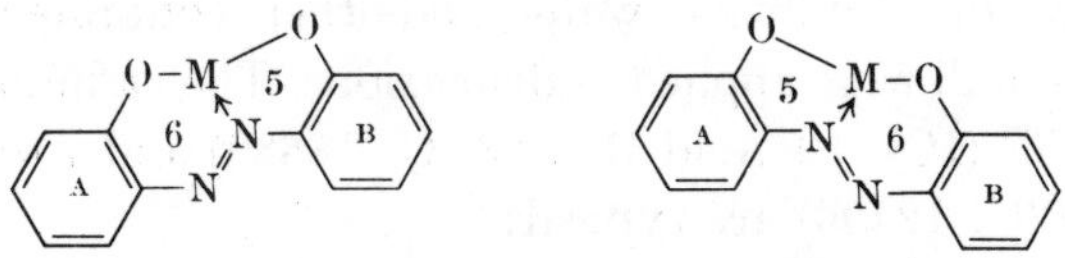

The existence of such isomers has not yet been confirmed experimentally. In order to represent structures such as that of CI Acid Blue 158 [19] an arbitrary choice of one of the isomers is made. Metal complexes of *o*-carboxy-*o'*-hydroxyazo dyes probably exist in one form only, the nitrogen atom nearer to the carboxy-substituted ring being linked to the metal atom so that two six-membered rings are formed [20].

The strongly acid bath from which these chromium complexes are applied results in appreciable degradation of wool fibre, and this led to a demand for fast dyes suitable for milder application condi-

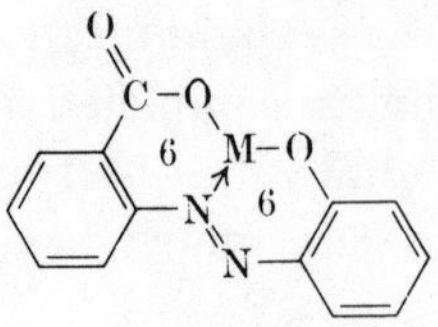

[20]

tions. After an extensive study of metal complex dyes by academic and industrial chemists it was discovered that a complex of the type already described will react in alkaline or weakly acid medium with a second molecule of the same dye to give a complex containing two molecules of dye and one atom of chromium. Drew and Fairbairn[6] assigned structures to several complexes of this type, for example [21].

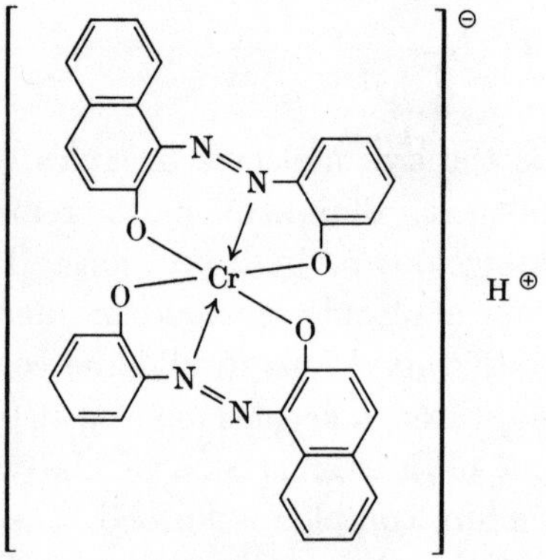

[21]

The *Perlon Fast* dyes manufactured by IG before the second world war for application to polyamide fibres consisted of complexes of this nature. Some of them contained sulphonamide groups, imparting a low degree of solubility in water, and others contained no solubilising groups, but all were applied as dispersions. The structures of *Perlon Fast Red BS* (IG) (CI Acid Red 38; CI 18880) and *Perlon Fast Violet BT* (IG) (CI 12196) are typical:

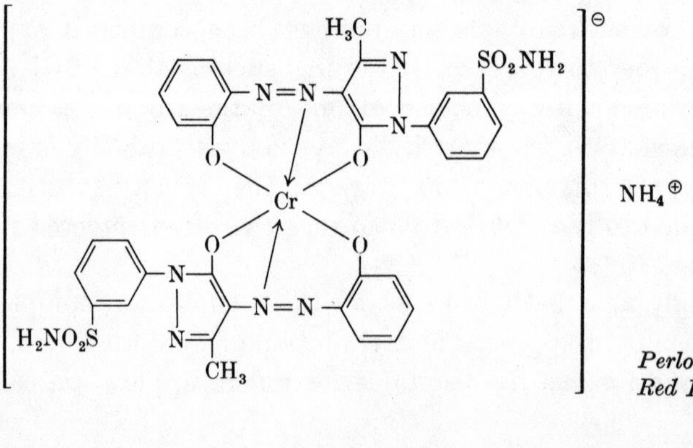

*Perlon Fast
Red BS* (IG)

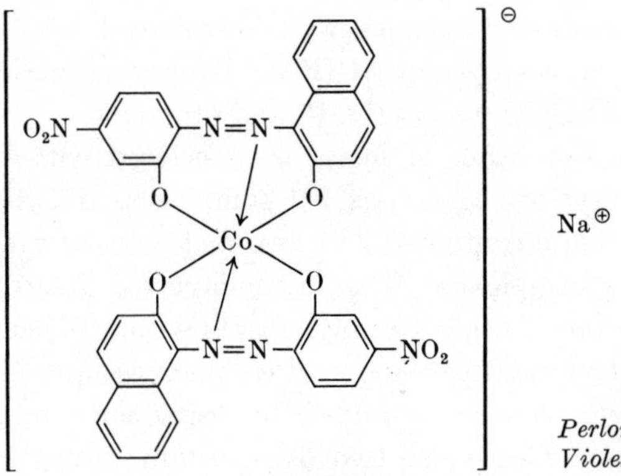

*Perlon Fast
Violet BT* (IG)

As shown by the structures illustrated, complexes of this type are monobasic acids. The location of the negative charge has not been established.

Similar structures containing sulphonic or carboxylic groups were examined for application to wool, but they proved exceptionally sensitive to natural variations in the fibre, and gave unlevel ('skittery') dyeings. Another means of solubilisation was therefore needed. The firm of Geigy examined several non-ionising hydrophilic substituents, and found that methylsulphonyl, sulphonamide or acetylamino groups conferred a sufficient degree of water-solubility without an adverse effect on dyeing or fastness properties. These groups are not acidic, and the solubilising effect is attributed to covalent association of water molecules with the sulphonyl oxygen atoms or keto groups, e.g.:

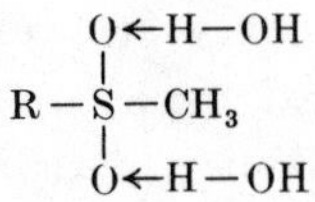

$$R-\overset{\displaystyle O\leftarrow H-OH}{\underset{\displaystyle O\leftarrow H-OH}{\overset{|}{\underset{|}{S}}}}-CH_3$$

This work led to the introduction of the *Irgalan* (Gy) range of dyes in 1949.[7] The constitutions of most of these dyes are unpublished, but Zollinger[8] has given the structure of *Irgalan Brown Violet DL* (Gy) (CI Acid Violet 78) as:

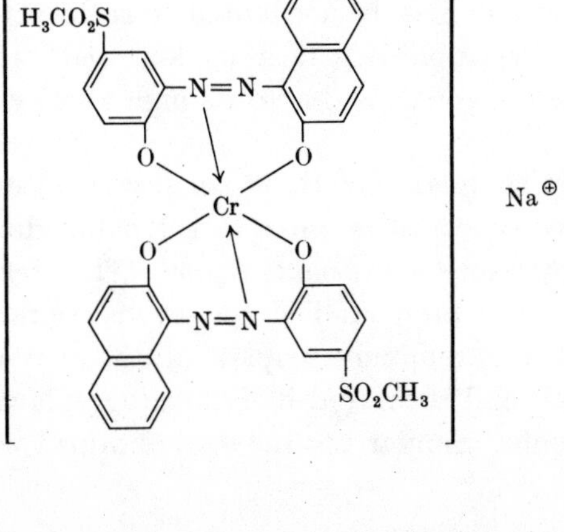

Ranges of dyes with similar properties were introduced later by other firms under the names *Cibalan* (CIBA), *Lanasyn* (Sandoz), *Isolan* (By), *Ortolan* (BASF), *Capracyl* (DuP) and others.

Complexes in which one atom of metal is associated with one molecule of a monoazo dye are known as 1:1 complexes, and those containing one atom of metal combined with two molecules of dye as 1:2 (or sometimes 2:1) complexes. The 1:2 complexes described above are symmetrical, but if a 1:1 complex reacts with a molecule of a different dye an unsymmetrical or mixed complex results. The range of available shades can be extended by using such mixed structures. It is also possible to use two dyes of which only one contains a sulphonic acid group, and in this way relatively cheap products having good solubility have been obtained which give level dyeings on wool from neutral baths with negligible damage to the fibre.[9] Such dyes have been described in many patent specifications, and it is probable that some of them are manufactured.

Pre-metallised dyes can be obtained from *o,o'*-dihydroxyazo, *o*-carboxy-*o'*-hydroxyazo, *o*-amino-*o'*-hydroxyazo or *o*-hydroxy-*o'*-methoxyazo structures. In the last case demethylation occurs during complex formation, and the product is identical with that from the corresponding *o,o'*-dihydroxyazo dye. Other octahedrally coordinating metals may be used in place of chromium, but of these only cobalt yields dyes of technical importance. 1:1 Cobalt complexes are not obtained by the methods used for corresponding chromium compounds, but 1:2 complexes are readily prepared. These are naturally of the symmetrical type. Attempts to prepare 'mixed' complexes from an equimolecular mixture of two different metallisable dyes by treatment with a cobalt salt invariably yield statistical mixtures of the three possible 1:2 complexes. The bathochromic effect of cobalt is less than that of chromium in corresponding structures, and the cobalt complexes often have somewhat higher light fastness. The general enhancement of light fastness resulting from metallisation of an azo dye may be attributed to stabilisation of the azo group towards electrophilic attack by lone pair withdrawal, and the effectiveness of cobalt is due to its high affinity for nitrogen donor ligands.

In chromium and cobalt complexes of the types described each dye molecule occupies three coordination sites in the octahedrally complexed metal, and is therefore a *tridentate ligand*. The stereochemistry of these systems has been studied by several workers. Schetty[10] examined the 1:2 chromium complex of the dye anthranilic acid → β-naphthol, and separated it chromatographically into four isomeric components. Similar results were obtained with related dyes carrying additional substituents, also with the corresponding cobalt complexes, but Schetty was unable to resolve complexes of the dye o-aminophenol → β-naphthol. He suggested that in 1:2 complexes derived from o-carboxy-o'-hydroxyazo and o-carboxy-o'aminoazo compounds, which consist of 6:6 chelate ring systems, the dye molecules lie in parallel planes (Pfeiffer form, sometimes called 'sandwich' or *fac* form), but that in 1:2 complexes derived from o,o'-dihydroxyazo or o-amino-o'-hydroxyazo compounds consisting of 5:6 chelate ring structures, the dye molecules lie in planes perpendicular to each other (Drew–Pfitzner, or *mer* form). This suggestion is based on the fact that the Drew–Pfitzner structure does not permit isomerism, but the Pfeiffer structure allows up to five isomers:

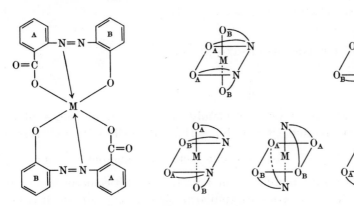

M = Cr, Co
X = —NH—, —O—

Drew–Pfitzner, or *mer* configuration

o, o'-Dihydroxyazo and
o-amino-o'-hydroxyazo structures

o-Carboxy-o'-hydroxyazo structures   Pfeiffer, sandwich or *fac* configuration
(o-Amino-o'-carboxyazo structures   (5 isomers)
show similar stereoisomerism)

Schetty's view was supported by crystal structure studies carried out by R. Grieb and A. Niggli.[11]

In the case of 1:1 chromium complexes of o,o'-dihydroxyazo dyes if *dl* pairs are disregarded there is no possibility of isomerism. On introducing a colourless bidentate ligand such as 2,4-pentanedione, which does not affect spectral properties and is unlikely to affect stereochemistry, three isomers become possible in the *fac* configuration, but there is still only one possibility in the *mer* configuration. Idelson and his co-workers[12] prepared such a chromium complex from the dye 1-naphthalene-8-sulphonyl piperidide $\rightarrow$ 3-methyl-1-phenylpyrazol-5-one, with 2,4-pentanedione as colourless ligand, and showed that it could be separated into three isomeric fractions. The dye must therefore be coordinated with chromium in a *fac* position. This is a surprising result in view of the *mer* configuration assigned to 1:2 complex dyes and it appears that complexes of *o,o'*-dihydroxyazo dyes are capable of existing in either configuration according to their structure or alternatively that a change occurs during formation of 1:2 complexes.

Copper complexes of metallisable azo dyes are of importance for application to cellulosic fibres, and are described in Section 5-8.

4-2 Dyes for silk

Cultivated silk is a natural fibre produced by larvae of the silkworm *Bombyx mori*, and wild silk is produced similarly by silkworms of various species. Raw silk consists of the protein *fibroin* surrounded by silk gum (*sericin*), and the latter is removed in the process of de-gumming or 'boiling off' which precedes dyeing. Fibroin consists of long parallel chains containing about 400 amino acid residues with a structure of the general type [22].

$$-NH-\overset{\overset{\displaystyle R}{|}}{CH}-CO-NH-\overset{\overset{\displaystyle R}{|}}{\underset{\underset{\displaystyle R}{|}}{CH}}-CO-NH-\overset{\overset{\displaystyle R}{|}}{CH}-CO-$$

[**22**]

The residues are derived mainly from the amino acids glycine (R = H), alanine (R = CH_3), serine (R = CH_2OH) and tyrosine (R = $-CH_2-\langle\bigcirc\rangle-OH$), but there are numerous others in small quantities. Fibroin differs from keratin in that it contains no sulphur. Its chemical properties are similar to those of keratin, but it is more sensitive to acids than the latter and less sensitive to mild alkalis. Silk can be dyed with dyes of almost every class, but some restrictions arise from the common practice of weighting the fibre with tin salts, which is carried out in order to improve handling properties and reduce cost.

So far as azo dyes are concerned the main classes applied to silk are the acid dyes and pre-metallised dyes already described as wool dyes, the direct dyes described in Chapter 5 and the reactive dyes described in Chapter 13. Mordant dyes applied to silk are mainly of the anthraquinone type (Chapter 9). It has never been necessary to develop dyes especially for silk.

4-3   Dyes for leather

Leather has a complex structure consisting largely of the fibrous protein *collagen*. Collagen has a molecular weight which has been estimated as at least 38,730, and it is built up from about 21 amino acid residues.[13] In the production of leather, skins are tanned by various processes with the object of suppressing chemical activity and protecting the peptide links so that a durable product is obtained. This treatment does not destroy affinity for dyes, however, and the amino acid residues confer binding power for acid and basic dyes. Mordant or pre-metallised dyes are used when high light fastness is required. Direct dyes (see Chapter 5) are used to some extent, but have in general poor penetration. Many direct dyes contain a free amino group which can be diazotised on the fibre and developed with β-naphthol or another coupling component, and this process is especially useful for the production of blacks. Insoluble azo dyes (Chapter 7) are increasingly used for gloves and other garments exposed to the weather.

Special problems arise in the dyeing of leather because of its non-uniformity. Dyes must therefore be chosen that are not highly sensitive to variations in the leather. The view has long been held that leather dyes should be homogeneous, but the advance of chromatographic techniques has shown that many dyes formerly regarded as homogeneous are in fact mixtures. Many azo dyes made from intermediates such as m-phenylenediamine, resorcinol or α-naphthol are undoubtedly mixtures of isomeric products, but properties of the components are similar and they can often be applied satisfactorily to leather.

Table 4-3 gives a few examples of azo dyes widely used for leather.

Table 4-3 Examples of azo dyes applied to leather

Chemical class	Application class	CI Ref. Nos.	Structure
Monoazo	Acid dye	CI Acid Orange 7 CI 15510	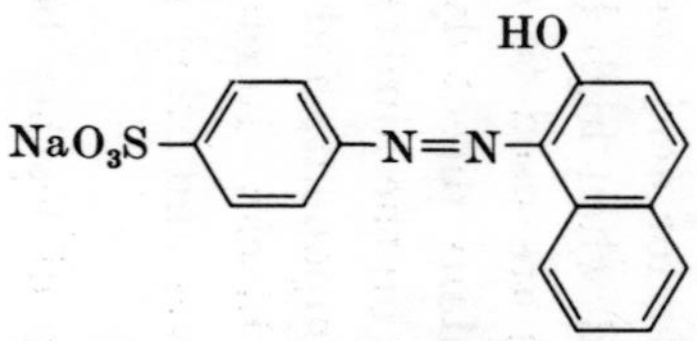
Monoazo	Acid dye	CI Acid Red 1 CI 18050	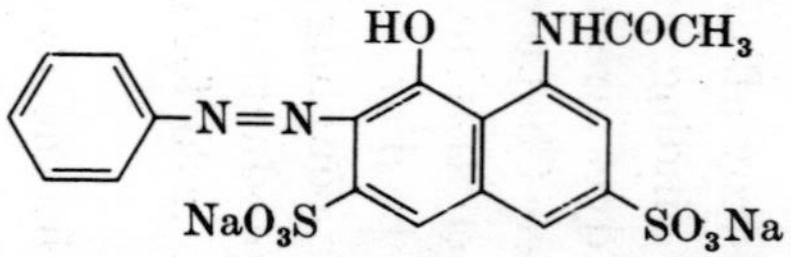
Pre-metallised Monoazo	Acid dye	CI Acid Blue 158 CI 14880	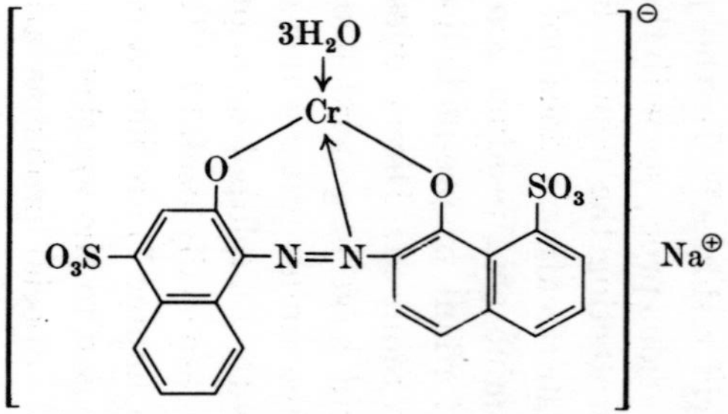

Monoazo	CI Acid Brown 6 CI 14625	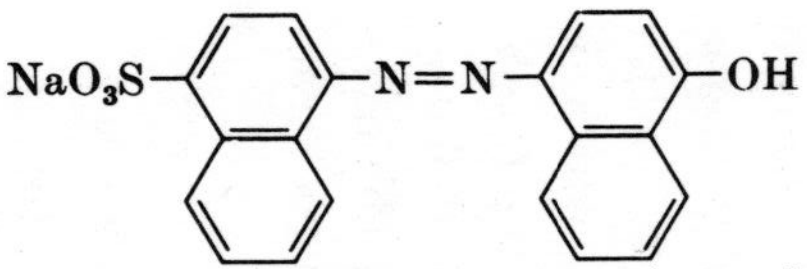 NaO$_3$S—[naphthalene]—N=N—[naphthalene]—OH
Disazo	CI Basic Brown 1 CI 21000	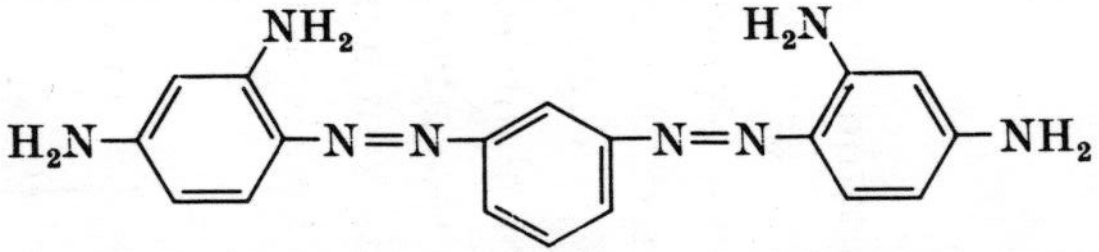 H$_2$N—[benzene]—N=N—[benzene(NH$_2$)]—N=N—[benzene]—NH$_2$ with H$_2$N
Trisazo	CI Direct Black 38 CI 30235	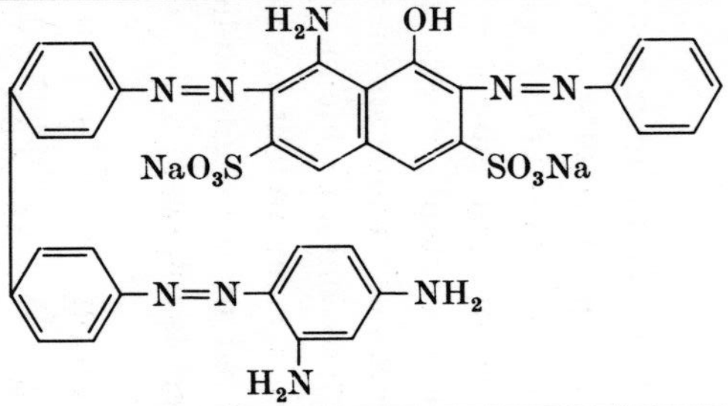 H$_2$N—[naphthalene with OH, SO$_3$Na, N=N—phenyl]—N=N—[benzene]—N=N—[benzene]—NH$_2$, NaO$_3$S
Disazo (as applied)	CI Direct Blue 2 CI 22590	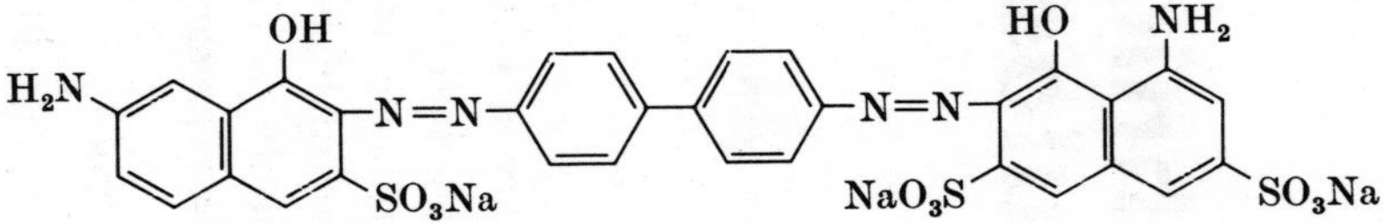 H$_2$N—[naphthalene with OH, SO$_3$Na]—N=N—[biphenyl]—N=N—[naphthalene with HO, NH$_2$, SO$_3$Na, NaO$_3$S] Diazotised on leather and developed with β-naphthol or m-tolylenediamine, giving black shades

5 Technical azo dyes for cellulosic fibres

The earliest cellulosic fibres were linen and cotton, both of which have been used since remote antiquity. Linen, or flax, is derived from 'bast' fibres of plants of the *Linum* family, especially *Linum usitatissimum*. After removal of glutinous and pectinous matter the fibre has a cellulose content of 82–83%. Cotton, which is fine hair attached to seeds of various species of plants of the *Gossypium* genus, has a cellulose content which may reach 96%. Cellulose is a polymer of high molecular weight consisting of long chains of D-glucose units connected by β-1,4-glucosidic bonds, and its structure may be represented as follows:

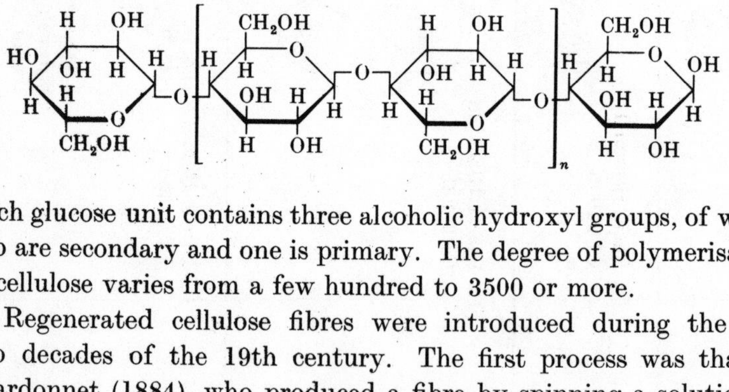

Each glucose unit contains three alcoholic hydroxyl groups, of which two are secondary and one is primary. The degree of polymerisation of cellulose varies from a few hundred to 3500 or more.

Regenerated cellulose fibres were introduced during the last two decades of the 19th century. The first process was that of Chardonnet (1884), who produced a fibre by spinning a solution of nitrocellulose in a mixture of alcohol and ether and subsequently removing nitro groups. The cuprammonium process followed (1890), and in 1891 Cross and Bevan introduced the viscose process whereby wood pulp cellulose is treated with caustic soda and carbon disulphide to form sodium cellulose xanthate, which, after a 'ripening' stage, is spun into an acid coagulating bath. The nitrocellulose process is now obsolete, but the cuprammonium process, which has the advantage of giving an exceptionally fine filament, is still used. The viscose process is of much greater importance, but it is declining in consequence of the development of the newer synthetic fibres.

The dyeing properties of the various cellulosic fibres are broadly similar, but application conditions are affected by differences in physical properties. Thus linen, which has a harder structure than cotton, is less readily penetrated by dyes. There are also differences in dyeing properties between the several types of regenerated cellulose fibres; cuprammonium rayon, for example, having fine filaments, is more easily dyed than viscose.

Dyes of many chemical classes are applied to cellulosic fibres. Azo dyes, which predominate numerically, are described here, and others are dealt with in the appropriate chapters.

The first substantive or 'direct' dyes discovered in 1884 (see Chapter 3, p. 22) were disazo dyes obtained from tetrazotised benzidine, but other structures have since been found to confer affinity for cellulose. The azo group itself favours substantivity but for adequate effect either a second azo group or another favourable group must also be present in the dye molecule. The structures which are chiefly important in substantive dyes are as follows:

Azo   Diphenyl 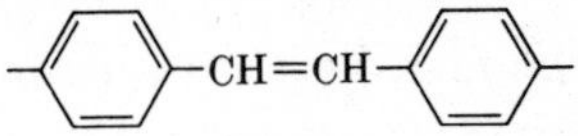   Stilbene   Carboxyamide

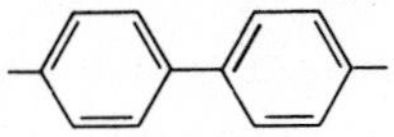

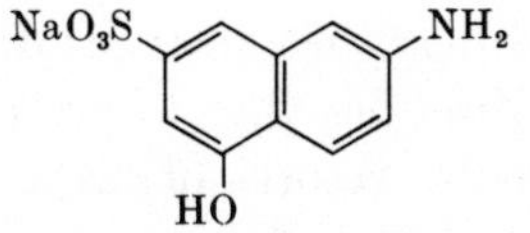

J acid 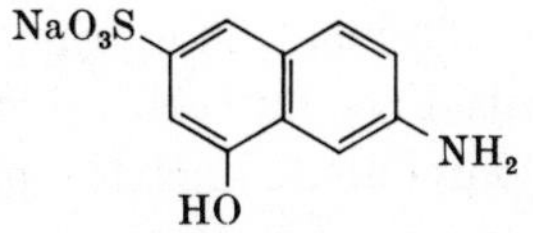   γ acid 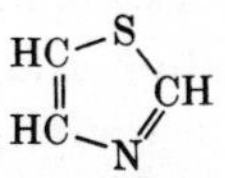   Thiazole

All of the other groupings listed find use in conjunction with the azo chromophore to give a great variety of dyes for cellulosic fibres. Others of smaller importance, such as the residues of pyrazol-5-one, resorcinol and m-phenylenediamine, also confer a measure of cellulose affinity. Apart from the presence of one or more of the favourable components there are other structural requirements for substantivity, and these are discussed in Chapter 19.

Typical substantive azo dyes of the various chemical classes are now described.

5-1 Monoazo dyes

About 35 monoazo direct dyes are in use, most of them containing either a thiazole or a J acid residue. Examples are CI Direct Yellow 8 (CI 13920), CI Direct Brown 30 (CI 17630) and CI Direct Red 118 (CI 17780) (diazotised and developed on the fibre with β-naphthol or 3-methyl-1-phenylpyrazol-5-one), with the structures shown:

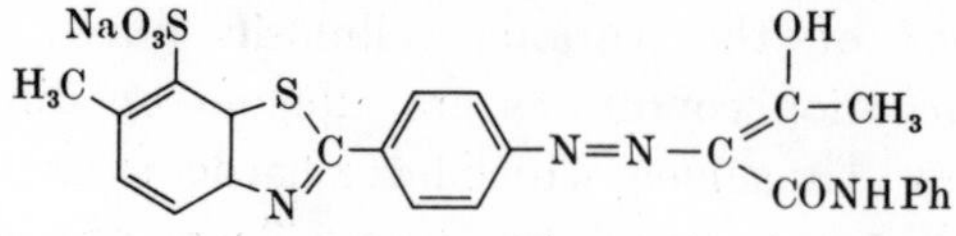

CI Direct Yellow 8

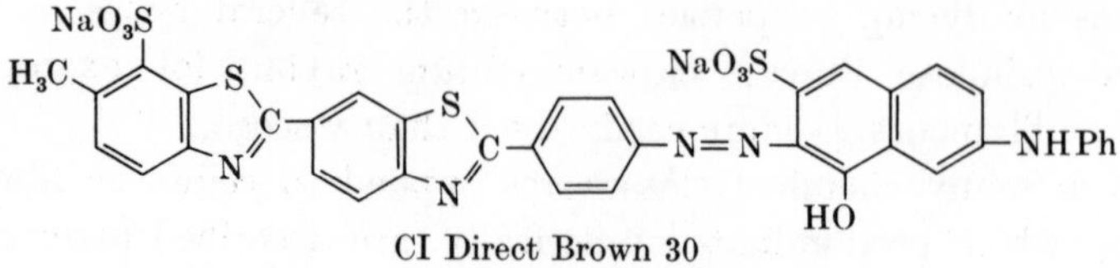

CI Direct Brown 30

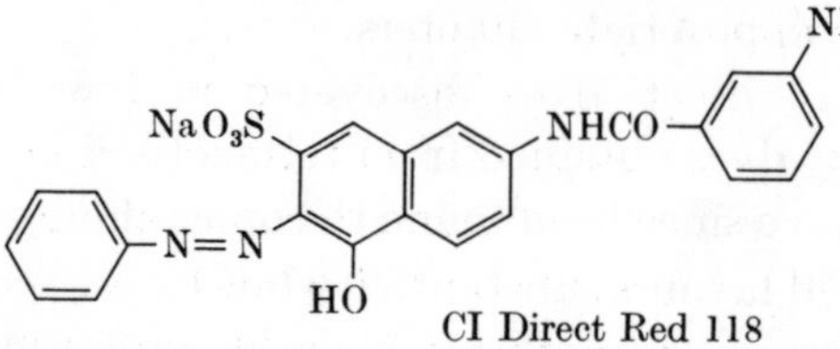

CI Direct Red 118

5-2 Disazo dyes of the type $D \overset{\nearrow E^1}{\underset{\searrow E^2}{}}$

Congo Red, the first direct dye manufactured, which was discovered by Böttiger in 1884, has the constitution benzidine $\Rightarrow$ (naphthionic acid)$_2$, and is therefore included under this heading. Many other dyes of the same type have been introduced, and the Colour Index includes about 300 of them. The principal diamines are benzidine, o-tolidine and dianisidine, but other benzidine derivatives are also used. Coupling components include phenols, resorcinol, salicylic acid, m-phenylenediamine, naphthols, naphtholsulphonic acids, naphthylaminesulphonic acids, aminonaphtholsulphonic acids and pyrazolones. In dyes of corresponding series the methyl and methoxy groups in tolidine and dianisidine have a progressive bathochromic effect, and an almost complete shade range is available. Fastness to light of dyes of the benzidine type is in general poor, but fastness to washing is very good. In spite of their shortcomings these dyes are in demand because of their moderate cost.

A few dyes of this type are made from arylenediamines as D components. Usually a nitroarylamine is diazotised and coupled with E^1, the nitro group is reduced, then the amine is diazotised and coupled with E^2. Alternatively a compound such as p-amino-acetanilide can be diazotised and coupled with E^1, the acetamidoazo compound hydrolysed and the resulting aminoazo compound diazotised and coupled with E^2.

Examples of dyes of the type $D \overset{\nearrow E^1}{\underset{\searrow E^2}{}}$ are shown in Table 5-1.

Table 5-1   Examples of disazo direct dyes of the type $D\underset{\searrow E^2}{\overset{\nearrow E^1}{}}$

CI Ref. Nos.	Structure
CI Direct Orange 1 CI 22375	Benzidine $\underset{2\ \searrow}{\overset{1\ \nearrow}{}}$ salicylic acid 3-methyl-1-p-sulphophenylpyrazol-5-one
CI Direct Red 39 CI 23630	o-Tolidine $\underset{2\ \searrow}{\overset{1\ \nearrow}{}}$ 2-naphthol-6,8-disulphonic acid phenol (ethylated)
CI Direct Violet 3 CI 22445	Benzidine $\underset{\searrow}{\overset{\nearrow}{}}$ 1-naphthol-4-sulphonic acid 1-naphthol-3,6-disulphonic acid
CI Direct Blue 1 CI 24410	o-Dianisidine $\rightrightarrows$ (1-amino-8-naphthol-2,4-disulphonic acid)$_2$
CI Direct Blue 96 CI 21620	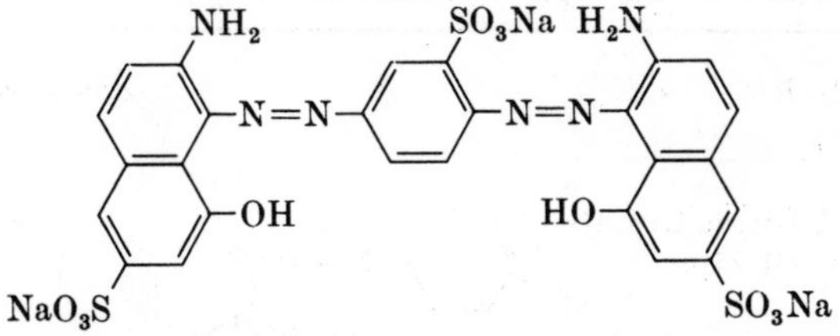

(Obtained from 2-amino-5-nitrobenzenesulphonic acid → γ acid by reducing the nitro group, diazotising and coupling with γ acid in acid medium)

5-3   Disazo dyes of the type A → M → E

This is a fairly large group. The A components are variously substituted anilines and naphthylamines. Suitable middle components are not numerous, and the commonest of them are 2,5-xylidine, 2-methoxy-5-methylaniline ('cresidine'), 1-naphthylamine, 2-ethoxy-1-naphthylamine-6-sulphonic acid, 1-naphthylamine-6- and -7-sulphonic acids (often mixed and called 'Cleve's acids'), and 6-amino-1-naphthol-3-sulphonic acid (J acid). There are several widely used end-components, including 1-naphthol-3-, -4- and -5-sulphonic acids, 1,8-dihydroxynaphthalene-4-sulphonic acid, 6-amino-1-naphthol-3-sulphonic acid (J acid) and its N-phenyl, N-acetyl and N-benzoyl derivatives, 7-amino-1-naphthol-3-sulphonic acid (γ acid), 1-amino-8-naphthol-2,4-disulphonic acid (Chicago or 2S acid).

1-benzoyl-amino-8-naphthol-3,6-disulphonic acid and 3-carboxy-1-phenylpyrazol-5-one. By far the most important of these are J acid and its *N*-phenyl, *N*-acetyl and *N*-benzoyl derivatives, which confer affinity for cellulose to a marked degree. γ Acid confers this property to a smaller extent.

Substituents such as sulphonic or carboxylic acid groups are introduced into these dyes in number sufficient to give the required degree of solubility in water, but in excess they lead to loss of fibre affinity. Of the direct dyes of the type $A \to M \to E$ included in the Colour Index about two-thirds contain two sulphonic groups, and in general only the larger molecules require more than this.

The hues are mainly red, violet or blue and are fairly bright. There are also a few orange, green and grey dyes of this type. Fastness to light is medium (mainly about 4–5 on the SDC 1–8 scale), and fastness to washing is moderate. Some examples are shown in Table 5-2.

Table 5-2   Examples of disazo direct dyes of the type $A \to M \to E$

CI Ref. Nos.	*Structure*
CI Direct Red 16 CI 27680	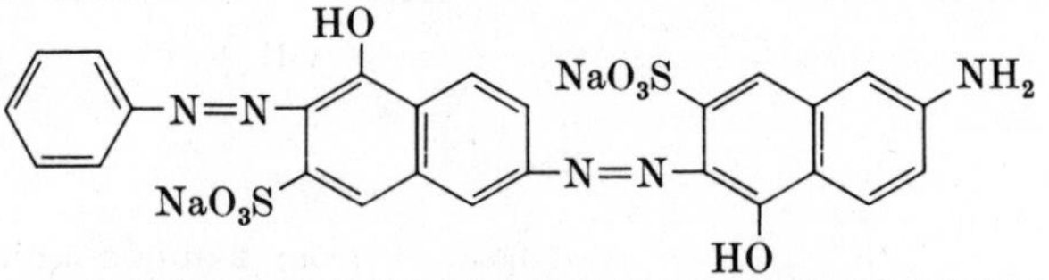
CI Direct Violet 51 CI 27905	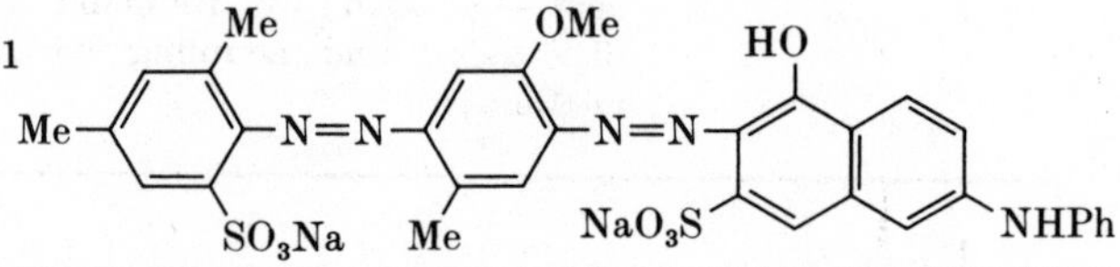
CI Direct Blue 67 CI 27925	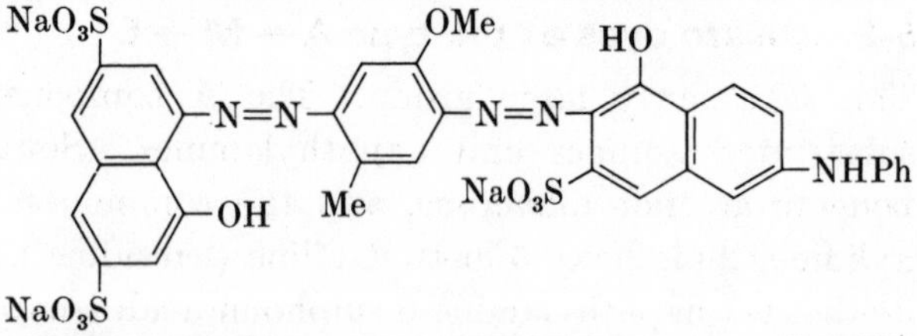
CI Direct Black 51 CI 27720	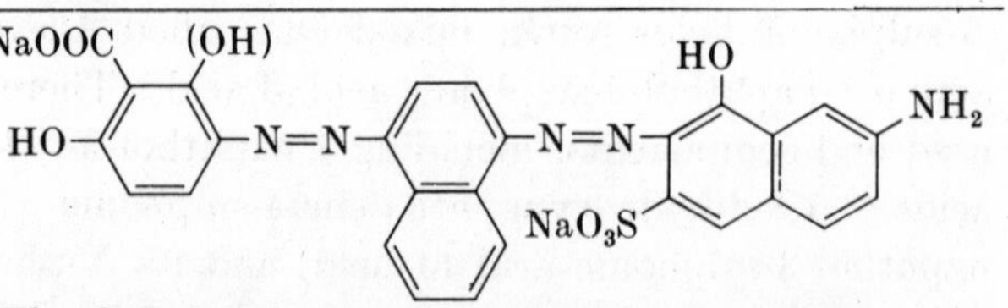

(The first component is a mixture of 3- and 5-aminosalicylic acid)

5-4   Disazo dyes of the type $A^1 \rightarrow Z \leftarrow A^2$

The dyes of this group are not numerous, but their importance is by
no means negligible. They fall into two groups. The first consists
of orange and brown dyes obtained from Z components such as
m-phenylenediamine, *m*-phenylenediaminesulphonic acid or resorcinol. The A components include anilines, naphthylamines and
their sulphonated derivatives, dehydrothio-*p*-toluidinesulphonic acid
and Primuline. Probably the most important example from this
group is CI Direct Orange 18, which is made in three versions, with
the following structures:

CI 20215 Dehydrothio-*p*-toluidinesulphonic acid $\xrightarrow{1}$ resorcinol
  $\xleftarrow{2}$ aniline

CI 20216 Primuline $\xrightarrow{1}$ resorcinol $\xleftarrow{2}$ aniline

CI 20230 (Primuline)$_2$ $\rightrightarrows$ resorcinol.

The chemistry of Primuline and dehydrothio-*p*-toluidine is described
in Section 12-9.

The second group consists of dyes derived from symmetrical Z
components containing two aromatic residues linked by groups
such as —NHCONH— or —NH—. Some of these are obtained by
phosgenation of aminoazo compounds and often contain no auxochrome. An example is CI Direct Yellow 50 (CI 29025), which is
obtained by phosgenating the compound 3-aminonaphthalene-
1,5-disulphonic acid → *m*-toluidine:

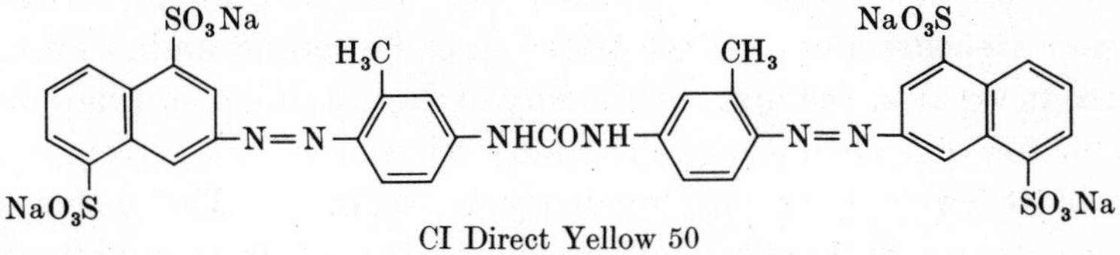

CI Direct Yellow 50

Other dyes containing urea groups are obtained from the intermediate
Carbonyl J acid [**23**], which is obtained by phosgenating J acid.

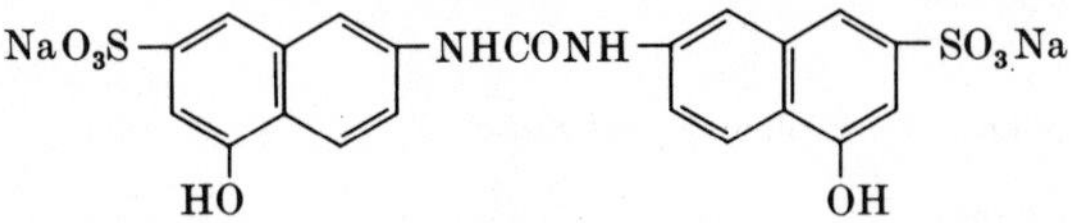

[**23**]

Carbonyl J acid can be coupled successively with two molecular
proportions of a diazo component giving symmetrical or unsymmetrical disazo dyes. Thus CI Direct Orange 26 (CI 29150) is
obtained by coupling two molecules of diazotised aniline with one
molecule of Carbonyl J acid, or CI Direct Red 23 (CI 29160) by

coupling one molecule of diazotised aniline and one molecule of diazotised 4-aminoacetanilide with the same component. These dyes have washing fastness of the same order as that of most benzidine dyes, but their light fastness shows a considerable improvement.

Disazo dyes of a similar character can be obtained from di-J acid [**24**], obtained by treating J acid with a boiling solution of sodium sulphite.

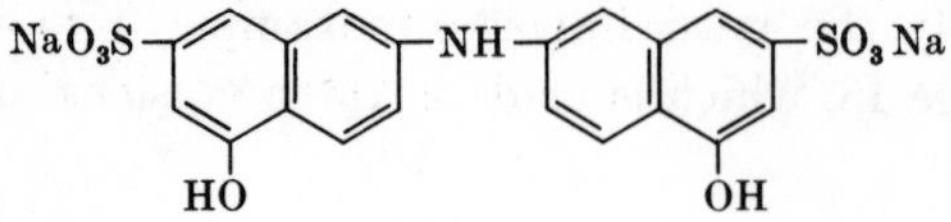

[**24**]

5-5 Trisazo and other polyazo dyes

These dyes are derived from components of the types used for disazo dyes, but the range of Z components is greater. It includes 1,8-dihydroxynaphthalene-4-sulphonic acid, 1,8-dihydroxynaphthalene-3,6-disulphonic acid (Chromotrope acid), 6-amino-1-naphthol-3-sulphonic acid (J acid), 1,8-aminonaphthol-4-sulphonic acid (S acid), 1,8-aminonaphthol-3,6-disulphonic acid (H acid) and 1:8-aminonaphthol-4,6-disulphonic acid (K acid).

Three of the various types of trisazo structure are of principal importance. The type D $\nearrow$ E^1, D $\searrow$ M $\rightarrow$ E^2 is numerically predominant, D being usually either a diamine of the benzidine series or *p*-phenylenediamine; in the latter case the second amino group is introduced after the first coupling by hydrolysis of an acetylamino or reduction of a nitro group. The hues are mainly blue, green, brown or black, with a general tendency to dullness. The increase in molecular weight in relation to disazo dyes results in an improvement in washing fastness. A typical dye is CI Direct Brown 57 (CI 31705), with the structure [**25**].

Benzidine $\xrightarrow{1}$ salicylic acid
Benzidine $\xrightarrow{2}$ (alk) γ acid $\xrightarrow{3}$ *m*-phenylenediamine

[**25**]

A second type D $\nearrow$ E, D $\searrow$ Z $\leftarrow$ A is well represented, mainly by dyes of the benzidine series. Their properties are similar to those of the first type. An example is CI Direct Black 4 (CI 30245), which has the structure [**26**].

$$\text{Benzidine} \begin{cases} 1 \rightarrow \text{(acid)H-acid (alk)} \overset{2}{\leftarrow} \text{aniline} \\ 3 \nwarrow m\text{-tolylenediamine} \end{cases}$$

[26]

Dyes with structures of the third type $A \rightarrow M^1 \rightarrow M^2 \rightarrow E$ are derived from components similar to those used in making disazo dyes of the type $A \rightarrow M \rightarrow E$. The dyes have high substantivity for cellulosic fibres, giving mainly blue or grey hues with good fastness to light. An example is CI Direct Blue 78 (CI 34200), with the structure aniline-2,5-disulphonic acid $\rightarrow$ 1,7-Cleve's acid $\rightarrow$ 1-naphthylamine $\rightarrow$ N-phenyl J acid. It gives blue shades on cellulosic fibres and is also used on chrome-tanned leather.

Tetrakisazo and other polyazo dyes give mainly dark brown or black shades. Their washing fastness is good in general, and light fastness is somewhat variable. An example with outstandingly good light fastness obtained by aftertreatment on the fibre with copper sulphate is CI Direct Blue 150 (CI 35110). This dye has the structure dianisidine $\overset{alk}{\rightarrow}$ (J acid)$_2$ $\overset{acid}{\leftarrow}$ (5-amino-4H-1,2,4-triazole-3-carboxylic acid)$_2$ and provides an interesting example of the use of a heterocyclic diazo component. The aftertreated dyeings on cotton or viscose are navy blue.

5-6   Developed dyes

Many azo dyes contain an amino group in the end-component, and amino groups may also be formed after coupling by reduction of a nitro group or hydrolysis of an acylamido group in the diazo component. In many cases such dyes can be diazotised on the fibre and coupled with suitable unsulphonated components. The hue is thereby deepened, and usually there is an improvement in washing fastness, since the molecular weight in increased without addition of solubilising groups. Sometimes, however, there is a fall in light fastness. Dyes applied in this way are known as *developed* colours; many of them are used only in the developed form. Developers commonly used include phenol, resorcinol, β-naphthol, m-phenylenediamine, m-tolylenediamine, 3-methyl-1-phenylpyrazol-5-one and 3-hydroxy-2-naphthoic acid.

Other dyes include a coupling component with an unoccupied coupling position, and after dyeing these may be developed on the fibre by treatment with a diazo solution (usually diazotised p-nitroaniline). Thus the dye CI Direct Blue 4 (CI 24380) with the structure [27] can be coupled on the fibre in the two positions *ortho* to the amino groups.

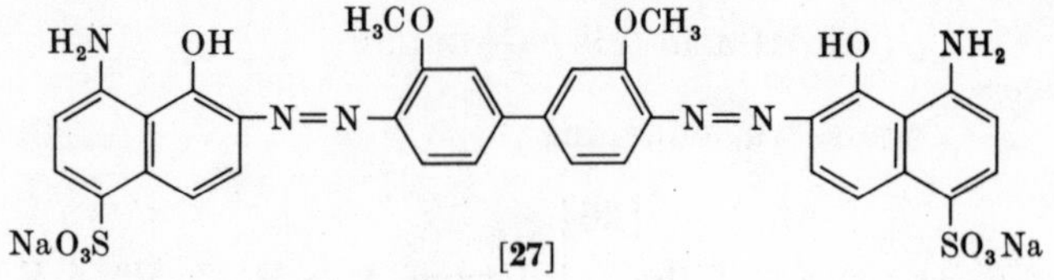

[27]

5-7 Other aftertreated dyes

Some direct dyes are aftertreated on the fibre with formaldehyde, and fastness to washing is thereby improved. The effect on light fastness tends to be adverse. Dyes containing salicylic acid residues are often aftertreated with a bichromate or chromium fluoride, an improvement in wet fastness properties being obtained without a marked change in hue. Other metallisable dyes may be treated on the fibre with copper sulphate with a great improvement in light fastness. It is possible with suitable dyes to apply copper sulphate and bichromate in a single bath.

o-Hydroxyazo dyes form loose coordination complexes of the type [28] and these tend to lose copper during washing. More stable complexes are formed by *o,o'*-dihydroxyazo and *o*-hydroxy-*o'*-carboxyazo dyes, with structures of the types [29] and [30].

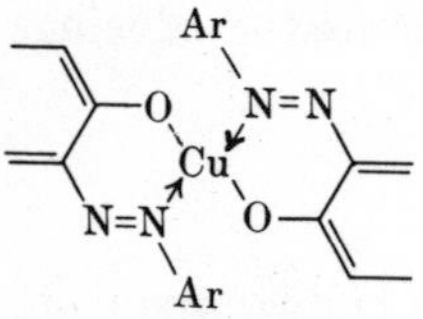

[28] 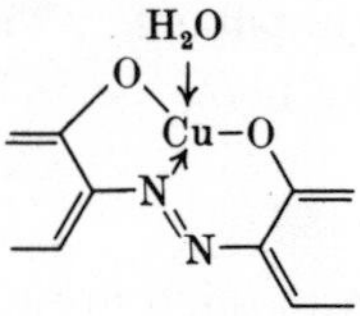   [29] 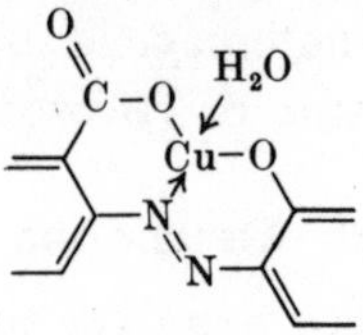   [30]

Ranges of direct dyes suitable for after-coppering have been marketed by several makers (*Coprantine*, CIBA; *Cuprophenyl*, Geigy; *Cuprofix*, Sandoz), and these usually form sparingly soluble complexes resistant to washing.

Various cationic fixing agents have been introduced for aftertreatment of dyed fibres which convert direct dyes into lakes with increased resistance to water. The lakes are often broken down by soap, however, and treatments of this kind also have disadvantages in change of shade and loss of fastness to light. Nevertheless these agents are of considerable value when applied with suitably selected dyes. The adverse effect on light fastness can often be countered by simultaneous treatment with copper sulphate, but allowance must be made for the effect on shade.

5-8 Pre-metallised dyes

Water-soluble copper complexes of *o,o'*-dihydroxyazo dyes were first prepared in substance by SCI (now CIBA) about 1915, and it was found that they could be applied to cotton in the same way as ordinary direct dyes.[1] Many copper complexes have been manufactured and are included in commercial ranges such as the *Chlorantine* (CIBA), *Sirius Supra* (FBy), *Durazol* (ICI) and *Solophenyl* (Gy) dyes. In many cases the complexes are easily obtained by heating an aqueous solution of the *o,o'*-dihydroxyazo dye with copper sulphate and ammonia at 80°–90°C. Sometimes a corresponding *o*-hydroxy-*o'*-methoxyazo dye is more readily accessible than the *o,o'*-dihydroxyazo dye, and it is usually possible to metallise the former with demethylation to yield the same complex as that given by the latter. In such cases the reaction may be carried out at 110°–125°C under pressure, or in an open vessel in presence of a catalyst such as pyridine[2] or an alkylamine.[3]

Copper complexes of *o,o'*-dihydroxyazo dyes are obtainable from *o*-chloro-*o'*-hydroxyazo dyes.[4] They can also be derived from *o*-hydroxy-*o'*- unsubstituted azo dyes by oxidation with hydrogen peroxide in acid medium in presence of copper salts.[5]

The following are examples of copper-containing direct dyes:

CI Direct Red 83 (CI 29225)	Bis copper complex of (2-aminophenol-4-sulphonic acid)$_2$ $\rightrightarrows$ Carbonyl J acid, obtained from (4-methoxymetanilic acid)$_2$ $\rightrightarrows$ Carbonyl J acid by demethylative coppering
CI Direct Violet 48 (CI 29125)	Bis copper complex of (2-aminophenol-4-sulphon-N-methylamide)$_2$ $\rightrightarrows$ di J acid
CI Direct Blue 98 (CI 23155)	Bis copper complex derived from dianisidine $\nearrow$ 1-naphthol-3,8-disulphonic acid $\searrow$ N-phenyl J acid by demethylative coppering
CI Direct Brown 95 (CI 30145)	Benzidine $\nearrow$ salicylic acid $\searrow$ (copper complex of 2-aminophenol-4-sulphonic acid → resorcinol)

5-9 Dyes with mixed chromophores

Polyazo dyes normally contain a single chromophoric system, and a conjugated chain runs through the whole molecule. It is possible, however, for a dye molecule to contain two or more independent chromophoric systems electronically insulated from each other. Such dyes were first introduced by CIBA, who utilised the triazinyl ring as a chromophoric block. This ring serves as a convenient link since it can be introduced by reaction of cyanuric chloride with two or three amino-containing dyes in succession.[6] Substitution of the first chlorine atom takes place easily in presence of alkali at atmospheric temperature. The second chlorine atom is less easily removed, and reaction with an amino compound may require a temperature of 55°–60°C, the optimum conditions varying with the basicity of the amine. Replacement of the third chlorine atom calls for still more vigorous conditions, and a temperature of 90°–100°C may be suitable; much higher temperatures are needed, however, in the case of weakly basic compounds. The progressive loss of activity at each stage enables condensation to be carried out with three different components to give a substantially homogeneous product. The residues of three dyes (Dye 1)-NH_2, (Dye 2)-NH_2 and (Dye 3)-NH_2 may be linked by a series of reactions in alkaline medium, as follows:

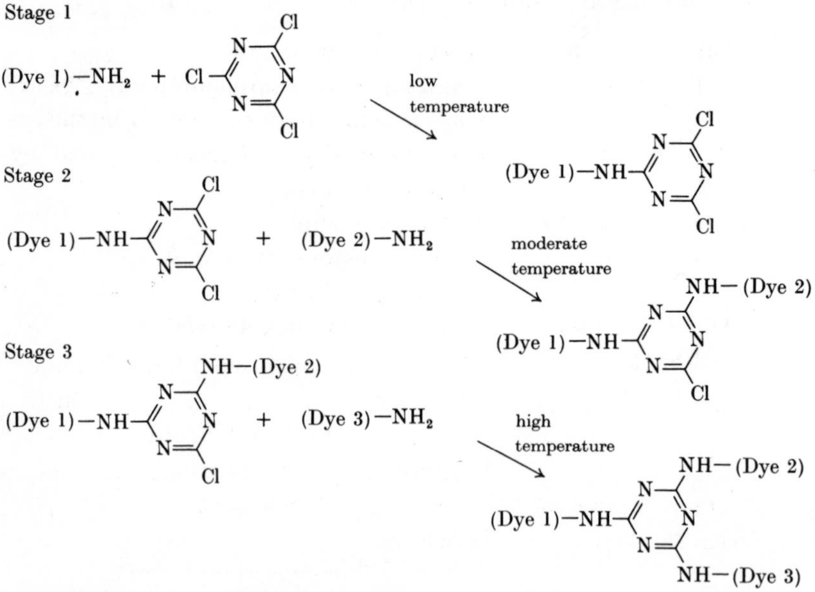

In the resulting product each dye residue contributes its own absorption characteristics; by combining yellow and blue components, green dyes can therefore be obtained that are much brighter than normal polyazo greens. Dyes containing three independent chromophoric systems are of limited interest and the third condensation is often carried out with a suitably reactive colourless compound such as aniline or phenol.

An example of a commercial dye containing two electronically insulated chromophores is *Chlorantine Fast Green BLL* (CIBA) (CI Direct Green 26; CI 34045) with the structure [31]; it gives a bluish green hue on cellulosic fibres. One of the aminoazo dye residues may be replaced by an amino-substituted anthraquinone dye residue. A commercial dye containing both azo and anthraquinone residues is *Chlorantine Fast Green* 5GLL (CIBA) (CI Direct Green 28; CI 14155), which has the structure [32] and gives bright yellowish green shades on cellulosic fibres.

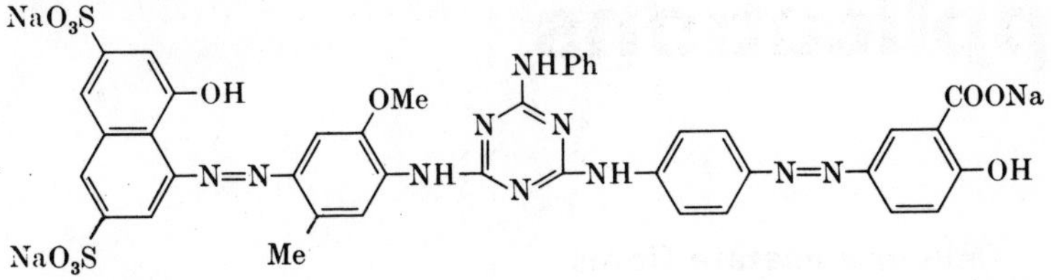

[31]

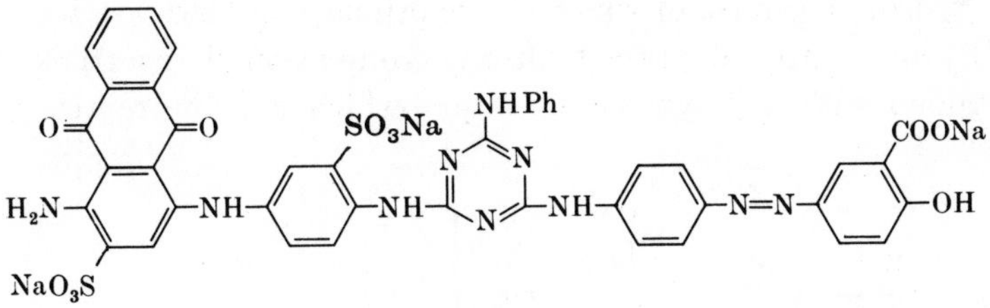

[32]

6 Technical azo dyes for synthetic fibres and miscellaneous applications

6-1 Cellulose acetate fibres

The D-glucose units in the cellulose polymer (see Chapter 5) contain three hydroxyl groups, of which one is primary and two are secondary. By acetylating all of the hydroxyl group in cellulose a triacetate is obtained with a polymeric structure which may be represented thus:

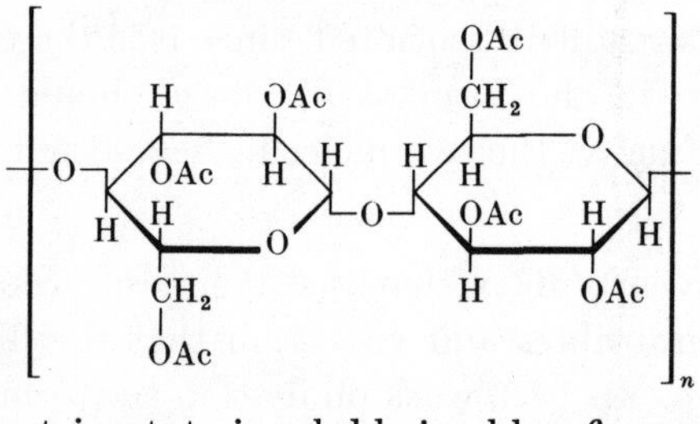

The triacetate is soluble in chloroform, and a fibre known as *Lustron* was spun from chloroform solution in early small-scale American manufacture (1914–1924). If the triacetate is partially hydrolysed to give a mixture with an average of $2\frac{1}{2}$ acetyl groups per glucose residue the product loses solubility in chloroform, but becomes soluble in acetone. A different product which is insoluble in acetone is obtained by direct introduction of $2\frac{1}{2}$ acetyl groups; presumably the less accessible hydroxyl groups are the last to be acetylated and the last to be re-formed on hydrolysis.

During the first World War incompletely acetylated cellulose was produced on a large scale for use as a dope for aircraft fabric. After the war efforts to find a new use for it led to the production of cellulose acetate fibre by British Celanese Corporation. The commercial product contains an average of 2·3 acetyl groups per glucose residue, and is known as secondary acetate, or simply 'acetate',

It is spun from acetone solution. In spite of an inconveniently low melting-point acetate fibre attained great success and is still extensively used, but in recent years it has been partly superseded by other synthetic fibres.

Although free hydroxyl groups remain, acetate fibre cannot be dyed by direct dyes, and in the early days the absence of suitable dyes seriously hampered development of the new product. The problem was first solved in 1922 by an invention of A. G. Green and K. H. Saunders which led to the introduction of the *Ionamine* dyes of British Dyestuffs Corporation.[1] These dyes were water-soluble ω-methanesulphonic acid derivatives of aminoazo compounds which were gradually hydrolysed in the dyebath so that the insoluble aminoazo compounds were adsorbed by the fibre as fast as they were formed. Some of the Ionamine dyes could be diazotised on the fibre and developed with a phenol or an amine to give a black or other deep shade. In the course of their work, Green and Saunders established some general principles relating to dyes for acetate. The presence of amino, substituted amino or hydroxyl groups is desirable, but sulphonic and other strongly acid groups reduce affinity for the fibre. Basic dyes may be applied in salt form provided that the salt is readily dissociated, since it is the free base that is adsorbed. Dyes in the form of free base should be sparingly soluble in water. Finally, the dye molecule should not be unduly large.

It was appreciated in the early days that the dyeing of acetate differs from that of the natural fibres and viscose in that the fibre serves as a solvent for the dye. In 1923 work on dyes in the form of aqueous dispersions was carried out independently by British Celanese Corporation and British Dyestuffs Corporation. The *SRA* colours of British Celanese Corporation were dispersions of aminoazo or hydroxyazo dyes obtained by means of the surface-active agent sulphated ricinoleic acid. Other dispersing agents used included alkyl sulphates, alkaryl sulphonates and fatty alcohol–ethylene oxide condensates (a long alkyl chain being usually present in the molecule), and the dispersions obtained by applying them with various milling techniques were often so fine as to be easily mistaken for true solutions.[2] British Dyestuffs Corporation marketed dispersed aminoazo and hydroxyazo dyes in their *Dispersol* range,[3] and this is still maintained by ICI (formed in 1926 by a union of British Dyestuffs Corporation with other firms). The *Duranol* range (see Section 9-3) is a parallel range of dispersed dyes of the anthraquinone series.

Dyes of these types are now produced by many manufacturers. Whereas the dyes were formerly supplied only as aqueous dispersions they are now usually marketed in the form of re-dispersible powders which yield suitable dispersions on stirring with water.

Hydroxyalkylamino groups impart a small degree of water-solubility and assist dispersibility; coupling components such as N-ethyl-N-β-hydroxyethylaniline or N,N-di(β-hydroxyethyl)aniline are therefore commonly used. Many of the earlier yellow and orange dyes proved to be phototropic (see Section 3-1), but it was found that this troublesome characteristic can be largely avoided by introducing nitro or other negative groups into the dye molecule; these substituents restrain *trans* → *cis* isomerisation. Since dye molecules must be fairly small in order that they may dissolve readily in the fibre monoazo dyes are commonly used, but a few disazo dyes are included in commercial ranges. Blacks are obtained by diazotising aminoazo dyes on the fibre and developing with a solution of 3-hydroxy-2-naphthoic acid.

Table 6-1 Examples of azo disperse dyes applied to acetate fibre

CI Ref. Nos.	Structure
CI Disperse Yellow 3 CI 11855	p-Aminoacetanilide → p-cresol
CI Disperse Yellow 4 CI 12770	Aniline → 2,4-quinolinediol
CI Disperse Orange 1 CI 11080	p-Nitroaniline → diphenylamine
CI Disperse Orange 3 CI 11005	p-Nitroaniline → aniline (*coupled with ω-methanesulphonate, then hydrolysed*)
CI Disperse Orange 5 CI 11100	2,6-Dichloro-4-nitroaniline → N-methyl-N-β-hydroxyethylaniline
CI Disperse Orange 13 CI 26080	Aniline → 1-naphthylamine → phenol
CI Disperse Red 1 CI 11110	p-Nitroaniline → N-ethyl-N-β-hydroxyethylaniline
CI Disperse Red 13 CI 11115	2-Chloro-4-nitroaniline → N-ethyl-N-β-hydroxyethylaniline
CI Disperse Violet 7 CI 11410	2-Bromo-4,6-dinitroaniline → 1-sec-butyl-1,2,3,4-tetrahydro-7-methyl-3-quinolinol
CI Disperse Blue 38 CI 11430	2-Chloro-4-nitroaniline-1,2,3,4-tetrahydrobenz [h] quinoline-3,7-diol
CI Disperse Black 1* CI 11365	p-Phenylenediamine → 1-naphthylamine [p-Nitroaniline → 1-naphthylamine, reduced]

* The black shade is obtained by diazotisation of the aminoazo compound on the fibre and coupling with 3-hydroxy-2-naphthoic acid.

In 1936 a range of water-soluble dyes for acetate was marketed by ICI under the name *Solacet*.[4] Their solubility was due to the presence of a sulphuric ester group (—OSO$_3$Na), usually introduced by sulphation of a β-hydroxyethylamino group, which did not seriously impair affinity for the fibre. The unsuitability of conventional water-soluble dyes for acetate fibres is apparently due to the presence of highly ionised —SO$_3$$^-Na^+$ groups rather than their solubility in water. In consequence of the development of dispersed dyes with improved dyeing and fastness properties the Solacet range has now been superseded.

Many dyes developed for acetate have now been applied to the newer synthetic fibres, and the manufactured ranges have been extended specially for these outlets. The term 'Acetate dyes' has therefore been discarded in favour of 'Disperse dyes' so that all applications may be included. Disperse dyes for fibres other than acetate are described later. Examples of azo disperse dyes applied to acetate are shown in Table 6-1; violet and blue dyes are included, but disperse dyes of these shades are derived mainly from the anthraquinone series.

6-2   Cellulose triacetate fibres

As already stated, cellulose triacetate was manufactured in the United States during the period 1914–24, but the process was unsatisfactory because the only suitable solvent then commercially available was chloroform, and this was both toxic and expensive. Methylene dichloride is a suitable solvent of low toxicity, and it became available fairly cheaply about 1930, but by that time secondary acetate was fully established. Later, however, when the hydrophobic fibres nylon and 'Terylene' had achieved great success, the possibilities of triacetate as an inexpensive fibre sharing some of their good properties became apparent, and it has now been introduced as a commercial fibre under names such as Tricel (Courtaulds Ltd), Arnel (Celanese Corporation of America) and Trilon (Canadian Celanese Ltd). It has good shrink- and crease-resistance, is quick-drying, shows good fastness to wet treatments and can be heat-set without loss of lustre. As it has a higher melting-point the hazards associated with the ironing of fabrics of secondary acetate are largely avoided.

Because of its hydrophobic character triacetate is less easily dyed than acetate, but suitable dyes can be selected from existing ranges of disperse dyes. Whereas acetate is dyed at 75°–80°C, triacetate requires a temperature at or near the boil. If the fabric is to be heat-set for pleats the dyes used must be stable at 200°C.

Dyes suitable for use on triacetate include CI Disperse Yellow 3, CI Disperse Oranges 1, 3, 5 and 13 and CI Disperse Red 1; constitutions of these are shown in Table 6-1. Many other dyes, usually with undisclosed structures, have been recommended for the purpose. Black shades can be obtained by diazotisation of aminoazo compounds on the fibre and development with suitable coupling components; reaction with nitrous acid is, however, somewhat slower than on acetate.[5]

6-3   Polyamide fibres

The earlier man-made fibres were not truly synthetic. Products such as viscose are composed of regenerated cellulose; acetate and triacetate are derivatives of cellulose. The first artificial fibre built up from non-polymeric starting materials was nylon, discovered by W. H. Carothers and initially manufactured by DuPont about 1938. The name 'nylon' is now regarded as a generic one and applies to a group of synthetic polyamides. Of the various types the first to be produced commercially, and still of major importance, was Nylon 6.6, obtained by polymerisation of the salt of adipic acid and hexamethylenediamine. It has a structure $[-NH(CH_2)_6NHCO(CH_2)_4CO-]_n$, where n varies within a range 50–90. Polymerisation is carried out in an inert atmosphere at about 280°C, and the chain length is controlled by introducing a suitable quantity of a monofunctional stabiliser, such as acetic acid. At a stage depending on the amount of stabiliser present the polymer has an acidic group at each end and further reaction is thus prevented. A similar result is obtainable by using adipic acid in slight excess.

Another nylon now manufactured on an increasing scale is Nylon 6. It is obtained by polymerisation of caprolactam by heating under pressure, with or without addition of water, and has a structure $[-NH(CH_2)_5CO-]_n$, where n has a value of about 200. Nylon 6 has advantages over Nylon 6.6 in greater elasticity, ease of dyeing and resistance to heat and light. Its melting-point, however, is considerably lower than that of Nylon 6.6 (about 215°–220°C as compared with 260°C).

Nylon 6.6 and Nylon 6 can be dyed by many disperse, acid and direct dyes. Since many suitable dyes are available, commercial ranges are usually selected from products already manufactured for other purposes, and (apart from the reactive dyes discussed later) new structures have not been required. It has proved very difficult to manufacture nylon with uniform dyeing properties, and for this reason dyes with good levelling properties are necessary. In this respect disperse dyes have a great advantage in that they conceal fibre irregularities. For high wet-fastness acid dyes are preferred, but very careful application is necessary in order to secure level dyeing. These dyes often show better wet-fastness properties on nylon than on wool because of the hydrophobic character of the former. Fastness to light, however, is often slightly lower on nylon than on wool. The affinity of acid dyes for Nylon 6 is higher than that for other types because polycaprolactam fibres contain a higher proportion of free amino groups. Ranges of acid dyes for nylon are classified by the makers so that users may select dyes with good levelling or good wet-fastness properties according to their requirements; there are also ranges with intermediate properties and others specially designed for fabric printing.

6-4 Polyester fibres

In the course of the exploratory work that led to the development of nylon W. H. Carothers examined aliphatic polyesters but abandoned them in favour of the more promising polyamides. Subsequently, however, the late J. R. Whinfield and J. T. Dickson of The Calico Printers' Association re-examined polyesters for the purpose. They extended the work to aromatic compounds and obtained a polymer with excellent fibre-forming properties from terephthalic acid and ethyleneglycol. This has the structure [33]. The important

$$HO-\left[-OC-\bigodot-CO\cdot O\cdot H_2C\cdot CH_2\cdot O-\right]_n H$$

[33]

fibre 'Terylene' was based on this work, and was first prepared in the laboratory in 1941. Development and production of the fibre were carried out by ICI, and this fibre is now manufactured under various names on a very large scale in many parts of the world. Dimethyl terephthalate is now commonly used in place of the free acid so that the terminal carboxylic acid group is esterified. Since n has a value of about 80 the properties of the fibre are not greatly affected. The ester is preferred as starting material because it is more easily purified, and purity is essential in the manufacture of high polymers.

'Terylene' fibre is highly hydrophobic, withstands attack by bacteria, moulds, moths, acid and alkali, has high strength even in wet conditions, is superior to nylon in resistance to light, can be heat-set and has good di-electric properties. It is largely used for manufacture of net curtains, in blends with wool for suitings and other outerwear, and for many industrial purposes.

The hydrophobic nature of 'Terylene', its tightly packed molecular structure and its lack of reactive groups all render it unreceptive to dye molecules. Certain disperse dyes can be applied, but under normal conditions adsorption is slow and only pale shades are obtained. Much better penetration is obtained by dyeing at about 120°C under pressure, and the special dyeing machinery required is now in general use. Since diffusion is slow in conditions of normal use, dyeings obtained in this way have good wet-fastness properties. Suitable dyes must be selected for this process since not all will withstand the high temperature without change of shade. Disperse dyes can also be applied at temperatures below 100°C by the aid of 'carriers' added to the dyebath. These agents are supplied under various brand names, such as 'Tumescal' (ICI), and usually consist of compounds such as o- or p-hydroxydiphenyl. Their presence greatly facilitates the dyeing process, but the mode of action is not fully understood; some possible explanations are discussed in Chapter 19. This process enables dyeing to be carried out in standard machines, but it is somewhat expensive and has disadvantages in that the carriers are often difficult to remove completely; their presence may cause a noticeable odour and sometimes impairment of light-fastness.

Polyester fibres can be dyed by the Thermosol process (DuPont), which consists in padding with a disperse dye and a thickening agent, then drying and heating at 175°–200°C for about one minute. Under such conditions the dye is adsorbed rapidly; after scouring to remove loose colour the dyed material is finished in the usual way.

The dyeing of polyester fibres with azoic dyes is described in Chapter 7.

6-5 Polypropylene fibres

Polyethylene has many applications in the plastics industry, but its low melting-point renders it unsuitable for fibre formation. Its homologue polypropylene exists in various forms according to the disposition of the substituent methyl groups; the isotactic polymers, in which these groups are all attached on the same side of the main carbon chain, can be spun and drawn into fibres. Catalysts promoting formation of isotactic polymers were discovered by Zeigler, and the process was further developed by Natta and others. Polypropylene fibres are hydrophobic and resist chemical attack, but they are not readily dyed. Certain disperse dyes can be applied, but only pale and medium shades are obtainable. Many methods have been described in the patent literature whereby the fibre may be modified to confer affinity for acid or basic dyes. Side chains carrying polar groups may be grafted to the main polymer chain, or basic substances may be included in the melt from which the fibre is spun. Much attention has been paid to a method whereby a compound of a polyvalent metal such as nickel, zinc or aluminium is incorporated in the fibre, which can then be dyed with metallisable dyes.[6]

6-6 Polyurethane fibres

Several elastomeric fibres developed in America are based on polymeric structures containing urethane (–NHCOO–) linkages. Full details of the processes used are not available, but complex cross-linked polymers with rubber-like properties are obtained from polyesters or polyethers containing terminal hydroxyl groups by means of a series of reactions involving di-isocyanates and diamines.[7] Typical examples of such fibres are Lycra (Du Pont) and Vyrene (U.S. Rubber Co.), which are extensively used for foundation garments and swimsuits. These fibres have advantages over rubber in strength, resistance to oxidation, perspiration and cosmetic oils, also in whiteness and affinity for dyes. They are readily dyed by acid, basic and disperse dyes, but fastness properties are in general rather low.

6-7 Polyacrylonitrile fibres

The simplest polyacrylonitrile fibres are straight polymers of acrylonitrile with the structure:

$$\left[\begin{array}{c} -CH_2-CH- \\ | \\ CN \end{array} \right]_n$$

, where n varies from

600 to 2000. The first commercial fibre of this type was Orlon, introduced by DuPont in 1948. It can be dyed by basic dyes or by acid dyes in presence of copper sulphate. Various modified acrylic fibres (often called 'modacrylic' fibres) are now obtained by co-polymerising acrylonitrile with other substances, and dyeing properties are thereby improved; Orlon as now manufactured is a co-polymer, but the identity of the second component has not been disclosed. Acrilan (Chemstrand Corporation), Dynel (Union Carbide Corporation) and Courtelle (Courtaulds Ltd) are other modified acrylic fibres. In general acid, disperse, basic and vat dyes can be applied to these fibres, but acid dyes are not recommended for Courtelle.

The older basic dyes often show better light fastness on acrylic fibres than on natural fibres, but new basic dyes have been developed with fastness properties on polyacrylonitrile that are fully compatible with modern standards.[8] A short account of recent work in this field is given in Chapter 8.

6-8   Miscellaneous applications

Azo dyes are used for many minor purposes, including the colouring of foodstuffs, cosmetics and anodised aluminium; some find application as drugs, biological stains or analytical indicators. For such uses monoazo acid dyes are of chief importance, but unsulphonated oil-soluble dyes are sometimes used for colouring food. In most countries the use of dyes in foods and cosmetics is now rigidly controlled, and products for these purposes must be included in a 'permitted list'. So far as water-soluble azo dyes are concerned it appears to be desirable that all reduction products likely to be formed in the body should be readily soluble in water and therefore easily eliminated. All dyes in the British permitted list do not yet conform to this principle, but further restrictions may be expected. In the United States control of food dyes is rather more stringent.

Azoic dyes

In 1880 Thomas and Robert Holliday,[1] of Read Holliday Ltd, dyemakers of Huddersfield, conceived the idea of producing water-insoluble azo dyes directly upon cotton fibre. They impregnated cotton with an alkaline solution of β-naphthol, then treated it with a diazo solution obtained from aniline, a toluidine, xylidine, naphthylamine, aminoazobenzene or aminoazotoluene, so that particles of an azo pigment were formed and became firmly fixed within the fibre. During the next ten years interest in this process gradually developed, and it was applied to piece dyeing by Weber in 1887, and to calico printing by Galland and von Gallois, also by Koechlin, in 1889.[2] Sodium β-naphtholate has no affinity for cotton, and in order to obtain level shades it was necessary to dry the padded fibre before development. In the early years β-naphthol was the only coupling component used, but α-naphthol and 2-naphthol-7-sulphonic acid (both of which give alkali-soluble dyes) were used to some extent for shading purposes. In 1895 the process was developed further by the firm of Meister, Lucius and Brüning (MLB), who used diazotised p-nitroaniline with β-naphthol to give *Para Red*, and this became of some importance. Other diazo components included α-naphthylamine (giving *Naphthylamine Bordeaux*), β-naphthylamine (giving *Vacanceine Red*), m-nitroaniline, 2-amino-4-nitrotoluene, 2-amino-4-nitroanisole, 4-amino-3-nitrotoluene, o-anisidine, 2-amino-4-chloroanisole, 2-amino-5-nitroanisole, 4-aminoazobenzene, benzidine and dianisidine. The shade from dianisidine is dull and uninteresting, but in 1893 MLB found that it can be brightened and rendered much faster to light by adding fatty acids to the naphthol bath and copper salts to the developing bath.[3]

Because of the need for ice in diazotising the arylamines the dyes became known as 'Ice colours'. Since the diazotisation process was often troublesome, many attempts were made to produce stabilised diazo compounds which could be stored until required. The first such product was *Nitrosamine Red*,[4] which consisted of the isodiazotate obtained by running a solution of diazotised p-nitroaniline into 18% caustic soda at 50°–60°C; the diazo compound was regenerated on treating the isodiazotate with dilute mineral acid. Soon various diazo compounds were marketed by MLB under the brand name of *Azophor*, and these were obtained by diazotising bases such as *m*- or *p*-nitroaniline or *o*-anisidine, evaporating the resulting solutions under reduced pressure to a high concentration, then absorbing the remaining water with anhydrous sodium sulphate or partly dehydrated aluminium sulphate.[5] *Nitrazol C* (Cassella) was obtained by diazotising *p*-nitroaniline in concentrated sulphuric acid and adding a dehydrated inorganic salt.[6] More satisfactory methods were developed in due course, and these are described later. The term 'azoic dyes' is now generally used instead of 'ice colours'; this name may not be ideal, but it is brief and serves to distinguish the class from other azo dyes.

The dyes obtained from β-naphthol are restricted in hue and have only moderate fastness to light. Great care is needed to produce level dyeings, and because of these shortcomings the early insoluble azo dyes were not widely used. In 1912, however, the situation was transformed by the discovery that the anilide of 3-hydroxy-2-naphthoic acid has great advantages over β-naphthol. In the form of its sodium salt it has affinity for cotton, and can be applied from a dyebath at about 30°C. Drying of the prepared cotton is usually unnecessary, and it can be stored for a week or more before development with a diazo solution. The dyed shades are usually superior in fastness to light, washing and rubbing in comparison with the corresponding β-naphthol derivatives. The anilide of 3-hydroxy-2-naphthoic acid was first described by Schöpff[7] in 1892, who prepared it with other products by condensing the acid with aniline. The discovery of its commercial value about twenty years later was made by the firm of Griesheim-Elektron, and they manufactured it by an improved process in which condensation was brought about in an inert solvent such as toluene in presence of an agent such as phosphorus trichloride.[8] The new product was sold as *Naphtol AS*, and during the next few years many other arylamides of the same acid were marketed under names such as *Naphtol AS-BS* (*m*-nitroanilide), *AS-RL* (*p*-anisidide) and *AS-E* (*p*-chloroanilide). At the same time the range of diazotisable amines was extended, and these were sold under names such as *Fast Orange GC Base* (*m*-chloroaniline hydrochloride), *Fast Red TR Base* (4-chloro-2-methylaniline) and *Fast Bordeaux GP* Base (4-methoxy-2-nitroaniline).

These Griesheim–Elektron products rapidly assumed commercial importance, and when the firm became part of the IG combine the ranges continued to be developed. In the first place the hues were

predominantly red, scarlet or orange, but new Naphtols and Fast
Bases were added to provide an almost complete range of shades.
Although the substituents in the arylamide residues of the Naphtols
have a considerable effect on the derived hues, the nature of the
diazo component has a greater influence. This no doubt accounts
for the naming of the Fast Bases in accordance with the shades
chiefly obtained; in some cases later developments caused the
chosen names to become inappropriate.

Although many of the Naphtols attained importance, Naphtol
AS has always been chiefly in demand. The following are typical
examples selected from the many combinations derived from it, and
the shades produced are indicated:

Fast Orange GR Base (*o*-nitroaniline)	orange
Fast Scarlet G Base (2-methyl-5-nitroaniline)	scarlet
Fast Scarlet GG Base (2,5-dichloroaniline)	scarlet
Fast Red GG Base (*p*-nitroaniline)	red
Fast Red GL Base (4-methyl-2-nitroaniline)	red
Fast Red RC Base (5-chloro-2-methoxyaniline hydrochloride)	red
Fast Red B Base (2-methoxy-4-nitroaniline)	bluish claret
Fast Garnet GBC Base (4-amino-2′,3-dimethylazobenzene hydrochloride)	claret
Fast Blue B Base (dianisidine)	reddish blue

The affinity of the Naphtols for cellulosic fibres tends to rise as the
molecular weight is increased by introduction of substituents, and
products such as Naphtols AS-BO (α-naphthylamide), AS-SW
(β-naphthylamide) and AS-BR (dianisidide of 3-hydroxy-2-naph-
thoic acid) are strongly adsorbed from alkaline solution. This is a
disadvantage in textile printing styles for which naphtholated
fabric is printed with a thickened diazo solution leaving in non-
printed areas Naphtol which must be washed out. For printing
purposes, therefore, less substantive Naphtols such as AS, AS-D
(*o*-toluidide) or AS-OL (*o*-anisidide) are preferred. Naphtols with
larger molecules such as AS-BO, AS-SW and AS-BR, mentioned
above, are used in dyeing applications for deeper shades such as
claret, bordeaux or brown. Naphtol AS-TR (4-chloro-2-methyl-
anilide of 3-hydroxy-2-naphthoic acid) gives with diazotised Fast
Red TR Base (4-chloro-2-methylaniline) a Turkey Red shade, with
outstanding fastness to kier-boiling (a bleaching process often
applied after dyeing). A combination introduced later which gives a
similar shade with outstanding fastness to light is obtained from

Naphtol AS-ITR (5-chloro-2,4-dimethoxyanilide of 3-hydroxy-2-naphthoic acid) with diazotised Fast Red ITR Base (2-methoxyaniline-5-sulphondiethylamide).

Since yellow shades are not obtained from 3-hydroxy-2-naphthoic arylamides, another chemical class was introduced into the Naphtol AS series. This consists of the acylacetic arylamides, and the first to be employed was diacetoacetic tolidide.[9] It will be seen that it is not a naphthol, but since it resembles the earlier products in application it was included in the same range, and called *Naphtol AS-G*. In alkaline solution it has affinity for cotton, and gives a lemon yellow shade with diazotised Fast Yellow GC Base (*o*-chloroaniline hydrochloride), or redder yellows with other diazo components. Dyes derived from Naphtol AS-G have somewhat low light-fastness, but later other yellow-yielding components giving dyes of better light-fastness were introduced.[10] These include *Naphtols AS-LG, AS-L3G* and *AS-L4G*. The newer products have not displaced Naphtol AS-G, which remains an important member of the range. The structures of these components are shown below:

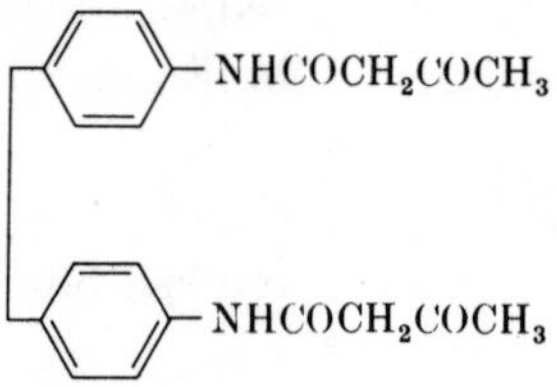

Naphtol AS-G

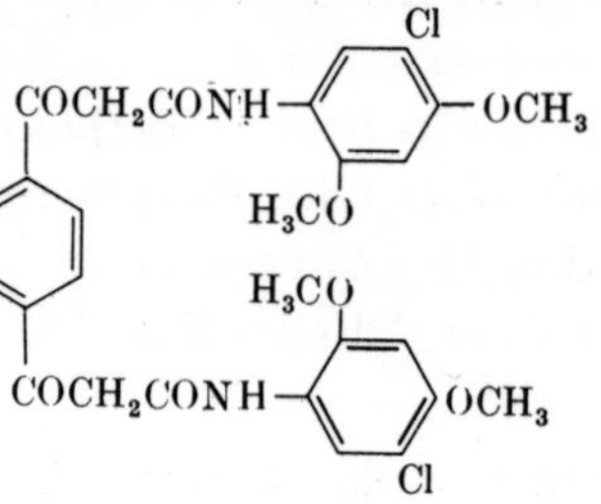

Naphtol AS-LG

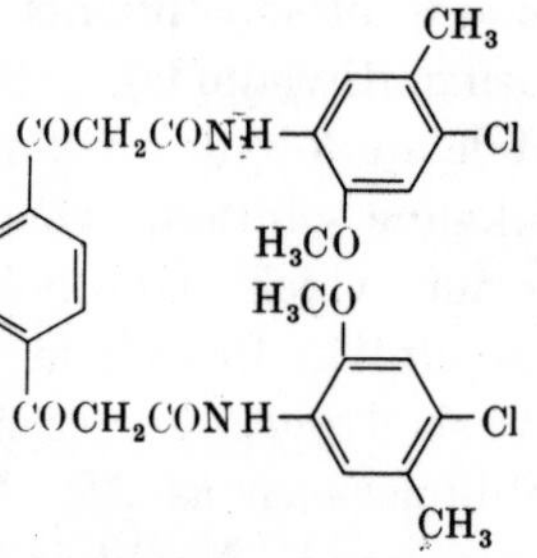

Naphtol AS-L3G

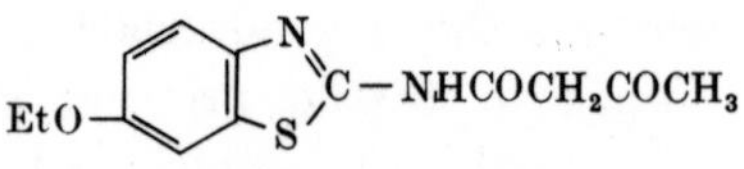

Naphtol AS-L4G

The use of dianisidine to give blues has been known from the time of the earliest azoic dyes, but it is associated with rather low fastness to light. Several *p*-aminodiphenylamine derivatives have been successfully used to give blue shades with Naphtol AS. Their diazonium salts have somewhat low coupling energy, and at one time it was customary to diazotise with an excess of nitrous acid so that the *N*-nitrosodiazonium salt was obtained; this has higher coupling energy, but in order to obtain the correct shade it was necessary to remove the N-nitroso group by aftertreatment with a soap bath containing sodium sulphide. These Fast Bases have fallen out of use, but the corresponding stabilised diazo compounds (in which the —NH— group is not nitrosated) are applied in textile printing, coupling being accelerated by treatment with steam. The most important product in this series is *Variamine Blue B Salt* and its equivalents, consisting of 4′-methoxydiphenylamine-4-diazonium chloride. Others are *Variamine Blue FG Salt* (3-methoxydiphenyl-amine-4-diazonium chloride) and *Variamine Blue RT Salt* (diphenyl-amine-4-diazonium chloride).[11]

About the year 1930 IG introduced two other blue-yielding components under the names *Fast Blue RR* and *Fast Blue BB Bases*. These are 4-benzoylamino-2,5-dimethoxyaniline and 4-benzoylamino-2,5-diethoxyaniline respectively, and they give very pleasing reddish blue and blue shades with Naphtol AS and other coupling components.[12]

For many years green shades presented a problem. In 1931 ICI obtained greens from diazotised 1-methylamino-4-p-aminoanilino-anthraquinone in conjunction with acetoacetarylamides, but the dyeings had rather low fastness to light, and the stabilised diazo salt was insufficiently stable for commercial use.[13] Later IG introduced *Naphtol AS-GR* (3-hydroxyanthracene-2-carboxylic o-toluidide) which gives somewhat dull greens with diazotised bases such as Fast Blue BB Base or the Variamine Blue Bases.[14] Copper tetra-4-(p-aminobenzoyl)phthalocyanines and similar substances were examined as green-yielding bases by ICI, but the fastness properties of the resulting dyes did not justify commercial use.[15] More recently *Naphtol AS-FGGR* has been introduced by Farbenfabriken Bayer, and this product gives bright yellowish greens with diazotised bases such as Fast Scarlet GG, Red TR, Red KB or Yellow GC (Table 7-1). The affinity of this Naphtol is very low, but it can be applied to cotton (not, however, to viscose) by padding. It is suitable for printing, but the printing of padded cloth gives only green or brown shades. This limitation can be avoided by using the Naphtol as a component of a *Rapidogen* mixture (see Section 7-5-2), which can be applied alongside other combinations.[16] The constitution of Naphtol AS-FGGR has not been disclosed, but in patent specifications the makers have described green-yielding coupling components obtained by tri- or tetra-chlorosulphonation of copper or nickel phthalo-cyanine (Chapter 15) and condensing the products with three or four molecular proportions of a 3-methyl-1-p-aminophenylpyrazol-5-

one or an amino-substituted acylacetic arylamide, and these are probably relevant.[17]

The range of brown shades was considerably extended in 1933 by the introduction of Naphtol AS-LB, which is used with a wide variety of diazo components.[18] For many years this Naphtol was believed to consist of 2-hydroxycarbazole-3-carboxylic *p*-chloroanilide, but it is now known to be 2-hydroxycarbazole-1-carboxylic *p*-chloroanilide.[19] Other brown-yielding components are Naphtols AS-BT (2 - hydroxydibenzofuran - 3 - carboxylic - 2′,5′ - dimethoxy - anilide)[20] and AS-KN (2-hydroxydibenzofuran-3-carboyxlic α-naphthylamide).

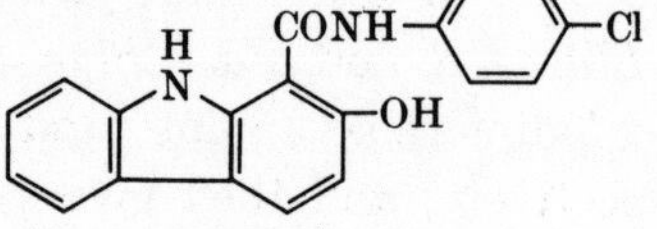

Naphtol AS-LB

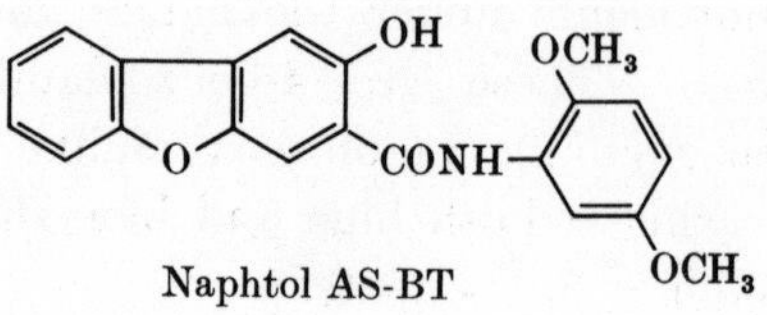

Naphtol AS-BT

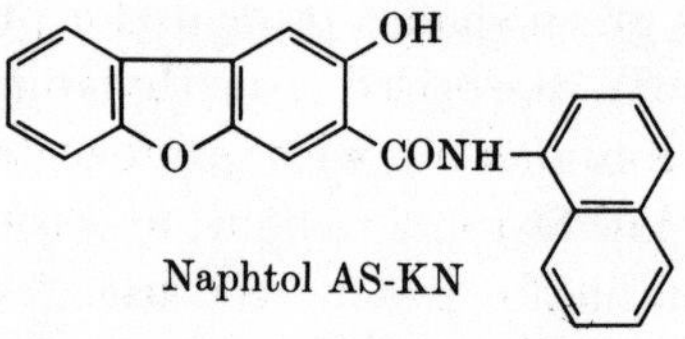

Naphtol AS-KN

The first attempts to produce azoic blacks actually gave navy blues, and heavy shades were needed in order to approach black. The use of 4,4′-diaminodiphenylamine (*Fast Black B Base*) in this way dates

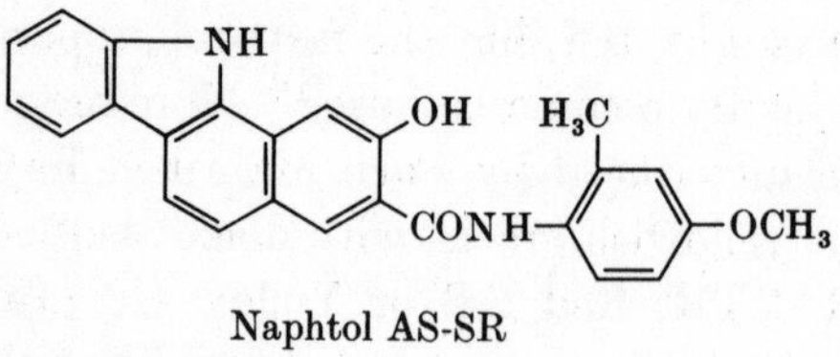

Naphtol AS-SR

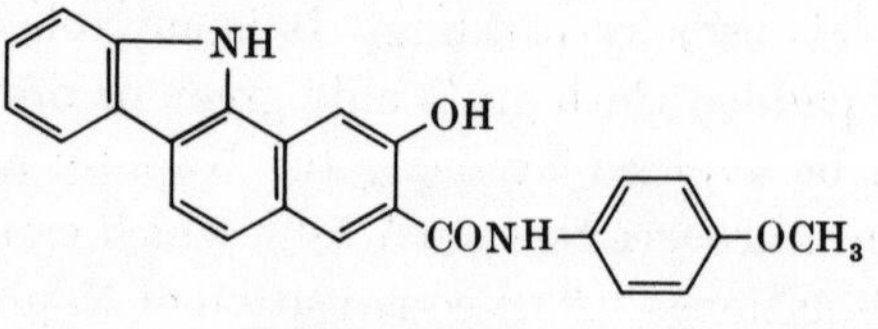

Naphtol AS-SG

from 1912.[21] *Fast Black Salt K* (a stabilised diazonium salt derived from the aminoazo compound *p*-nitroaniline → 2,5-dimethoxy-aniline), introduced in 1923, also gives bluish blacks with various Naphtols, but is now largely used for printing with Naphtol AS-G to give chocolate shades.[22] Better blacks are obtained from *Fast Black Salt G* (tetrazotised 4,4'-diaminodiphenylamine coupled with one equivalent of 2-ethoxy-5-methylaniline, the amino group diazotised, and the resulting tetrazo compound isolated as the zinc chloride double salt), also introduced in 1923.[23] Two Naphtols, *AS-SR* and *AS-SG*, were designed especially for blacks and placed on the market in 1929. They are used mainly in conjunction with diazotised Fast Red B Base (2-methoxy-4-nitroaniline), the former giving a reddish and the latter a greenish black;[24] a good black results from a suitable mixture of the two Naphtols. Their structures are shown on p. 82.

7-1 Stabilised diazo compounds

As the azoic dyes grew in importance the need for improved forms of stable diazo compounds became pressing, and in 1923 BASF made commercial use of zinc chloride double salts of various diazonium compounds.[25] The improved stability of such derivatives had been mentioned by A. Feer in footnotes to papers published in 1891,[26] and MLB had described the use of zinc double chlorides of diazotised aminoazo compounds in 1896,[27] but these compounds appear to have been then forgotten. The complex salts have structures of

the type $\left[R - \overset{\ominus}{\underset{\underset{N}{|||}}{N^{\oplus}}} \right]_2 ZnCl_4$, and they are easily prepared by adding

zinc chloride to a concentrated solution of the diazonium chloride. In most cases crystals of the double salt separate at once, and the yield may be increased by addition of common salt. The arylamine may be diazotised in sulphuric acid medium if required, and in that case an addition of salt must be made in order to provide the necessary chloride ions. The resulting products are readily soluble in water; in solution they are ionised and show the normal properties of diazonium salts. There is a wide variation in stability, sometimes even between compounds with small structural differences, but in general the most stable molecules are those of greatest weight. The simpler structures are so unstable as to be unsafe to handle in the dry state, especially if a nitro group is present. If the moist filter-cake is mixed with an inorganic diluent such as anhydrous sodium sulphate the inert particles in the mixture restrict the propagation of any local exothermic decomposition that may occur, and in many cases such mixtures can be dried safely at 40°–50°C.

Zinc chloride is still the most generally useful stabilising agent, but the complex salts obtained with a few diazo compounds are too readily soluble for satisfactory isolation, and others have poor stability in dry storage. In many such cases salts with satisfactory properties have been obtained by using other stabilisers. Naphthalene-1,5-disulphonic acid yields two series of salts, the acid salts of structure [34][28] and the neutral salts of structure [35][29]. The acid

RN_2O_3S — [naphthalene] — SO_3H

[34]

RN_2O_3S — [naphthalene] — SO_3N_2R

[35]

salts are used commercially, but the neutral salts are in general too sparingly soluble in water. The neutral salts are liable to be precipitated from concentrated solutions of the acid salts (a molecule of naphthalene-1,5-disulphonic acid being liberated from two molecules of the acid salt), but this transformation can be restrained by addition of a free arylsulphonic acid.[30] The sodium salts of arylsulphonic acids such as naphthalene-1,6-disulphonic or 1,3,6-trisulphonic acid are used as solubilising agents.[31]

In many cases diazonium borofluorides are easily isolated by adding sodium borofluoride or hydrofluoric acid and borax to a concentrated diazo solution. The resulting complex salts, with structures of the type RN_2BF_4, are often somewhat sparingly soluble in water, but their solubility can be increased to some extent by mixing with common salt or a solubiliser of the type mentioned above.[32] Several commercial Fast Salts are based on borofluoride complexes.

Diazonium compounds with larger molecules can be isolated as diazonium chlorides (e.g., the Variamine Blue Salts)[33] or acid sulphates (e.g., Fast Garnet GBC Salt, derived from 4-amino-2', 3-dimethylazobenzene)[34], and these are sufficiently stable for commercial use. Stabilisers such as cobalt chloride,[35] ethyl hydrogen sulphate[36] and acetylsulphanilic acid[37] have limited commercial use, but have advantages for particular products.

It will be seen that stabilisers such as zinc chloride, cobalt chloride and boron trifluoride form complex salts, but naphthalene-1,5-disulphonic acid, acetylsulphanilic acid and ethyl hydrogen sulphate merely provide anions for simple salt formation with the diazonium cation.

Stabilised diazonium salts marketed first by IG and later by many other firms are adjusted to a standard strength (often 20%, calculated as the corresponding Fast Base) by inclusion of one or more inorganic diluents, and one of the commonest of these is aluminium sulphate. This diluent fulfils three functions, since it is an excellent fire retardant, a buffer preventing diazo decomposition that would result from the introduction of alkali into the developing bath with naphtholated cotton, and also a desiccant.

Aluminium sulphate can be used as a buffer only for strongly coupling diazo salts for which a bath at pH 5–6 is suitable. Diazo salts having lower activity such as Fast Blue BB Salt (derived from 4-benzoylamino-2,5-diethoxyaniline) and Fast Violet B Salt (derived from 4-benzoylamino-2-methoxy-5-methylaniline) are usually buffered with zinc sulphate, giving pH 6–7. The Variamine series of Salts (obtained from 4-aminodiphenylamine or its derivatives), require pH 7 for satisfactory coupling, and for these the most suitable buffer is magnesium sulphate. In the case of many diazo salts, however, coupling proceeds rapidly in presence of an excess of aluminium sulphate, and for these products this versatile diluent is used in a partially dehydrated form in which it functions as a convenient desiccant.[38] The crystalline diazonium salt is centrifuged or well drained on a vacuum filter, then mixed with the partially dehydrated aluminium sulphate, and in this way a dry product is quickly obtained. This process is not only more rapid than oven drying, but it is less hazardous, and avoids the slight discoloration that sometimes arises during oven drying. Other dehydrated inorganic salts are less suitable for use in this way, since water is less firmly bound in the hydrates finally formed and has an adverse effect on diazo stability during storage.

7-2   Commercial ranges of azoic components

Many manufacturers now supply ranges of Fast Bases, Fast Salts and azoic coupling components under their own brand names. Thus such products are marketed by ICI as *Brentamine Fast Bases*, *Brentamine Fast Salts* and *Brenthols*, by CIBA as *Ciba Bases*, *Ciba Salts* and *Cibanaphthols*, by Sandoz as *Devol Bases*, *Devol Salts* and *Celcots*, and by DuPont as *Naphthanil Bases* and *Naphthanils*. The *Solunaptols* introduced by J. W. Leitch & Co. in 1936 and later manufactured by Fine Dyestuffs and Chemicals Ltd are mixtures of conventional coupling components with an alkali and a dispersing agent which have the advantage of being readily soluble in boiling water.[39] These and many similar azoic products are widely used by dyers and textile printers.

In this chapter azoic coupling components in general are referred to as 'Naphthols', the spelling 'Naphtol' being reserved for commercial products so named.

Table 7-1 Constitutions of selected azoic diazo components

Name	Constitution of Fast Base	Constitution of Fast Salt
Fast Black K Salt	—	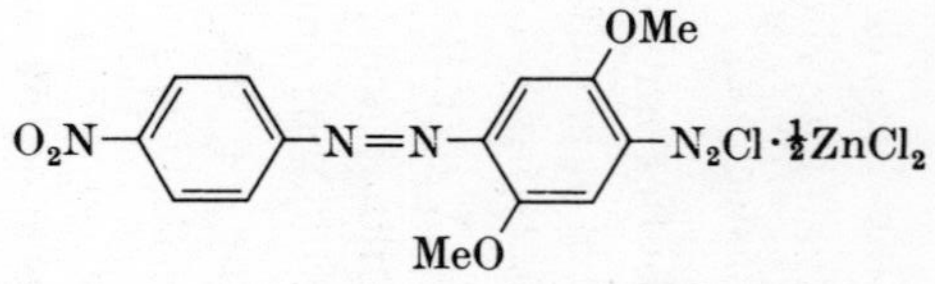 O_2N—C$_6$H$_4$—N=N—(ring: OMe, $N_2Cl \cdot \frac{1}{2}ZnCl_2$, MeO)
Fast Blue BB Base Fast Blue BB Salt	4-Benzoylamino-2,5-diethoxyaniline	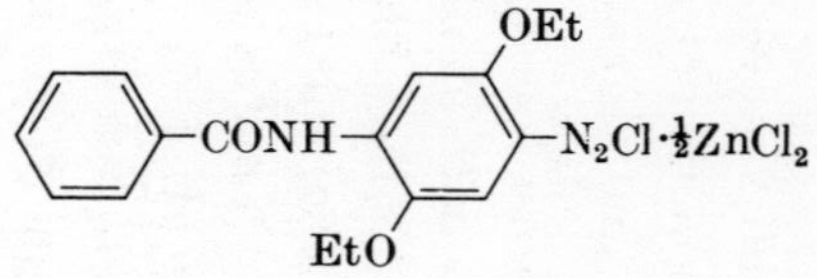 C$_6$H$_5$—CONH—(ring: OEt, $N_2Cl \cdot \frac{1}{2}ZnCl_2$, EtO)
Variamine Blue B Salt	—	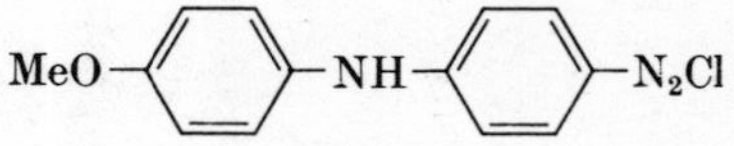 MeO—C$_6$H$_4$—NH—C$_6$H$_4$—N_2Cl
Fast Garnet GBC Base Fast Garnet GBC Salt	4-Amino-2',3-dimethylazobenzene	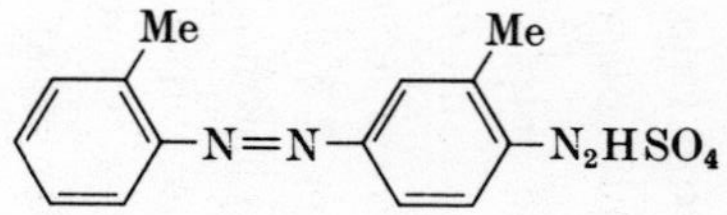 Me—C$_6$H$_4$—N=N—(ring: Me, N_2HSO_4)
Fast Golden Orange GR Salt	—	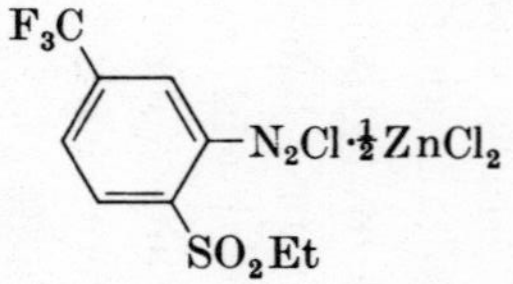 F_3C—(ring: $N_2Cl \cdot \frac{1}{2}ZnCl_2$, SO_2Et)

Fast Orange GC Base Fast Orange GC Salt	*m*-Chloroaniline hydrochloride	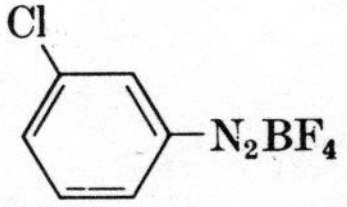 Cl—C₆H₄—N₂BF₄ ; anthraquinone—N₂Cl·½ZnCl₂
Fast Red AL Salt	—	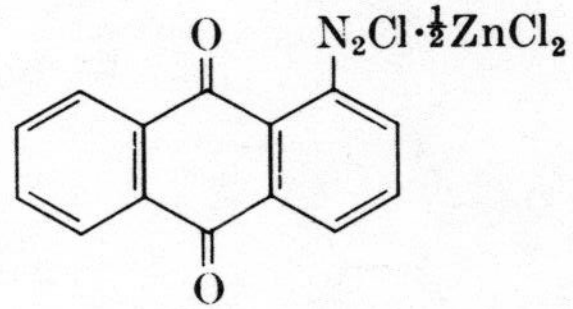 naphthalene SO₃H / N₂O₃S
Fast Red B Base Fast Red B Salt	2-Methoxy-4-nitroaniline	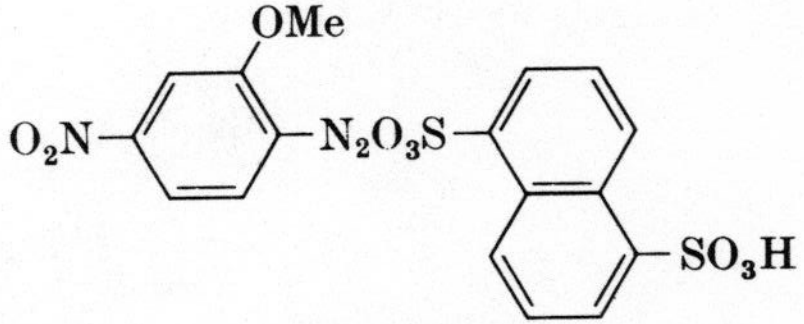 OMe, O₂N, N₂O₃S
Fast Red FR Base Fast Red FR Salt	2-Amino-4,4′-dichlorodiphenyl ether	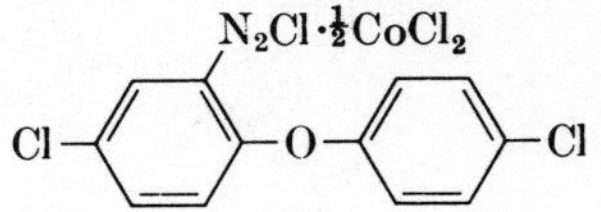 Cl—C₆H₃(N₂Cl·½CoCl₂)—O—C₆H₄—Cl
Fast Red 3GL Base Fast Red 3GL Salt	4-Chloro-2-nitroaniline	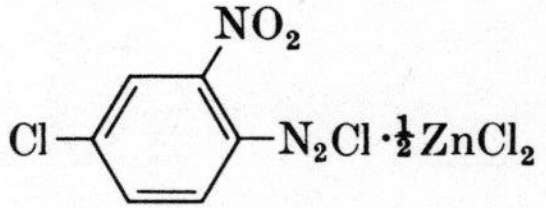 NO₂, N₂Cl·½ZnCl₂, Cl
Fast Red ITR Base Fast Red ITR Salt	2-Methoxyaniline-5-sulphondiethylamide	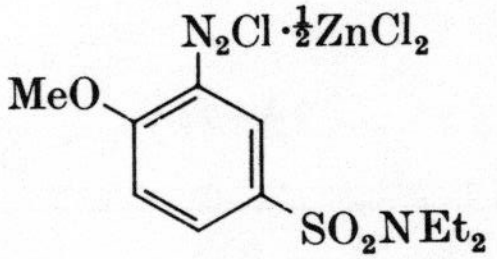 MeO, N₂Cl·½ZnCl₂, SO₂NEt₂

Table 7-1   Constitutions of selected azoic diazo components   (Contd.)

Name	Constitution of Fast Base	Constitution of Fast Salt
Fast Red KB Base Fast Red KB Salt	5-Chloro-2-methylaniline	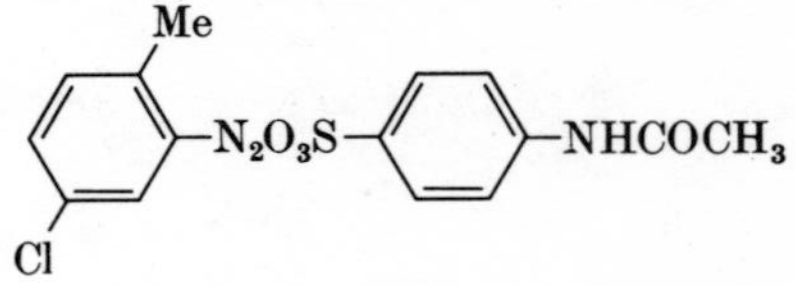
Fast Red RC Base Fast Red RC Salt	5-Chloro-2-methoxyaniline	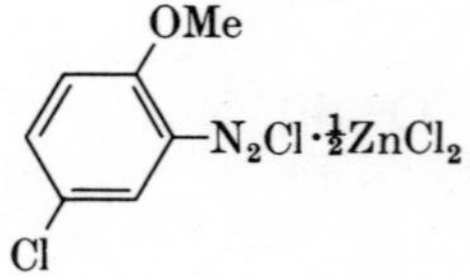
Fast Red TR Base Fast Red TR Salt	4-Chloro-2-methylaniline	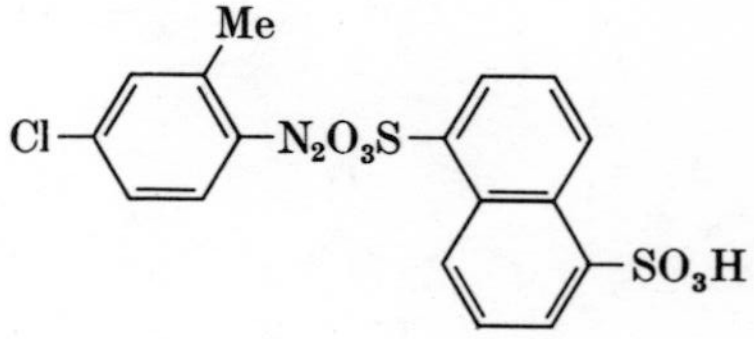
Fast Scarlet GG Base Fast Scarlet GG Salt	2,5-Dichloroaniline ½ sulphate	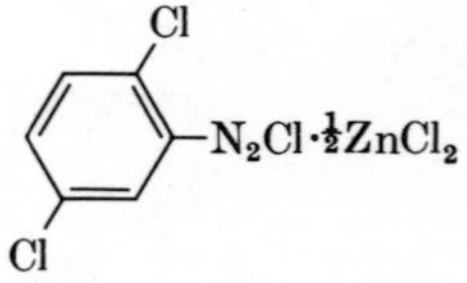

Fast Scarlet R Base
Fast Scarlet R Salt

2-Methoxy-5-nitroaniline

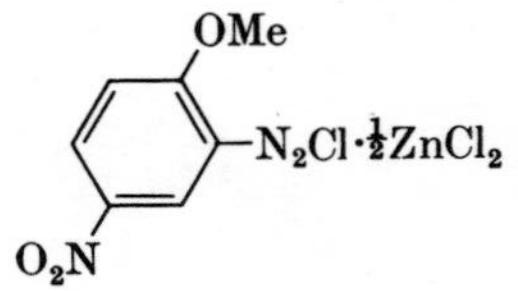

$$O_2N \quad \overset{OMe}{\bigcirc} \quad N_2Cl \cdot \tfrac{1}{2}ZnCl_2$$

Fast Yellow GC Base
Fast Yellow GC Salt

o-Chloroaniline hydrochloride

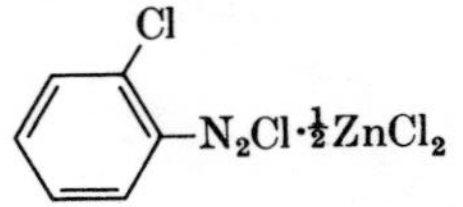

$$Cl \quad \overset{}{\bigcirc} \quad N_2Cl \cdot \tfrac{1}{2}ZnCl_2$$

Note: Several manufacturers produce azoic diazo components under the above names. In the former IG ranges these names were used for the Fast Bases, but the names of Fast Salts were rearranged as in Fast Blue Salt BB. This practice has been retained by FBy, but not in general by FH.

Table 7-2 Selected azoic coupling components

Naphtol	Constitution
AS	3-Hydroxy-2-naphthoic anilide
AS-BG	3-Hydroxy-2-naphthoic 2,5-dimethoxyanilide
AS-BO	3-Hydroxy-2-naphthoic α-naphthylamide
AS-BR	3-Hydroxy-2-naphthoic dianisidide
AS-BS	3-Hydroxy-2-naphthoic m-nitroanilide
AS-D	3-Hydroxy-2-naphthoic o-toluidide
AS-E	3-Hydroxy-2-naphthoic p-chloroanilide
AS-ITR	3-Hydroxy-2-naphthoic 5-chloro-2,4-dimethoxyanilide
AS-LC	3-Hydroxy-2-naphthoic 4-chloro-2,5-dimethoxyanilide
AS-LT	3-Hydroxy-2-naphthoic 4-methoxy-2-methylanilide
AS-OL	3-Hydroxy-2-naphthoic o-anisidide
AS-PH	3-Hydroxy-2-naphthoic o-phenetidide
AS-RL	3-Hydroxy-2-naphthoic p-anisidide
AS-SW	3-Hydroxy-2-naphthoic β-naphthylamide
AS-TR	3-Hydroxy-2-naphthoic 4-chloro-2-methylanilide

AS-G CH_3COCH_2CONH ... $NHCOCH_2COCH_3$ (with Me groups)

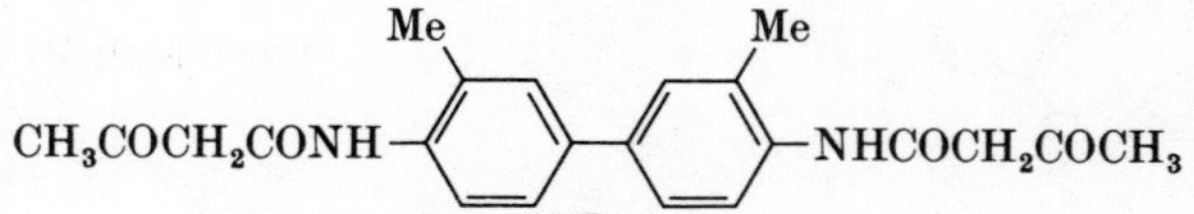

AS-IRG CH_3COCH_2CONH ... OMe, Cl, MeO

AS-LG   MeO ... $NHCOCH_2CO$ ... $COCH_2CONH$ ... Cl, OMe

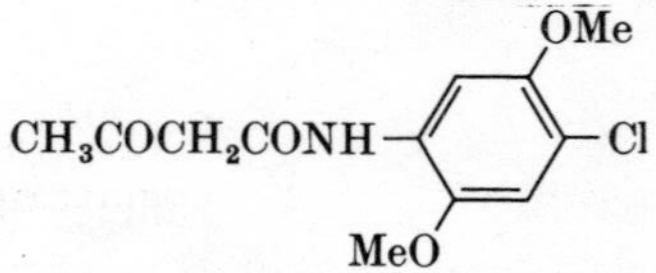

AS-L3G

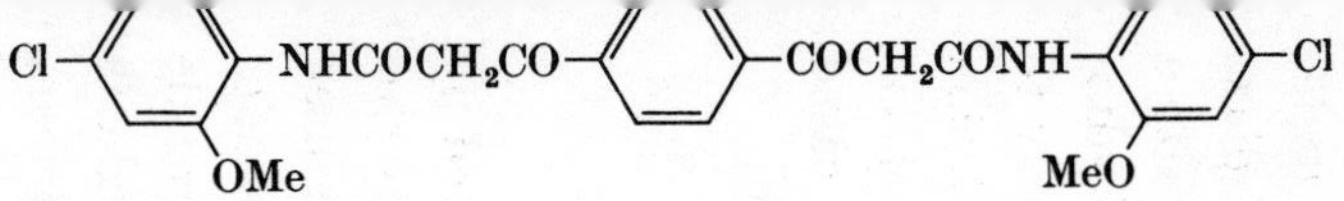

AS-L4G

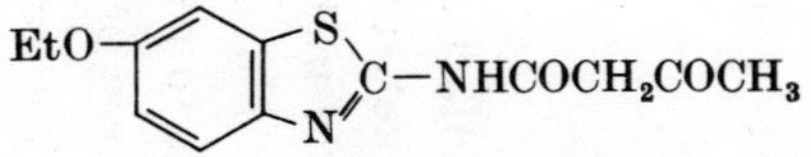

AS-BT

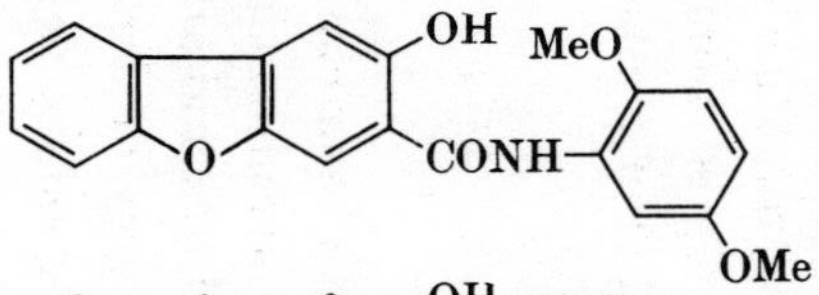

AS-GR

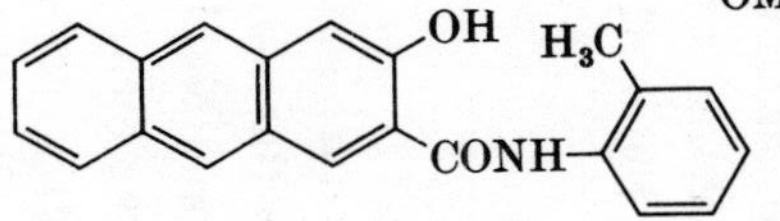

AS-LB

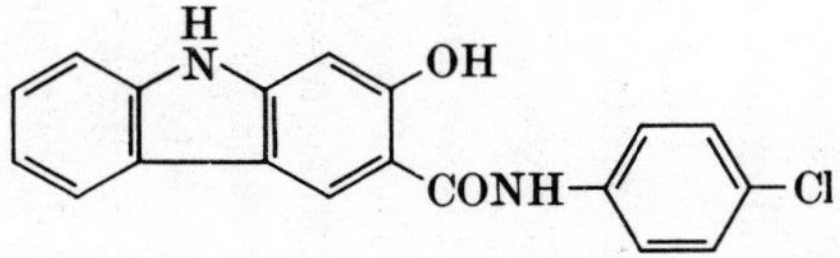

AS-SG

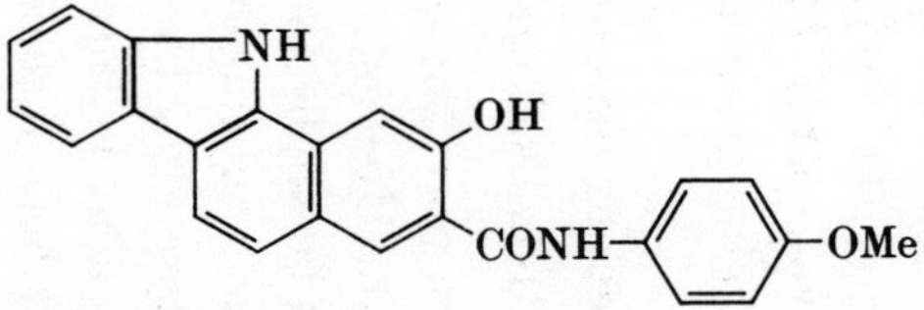

AS-SR

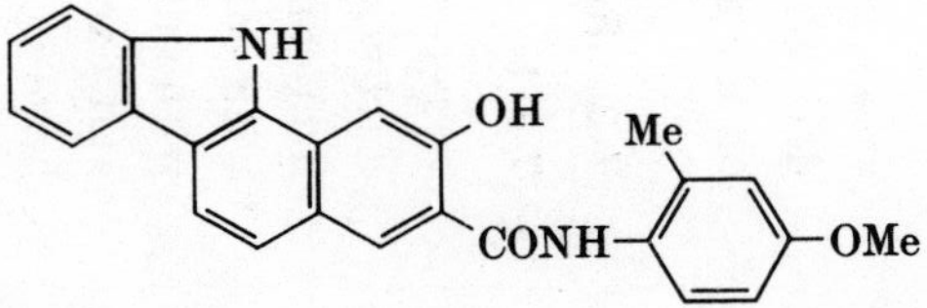

The Colour Index and its Supplement include 130 Azoic Diazo Components and 108 Azoic Coupling Components, but the constitutions of some of them are undisclosed. The examples shown in Tables 7-1 and 7-2 have been selected to illustrate the range of structures, and many technically important products are omitted. It should be noted that azoic bases not readily diazotised under dyehouse conditions are marketed only in the form of stable diazo salts. In the dyeing and printing trades the term Base relates to a diazotisable amine, whether it is in the form of a free base, hydrochloride or half sulphate, and the term Fast Salt is applied only to stabilised diazo compounds. A further source of possible confusion arises from the varying practice in naming toluidine and anisidine derivatives, some publications having adopted numbering based on the amino group and others on the methyl or methoxy group.

7-3   Recent developments

7-3-1   Metallised azoic dyes

In recent years metallisable azoic dyes have been manufactured by Farbwerke Hoechst. The *Variogen* Bases and Salts marketed by this firm can be applied with conventional Naphtols and after-metallised with cobalt or copper salts to give green, grey or dark blue shades with outstanding fastness to rubbing, very good fastness to peroxide and excellent fastness to light.[40] The structures of these products have not been disclosed, but metallisable azoic dyes obtained from various heterocyclic amines have been described in the patent literature. Thus, cotton impregnated with Naphtol AS-ITR (5-chloro-2,4-dimethoxyanilide of 3-hydroxy-2-naphthoic acid) and developed with diazotised 3-amino-6-methoxyindazole gives a bright green dyeing on aftertreatment with cobalt chloride.[41] Brown shades are obtained by developing naphtholated cotton in a suitably buffered bath containing a diazotised aminoarylbenzotriazole oxide such as [36] and aftertreating with a salt of copper,

[36]

cobalt or nickel.[42] The use of 8-aminoquinoline and its derivatives as Fast Bases, giving predominantly brown shades with azoic coupling components when after-metallised with copper, cobalt or nickel salts has also been described.[43] More recently, metallised coupling components have been obtained by coupling a diazotised aminobenzimidazole, aminobenzotriazole or aminobenzothiazole with resorcinol, 2,6- or 2,7-dihydroxynaphthalene, and treating the product with a salt of copper, cobalt or nickel. Such components give brown or black shades with conventional diazo components without aftertreatment.[44] The fastness to washing is said to be superior to that of somewhat similar metal complexes obtained earlier from the product of coupling diazotised aminoindazoles with resorcinol.[45]

7-3-2 Azanil salts

A short range of *Azanil* colour salts has recently been introduced by Farbwerke Hoechst. These are water-soluble diazoamino compounds intended for application to cellulosic fibres from dyebaths which also contain a highly substantive member of the Naphtol AS series. When the components have been adsorbed by the fibre dye formation is brought about by acidification of the dyebath. These products therefore enable standard azoic combinations (so far as available in the range) to be applied in a single bath. It is also possible to apply Azanil salts by a two-bath process, since on acidifying the solution of an Azanil salt it is converted into the corresponding diazotised base, which can be used in a conventional manner with Naphtols of high or low substantivity. This system is likely to be useful in cases such as that of Fast Scarlet TR Base (3-chloro-2-methylaniline) in which no satisfactory stabilised diazo salt is available, and others such as that of Fast Red KB Base where the available diazo salt has very low stability.

The structures of the Azanil Salts have not been disclosed, but may correspond to the diazoamino compounds described in UK 443,222 (IG) and UK 1,077,777 (FH), obtained by coupling diazotised arylamines or tetrazotised diamines with a compound such as sodium cyanamide or cyanamidecarboxylate.[46] According to the inventors active diazonium salts are regenerated by a reaction with aqueous acid (HX) which may be represented as follows:

$$R.N_2.N\begin{array}{c} {}^{CN} \\ {}_{(COO)Na} \end{array} + 2HX + H_2O \rightarrow RN_2^{\oplus} X^{\ominus} + CO(NH_2)_2 + NaX\ (+CO_2)$$

In contrast with the liberation of diazonium salts from conventional diazoamino compounds this reaction is not reversible.

7-4   The dyeing of cellulosic fibres

The dyeing process consists of three stages:

1. Impregnation of the fibre with an alkaline solution of the Naphthol.
2. Development with the diazo solution.
3. Aftertreatment with a solution of soap or other surface-active agent.

Cotton may be dyed as yarn (in hank, cop, cheese or beam form) or as cloth, and the details of the process vary accordingly. Since the substantivity of Naphthols (except Naphtol AS-BR) declines as the temperature is raised, impregnation is normally carried out at a temperature not exceeding 40°C. In the case of the simpler structures the degree of exhaustion is low (sometimes about 10%), so a standing bath is often used, with addition of fresh Naphthol as required. If impregnated cotton is to be stored, care must be taken to avoid spotting with water and exposure to an acid atmosphere. Drying is not essential, but piece goods are often dried to obtain better fastness to rubbing. In the case of many Naphthols the stability of the treated fibre may be improved by addition of formaldehyde to the bath. Brass and Sommer showed that in the case of Naphtols AS, AS-BO and AS-SW formaldehyde forms a methylene bridge linking two molecules in the 1 positions, and that the methylene group is displaced by most diazo compounds to give normal azo derivatives.[47] Formaldehyde is not used with acetoacetarylamides and must be avoided in combinations with low coupling energy.

The development operation is simple and rapid. If a stabilised diazo salt is used it has only to be dissolved in water and is then ready for use, the necessary buffer being usually present in the marketed product. For large-scale work the dyer may find it cheaper to carry out diazotisation himself, and in that case excess mineral acid must be removed afterwards by means of sodium acetate or other agent, and an alkali-binding agent such as aluminium sulphate, zinc sulphate, magnesium sulphate or acetic acid is added to prevent decomposition that would be caused by alkali introduced with the impregnated cotton. The diazo compound is normally used in excess, especially when the ratio of liquor to goods is high; at 20:1, for example, the excess may be 100%. Standing baths may be used for periods depending on the stability of the diazo compound concerned.

The aftertreatment with soap or other surface-active agent is designed to remove loosely adhering particles of pigment, to develop the true shade and to improve the fastness properties. There is often a marked change in shade during this treatment, and fastness to light and chlorine may be considerably improved. These changes were studied by Bean and Rowe,[48] who showed that soaping causes the pigment particles to aggregate and assume a crystalline structure. Prolonged soaping results in migration of the crystals partly into the lumen (the cavity within the cotton fibre) and partly to the outer surface, from which they are eventually detached. Soaping is continued in practice for half an hour, during which aggregation proceeds far enough to bring about the desired improvement in properties, and the dyed material is then rinsed and dried.

7-5 Textile printing

There are several methods whereby azoic dyes may be printed on fabrics of cellulosic fibres, and one of the most important of these consists in impregnating the cloth with an alkaline solution of a Naphthol, drying, printing with a thickened solution of a Fast Salt or diazotised Fast Base, and finally removing uncoupled Naphthol in an alkaline soap bath. Only Naphthols of low substantivity are suitable, and by far the most important in printing are Naphtol AS and Naphtol AS-G (and their equivalents). The range of shades obtainable from these two components with a selection of Fast Bases or Salts is illustrated in Table 7-3.

Table 7-3   Shades obtained from selected Fast Bases or Fast Salts by printing on cloth impregnated with Naphtol AS or Naphtol AS-G

Fast Base or Fast Salt	Shade with Naphtol AS	Shade with Naphtol AS-G
Fast Orange GC	Orange	Greenish yellow
Fast Scarlet GG	Scarlet	Greenish yellow
Fast Scarlet R	Scarlet	Yellow
Fast Red 3GL	Red	Golden yellow
Fast Red TR	Red	Bright yellow
Fast Red B	Bluish red	Golden yellow
Fast Blue BB	Blue	Orange
Fast Black K	Black	Bordeaux

In another process cloth is printed with a thickened solution of a Naphthol and developed in a bath of a diazo solution. A white discharge effect can be obtained on cloth dyed with an azoic combination by printing a thickened solution of a reducing agent which destroys the colour in printed areas. By printing similarly dyed cloth with a thickened solution of a reduced vat dye containing an excess of the reducing agent a coloured discharge is obtained, the azoic dye being destroyed and the vat dye applied simultaneously.

7-5-1   Rapid Fast colours

Printing mixtures containing both diazo and coupling components were first produced by BASF in 1894, when they marketed mixtures of nitrosamines (isodiazotates derived from p-nitroaniline and other arylamines) with sodium β-naphtholate.[49] These were printed on cotton and the dyes were developed by hanging in air. Griesheim-Elektron extended the use of this method with their *Rapid Fast* colours, placed on the market in 1914–15.[50] Each of these contained an alkali metal isodiazotate, a Naphtol AS coupling component and an excess of caustic alkali. The mixtures were printed on cloth, then exposed to acid steam so that the active diazonium compound was regenerated and coupling took place. As with the earlier products, some printers simply hung the printed cloth in air so that the carbon dioxide present gradually brought about development. The range of printed shades was greatly increased by the use of these preparations, since in a complex pattern both components could be varied, whereas in earlier processes one component was applied to the whole of the cloth. The original Rapid Fast mixtures were supplied in paste form, but afterwards powder brands were produced by mixing the moist isodiazotates with anhydrous sodium acetate and then adding the Naphtol and alkali.[51]

Products equivalent to the Rapid Fast colours have been made by several firms. Constitutions of some of the mixtures are given in Table 7-4, but many of them have been superseded by more modern printing preparations.

Table 7-4   Composition of selected Rapid Fast colours

Name	Diazo component	Naphtol
Rapid Fast Yellow GH	Fast Scarlet GG Base	AS-G
Rapid Fast Yellow I3GH	Fast Red TR Base	AS-IRG
Rapid Fast Orange RH	Fast Scarlet GG Base	AS-PH
Rapid Fast Scarlet ILH	Fast Scarlet GG Base	AS-OL
Rapid Fast Scarlet IRH	Fast Red KB Base	AS-PH
Rapid Fast Red RH	Fast Red RC Base	AS-OL
Rapid Fast Red FGH	Fast Red KB Base	AS-D
Rapid Fast Bordeaux IBN	Fast Red B Base	AS-BO
Rapid Fast Bordeaux RH	Fast Red RC Base	AS-BS
Rapid Fast Blue B	Fast Blue B Base (dianisidine)	AS
Rapid Fast Brown IBH	Fast Red RC Base	AS-LB
Rapid Fast Olive Brown IGH	Fast Orange GC Base	AS-LB

7-5-2 Rapidogen colours

In 1930 printing mixtures of a new type were marketed by IG under the name *Rapidogen* colours. These differed from the Rapid Fast range in that the diazo components were present in the form of diazoamino compounds obtained by coupling a diazotised azoic base in alkaline medium with a secondary amine such as sarcosine (CH_3NHCH_2COOH), N-methyltaurine $(CH_3NHC_2H_4SO_3H)$ or 2-N-ethylamino-5-sulphobenzoic acid; in a few cases the primary amine 4-sulphoanthranilic acid was used. When printed on textile fabric with a Naphthol and developed with acid steam the active diazo compound is regenerated and coupling takes place.[52] The formation of a diazoamino compound (or triazene) in alkaline medium and its scission in acid may be represented thus:

$$RN_2Cl + NHR'R'' \xrightarrow[\text{scission}]{\text{formation}} RN_2NR'R'' + HCl$$

In practice acetic or formic acid is used for development.

Diazoamino compounds are in general more easily manufactured than the isodiazotates, since there is no necessity for the hot concentrated solution of caustic alkali required by the latter. The greater stability of the diazoamino compounds allows them to be dried at moderate temperatures, and confers better storage properties on the mixtures with Naphthols. In application the printing paste remains serviceable for longer periods, and the resulting shades are somewhat brighter than those obtained from the corresponding Rapid Fast colours.

The Rapidogen colours became very widely used, and in due course many manufacturers marketed similar products. The

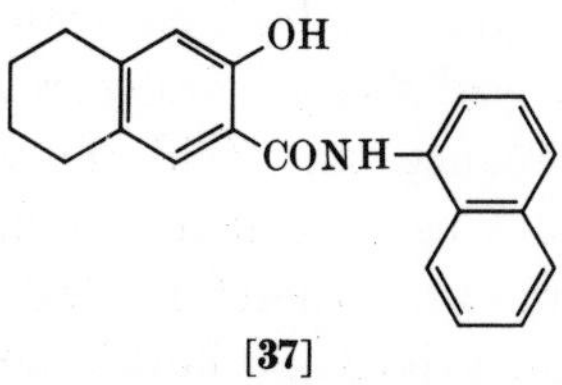

[37]

constitutions of some of them are given in Table 7-5. It will be seen that one of them (*Rapidogen Black IT*) includes the special coupling component 5,6,7,8-tetrahydro-2-naphthol-3-carboxylic α-naphthylamide [37][53].

Table 7-5   Composition of selected Rapidogen colours

Name	Stabiliser (see key)	Diazo Component	Naphthol
Rapidogen Yellow G	SA	Fast Red KB Base	AS-G
Rapidogen Yellow GS	S	Fast Red KB Base	AS-G
Rapidogen Yellow I4G	MT	Fast Red TR Base	AS-IRG
Rapidogen Orange G	SA	Fast Orange GC Base	AS-D
Rapidogen Orange R	EA5SB	Fast Scarlet GG Base	AS-PH
Rapidogen Scarlet IR	S	Fast Red KB Base	AS-PH
Rapidogen Red R	S	Fast Red RC Base	AS-OL
Rapidogen Red G	S	Fast Red KB Base	AS-D
Rapidogen Red ITR	EA5SB	Fast Red ITR Base	AS-ITR
Rapidogen Bordeaux RN	EA5SB	Fast Red RL Base	AS-D
Rapidogen Bordeaux IB	MA5SB	Fast Red B Base	AS-BO
Rapidogen Violet B	S	Fast Violet B Base	AS
Rapidogen Navy Blue IB	S	Variamine Blue B	AS
Rapidogen Blue B	S + MT	Fast Blue BB Base	AS
Rapidogen Green B	S + MT	Fast Blue BB Base	AS-GR
Rapidogen Brown IB	S	Fast Red RC Base	AS-LB
Rapidogen Brown IRRN	EA5SB	Fast Red RL Base	AS-LB
Rapidogen Black IT	MA5SB	Fast Red B Base	AS-SR + 2-Tetralol-3-carboxylic α-naphthyl-amide

Key to Stabilisers
S   Sarcosine
MT   N-Methyltaurine
SA   4-Sulphoanthranilic acid
MA5SB   2-Methylamino-5-sulphobenzoic acid
EA5SB   2-Ethylamino-5-sulphobenzoic acid

7-5-3   Neutral-developing printing mixtures

The main disadvantage of the Rapidogen dyes and their equivalents arose from the necessity of developing in acid steam. Its corrosive character resulted in costly plant maintenance, and acid development was also a barrier to the simultaneous use of vat dyes, which require alkaline conditions. Many attempts were therefore made to devise means whereby dyes of the Rapidogen type might be developed in neutral steam. In one of the early methods an auxiliary substance such as sodium chloroacetate which generated acid by hydrolysis was incorporated in the print paste, but this system proved inefficient.[54] Other methods depended on the use of a volatile base to form a salt with the triazene, the Naphthol or both components which dissociated to form a self-splitting triazene or an acidic Naphthol.[55] Various developing agents, based chiefly on diethyl-aminoethanol, were marketed, and were used fairly extensively in neutral-developing processes, but they were somewhat costly.

The problem has been solved by the use of new diazoamino compounds derived from stabilisers that allow scission to take place at a higher pH value. The first successful neutral-developing azoic printing mixtures were placed on the market in 1953 under the brand name *Neutrogene* by the Compagnie Française des Matières Colorantes. Stabilisers used in the manufacture of the range included *o*-carboxyphenylglycine and some related compounds. Suitable stabilisers are said to include the 3-, 4- and 5-chloro derivatives of *o*-carboxyphenylglycine, methoxy and dichloro derivatives, the esters and amides of these compounds, also *N*-alkoxyanthranilic acids, *N*-alkylanthranilic acids, *N*-*o*-carboxyphenyl-*β*-aminopropionic acid, *N*-*β*-hydroxy-*γ*-sulphopropylanthranilic acid and substituted derivatives of these compounds.[56]

Previous experience suggested that as a general rule the stability of triazenes is roughly proportional to the reactivity of the diazotised base and to the basicity of the stabiliser. Negatively substituted diazo compounds therefore require weakly basic stabilisers and less reactive diazo components require more strongly basic stabilisers. The neutral-developing triazenes, however, were derived from strongly basic diazo components and weakly basic stabilisers and thus do not conform to this principle. Siegrist[57] concluded from this that scission of triazenes may take place by one of two mechanisms which are influenced oppositely by the basicity of the stabiliser. Whereas triazenes requiring acid conditions yield the diazonium compound by mechanism (1) Siegrist suggested that neutral-developing triazenes are catalysed by water in accordance with mechanism (2):

Mechanism (1)

$$R-N=N-N\begin{array}{c}R^1\\\diagup\\\diagdown\\R^2\end{array} + \overset{\oplus}{H} \rightleftharpoons R-N=N-\overset{\overset{\oplus}{\overset{H}{\uparrow}}}{N}\begin{array}{c}R^1\\\diagup\\\diagdown\\R^2\end{array}$$

$$\updownarrow$$

$$R-\overset{\oplus}{\underset{\underset{N}{|||}}{N}} + HN\begin{array}{c}R^1\\\diagup\\\diagdown\\R^2\end{array}$$

Mechanism (2)

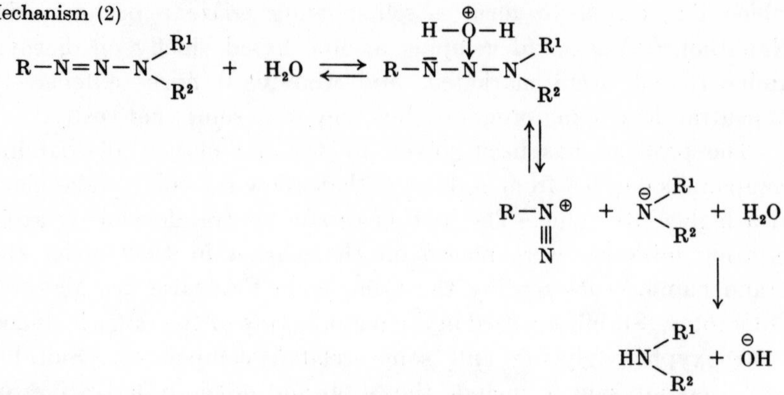

$$R-N=N-N\begin{array}{c}R^1\\R^2\end{array} + H_2O \rightleftharpoons R-\bar{N}-N-N\begin{array}{c}R^1\\R^2\end{array}$$

with $H-\overset{\oplus}{O}-H$ above

$$R-N\overset{\oplus}{\underset{N}{\overset{|||}{}}} + N\overset{\ominus}{\begin{array}{c}R^1\\R^2\end{array}} + H_2O$$

$$HN\begin{array}{c}R^1\\R^2\end{array} + \overset{\ominus}{O}H$$

Other proposals were put forward by Petitcolas and Thirot.[58]

The new stabilisers enabled products to be manufactured that are sufficiently stable to be stored for reasonable periods but very easily developed on the fibre in neutral steam.

A range of neutral-developing *Rapidogen N* colours was marketed by Farbenfabriken Bayer in the early 1950s. These may have been based on a stabiliser with the structure [**38**] which had been described

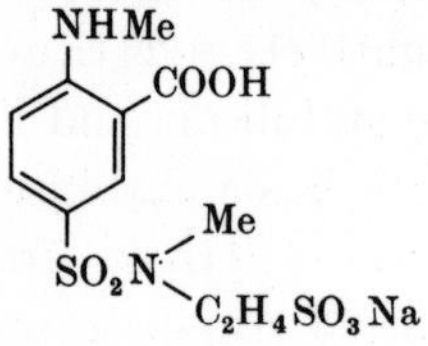

NHMe, COOH, SO$_2$N with Me and C$_2$H$_4$SO$_3$Na

[**38**]

in 1943 and was later stated to give neutral-developing triazenes.[59,60] In 1954 an improved range was produced by the same firm under the name *Rapidogen N54*. Extensive patent activity of the period[61] suggests that the stabilisers chiefly concerned were 2-alkylamino-4- and -5-sulphobenzoic acids. Triazenes derived from such stabilisers give satisfactory development in neutral steam if the use of excess alkali is avoided in preparation of printing pastes. 2-Ethylamino-sulphobenzoic acid had already been used as a stabiliser by IG, but only for diazo compounds derived from weak bases or rather complex molecules; diazotised bases such as 5-chloro-2-methylaniline or 5-chloro-2-methoxyaniline give highly soluble triazenes which are not readily isolated by normal salting. Methods have been devised for isolating these triazenes by salting with caustic soda[62] or an alkaline earth metal salt.[63]

In 1956 the firm of Rohner introduced a range of neutral-developing printing mixtures called *Sinagenes*. These are mixtures of diazoamino compounds with Naphthols supplied in the form of solutions in organic solvents. The diazoamino compounds are obtained mainly from stabilisers consisting of N-alkylanthranilic acids carrying strongly electronegative substituents such as —SO$_2$N-(alkyl)$_2$ or —SO$_2$alkyl groups, and suitable solvents are said to include alcohols, glycol monoethyl ether and thiodiethyleneglycol.[57]

A short range of *Rapidazol* colours has been marketed by Farbwerke Hoechst, consisting of mixtures of aryldiazosulphonates with Naphtols; these can be applied by printing and developed by neutral steam, preferably in presence of an oxidising agent such as sodium chromate. The range provided only violet, blue, green, brown and black shades. Most of these products were originally introduced by IG; an example is *Rapidazol Blue IB*, consisting of a standardised mixture of the diazosulphonate derived from 4-amino-4'-methoxydiphenylamine [**39**][64] with Naphtol AS. The Rapidazol

MeO—⟨ ⟩—NH—⟨ ⟩—N=N—SO$_3$Na

[**39**]

range was probably introduced as a means of avoiding technical problems in the production of diazoamino compounds from diazo compounds of low reactivity which are unstable in alkaline media.

The importance of azoic dyes applied to cellulosic fibres has declined considerably since the development of reactive dyes which enable bright shades with good fastness properties to be obtained by simple dyeing and printing processes.

7-6   Application to non-cellulosic fibres

Azoic dyes are not applied extensively to non-cellulosic fibres, and a brief description of the processes available for such applications will therefore suffice.

Wool and silk. Since these fibres are seriously damaged by alkali, the methods used for cotton require modification. Protective colloids have been used to reduce the damage, but they are incompletely effective. An improved process was devised by Everest and Wallwork[65] depending on the application of Naphthols as dispersions in soap solution. Their work related mainly to wool, but the process has also been applied to silk.

Acetate fibre. Various methods for applying azoic dyes to cellulose acetate have been used, and one of the more important of them consists in applying both components to the fibre, preferably as a dispersion, then treating with nitrous acid so that diazotisation and coupling take place.[66] The *Brentacet* dyes (ICI) are mixtures designed for such methods; they are also suitable for use on nylon.

Triacetate fibre. The methods used for acetate can be adapted for triacetate, application temperatures usually being higher and sometimes over 100°C. Coupling components are supplied in redispersible form for use on hydrophobic fibres; thus the *Brentosyns* (ICI) are special preparations of correspondingly named members of the Brenthol range. These coupling components are also used in conjunction with diazotisable aminoazo dyes such as CI Disperse Black 1 (Table 6-1).

Nylon. Azoic dyes may be applied to nylon by means of an alkaline bath containing both components, with subsequent diazotisation and coupling. Several processes have been described in which the diazo component is used in the form of a dispersed water-insoluble triazene.[67] It has been suggested that *Ofna-Perl Salt RRA* (FH) (CI Azoic Diazo Component 129) may be a product of this type, and if so presumably the other members of this short range are chemically similar.[68]

'Terylene'. Red, maroon, navy blue, brown and black shades are produced on 'Terylene' fibre by means of azoic dyes. Diazo components are applied in the form of free base since salts and diazonium compounds are not readily adsorbed. Similarly coupling components must be in the form of a dispersion of the free naphthol and not a sodium or other salt. Components with small molecules are preferred since they can usually be applied at the boil whereas more complex products can only be applied with the aid of a 'carrier' (see Section 6-4)[69] or under pressure. 3-Hydroxy-2-naphthoic acid is extensively used as a coupling component. Many combinations can be produced by applying the components simultaneously, but in a few cases separate baths give better results. On 'Terylene' and other hydrophobic fibres diazotisation and coupling take place somewhat slowly, and a temperature of 85°C may be needed. An excess of nitrous acid is necessary to compensate for loss in open equipment; closed vessels are therefore often used in order to avoid the nuisance of nitrous fumes.

Cationic and related dyes

The term 'Basic dyes' is conveniently used to distinguish an application class of dyes that, by virtue of the presence of basic groups in their molecules, have affinity for protein fibres and cellulosic fibres mordanted with tannic acid. If acid as well as basic groups are present *zwitterions* are formed, but the groups are ionised independently, and negatively charged dye ions usually predominate; such dyes therefore function as acid dyes. In a chemical classification the term 'Cationic dyes' is usually preferred; this relates to dyes consisting of salts in which the chromophoric system resides in the cation. For the purposes of the present chapter zwitterionic dyes (i.e. acid or mordant cationic dyes) are treated as cationic dyes. This arrangement, which is convenient for presentation, is justified in that a zwitterion is both cation and anion, but does not conform to a recent definition of a cationic dye as one in which the balance of charge on the ion is positive.[1]

The earliest synthetic dyes were cationic, and many such dyes now manufactured were discovered in the nineteenth or early twentieth century. Various chemical classes are represented, all characterised by exceptional brilliance, high tinctorial strength and low fastness to light. These dyes were formerly applied extensively to wool, silk and tannin-mordanted cotton, but dyes of other classes with better fastness properties are now generally preferred for such purposes, and basic dyes of the older types are used mainly for colouring paper (in applications for which brilliance rather than permanence is chiefly required), printing inks, crayons, cosmetics, copying papers, foodstuffs, military smoke signals and other minor applications.

With the advent of synthetic fibres based on polyacrylonitrile and its co-polymers a new textile application for cationic dyes has been found, but many new dyes have been developed especially for these fibres, and older dyes are used to only a small extent.

The chemistry of classical cationic dyes has been fully described in many reference books, and there are few recent developments. For the present purpose a brief description of some representative examples may therefore suffice; readers needing more detailed information should consult the *Colour Index* or one of the larger textbooks. The chief chemical classes are here now considered in turn. Most of the dyes discussed are basic in character, but a few acid and mordant dyes closely related to the main types described are included.

8-1   Diphenylmethane dyes

There are only two important commercial dyes of this class, *Auramine O* and *Auramine G* (CI Basic Yellows 2 and 3; CI 41000, CI 41005). Auramine O was first prepared in 1883 by Caro and Kern from 4,4′-bis(dimethylamino)benzophenone (Michler's ketone) by heating it with ammonium chloride and zinc chloride at 150°–160°C. A more recent method consists in passing ammonia over a mixture of 4,4′-bis(dimethylamino)diphenylmethane, sulphur, oxalic acid and salt at a temperature which is gradually raised from 125° to 170°C, and converting the resulting dye-base into its hydrochloride.[2]

Auramine G is made similarly from 3,3′-dimethyl-4,4′-di(methyl-amino)diphenylmethane, obtained by condensing *N*-methyl-*o*-toluidine with formaldehyde. These dyes are used for the dyeing and printing of tannin-mordanted cotton, wool, silk, leather and paper, also in spirit inks and as a lake for printing inks. The shades are golden yellow. In boiling water the Auramines decompose, with loss of ammonia and formation of the corresponding ketones. It is of interest to note that acetylation of Auramine O yields a deep violet dye. In this derivative resonance evidently takes place through a chain of 11 atoms ending in the dimethylamino groups, but in Auramine O salt formation occurs chiefly at the $\diagup$C=NH group, so that resonance is confined mainly to the chains of 7 atoms by which the amino group is linked to the two dimethylamino groups; the shorter resonating system accounts for the yellow hue.[3]

8-2   Triphenylmethane dyes

These dyes are derived from triphenylmethane or its homologues. On oxidation this hydrocarbon yields triphenylmethanol, and the dyes are salts of amino or hydroxy derivatives of compounds of this type. Only di- and tri-substituted derivatives are of commercial value, and the amino or hydroxyl groups are always in different rings in the *para* positions with respect to the methane carbon atom.

The resonance hybrid of a triphenylmethane dye embraces many cationic structures. In the case of the amino derivatives ammonium and carbonium structures contribute to the system; thus the cation of one of the methylated triaminotriphenylmethane dyes of the Methyl Violet series may be represented as a hybrid of structures [**40**–**43**], and intermediate forms such as [**44**] are probably also present. Of these [**40**] and [**41**] are identical.

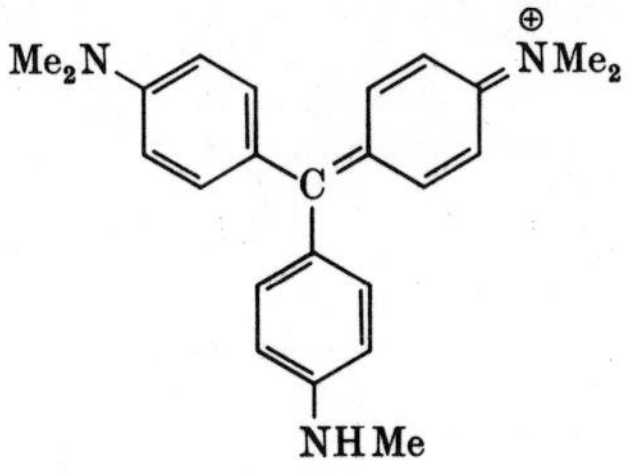

[**40**]

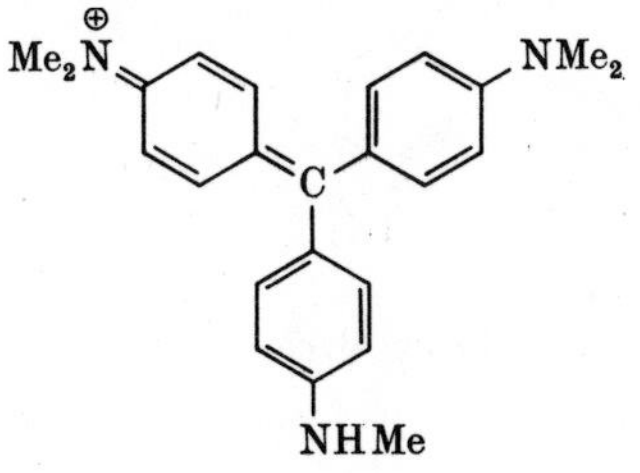

[**41**]

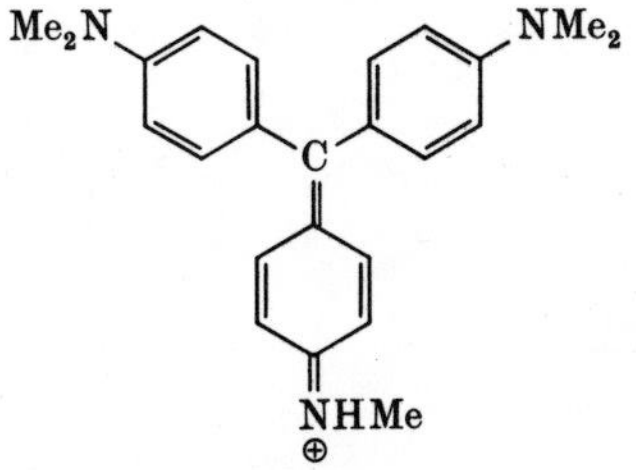

[**42**]

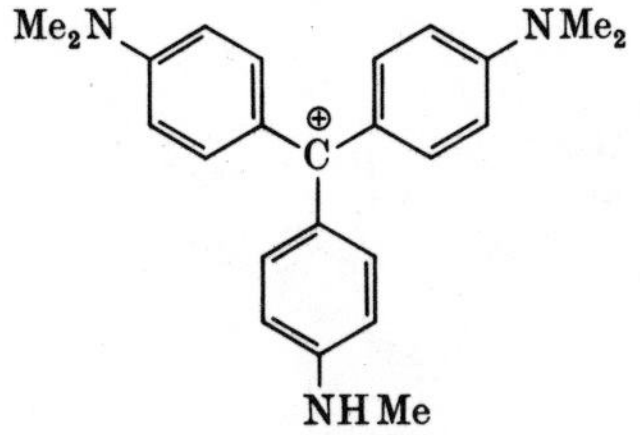

[**43**]

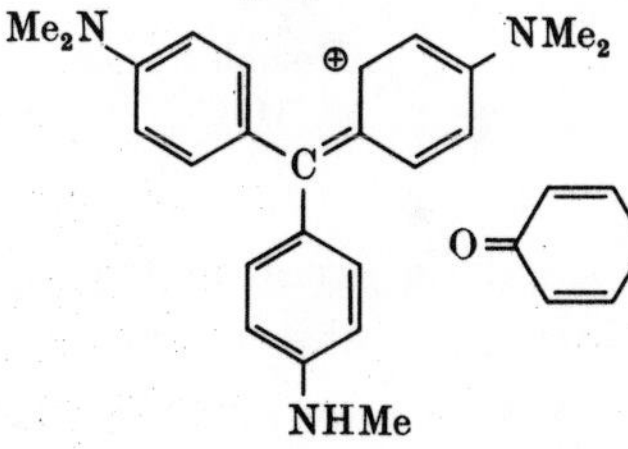

[**44**]

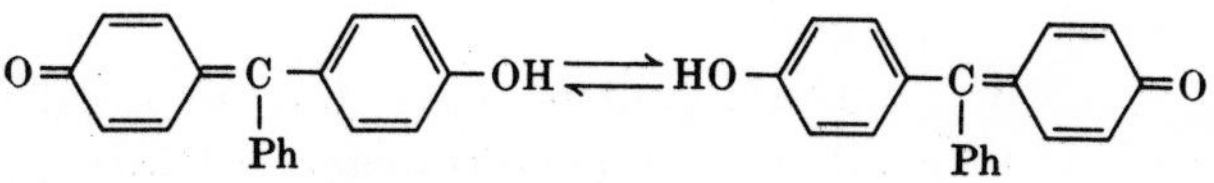

Resonance in the dihydroxytriphenylmethane dye benzaurine has already been referred to (Chapter 2). In the free acid form this dye exhibits tautomerism, as above (last two structures). A series of free bases may be obtained by treating a triphenylmethane dye with alkali, and on reduction a leuco base is formed. The reactions shown on page 106 relating to the red triaminotriphenylmethane dye Pararosaniline are typical of the whole class:

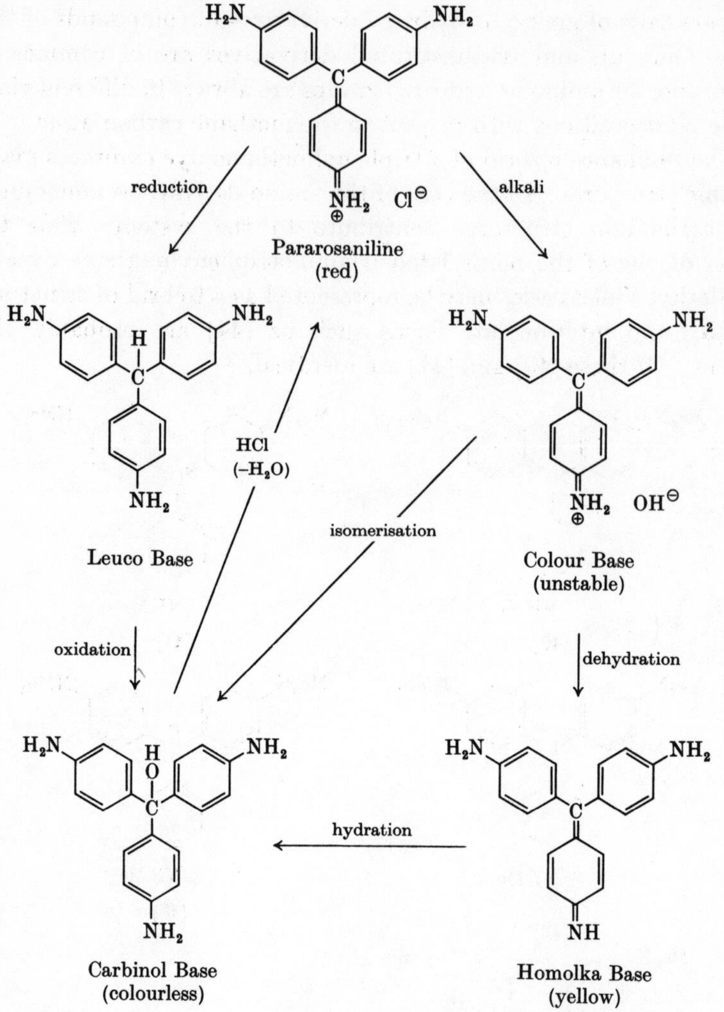

reduction / alkali

NH₂ Cl⊖

Pararosaniline
(red)

HCl
(–H₂O)

isomerisation

Leuco Base

Colour Base
(unstable)

OH⊖

oxidation

dehydration

hydration

Carbinol Base
(colourless)

Homolka Base
(yellow)

The unstable colour base first obtained on treating the dye salt with alkali is rapidly transformed into the isomeric carbinol base. By elimination of water from the colour base a more stable Homolka base is formed, but it is gradually hydrolysed in aqueous medium.

The triphenylmethane dyes are of four main types.

8-2-1 Malachite Green series, containing two amino or substituted amino groups

The simplest of these dyes is *Döbner's Violet*, which has already been mentioned (Chapter 2). It is of no technical value, but its tetramethyl derivative *Malachite Green* (CI Basic Green 4; CI 42000) is important. This dye is obtained by refluxing benzaldehyde with a slight excess of dimethylaniline in the presence of a deficiency of hydrochloric or sulphuric acid. When condensation is complete the mixture is made alkaline, excess dimethylaniline is removed by steam distillation, the resulting leuco base [4,4'-bis(dimethylamino)-triphenylmethane] is oxidised with lead peroxide to the carbinol base [4,4'-bis(dimethylamino)triphenylmethanol], and after removal of lead this is converted into the hydrochloride.[4] Malachite Green is usually marketed as a zinc chloride double salt, but some brands consist of the hydrochloride, sulphate or oxalate. The reactions on which manufacture is based are as follows:

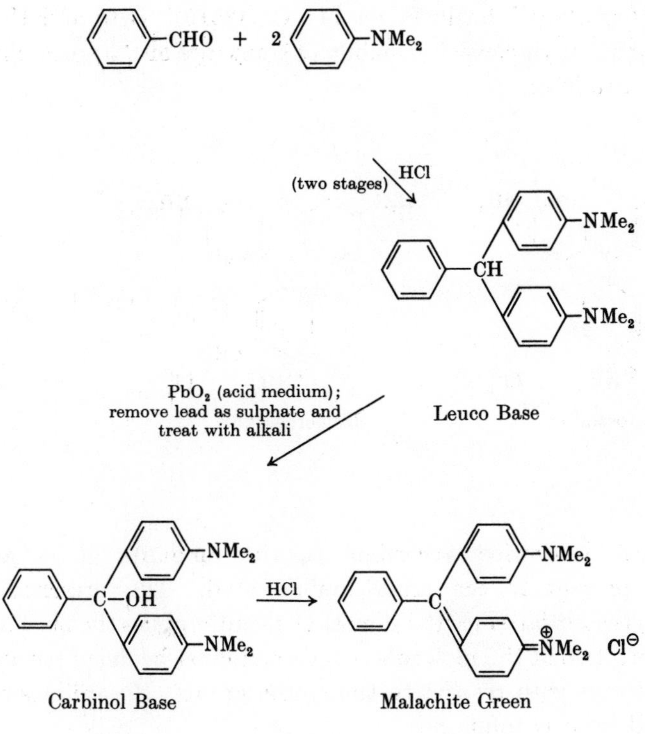

The corresponding dye obtained from N,N'-diethylaniline, known as *Brilliant Green* (CI Basic Green 1; CI 42040), gives somewhat yellower shades; apart from its value as a dye it has powerful antiseptic properties.

By carrying out similar reactions with o-chlorobenzaldehyde and dimethylaniline *Setoglaucine* (Gy) (CI Basic Blue 1; CI 42025) is obtained. It gives bluish green shades with fastness properties rather better than those of Malachite Green.

8-2-2   Rosaniline series, containing three amino or substituted amino groups

Manufacture from crude aniline. In 1856 Natanson observed the formation of a red dye on oxidation of crude aniline, and some three years later Verguin obtained a dye of the same type by oxidising crude aniline with stannic chloride. It was manufactured under the name *Fuchsine*, and its valuable properties attracted much interest. Processes using other oxidising agents, such as mercuric chloride, arsenic acid or nitrobenzene, were discovered, and the dye was manufactured by several firms; in England it became known as *Magenta* (CI Basic Violet 14; CI 42510). Otto and Emil Fischer showed that it consisted mainly of a mixture of Pararosaniline and Homorosaniline:

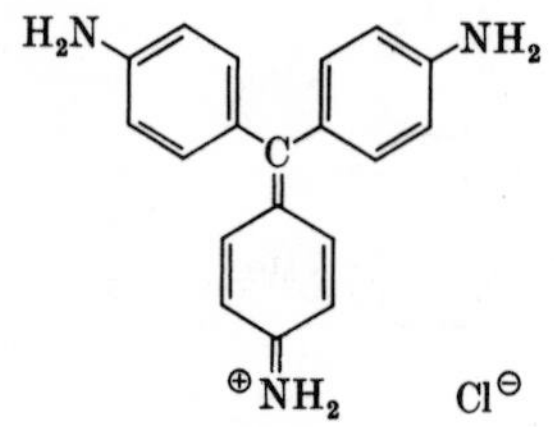

Pararosaniline 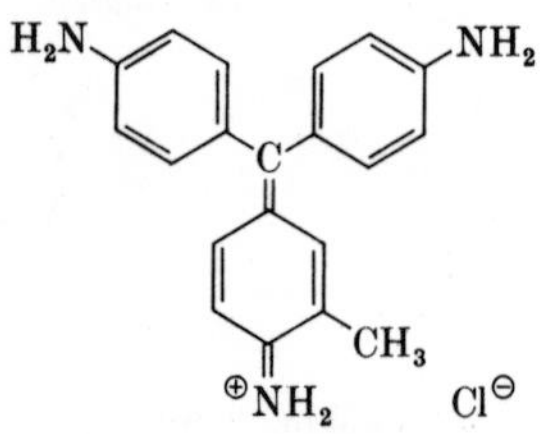   Homorosaniline

The composition varied according to the amounts of *o*- and *p*-toluidine present in the crude aniline used. The presence of *p*-toluidine is essential, since the *p*-methyl group supplies the methane carbon atom; two of the molecules concerned must be unsubstituted in *para* positions with respect to the amino group. Rosanilines are not obtained from *m*-toluidine.

Other reactions are used for producing rosanilines, and some of the more important of them are now briefly described.

Formaldehyde process. Formaldehyde reacts with aniline and aniline hydrochloride to give 4,4′-diaminodiphenylmethane; this can then be condensed with a further molecule of aniline in presence of iron filings and an oxidising agent such as nitrobenzene, and on converting the product into its hydrochloride Pararosaniline is obtained.[5] This process has the advantage of giving a homogeneous dye.

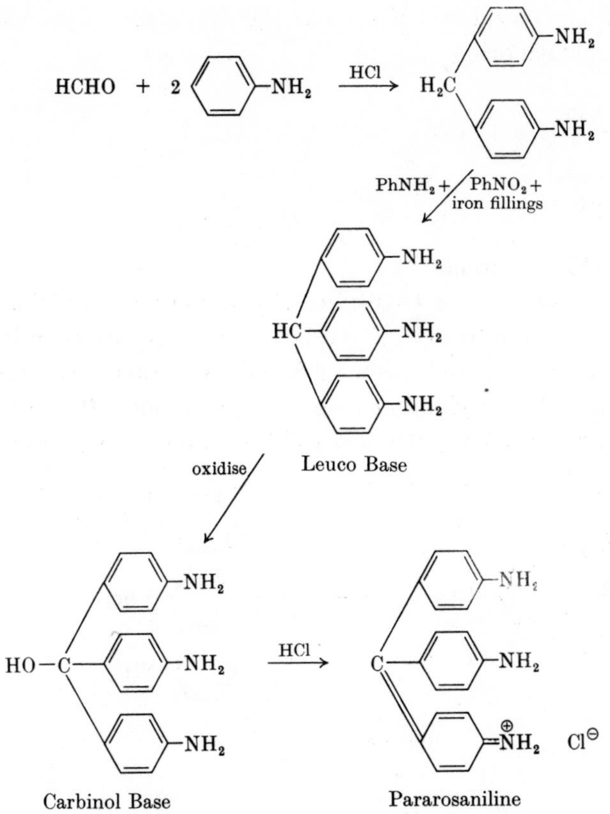

Leuco Base

Carbinol Base   Pararosaniline

Phosgene process. Reaction of N,N-dimethylaniline with phosgene in presence of zinc chloride yields 4,4'-bis(dimethylamino)-benzophenone (Michler's ketone), and this may be condensed with a further molecule of dimethylaniline (or another base) to yield a rosaniline base. The dye *Crystal Violet* (CI Basic Violet 3; CI 42555) is obtained in this way.[6]

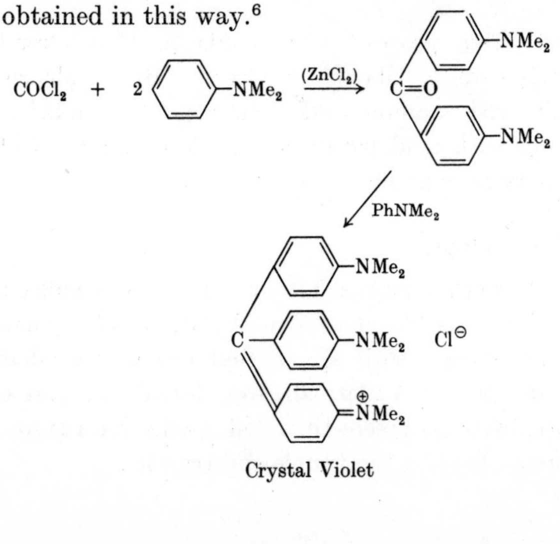

Crystal Violet

According to Fierz-David and Koechlin[7] the first stage of the reaction yields the ketochloride

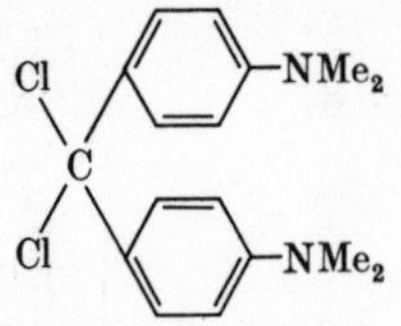

rather than Michler's ketone.

Carbinol   process.   4,4'-Bis(dimethylamino)phenylmethanol (Michler's hydrol), obtained by oxidation of 4,4'-bis(dimethylaminophenyl)methane or reduction of Michler's ketone, condenses with bases such as dimethylaniline to give triphenylmethanes which by oxidation and treatment with acid yield rosanilines. The process is of minor importance.

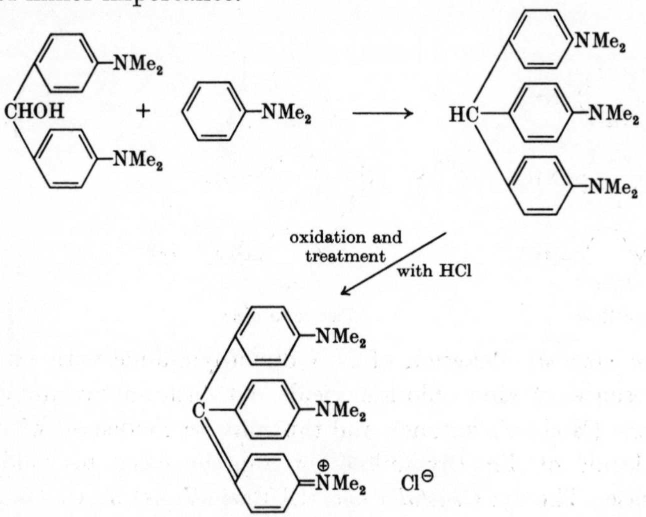

Aldehyde process. This process corresponds to that already described for manufacture of Malachite Green. By condensing *p*-aminobenzaldehyde with aniline under appropriate conditions, oxidising and treating with acid pararosaniline is obtained. Substituted rosanilines may be manufactured similarly.

8-2-3   N-Alkylated rosanilines

The introduction of *C*-methyl groups into the rosaniline molecule results in slightly bluer shades, but *N*-methylation has a more marked bathochromic effect; with six methyl groups the shade becomes violet (as in Crystal Violet, already described), and on further methylation it becomes green, then yellow (the main absorption band having passed beyond the visible spectrum).

Dyes of the Methyl Violet series (CI Basic Violet 1; CI 42535) are important methylated rosanilinés, with shades varying from reddish to bluish violet according to the degree of methylation. The redder brands can be made by methylation of rosaniline, but the bluer ones are made by an interesting process consisting in oxidising dimethylaniline with copper sulphate in presence of common salt and phenol. In the first reaction stage one methyl group is removed from a molecule of dimethylaniline with formation of formaldehyde. The formaldehyde then condenses with two molecules of unchanged dimethylaniline, giving 4,4′bis(dimethyl-amino)diphenylmethane, and this is oxidised to the corresponding hydrol. Condensation between the hydrol and the monomethyl-aniline formed in the first stage yields the required triphenylmethane derivative and this by oxidation and acidification gives Methyl Violet. The series of reactions may be represented as follows, but it should be understood that others also occur, and that the product is a mixture:

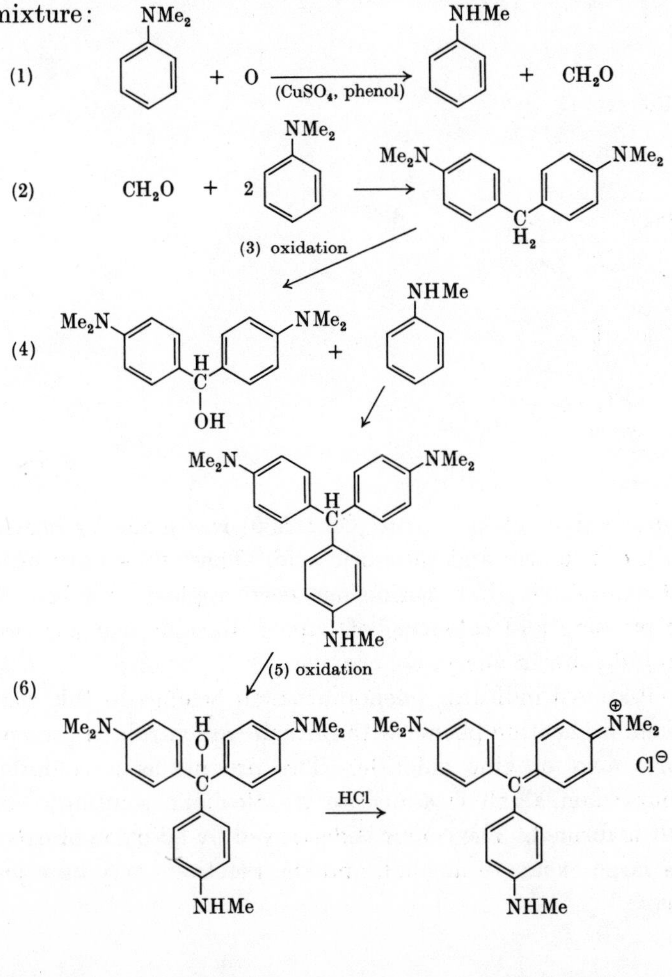

Methyl Violets are extensively used for hectograph inks, ball-pen inks, typewriter ribbons and copying paper, also for dyeing paper, leather and plastics.

8-2-4   Rosolic acid series, containing hydroxyl groups

Rosolic acid was one of the earliest artificial dyes, having been prepared by Runge[8] in 1834 by oxidation of crude phenol (containing cresols). Its structure is shown below:

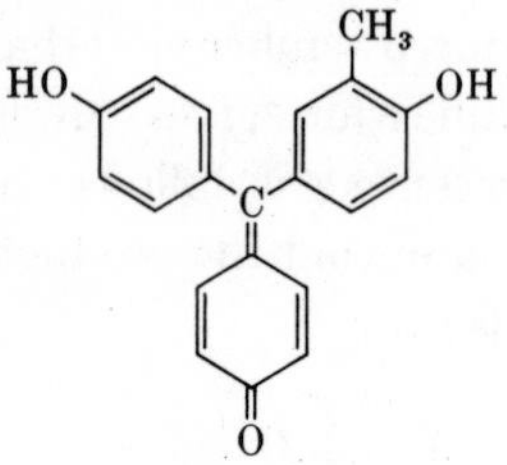

Rosolic acid

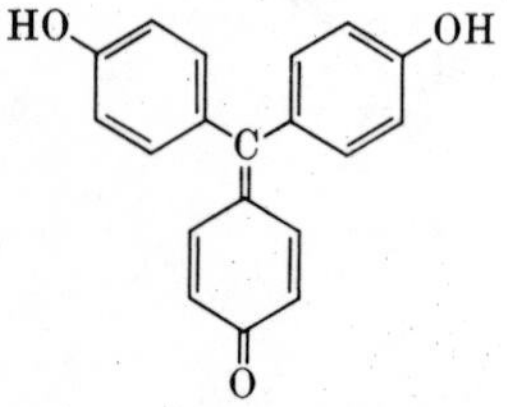

Aurine

Later a similar dye called *Aurine* (CI 43800) was made by heating phenol with oxalic acid and sulphuric acid. These dyes have never been used extensively, but Aurine has been applied as a lake for wallpaper printing and colouring of paper. Rosolic acid has been used as an indicator in analytical chemistry.

The well-known indicator phenolphthalein belongs to this class. It is obtained by heating phenol with phthalic anhydride in presence of sulphuric acid or zinc chloride. The product is a colourless lactone, but when alkali is added to its alcoholic solution a red sodium salt is formed. The colour is destroyed by addition of excess alkali or a large excess of alcohol, and the reactions may be represented thus:

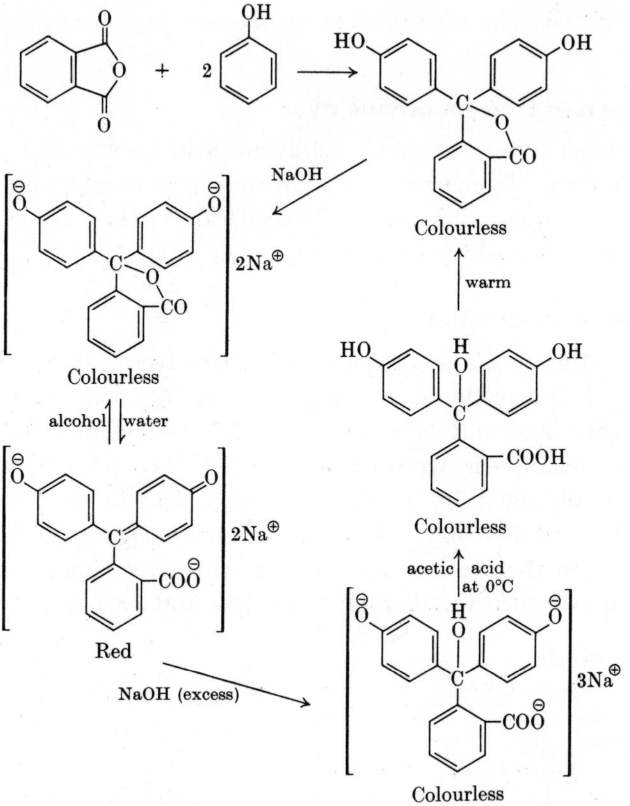

Colourless

2Na⊕

Colourless

alcohol | water

warm

HO ... OH

Colourless

2Na⊕

Red

NaOH (excess)

acetic | acid
at 0°C

Colourless

3Na⊕

Colourless

-3　Other triarylmethane dyes

In this class the *Victoria Blues* are of prime importance. They are triamino derivatives of α-naphthyldiphenylmethanes, the chief examples being *Victoria Blues B* (CI Basic Blue 26; CI 44045), R (CI Basic Blue 11, CI 44040) and 4R (CI Basic Blue 8; CI 42563), with the structures shown:

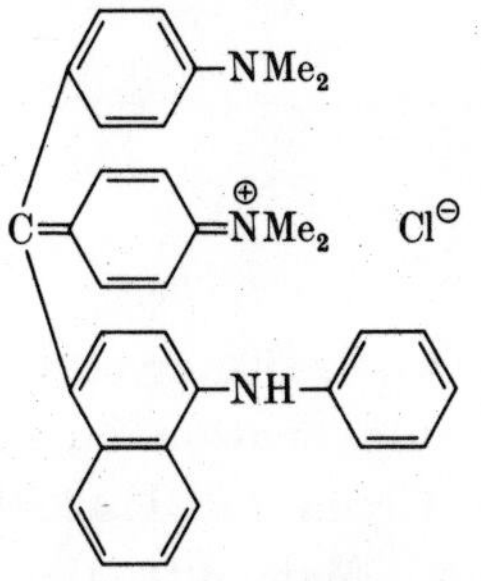

Victoria Blue B 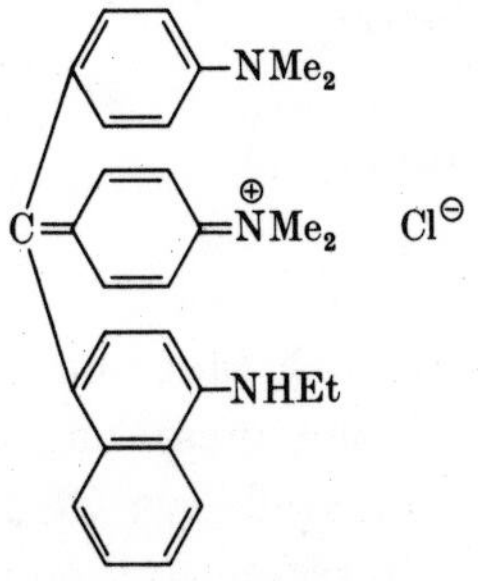　　　　Victoria Blue R 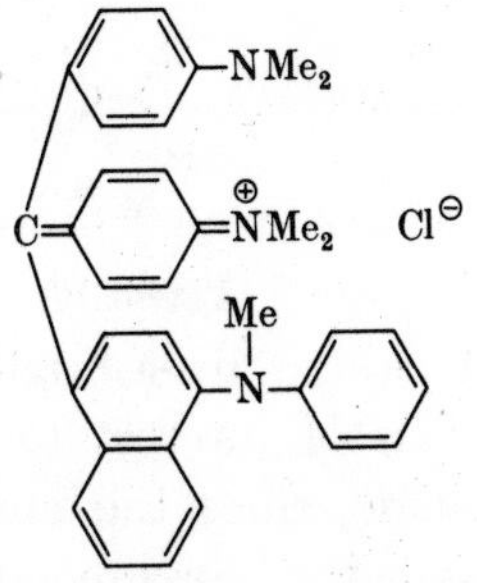　　　　Victoria Blue 4R

These dyes are obtained by condensing 4,4′-bis(dimethylamino)-benzophenone chloride with *N*-phenyl-α-naphthylamine, *N*-ethyl-α-naphthylamine and *N*-methyl-*N*-phenyl-α-naphthylamine, respectively. They give bright blue or reddish blue shades on wool, silk or cotton.

8-4 Sulphonated triarylmethane dyes

Triphenylmethane dyes containing sulphonic acid groups may be applied as acid dyes. In general they show the characteristic brightness of the parent basic dyes, with only moderate fastness to light, but their fastness to washing is often very good.

8-4-1 Malachite Green series

Direct sulphonation of diaminotriphenylmethane dyes is in general unsatisfactory, but benzylated derivatives are readily sulphonated. Alternatively, the dyes may be made from sulphobenzylated aniline derivatives. An example is *Naphthalene Green G* (ICI) (CI Acid Green 3; CI 42085), obtained by condensing benzaldehyde with two molecules of N-m-sulphobenzyl-N-ethylaniline, oxidising the product and coverting into the sodium salt. This bright green dye is now little used on wool, but it is still applied to paper and leather.

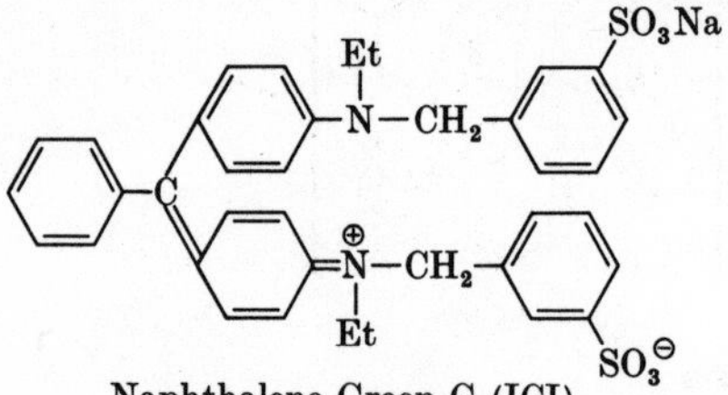

Naphthalene Green G (ICI)

In *Patent Blue V* (CI Acid Blue 1; CI 42045), made by several firms, sulphonic acid groups are introduced into the amino-free phenyl ring. It is obtained in the usual way from 2,4-disulphobenzaldehyde and N,N-diethylaniline, and has the structure shown:

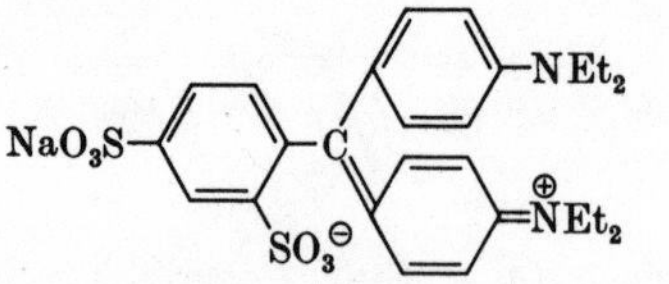

Patent Blue V

This dye gives bright greenish blue shades on wool, silk or cotton. It is of interest to note the great effect of sulphonation on the shade, since the unsulphonated dye CI Basic Green 1 (CI 42040) and the corresponding tetramethyl compound Malachite Green (Section 8-2-1) are both green. The effect may be attributed to molecular distortion caused by the *ortho* sulphonic acid group. It may be compared with the similar effect of two methoxy groups in Caledon Jade Green XBN (Section 10-5-1).

8-4-2 Rosaniline series

One of the earliest sulphonated dyes of this class was *Acid Magenta* (CI Acid Violet 19; CI 42685), discovered by Caro in 1877. It may be obtained by trisulphonation of Magenta (the sulpho groups entering in the positions *ortho* to the amino groups). This dye is now little used except for colouring leather, paper, soap, photographic films, and as a biological stain. An example of a sulphobenzylated rosaniline dye is *Fast Acid Violet 10B* (FBy and other firms) (CI Acid Blue 13; CI 42571), made by the carbinol process from Michler's hydrol and *N*-*m*-sulphobenzyl-*N*-ethylmetanilic acid. The commercial dye contains a monosulphonated derivative.

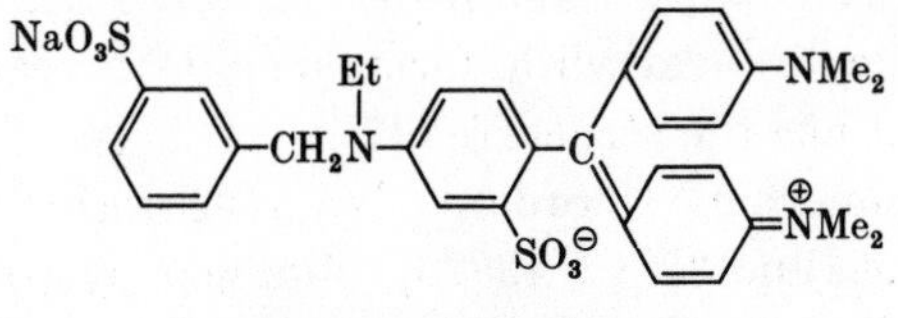

Fast Acid Violet 10B
(Main component)

It gives reddish blue shades, and is used to some extent on wool, also on leather and paper.

A marked bathochromic effect is obtained by phenylation of the amino groups in rosanilines; the shades resulting from the introduction of one, two and three phenyl groups are reddish violet, bluish violet and blue, respectively. Examples are CI Acid Blue 22 (CI 42755; a trisulphonated diphenyl derivative of Homorosaniline), CI Acid Blue 48 (CI 42770; a disulphonated diphenylrosaniline) and CI Acid Blue 93 (CI 42780; a trisulphonated triphenylrosaniline). The last-named dye is sometimes made by condensing formaldehyde with two molecular proportions of diphenylamine-4- (or -3-)sulphonic acid and oxidising in presence of a further molecular proportion of the latter compound. These Soluble Blues are now little used for textile coloration, but are applied to leather, paper and (sometimes as lakes) in printing inks.

8-5 Mordant triphenylmethane dyes

Many dyes containing salicylic acid residues have been manufactured for use as mordant dyes. They are applied to wool by any of the methods described in Section 4-1-2, to silk by the chrome mordant or afterchrome method, and to nylon, usually by the afterchrome method. In some cases cotton padded with chromium acetate can be dyed, and various printing processes are in use on wool, silk and cotton. Some examples of these dyes are now described.

Eriochrome Brilliant Violet R (Gy) (CI Mordant Violet 1; CI 43565), introduced by Geigy in 1908, is obtained by condensing *p*-diethylaminobenzaldehyde with 2,3-cresotic acid (2 molecular proportions) in sulphuric acid medium and oxidising the product with nitrous acid. It contains a diethylamino group and two salicylic acid residues, and has the structure [45]. An example of a dye containing two salicylic acid residues and no basic group is *Erio-chrome Azurol B* (Gy) (CI Mordant Blue 1; CI 43830). This is obtained by condensation of 2,6-dichlorobenzaldehyde with 2,3-cresotic acid, oxidising and coverting into the sodium salt [46]. A dye having three salicylic acid residues is *Chrome Violet* (Gy) (CI Mordant Violet 39; CI 43810), discovered by Sandmeyer in 1889. It is obtained by condensing salicylic acid with formaldehyde in concentrated sulphuric acid, and has the structure [47].

A sulphonated triphenylmethane mordant dye is *Eriochrome Cyanine R* (Gy) (CI Mordant Blue 3; CI 43820), obtained by condensing *o*-sulphobenzaldehyde with 2,3-cresotic acid, oxidising and converting the product into its sodium salt [48].

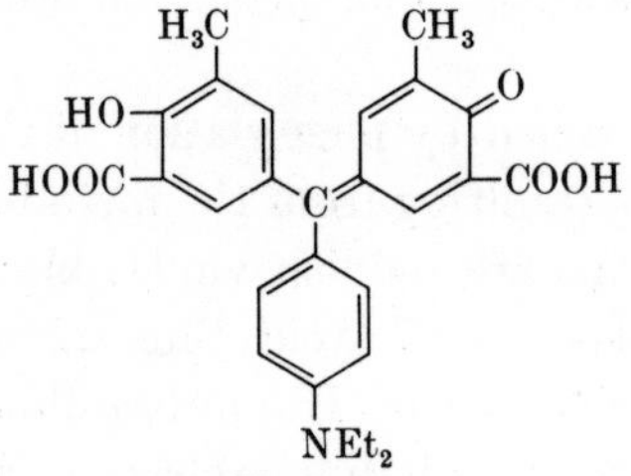

Eriochrome Brilliant
Violet R (Gy)

[45]

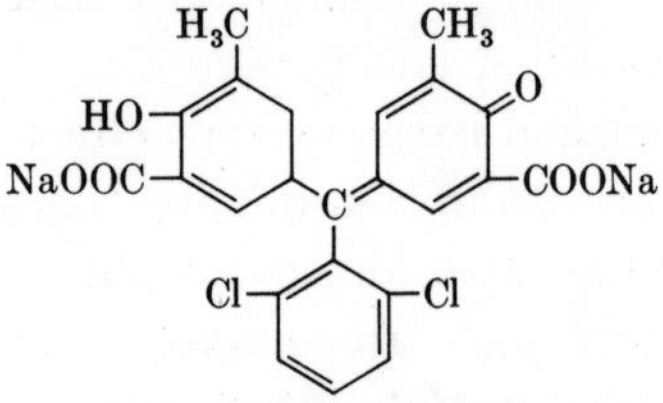

Eriochrome Azurol B
(Gy)

[46]

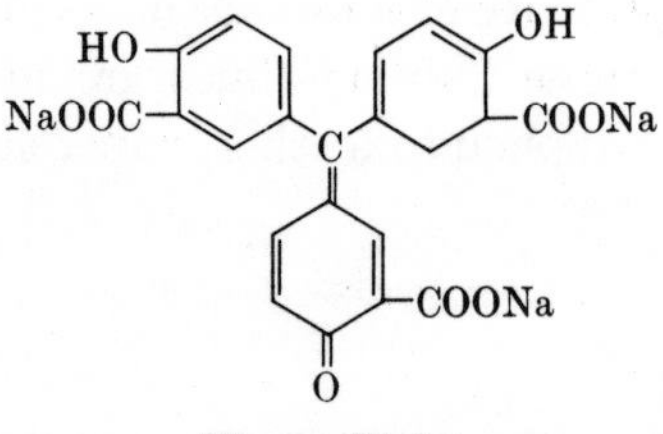

Chrome Violet
(Gy)

[47]

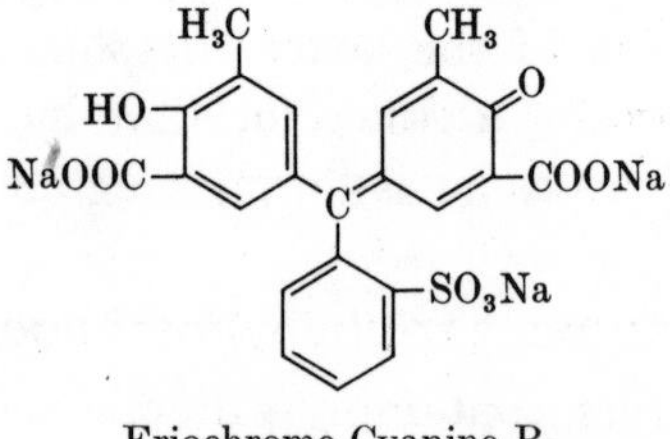

Eriochrome Cyanine R
(Gy)

[48]

As illustrated by these examples, triphenylmethane mordant dyes give deep shades, mainly violet or blue, and in many cases they are very bright. Light fastness varies, and is often affected by the

method of application, but in heavy shades sometimes reaches grade
6–7 or even 7. Fastness to milling and washing is usually fairly good
or very good.

8-6 Xanthene dyes

All the dyes of this group are based on the xanthene (or dibenzo-
1,4-pyran) structure [49], and contain amino or hydroxyl groups

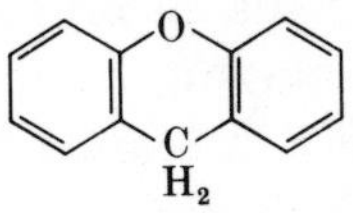

[49]

(or both) in the *meta* positions with respect to the oxygen bridge.
The chromophore of the amino derivatives is a resonance-hybrid of
ammonium and oxonium structures [50], and that of the hydroxy
derivatives is an equilibrium (with proton transfer) between
p-quinonoid and oxonium structures [51]. In this chapter dyes are
shown in the p-quinonoid forms, but it should not be assumed that
these predominate.

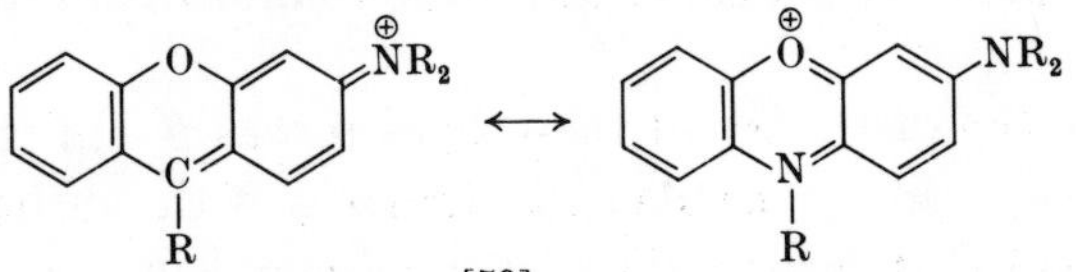

[50]

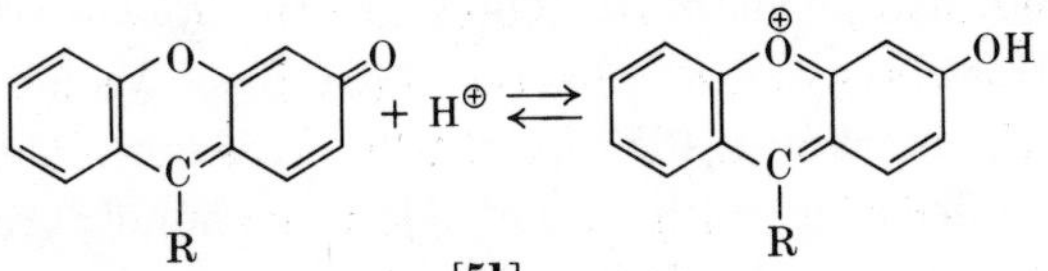

[51]

It will be seen that when the radical R attached to the pyran ring
is hydrogen, the dyes are derivatives of diphenylmethane; they are,
in fact, internal ethers derived from o,o'-dihydroxydiphenyl-
methanes. Similarly when this radical R is phenyl the dyes are
corresponding derivatives of triphenylmethanes.

In the Colour Index the Xanthene dyes are arranged in chemical
classes, but since the present account is restricted to the few dyes
still of major technical importance details of the classification are
omitted.

One of the earliest Xanthene dyes was *Fluorescein* (CI Acid
Yellow 73; CI 45350) [52] obtained by condensing phthalic anhydride

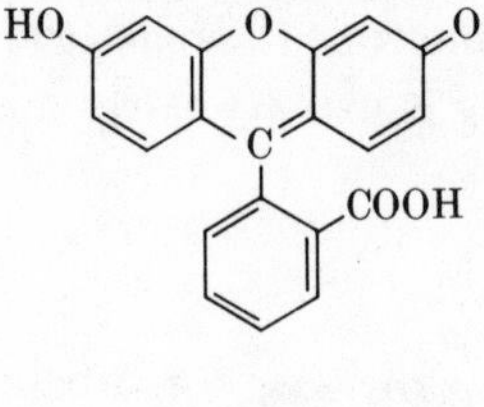

[52] 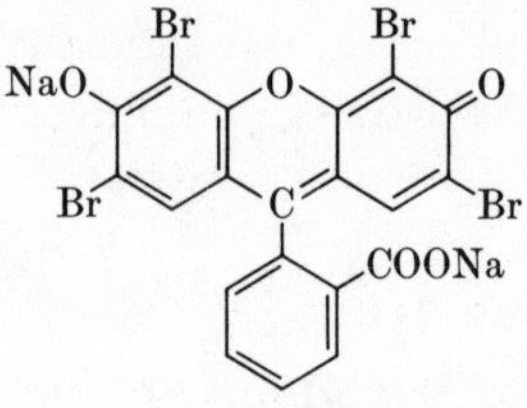   [53]

with resorcinol (Baeyer, 1871). The sodium (or potassium) salt was formerly used under the name *Uranine* for dyeing silk in brilliant yellow shades. Its strong green fluorescence in solution, even at very great dilution, enables Fluorescein to be used as a marker for life saving at sea, for tracing the course of underground streams, and in medical practice for detection of weak circulation of blood. Fluorescein is now used mainly as an intermediate for manufacture of its tetrabromo derivative *Eosine* (CI Acid Red 87; CI 45380) [53], discovered in 1874 by Caro. This is a brilliant red acid dye which is applied on textile materials to only a small extent because of its poor fastness properties, but widely used for colouring leather, paper, inks, stains, crayons and (in purified form, often as an aluminium lake) in drugs and cosmetics. The corresponding tetraiodo compound *Erythrosine* (CI Acid Red 51; CI 45430) gives bluer shades and is used for similar purposes, also (when suitably purified) for colouring food.

Some years after the discovery of these dyes it was found that *m*-dialkylaminophenols can be condensed similarly with phthalic anhydride to give dyes that surpass those of the fluorescein series in tinctorial strength and also in fastness. These are the *Rhodamines*. The first member of this class was *Rhodamine B* (CI Basic Violet 10; CI 45170), placed on the market in 1887 by BASF. It is obtained by condensing phthalic anhydride with *m*-diethylaminophenol; reaction takes place in two stages, the first giving the intermediate [54] and the second the dye base [55], which is converted into the dye [56] by acidification:

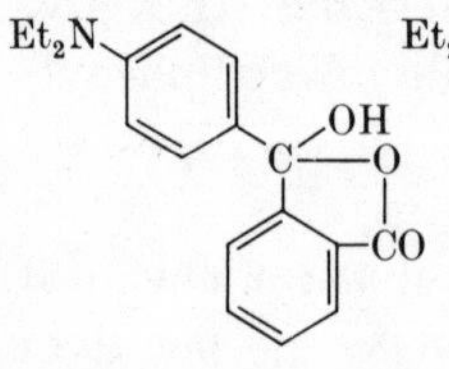

[54] 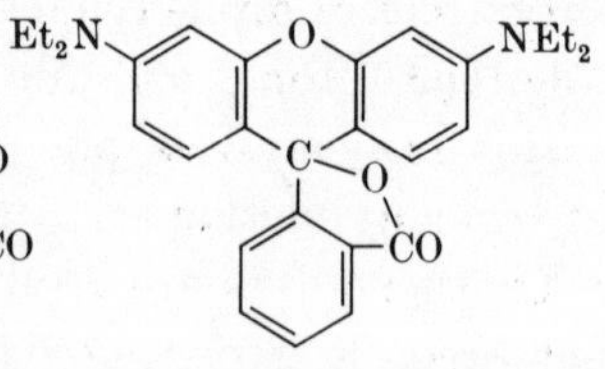   [55] 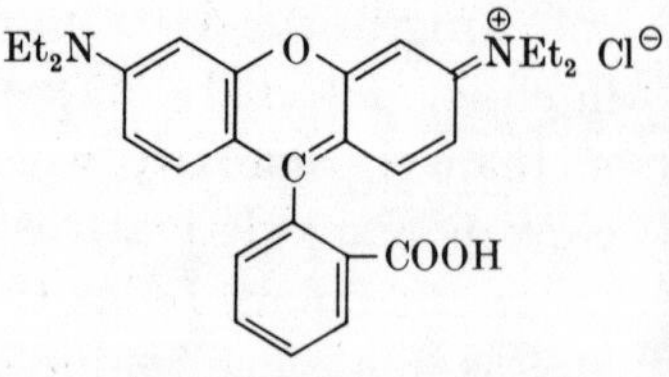   [56]

Whereas the fluorescein derivatives are acid dyes, the dialkylamino groups confer basic properties, and the Rhodamines can be applied to mordanted cotton as well as to silk. The shades on silk are bright bluish red, with a strong fluorescence. On tannin-mordanted cotton the fluorescence is lacking, the shade being a dull lilac, but it is present when the dye is applied to cotton mordanted with alumina and Turkey Red Oil. The analogue of Rhodamine B containing dimethylamino groups is little used on account of its low solubility.

Esterification of the carboxylic acid groups yields a more strongly basic dye. Manufacture of the ethyl ester (CI Basic Violet 11; CI 45175) has now been discontinued, but the related dye *Rhodamine 6G* (CI Basic Red 1; CI 45160) remains of some importance.

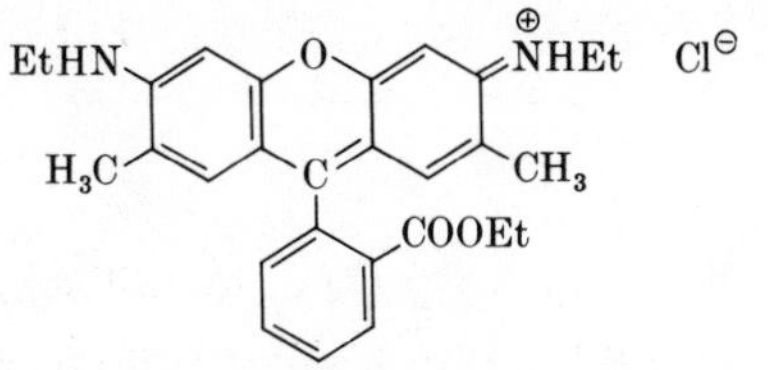

Rhodamine 6G

Since the condensations with phthalic anhydride occur in two stages it is possible to make unsymmetrical xanthene dyes by using different *m*-substituted phenols in succession. Several such dyes have been marketed, but (except for some members of the Rhodol series, discussed later) they have fallen out of use.

Sulphonated derivatives of Rhodamines provide acid dyes of this class with good fastness to light. They are obtainable by sulphonation of Rhodamines or, more usually, by condensation of phthalic anhydride with *m*-chlorophenol, reaction of the resulting dichlorofluorane with a primary aromatic amine and sulphonation of the product. An example is *Coomassie Violet 2R* (ICI) (CI Acid Violet 9; CI 45190), with the structure [57]. This dye gives bright

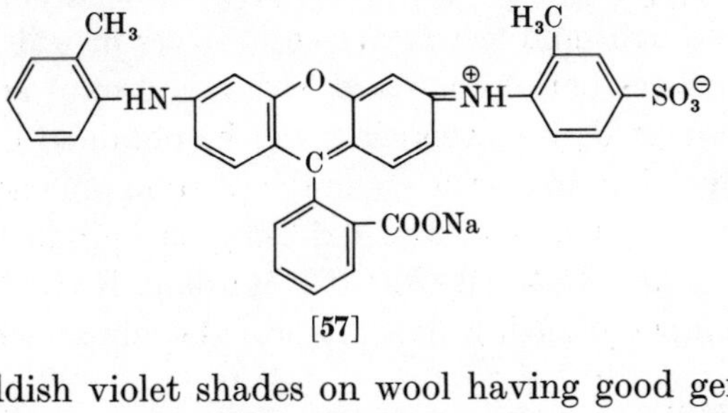

[57]

reddish violet shades on wool having good general fastness properties. In deep shades the light fastness reaches grade 5 of the SDC scale.

An example of a disulphonated Xanthene dye is *Lissamine Rhodamine B* (ICI) and its equivalents (CI Acid Red 52; CI 45100). This is obtained by condensing 2,4-disulphobenzaldehyde with *m*-diethylaminophenol (2 mol.) in sulphuric acid medium, heating with sulphuric acid at 135°C to form the pyrone derivative, then oxidising with bichromate and sulphuric acid. The resulting dye [58] gives bright bluish pink shades on wool, silk or nylon, and is often used for knitting yarn. The light-fastness varies from grade 2 to grade 3 according to the depth of shade.

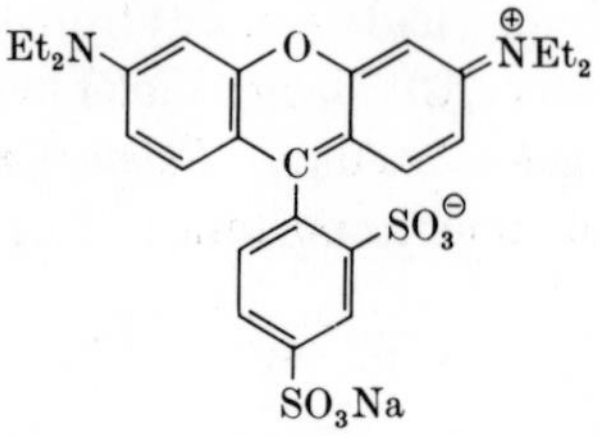

[58]

Xanthene dyes containing salicylic acid or other metallisable structures are manufactured as mordant dyes. An example is *Solochrome Brilliant Red 3B* (ICI) and its equivalents (CI Mordant Red 27; CI 45180); this dye is obtained by condensing 5-hydroxy-trimellitic acid and *m*-diethylaminophenol with sulphuric acid in *o*-dichlorobenzene, and has the structure [59]. It will be seen that

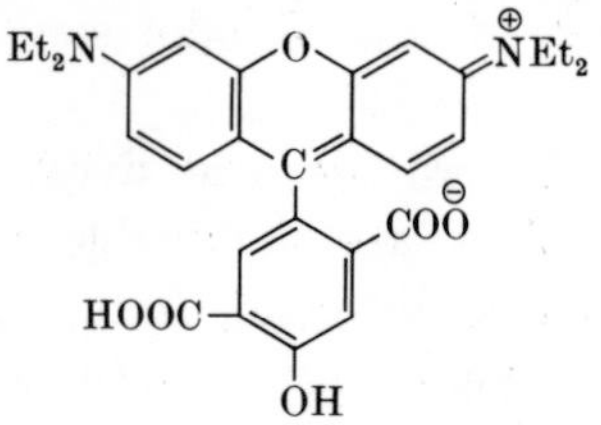

[59]

this is a derivative of Rhodamine B. It can be applied to wool by any of the three mordant dyeing methods, and gives bright bluish pink shades of good fastness to light and wet treatments. Dyes in which the xanthene residue contains both amino and hydroxyl groups are known as Rhodols. Mordant dyes of this class can be obtained by condensing phthalic anhydride first with a suitable *m*-aminophenol derivative, then with β-resorcylic acid and oxidising the product. *Basolan Chrome Brilliant Red 3BM* (BASF) (CI Mordant Red 15; CI 45305) [60] is an example of such a dye; it provides bluish red

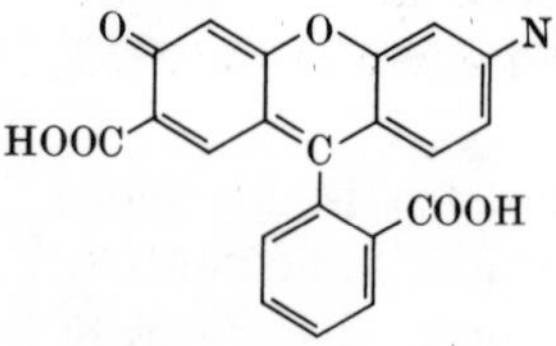

[60] 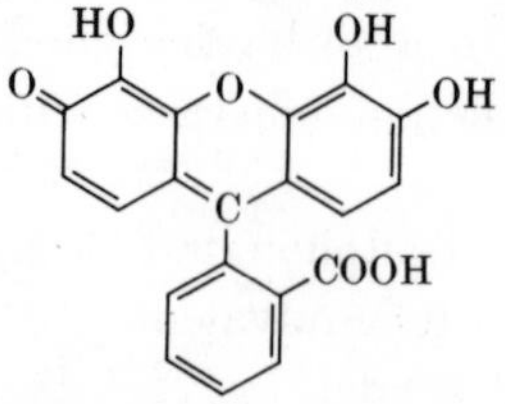   [61] 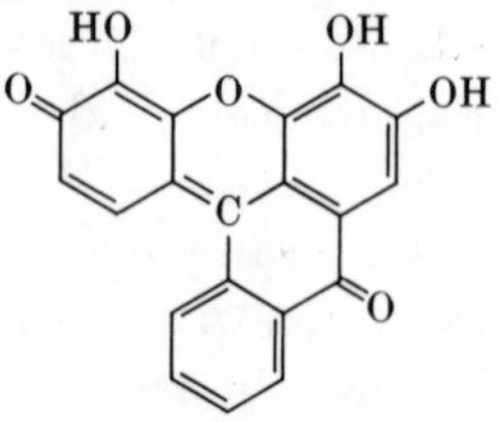   [62]

shades with good general fastness properties, and is applied to wool by the afterchrome or metachrome process. The analogue in which a sulphonic acid group takes the place of the carboxylic acid group is marketed by Durand & Huguenin (now Sandoz) as *Chromorhodine B* (CI Mordant Red 77; CI 45300). It gives bluish pink shades on cotton when applied with a chromium acetate mordant.

One of the earliest mordant dyes of this class was *Gallein* (CI Mordant Violet 25; CI 45445) [61], discovered in 1871 by Baeyer. It is obtained by heating gallic acid or pyrogallol with phthalic anhydride. This dye is now little used, but it is sometimes applied to chrome-tanned leather, giving bluish violet shades. By heating Gallein with concentrated sulphuric acid at 200°C it is converted into *Coerulein* [62], which is not only a xanthene but also an anthraquinone derivative. Its water-soluble bisulphite compound is manufactured by several firms as a mordant dye (CI Mordant Green 22; CI 45510), and gives dull green shades on chrome-mordanted wool or silk. It can also be printed on cotton with a chromium acetate mordant.

8-7 Acridine dyes

The dyes of this class are derivatives of the basic compound acridine [63]. This structure provides the chromophore, and an amino or alkylamino group is usually present in a *para* position with respect to the methane carbon atom:

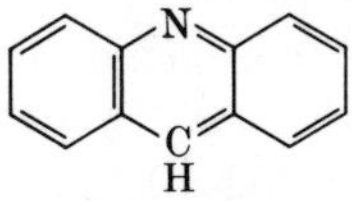

[63]

The dyes are salts of aminoacridine derivatives, consisting of resonance hybrids such as [64] and [65]. Acridine dyes yield mainly

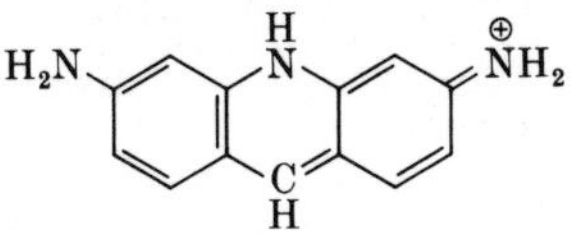

[64] 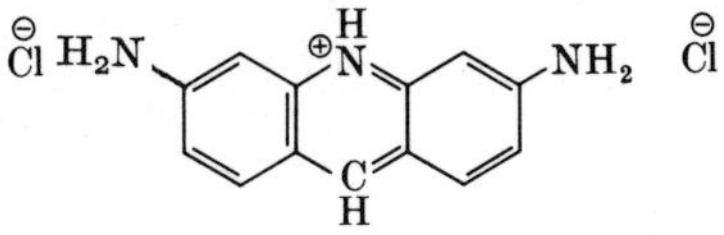   [65]

yellow, orange, red or brown shades, and they are largely used on leather. Textile applications are chiefly in the printing and dyeing of silk and cellulosic fibres; fastness properties do not reach the standard required on wool. Several acridine dyes are in use as antiseptics or medicinals although no longer applied as dyes.

The first acridine dye was *Chrysaniline* (CI Basic Orange 15; CI 46045), which was isolated by Hofmann in 1862 as a by-product from the magenta melt. The corresponding nitrate was introduced by Nicholson under the name *Phosphine* as a yellowish orange basic dye, and in 1884 its structure [66] was established by Fischer and Körner:[9]

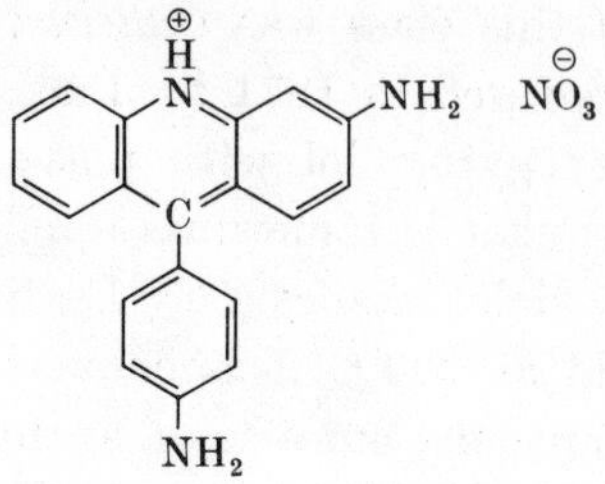

[66]

Phosphine is a triphenylmethane derivative, but most of the acridine dyes now in use are of the diphenylmethane type. An example is *Acridine Orange R* (ICI) (CI Basic Orange 14; CI 46005), with the structure [67]. It is manufactured from 4,4'-bis(dimethyl-

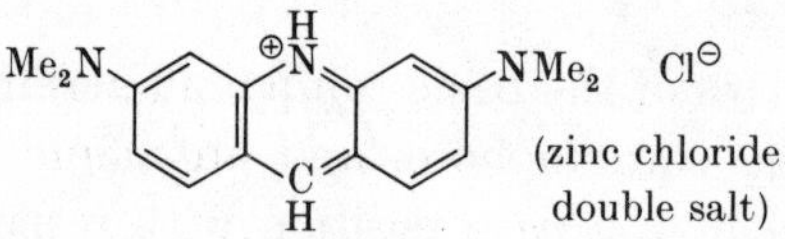

(zinc chloride double salt)

[67]

amino)diphenylmethane by dinitration, reduction to the diamine, cyclisation to the dihydroacridine by heating with an acid, then oxidising and converting into the zinc double chloride. Acridine Orange R is applied by dyeing processes to bast fibres, but not extensively to other textile fibres; it is used in textile printing, however, and also on leather. The shade is a bright yellowish orange.

Several orange dyes (CI Basic Oranges 4–11), the precise constitutions of which are unpublished, are obtained by alkylation of a dye such as [68] with dimethyl sulphate or methyl *p*-toluenesul-

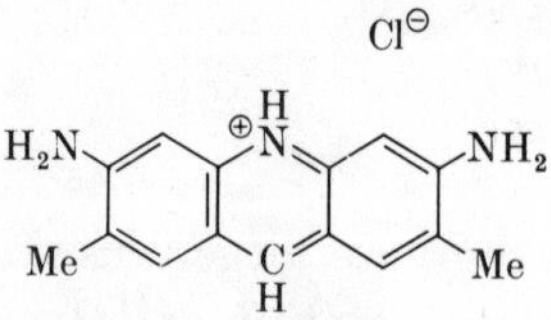

[68]

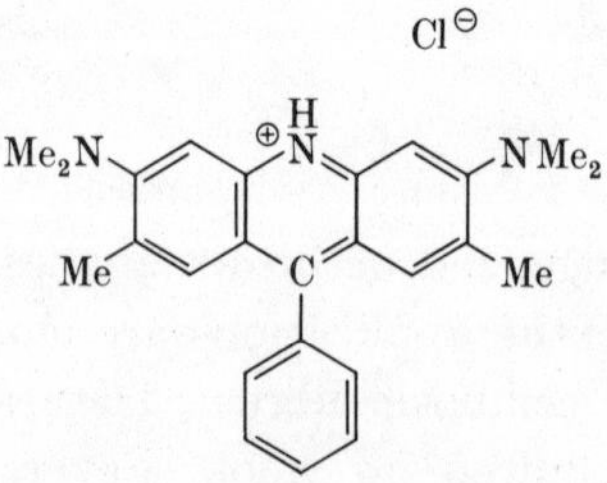

[69]

phonate. These reagents are stated to yield N-alkylacridinium derivatives, but the amino groups may be alkylated by alkyl halides or alcohols with mineral acids. Triphenylmethane derivatives such as CI Basic Orange 18 (CI 46070) [**69**] are obtained by alkylating the corresponding diaminoacridines. All of these dyes are used largely for application to leather.

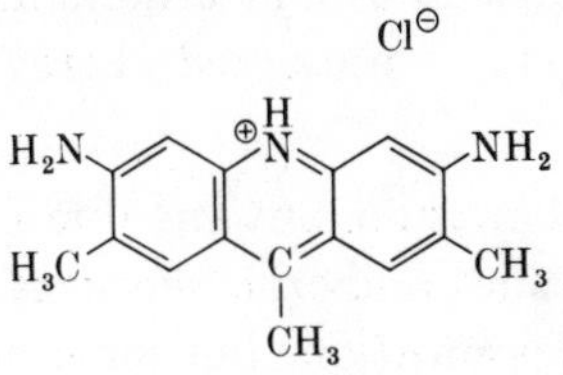

[**70**] 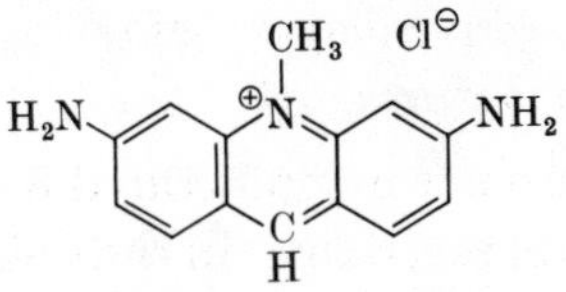   [**71**]

A greenish yellow dye, CI Basic Yellow 9 (CI 46040) [**70**] is obtained by condensing m-tolylenediamine (2 mol.) with acetaldehyde (1 mol.), cyclising and oxidising with ferric chloride.[10] It is applied to bast fibres, cotton and wool, and also to leather.

The well-known antiseptic *Acriflavine* (CI 46000) [**71**], discovered by Ehrlich and Benda, is no longer used as a dye. It is obtained by melting together m-phenylenediamine, oxalic acid, zinc chloride, glycerol and water, then methylating and oxidising the product.[11]

8-8 Azine dyes

Azine dyes are derivatives of the parent compound dibenzopyrazine (or phenazine) [**72**]. The central pyrazine ring is the chromophore,

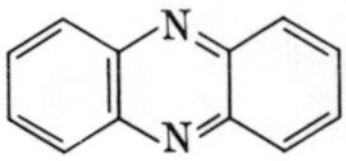

[**72**]

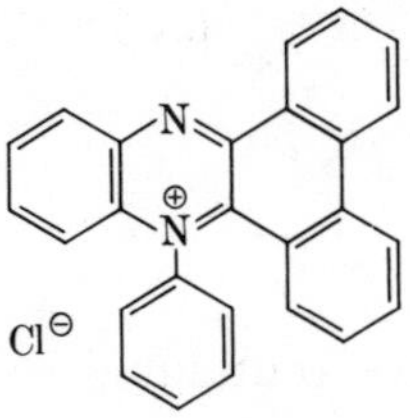

[**73**]

and with the two benzene rings forms the chromogen. There is usually at least one auxochrome standing in a *para* position with respect to one of the nitrogen atoms, but dyes containing no auxochrome are known; an example is the obsolete dye *Flavinduline* (CI 50000) [**73**].

As with other classes discussed in this chapter the azine dyes are resonance-hybrids. The structure of aminophenazine dyes may be represented thus:

In unsymmetrical diamino derivatives another *p*-quinonoid form is possible. Hydroxyphenazines may also exist in *o*- and *p*-quinonoid forms. For convenience azine dyes are represented here as *o*-quinonoid structures.

The dyes are not manufactured from phenazine, but are obtained by condensation reactions. In the Colour Index and other works they are arranged according to a structural classification, but since the more important products all fall into two of the classes the others will not be described here. The azines are basic dyes which may be applied to wool, silk or tannin-mordanted cotton. Some of them are used for colouring oils, fats, lacquers, etc. Many sulphonated azine dyes are acid dyes suitable for application to wool, silk or nylon, and some of them are moderately fast to light, especially in heavy shades.

Mauveine, the first commercial synthetic dye, which was discovered by W. H. Perkin in 1856 (Section 1-3), was an azine dye belonging to the Safranine class. The safranines are diamino*meso*arylphenazines, and Mauveine (which is no longer in commercial use) consisted mainly of a dye with the structure [74]. It was obtained

[74]   [75]

by oxidation of aniline containing *o*- and *p*-toluidines; Perkin prepared a similar dye *Pseudomauveine*, containing no methyl group, from pure aniline. A closely related dye *Safranine T* (CI Basic Red 2; CI 50240) [75] is still widely used. It was first obtained by Perkin as a by-product of the manufacture of Mauveine, and was later produced by oxidation of aniline with lead peroxide or other agents.[12] A more recent process consists in reducing 4-amino 2′,3-dimethylazobenzene to *o*-toluidine and 2-methyl-*p*-phenylenediamine, oxidising with acid dichromate in presence of aniline, and converting into the chloride. Safranine T is used for dyeing tannin-mordanted cotton, bast fibres, wool, silk, polyacrylonitrile fibres, leather and paper; it has also various applications in textile printing. It gives a bright bluish pink shade, but has poor fastness properties. By diazotising one of the amino groups in Safranine T and coupling with β-naphthol *Indoine Blue R* (CI Basic Blue 16; CI 12210) is obtained. This gives an indigo blue on tannin-mordanted cotton, with good fastness to light and washing.

Other basic azine dyes of the Safranine class which are still manufactured under various names are CI Basic Violets 5 and 8 (CI 50215, CI 50210) [76] and [77]. They give bright reddish violet

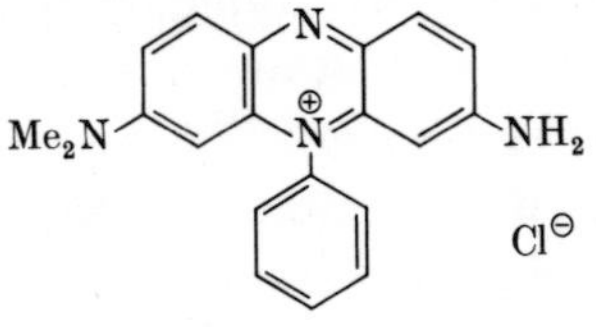

[76]

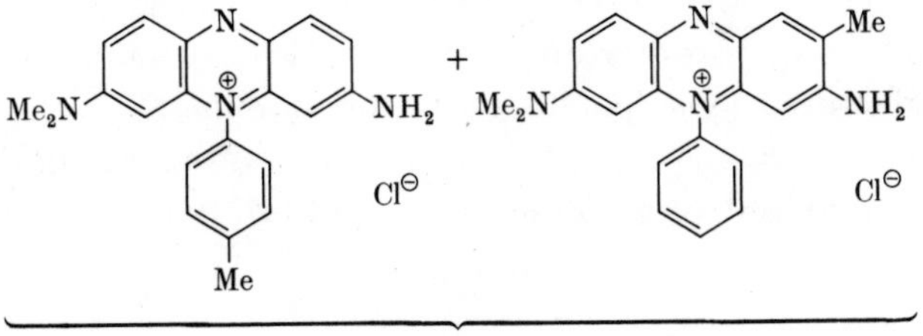

[77]

shades, and are used mainly on leather and paper. A related acid dye is *Lissamine Blue BF* (ICI) and its equivalents (CI Acid Blue 18; CI 50230) [78]. It gives reddish navy blue shades on wool or

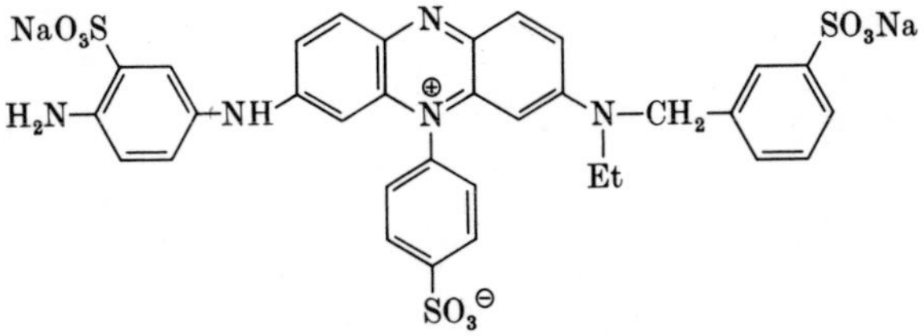

[78]

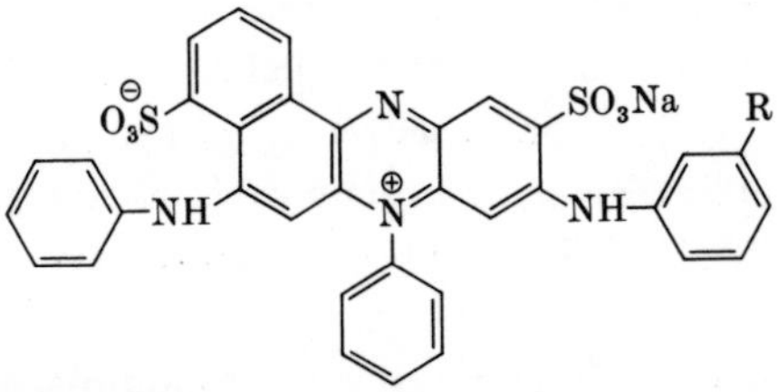

[79]

leather, with fairly good general fastness properties. Blue acid dyes of greater importance are *Coomassie Blue BL* (ICI) (CI Acid Blue 59; CI 50315) [**79**; R = H], *Coomassie Blue GL* (ICI) (CI Acid Blue 102; CI 50320) [**79**; R = OCH₃] and their equivalents. These give reddish blue and blue shades, respectively.

The second important class of azine dyes comprises the Indulines and Nigrosines, which are usually considered together.

Indulines are obtained by heating azo compounds, especially 4-aminoazobenzene, with aniline and aniline hydrochloride. The product is a mixture of azine bases of varying complexity, insoluble in water, but giving violet or blue solutions in ethanol. The conditions used differ widely, higher temperatures and more prolonged heating being adopted when bluer shades are required. Products with a degree of water-solubility are obtained by carrying out the reaction in aqueous or alcoholic medium. By including *p*-phenylenediamine in the reaction mixture more strongly basic products with greater solubility in water are obtained. Readily soluble acid dyes are manufactured by sulphonation of the indulines.

The products of such reactions are mixtures containing aminodianilino-, trianilino and tetra-anilinophenylphenazinium chlorides.

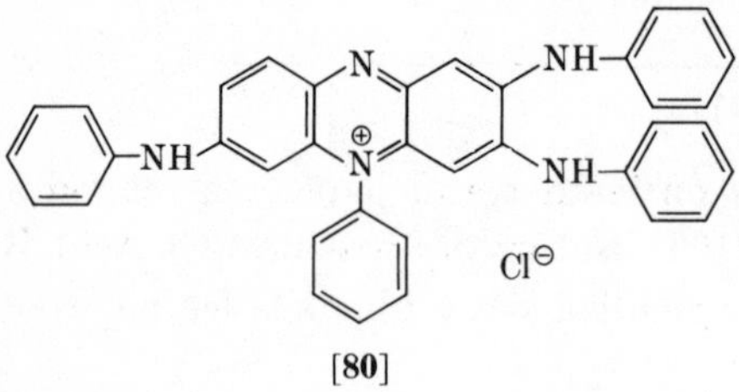

[**80**]

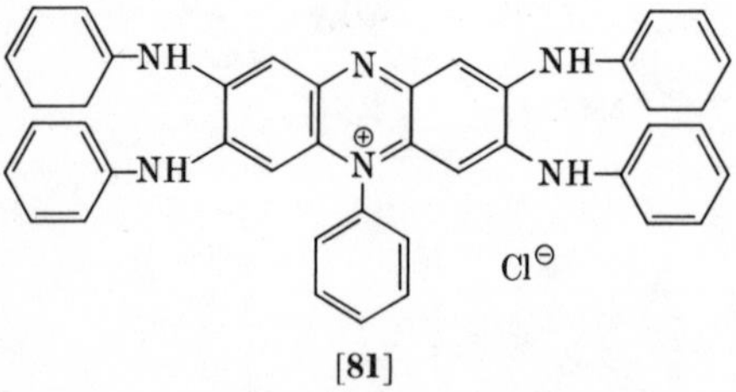

[**81**]

Examples of such compounds are *Induline 3B Base* [**80**] and *Induline 6B Base* (both CI Solvent Blue 7; CI 50400) [**81**]. These dyes are used for colouring fats, printing inks, copying paper, typewriter ribbons and similar applications. Sulphonated derivatives of the spirit-soluble dyes (CI Acid Blue 20; CI 50405) are used to produce navy blue shades on leather.

Nigrosines are obtained by heating nitro compounds such as nitrobenzene or nitrophenols with aniline and aniline hydrochloride in presence of iron or copper or their compounds at 180°–200°C. Here again the products are mixtures of complex azines, but less is known about their structures than in the case of the indulines. They are insoluble in water, but soluble in ethanol, and are used mainly for non-textile coloration, giving black or dark grey shades. The oleates or stearates are used in waxes, varnishes, shoe creams, copying papers, typewriter ribbons, stamping inks, leather finishes and allied applications. Sulphonated derivatives (CI Acid Black 2; CI 50420) are extensively used for dyeing leather, paper and many miscellaneous products. Nigrosines are manufactured more cheaply than indulines, but both types are produced in very large quantities.

An important complex azine dye is *Aniline Black* (CI 50440), first used successfully by Lightfoot in 1863. It is obtained by oxidation of aniline on cotton fibre, and gives fast deep black shades. The conditions used vary considerably, but one of the more important processes uses a dyebath containing aniline oil, aniline hydrochloride, sodium chloride, ammonium chloride, aluminium acetate and a copper or vanadium salt. Cotton yarn padded with this mixture is dried, then 'aged' at 60°–70°C, chromed and finally soaped. A modified process is extensively used in textile printing. Aniline Black is also made in substance for use as a pigment.

The chemistry of the Aniline Black process was studied in great detail by Willstätter, and independently by A. G. Green. It was found that oxidation and condensation reactions occur in six stages until a polyazine derived from eleven aniline residues is formed. Green[13] assigned to this the structure [**82**], and it has been generally accepted. In recent publications, however, R. Lantz[14] has suggested that some aspects of the matter require further investigation.

($X^{\ominus}$ = acid radical, probably chromate in aged and chromed blacks)

[**82**]

In printing applications Aniline Black has now been partly superseded by *Solanile Black* (CFMC) (CI Oxidation Black 3) and equivalent products. These are water-soluble sulphamino derivatives of diphenylamine which enable fast black shades to be obtained without the risk of fibre degradation associated with Aniline Black, and also have advantages in better print paste stability.[15] The black pigments produced on the fibre are believed to be closely related to Aniline Black.[14]

8-9 Oxazine dyes

Dyes of this class are characterised by the oxazine chromophore:

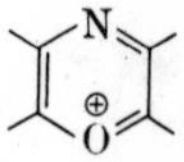

and are therefore related to the azines, just described, and still more closely to the thiazines (Section 8-10). The dyes contain three or more condensed rings, and auxochromes are usually present in benzene rings in positions *para* to the nitrogen atom. As with the related dyes the structures are resonance hybrids of *o-* and *p*-quinonoid systems, but they are mostly represented here as the former.

The oxazines give mainly violet or blue shades. The earlier dyes were basic dyes applied to tannin-mordanted cotton, but within a few years metallisable structures were introduced; the resulting mordant dyes have not only brilliant shades but also good fastness to light and moderate fastness to washing, and they have now surpassed the basic dyes in importance. More recently manufacturers have produced dioxazine dyes with direct dyeing properties for cellulosic fibres. Other dioxazines containing no solubilising group are now applied as pigments.

The first oxazine dye was discovered by Meldola in 1879. By condensing *p*-nitrosodimethylaniline hydrochloride with β-naphthol in glacial acetic acid he obtained *Meldola's Blue* (CI Basic Blue 6;

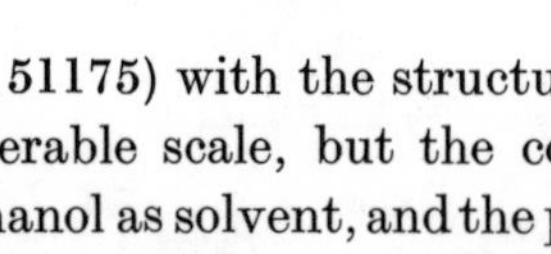

$Cl^{\ominus}$

[83]

CI 51175) with the structure [83]. It is still manufactured on a considerable scale, but the condensation is now usually performed in ethanol as solvent, and the product is isolated as a zinc double chloride. The dye is chiefly applied to leather. Other basic dyes of this series still in use are *Basic Pure Blue 3G* (FH) (CI Basic Blue 3; CI 51005) [84; R = OEt] and *Acronol Sky Blue 3G* (ICI) (CI Basic Blue 4; CI 51004) [84; R = OMe]. These dyes give bright greenish blue shades, and are used mainly on bast fibres and leather.

The first oxazine mordant dye was *Gallocyanine* (CI Mordant Blue 10; CI 51030) discovered by Koechlin in 1881. It is obtained by condensation of *p*-nitrosodimethylaniline hydrochloride with

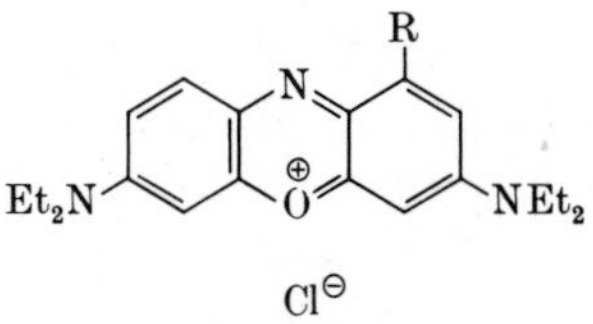

[84]

allic acid in methanol and conversion into the bisulphite compound. The structures of this and other oxazine mordant dyes [*Celestine Blue B* (S), CI Mordant Blue 14, CI 51050; *Delphine Blue*, CI Mordant Blue 56, CI 51120; *Chromazol Blue 5G* (ICI), CI Mordant Blue 59, CI 51125] are shown below:

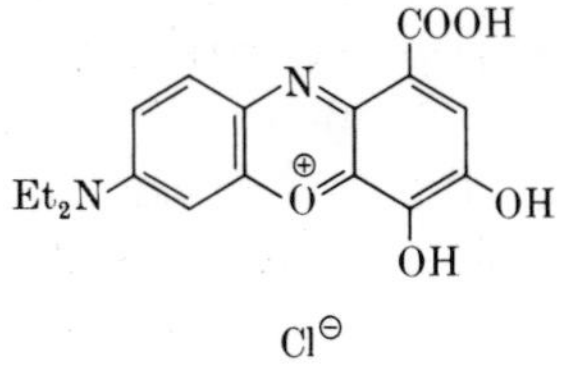

Gallocyanine

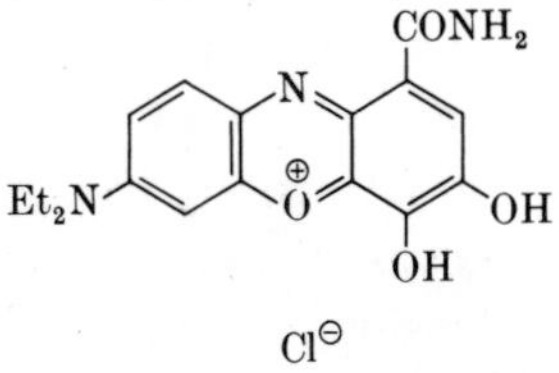

Celestine Blue B (S)

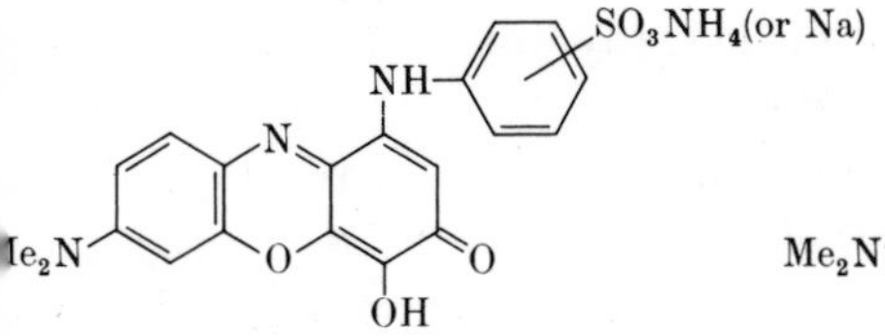

Delphine Blue

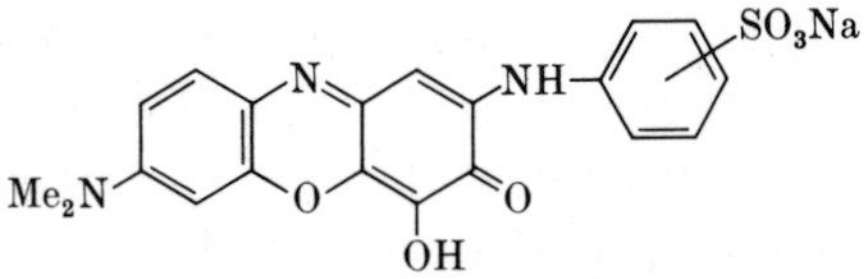

Chromazol Blue 5G (ICI)

These dyes are applied to wool, cotton or silk with a chromium mordant. They give reddish to greenish blue shades with moderately good fastness to light and washing.

Several dioxazines were introduced by IG as direct dyes from 1928 onwards. One of the simplest of them was *Sirius Light Blue FF2GL* (CI Direct Blue 106; CI 51300) [85], obtained by condensing

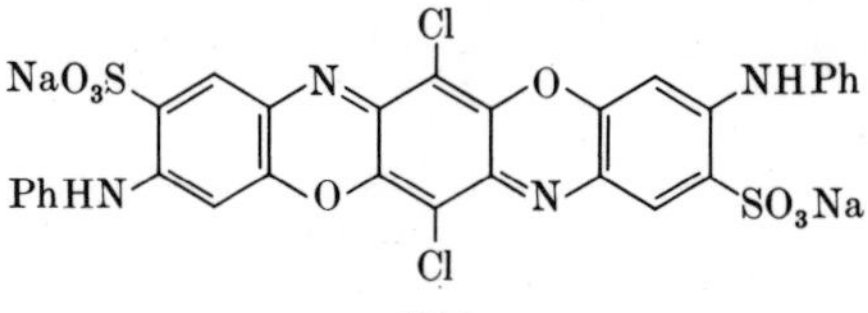

[85]

-aminodiphenylamine-2-sulphonic acid (2 mol.) with chloranil 1 mol.) in presence of magnesium oxide, cyclising with oleum and onverting into the disodium salt. More complex dyes are manufactured by similar processes using as starting materials chloranil with either 3-aminocarbazole or 1-aminopyrene; these are respectively CI Direct Blues 107 and 109 (CI 51315, 51310). A triphendioxazine pigment is described in Chapter 16.

8-10 Thiazine dyes

These dyes are analogues of the oxazines, an atom of sulphur replacing oxygen in the heterocyclic ring. Only five of them are known to be still manufactured (under various names). All but one are blue or green basic or solvent dyes; the exception is a vat dye.

The most important thiazine dye is *Methylene Blue* (CI Basic Blue 9, CI Solvent Blue 8; CI 52015), discovered by Caro in 1876 and having the structure shown below. It was originally obtained by ferric chloride oxidation of N,N-dimethyl-p-phenylenediamine in presence of hydrogen sulphide, but the commercial process developed later by Bernthsen consists in oxidation of the same intermediate by means of acid dichromate in presence of sodium thiosulphate, condensing the resulting 4-(dimethylamino)aniline-2-thiosulphonic acid with dimethylaniline to form an indamine, and oxidising by dichromate and copper sulphate to yield Methylene Blue.[16] The chloride is used medicinally, but the zinc chloride double salt is normally used for dyeing.

Other thiazine dyes are obtained by similar reactions, and the structures of typical examples are shown below; *Methylene Green* (CI Basic Green 5; CI 52020), however, is derived from Methylene Blue by nitration:

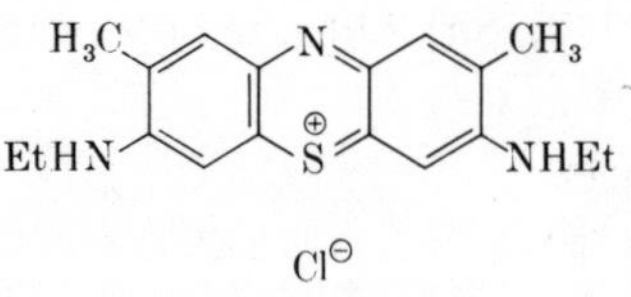

Me₂N ... N ... S⊕ ... N Me₂
Cl⊖
Methylene Blue

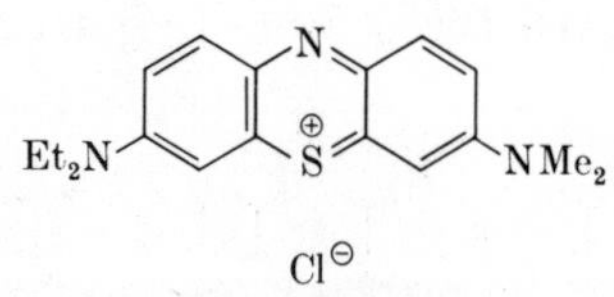

Me₂N ... N ... S⊕ ... NMe₂ ... NO₂
Cl⊖
Methylene Green

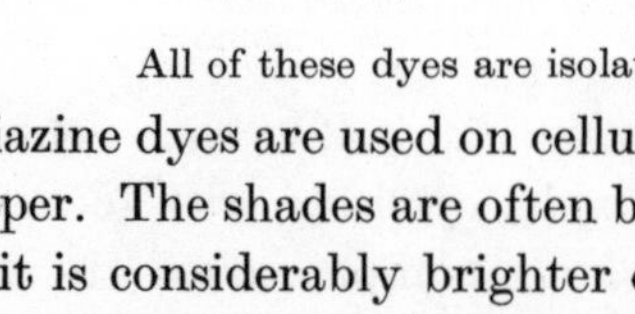

H₃C ... N ... CH₃
EtHN ... S⊕ ... NHEt
Cl⊖
CI Basic Blue 24
(CI 52030)

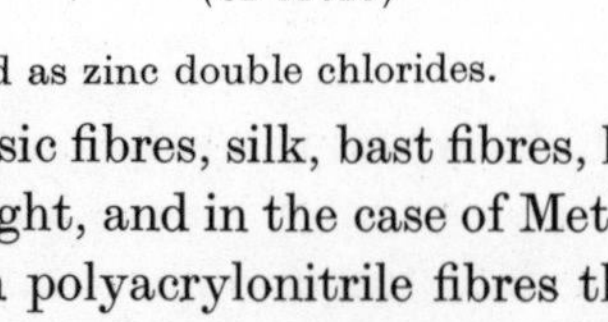

Et₂N ... N ... S⊕ ... NMe₂
Cl⊖
CI Basic Blue 25
(CI 52025)

All of these dyes are isolated as zinc double chlorides.

Thiazine dyes are used on cellulosic fibres, silk, bast fibres, leather and paper. The shades are often bright, and in the case of Methylene Green it is considerably brighter on polyacrylonitrile fibres than on tannin-mordanted cotton. Fastness to light is usually only fair.

The thiazine vat dye mentioned above is *Indanthren Printing Blue 3R* (Cassella) (CI Vat Violet 19; CI 52100), with the structure shown. It gives bluish violet shades with fairly good fastness to light and washing.

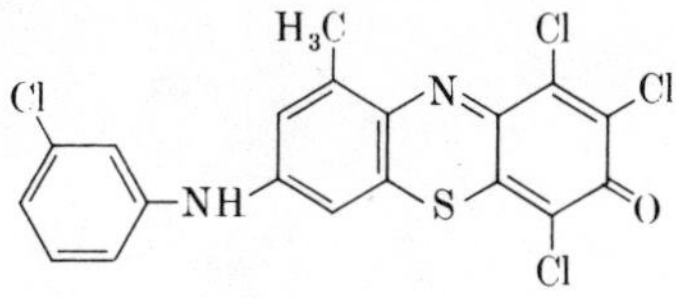

Indanthrene Printing Blue
3R (Cassella)

8-11   Newer cationic dyes for polyacrylonitrile fibres

The chemistry of polyacrylonitrile fibres has been briefly discussed in Section 6-7. The first of these fibres to be manufactured were dyed with difficulty, but various co-polymers containing sulphonic or carboxylic groups were introduced later, and these readily absorb cationic dyes. It has become customary to refer to fibres containing not more than 15% of a co-polymer as '100% polyacrylonitrile' and to fibres containing more than 15% of co-polymer as 'modacrylic' fibres. In general the older cationic dyes described in the preceding sections of this chapter have inadequate fastness properties for present-day requirements (although their light fastness is usually better on polyacrylonitrile than on natural fibres); since they are fairly cheap, however, dyes such as Malachite Green, Magenta, Bismarck Brown and Meldola's Blue have been used to some extent.

In the 1930s cationic dyes were developed in Germany for application to acetate fibre by printing processes, and were marketed as the *Astrazon* range (IG).[17] Blue dyes of the triphenylmethane and oxazine classes were included, and many members of the range were polymethine dyes (see Section 12-3). The two general methods for manufacture of polymethine dyes are illustrated on page 132. Examples (2) and (3) are obtained by the same method, differing only in the type of base used. An outline of the chemistry of Fischer's Base and Aldehyde is given in reference 17.

On acetate fibre the IG Astrazon dyes had light fastness mainly in the range of grades 3 to 6 (SDC 1–8 scale), but on cotton the ratings had a maximum of 3. With the advent of polyacrylonitrile fibres from 1948 onwards the known cationic dyes were re-examined for these fibres and many new ones were developed. Ranges for the purpose were marketed by various manufacturers under names such as *Astrazon* (FBy), *Basacryl* (BASF), *Calcozine* (ACY), *Deorlene Fast*

(1)

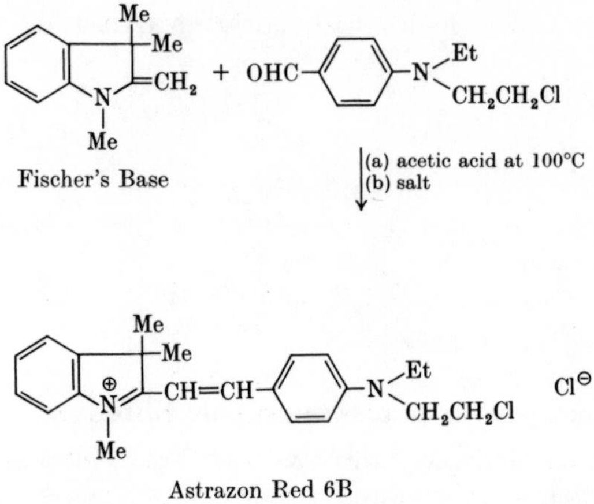

Fischer's Base

OHC—⟨ ⟩—N⟨Et, CH₂CH₂Cl⟩

(a) acetic acid at 100°C
(b) salt

Astrazon Red 6B

(2)

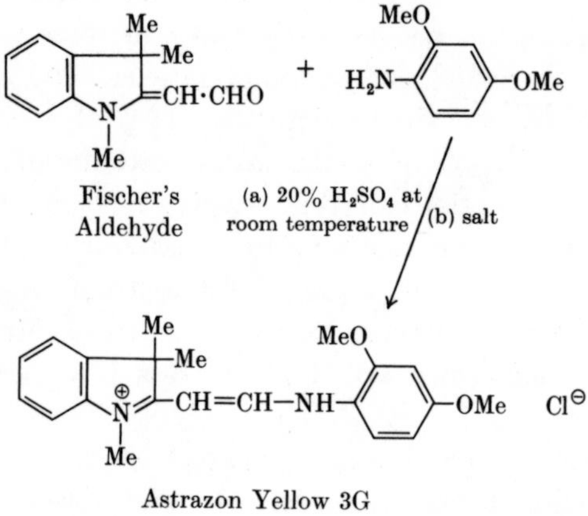

Fischer's
Aldehyde

H₂N—⟨ ⟩—OMe (MeO)

(a) 20% H₂SO₄ at room temperature
(b) salt

Astrazon Yellow 3G

(3)

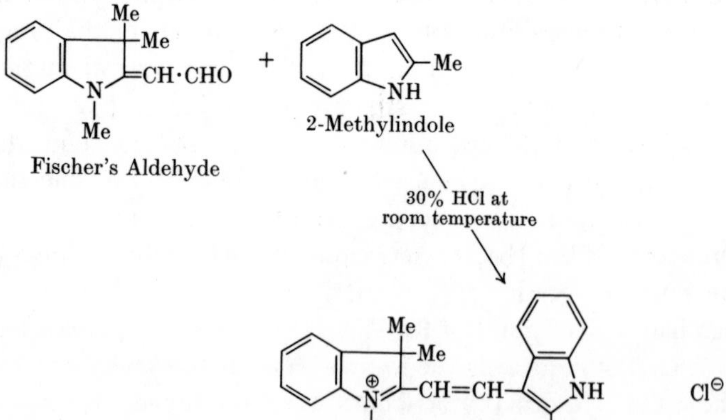

Fischer's Aldehyde

2-Methylindole

30% HCl at room temperature

Astrazon Orange G

(CIBA), *Lyrcamine* (Fran), *Maxilon* (Gy), *Novacryl* (YDC), *Panacryl* (LBH), *Sevron* (DuP), *Sandocryl* (S) and *Synacril* (ICI). Very few constitutions have been published, but it is probable that the ranges include equivalents of some of the pre-war German dyes and also representatives of the azo and anthraquinone classes. Constitutions of some of the Astrazon dyes (mainly older members of the range) are shown in Table 8-1. Equivalents to most of these are made by several other firms. Whereas the IG dyes mainly gave light-fastness on polyacrylonitrile of grade 4 or 4–5, more recent cationic dyes often attain grade 6 or 6–7, and one (*Astrazon Blue GL*, FBy) is stated by the makers to give grade 7–8.[18] There is some evidence that on polyacrylonitrile fibre light fastness is affected by basicity, and tends to increase as the dye–fibre bond becomes more weakly polar.[19]

The newer cationic dyes are described in an extensive patent literature, and only a few specifications can be quoted here. Dyes containing at least one quaternary nitrogen atom that is not a member of an aromatic ring have been applied to polyacrylonitrile fibre; red shades, for example, are obtained from the dye with structure [86].[20] Azo dyes containing at least one non-aromatically

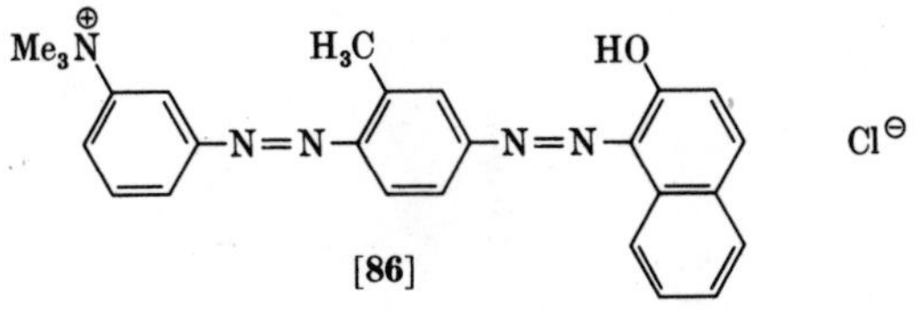

[86]

bound primary, secondary or tertiary amino group or quaternary ammonium group, such as [87][21] giving red shades, or [88][22] giving

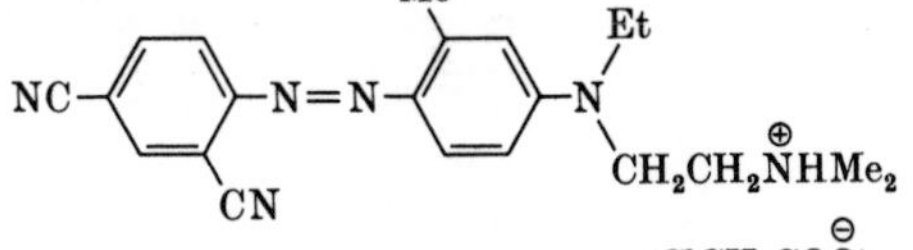

[87]

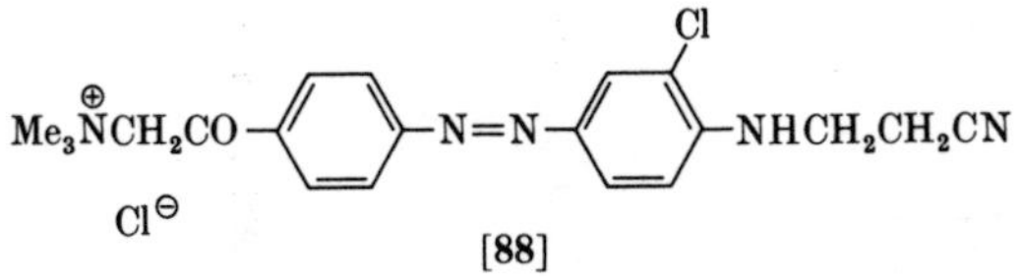

[88]

orange shades, have been used similarly. The use of arylaminoanthraquinones containing externally bound quaternary ammonium groups has also been described;[23] thus the dye [89] gives reddish blue shades on polyacrylonitrile fibre.

Table 8-1 Some dyes of the Astrazon range (FBy)

Name of dye	CI Generic Name	CI Constitution No.	Structure
Astrazon Blue B	CI Basic Blue 5	CI 42140	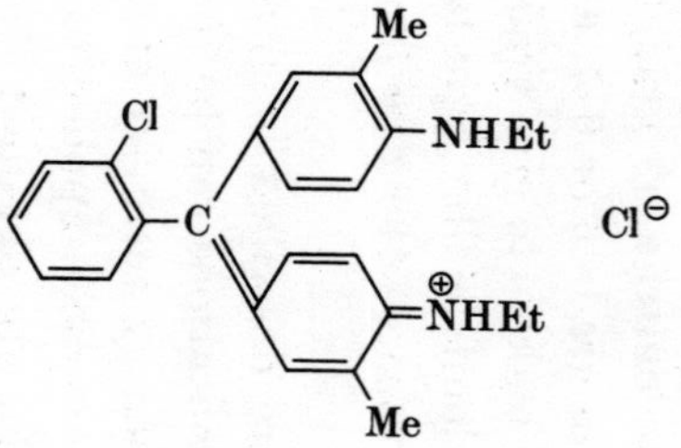 Me, NHEt, ⊕NHEt, Me, Cl, C, Cl⊖
Astrazon Blue BG	CI Basic Blue 3	CI 51005	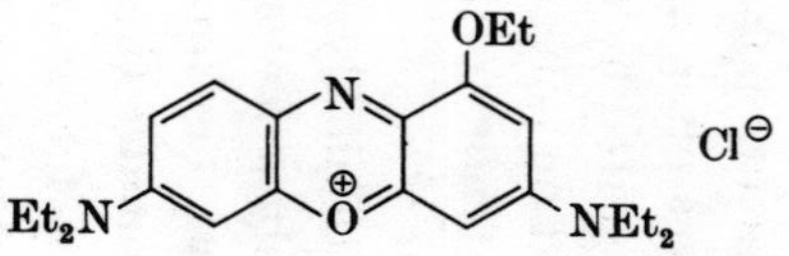 OEt, NEt$_2$, N, ⊕O, Et$_2$N, Cl⊖
Astrazon Blue G	CI Basic Blue 1	CI 42025	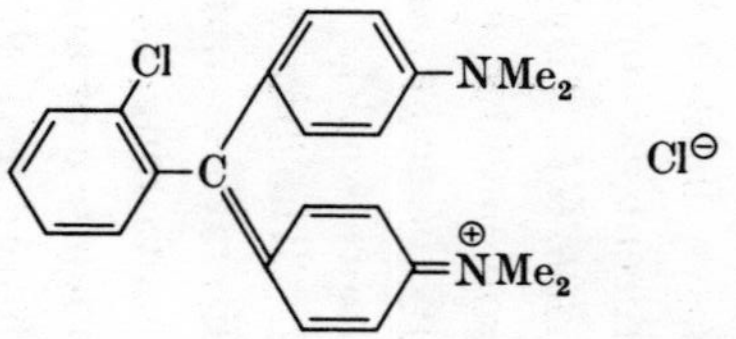 NMe$_2$, ⊕NMe$_2$, Cl, C, Cl⊖

Dye name	CI name	CI number
Astrazon Orange G	CI Basic Orange 21	CI 48035 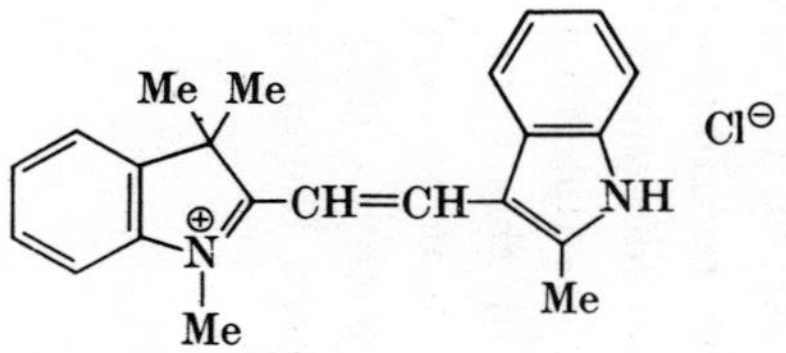
Astrazon Pink FG	CI Basic Red 13	CI 48015 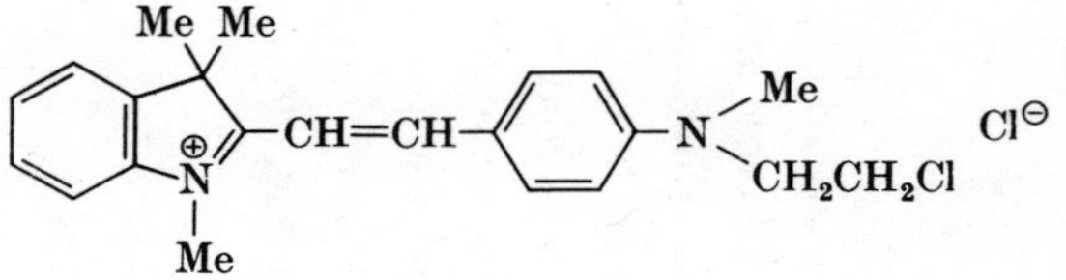
Astrazon Red 6B	CI Basic Violet 7	CI 48020 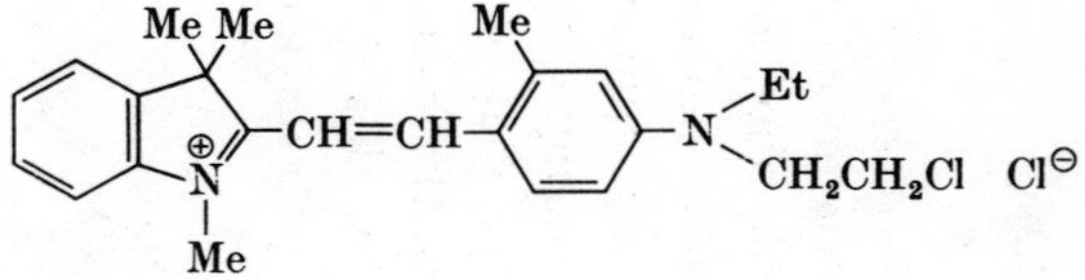
Astrazon Red GTL	CI Basic Red 18	CI 11085 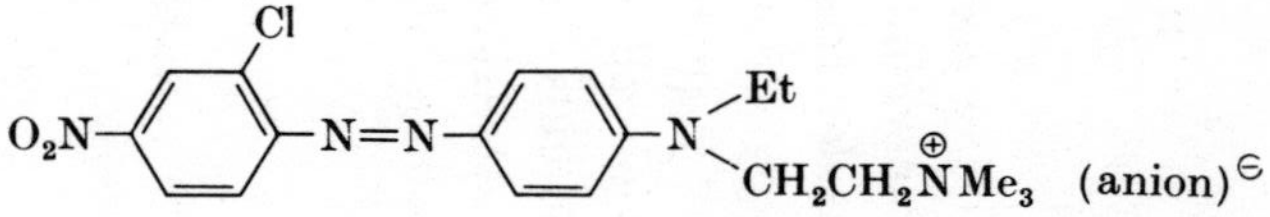
Astrazon Yellow 3G	CI Basic Yellow 11	CI 48055 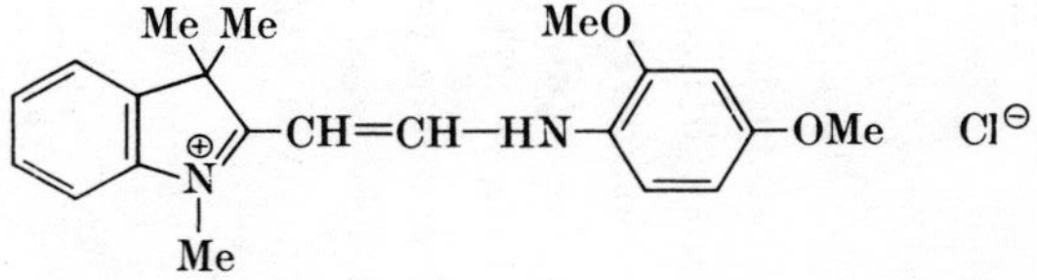

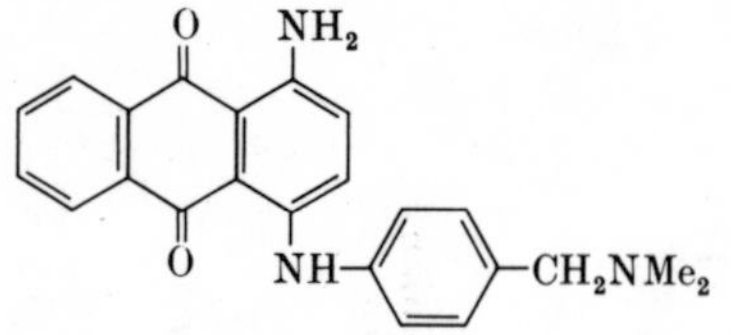

[89]

Azo dyes containing a cyclammonium group are of interest for application to polyacrylonitrile fibre, and many azo derivatives of thiazole, benzothiazole, triazole, indazole, thiadiazole, benzimidazole, benzoxazole, pyridine and quinoline have been described; they are solubilised by quaternising with an agent such as dimethyl sulphate.[24] The wine-red dye [90] is an example of this type. Hydrazinium compounds form the basis of another cationic system that has received attention in this field, and dyes such as [91], which gives a red shade on polyacrylonitrile, have been found of value.[25]

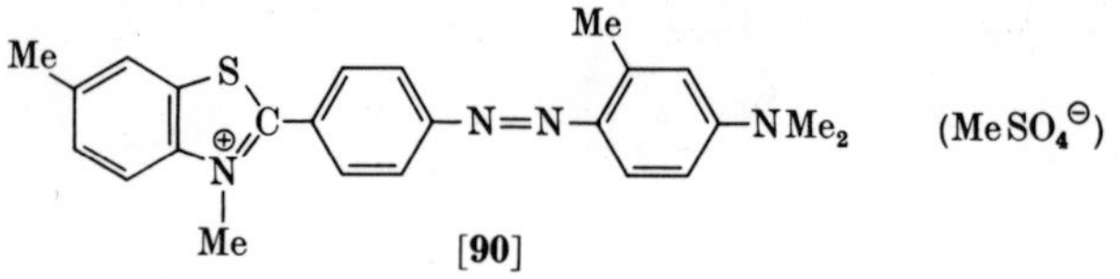

[90]

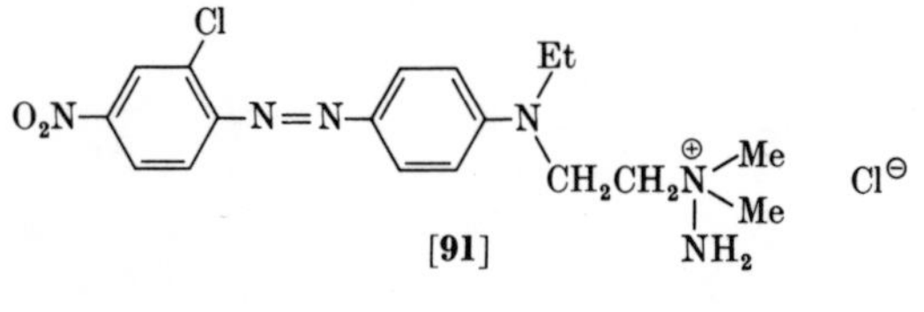

[91]

These and many other patent specifications show that all the common chromophores have been used. In general dyes of the anthraquinone and azo classes have good fastness properties, and those of the triphenylmethane, oxazine and methine classes are characterised by brightness of shade. Many azamethine dyes have been described. Dyes containing primary, secondary or tertiary amino groups are solubilised by quaternisation with an agent such as dimethyl sulphate. Alternatively dyes containing reactive halogen or sulphate groups may be quaternised by reaction with a tertiary base such as trimethylamine, pyridine or tetramethyl-thiourea.

In polymethine dyes the methine chain normally contains not more than three —CH= units, probably because increase in the length of this chain is associated with loss of fastness to light. Whereas in the older cationic dyes the positive charge is normally located within the chromophoric system in more recently developed dyes it is often isolated from the system by a saturated hydrocarbon link; this may have a bearing on light fastness, in respect of which a considerable improvement has been effected.

The affinity of cationic dyes for polyacrylonitrile fibre is so great that special precautions are needed to obtain level dyeing. It is believed that the dyeing process takes place in three overlapping stages:

(1) Absorption of dye cations on the surface of the fibre;
(2) Diffusion; and
(3) Salt formation between dye cation and anionic groups in the fibre.

Under normal conditions the final stage is almost irreversible, and this accounts for the poor levelling and high fastness properties. The first and third stages are rapid, and the slower second is the rate-determining stage. Dyeing is regulated by (a) careful control of temperature, (b) reduction of the pH of the dyebath in order to restrict the degree of dissociation of ionising groups in both dye and fibre, (c) addition of an electrolyte such as Glauber's salt to reduce dissociation and promote migration, and (d) addition of an anionic or cationic retarding agent. The dyeing conditions required vary with the dyes used and the depth of shade required, but in many cases the temperature is raised slowly from 80°C to the boil at pH 4–5, the usage of acid being greater when pale shades are desired. The principles governing the use of retarding agents and other details of the dyeing process are discussed in a recent paper by Kellett.[26]

9 Anthraquinone dyes

This chapter is concerned with anthraquinone dyes other than those of the vat and solvent classes discussed in Chapters 10 and 17, respectively. The dyes to be described here belong to the Acid, Mordant and Disperse application classes, and are dealt with under these headings.

In a chronological treatment the Mordant dyes would come first, since the important natural mordant dye *alizarin* (Section 9-2) is an anthraquinone derivative known since remote times. In 1871 Graebe and Liebermann prepared a sulphonated derivative of alizarin (described in Section 9-2), and this was the first water-soluble mordant dye. It was not until 1894 that the first anthraquinone acid dye, Alizarine Cyanine Green G (Section 9-1-1) was prepared by Schmidt. Since then many dyes of that type have been manufactured, and they now outnumber the anthraquinone mordant dyes in use. Many commercial dyes can be applied to the fibre either with or without a mordant and thus fall into both mordant and acid classes. Some are unaffected by the presence of chromium salts in the dyebath, and these are sometimes applied together with mordant dyes. The classification system of the Colour Index is followed here, and this treats dyes applied by both acid and afterchrome methods as acid dyes.

9-1 Acid dyes

The dyes of this class may be divided into three main types, and some important examples of each of them are described below. The hues fall within the range red to black, but are mainly violet, blue or green. In general dyeings on wool have good fastness to light, and their fastness to washing varies from poor to fairly good.

9-1-1 Sulphonated Aminoanthraquinone Derivatives

One of the earliest dyes of this type was *Alizarine Pure Blue B* (CI Acid Blue 78; CI 62105), introduced by Farbenfabriken Bayer in 1899. It is obtained by condensing 1-amino-2,4-dibromoanthraquinone with *p*-toluidine, then sulphonating the product, and has the structure [92]. This dye is now made by many firms and is widely used. A somewhat similar dye having the structure [93] was produced by Agfa in 1913 and later sold by Bayer under the name *Alizarine Saphirol A* (CI Acid Blue 25; CI 62055). It is

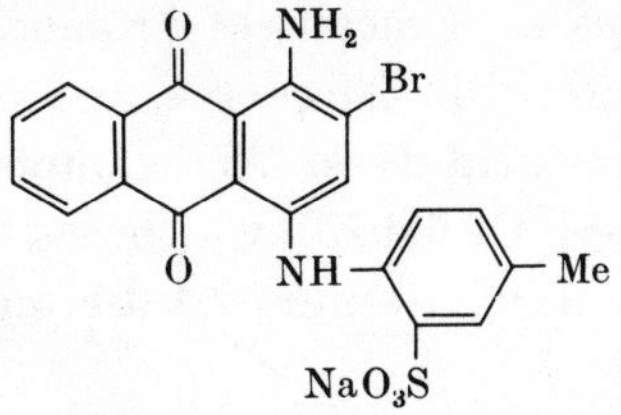

[92] 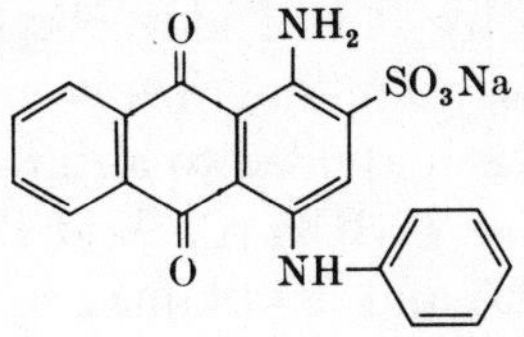   [93]

manufactured either by condensing 1-amino-2,4-dibromoanthraquinone with aniline, then treating the product with sodium sulphite in phenol under pressure, or by condensing sodium 1-amino-4-bromoanthraquinone-2-sulphonate ('Bromamine acid') with aniline in presence of a copper salt. In 1924 this dye was found to be suitable for dyeing acetate fibre, but it is now little used for that fibre except by printing methods. It is still in general use for the dyeing of wool, silk and nylon in bright shades with good fastness properties. Another dye discovered by Agfa at about the same date was marketed by Farbwerke Hoechst under the name *Alizarine Light Blue AGG* (now known as *Anthralan Blue G*) (CI Acid Blue 40; CI 62125); it is similar in structure to Alizarine Saphirol A except in that the anilide residue bears an acetylamino group in the 4' position. This dye gives greenish blue shades, and is widely used for woollen dress goods, upholstery, carpets, etc. A related dye containing an additional sulphonic acid group was produced by Sandoz in 1928 by condensing 1-amino-4-bromo-2,5- (or 2,8-) anthraquinonedisulphonic acid with *p*-aminoacetanilide. This was marketed under the name *Alizarine Light Blue 4GL* (S) (CI Acid Blue 23; CI 61125). On wool or nylon it gives a greenish blue shade with good fastness to light and rather better fastness to washing than the corresponding monosulphonic acid. A dye with even better washing fastness was

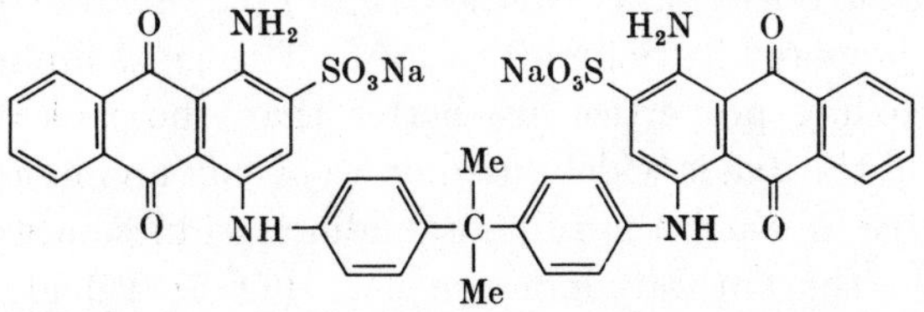

[94]

obtained later by IG by condensing 1-amino-4-bromoanthraquinone-2-sulphonic acid ('Bromamine acid') (2 mol.) with 4,4'-diaminodimethyldiphenylmethane (1 mol.). The product, with the structure [94] was sold as *Supranol Blue GG* (IG) (CI Acid Blue 127; CI 61135);[1] its good wet-fastness properties may be attributed to its large molecular size. This dye is now made by numerous firms and sold under various names.

The use by ICI of long alkyl chains as a means of promoting good fastness to milling has been mentioned in Chapter 4, and this device has been applied to anthraquinone acid dyes. An example is *Carbolan Blue B* (ICI) (CI Acid Blue 138; CI 62075), which has the structure [95] and is obtained by condensing 1-amino-2,4-dibromo-

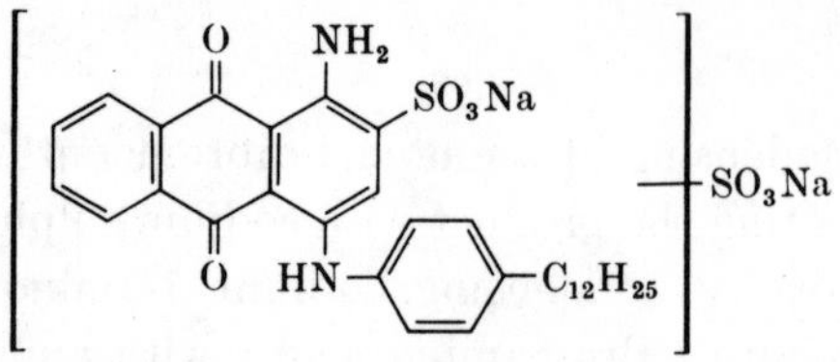

[95]

anthraquinone with *p*-dodecylaniline, treating with sodium sulphite at 170–175°C, sulphonating and converting into the sodium salt. Instead of the dodecyl residue two n-butyl residues may be used with similar effect, as in *Carbolan Green G* (ICI) (CI Acid Green 27; CI 61580). This dye, with the structure [96], is obtained by reaction of

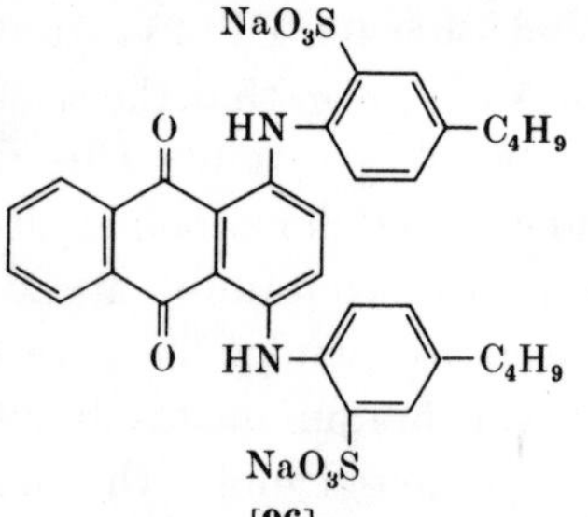

[96] 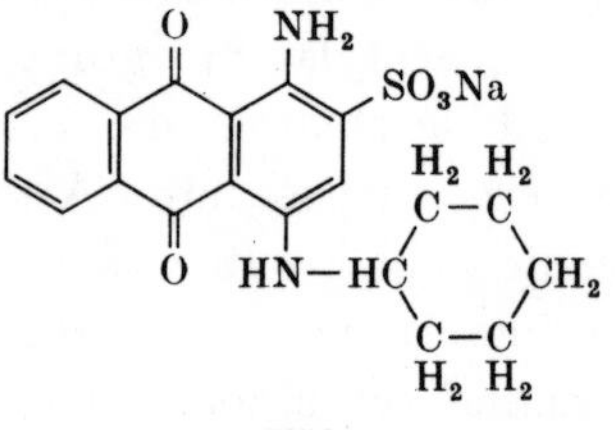   [97]

leucoquinizarin with *p*-butylaniline (2 mol.), sulphonation of the product and conversion into the sodium salt.[2]

The dye corresponding to [96] in which methyl groups replace the n-butyl groups is *Alizarine Cyanine Green G* (FBy) (CI Acid Green 25; CI 61570), first prepared by Schmidt in 1894. This lacks milling fastness, but its levelling properties are better than those of the dibutyl analogue, and the dye is widely used on wool, silk and nylon. The corresponding dye in which the sulphotoluidino residues occupy positions 1 and 5 in the anthraquinone nucleus (CI 61710) gives violet shades, and when these groups are in positions 1 and 8 (CI 61800) the shade is even redder; mixtures of the 1,5 and 1,8 derivatives are sometimes used for intermediate shades (CI Acid Violet 34 includes these isomeric dyes).

An example of an anthraquinone acid dye bearing amino and cyclohexylamino substituents is *Alizarine Brilliant Sky Blue R* (FBy) (CI Acid Blue 62; CI 62045), with the structure [97]. It is used for dyeing knitting yarns, especially in pale shades for baby clothes.

The sulphonated di(aminoanthraquinonyl)amine with the structure [98] (CI Acid Black 48; CI 65005), obtained by condensing

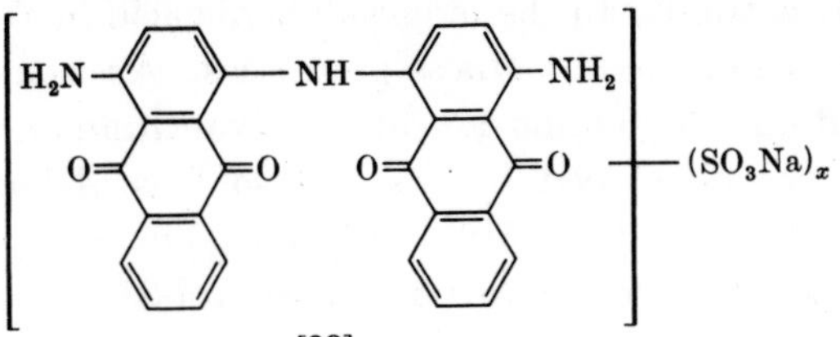

[98]

1,4-diaminoanthraquinone with 1-amino-4-bromoanthraquinone in presence of copper and sodium acetate, sulphonating the product and converting into the sodium salt, illustrates the effect of increase in molecular size on hue and fastness properties. The dye, introduced by Bayer in 1922 under the name *Alizarine Light Grey BBL*, has excellent fastness to light and good fastness to milling and other wet treatments. It is used for bluish grey shades on wool or nylon.

9-1-2 Sulphonated aminohydroxyanthraquinone derivatives

The few important dyes of this type were mostly discovered by Schmidt during the last decade of the nineteenth century. One of these was CI Acid Violet 43 (CI 60730), now made by many firms and sold under a variety of names. The dye is obtained by condensing quinizarin (or leucoquinizarin or 1-bromo-4-hydroxyanthraquinone) with *p*-toluidine and sulphonating the product; it has the structure [99]. This product has good levelling properties and gives bright bluish violet shades on wool, silk or nylon. Another dye discovered by Schmidt is *Alizarine Saphirol SE* (FBy) (CI Acid Blue 43; CI 63000), with the structure [100]. It may be obtained in various

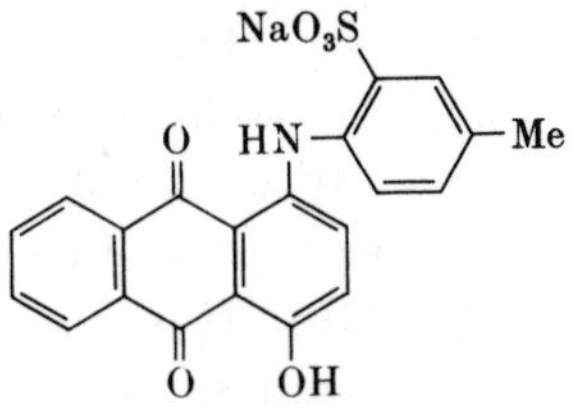

[99]

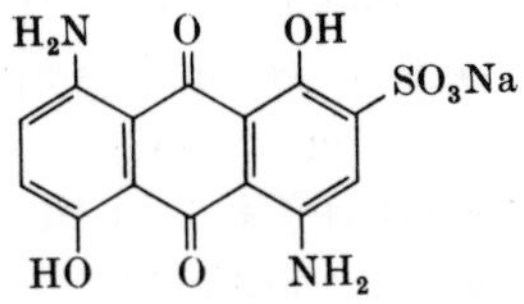

[100]

ways, for example by dinitrating anthrarufin (1,5-dihydroxyanthraquinone) in positions 4 and 8, disulphonating in positions 2 and 6, reducing with sodium sulphide removing one sulphonic group and forming the leuco diamino compound) and oxidising to the desired product. This dye has good fastness to light, but its fastness to wet treatments is only fair. It is still quite widely used on wool and nylon. The corresponding disulphonic acid 4,8-diamino-1,5-dihydroxyanthraquinone-2,6-disulphonic acid), originally called *Alizarine Saphirol B*, (CI Acid Blue 45; CI 63010) is now sold under many commercial names. It is similar to the monosulphonic acid in shade and marginally superior in general fastness properties. An isomeric dye with the constitution 4,5-diamino-1,8-dihydroxyanthraquinone-2,7-disulphonic acid was developed by IG and sold as *Alizarine Saphirol WS* (CI Acid Blue 69; CI 63610). It is a levelling dye with general properties similar to those of Alizarine Saphirol SE.

9-1-3 Sulphonated heterocyclic anthraquinone derivatives

One of the more important dyes of this type is *Alizarine Rubinol R* (FBy) (CI Acid Red 80; CI 68215). It has the structure [101] and is

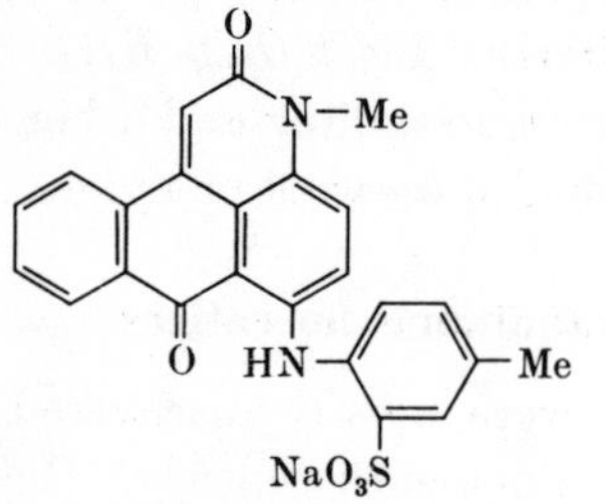

[101]

obtained from 4-bromo-1-methylaminoanthraquinone by acetylation and treating the *N*-acetyl derivative with caustic soda solution at 120°C under pressure to convert it into 4-bromoanthrapyridone, condensing this with *p*-toluidine and sulphonating the resulting 4-*p*-toluidino derivative. This dye, which is manufactured by various firms under their own brand names, gives bright bluish red shades on wool, silk or nylon. It has good levelling properties, good fastness to light and fairly good fastness to washing. On nylon the light-fastness is somewhat lower than on wool, but the hydrophobic properties of the fibre result in improved fastness to washing.

A dye with a heterocyclic structure of another type is *Alizarine Fast Brown G* (CIBA) (CI Acid Brown 27; CI 66710). It is obtained by condensing 1-amino-4-bromo-2-methylanthraquinone with β-naphthylamine, benzoylating the amino group and heating the product with concentrated sulphuric acid or oleum; in the last stage ring closure to the carbazole derivative and sulphonation take place together, and a dye with the structure [102] is obtained. It has

[102]

excellent fastness to light and also good fastness to washing and milling. Several firms have abandoned manufacture of this dye, probably because of the carcinogenic hazards associated with the handling of β-naphthylamine.

9-2   Mordant dyes

The natural dyes on which the dyeing industry depended for many centuries were mainly mordant dyes. In the latter part of the nineteenth century the important dye *alizarin* was manufactured synthetically and some analogous dyes were discovered. Only natural fibres were then known, and these were coloured by applying the dyes in conjunction with mordants consisting of various metal salts. Strongly coloured insoluble metal complexes thereby formed were precipitated within the fibre, and the resulting dyeings had excellent fastness properties. By varying the metal salt it was often possible to obtain several hues from a single dye. Alizarin and some of its derivatives are still used in this way, but their importance has declined.

The term *Mordant dyes* has sometimes been applied exclusively to products of this kind, but in this book (following the Colour Index practice) it covers all dyes applied to the fibre solely in conjunction with a metal salt which is necessary to yield the desired shade or fastness properties. Many of these dyes (especially in the azo series) contain sulphonic acid groups, and their metal derivatives (such as chromium, cobalt or nickel complexes) are to some extent soluble in water. Attachment to the fibre probably depends partly on the formation of metal–fibre bonds, and the strength of such bonds may be a factor contributing to the good wet-fastness properties often attained. This subject is discussed in Chapter 4.

Mordant dyes of the anthraquinone class in use at the present time are not numerous, and only a few are sufficiently important to cause many manufacturers to compete in meeting the demand.

One of the most important of the ancient natural dyes was *Madder*, extracted from the ground root of the plant *Rubia tinctorum*. The main colouring matter is *alizarin*, present in the form of a glucoside known as ruberythric acid, and a related colouring matter also present is *purpurin*. Alizarin was obtained by acid hydrolysis of ruberythric acid, and it was identified as 1,2-dihydroxyanthraquinone by Graebe and Liebermann[3] in 1868. In the following year

Alizarin

alizarin was prepared synthetically by Caro, Graebe and Liebermann by fusion of anthraquinone-β-sulphonic acid with caustic soda; their British patent application[4] dated 26th June, 1869 was followed on the next day by one submitted by W. H. Perkin[5] describing an almost identical process. The inventors collaborated, and manufacture by the new process was rapidly established. The total production in Europe is said to have reached 65 tons of 10% paste per working day by 1886.[6]

It was originally believed that alizarin is derived from anthraquinonedisulphonic acid, but later it was found that only the β-monosulphonic acid is suitable for the purpose, the second hydroxyl group being introduced by oxidation. In later modifications of the process an oxidising agent such as sodium nitrate was included in the fusion mixture, and this led to improvement in the yield.

Purpurin is 1,2,4-trihydroxyanthraquinone. It was formerly manufactured synthetically but never attained major importance.

The di- and tri-hydroxyanthraquinones are insoluble in water, but form readily-soluble sodium salts. In dyeing and printing processes they are used as aqueous suspensions or as water-soluble bisulphite compounds. Alizarin (CI Mordant Red 11; CI 58000) has been used with many different mordants, the chief being aluminium (red), ferrous iron (deep violet), ferric iron (brownish black), stannous tin (reddish violet), stannic tin (violet) and chromium (brownish violet). The famous *Turkey Red* process, formerly of great importance, was a long and complex operation whereby red shades of great fastness were produced on cotton from alizarin with an aluminium–calcium mordant; shorter processes were devised later, but none of them is now extensively used.

The structure of the Turkey Red alizarin lake has been studied by Fierz-David and Rutishauser[7] and more recently by Kiel and Heertjes.[8] The latter workers found that the lake is formed from two alizarin residues with one atom of aluminium and one of calcium, and they assigned to it the structure [103]. Free alizarin forms an

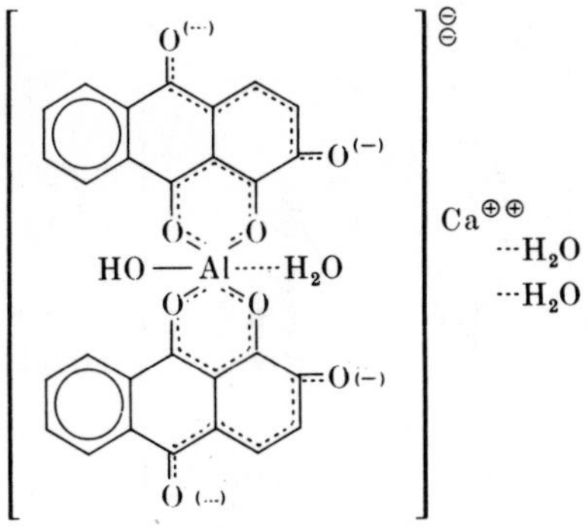

[103]

aluminium lake very slowly, but the calcium salt reacts much more readily.

A derivative of alizarin still widely used is *Anthragallol* (CI Mordant Brown 42; CI 68200). It consists of 1,2,3-trihydroxy-anthraquinone, and is obtained either by heating benzoic and gallic acids with concentrated sulphuric acid or by condensing phthalic anhydride with pyrogallol in concentrated sulphuric acid. It gives dull brown hues on wool by the afterchrome method or on nylon with a reduced chrome mordant; the dyeings have good fastness to light and excellent resistance to wet treatments.

The 3-sulphonic acid derivative of alizarin, discovered by Graebe and Liebermann in 1871, is manufactured in the form of its sodium salt and marketed by numerous firms under names such as *Alizarine Red S* (CI Mordant Red 3; CI 58000). It gives bright yellowish red shades on wool when aftertreated with an aluminium salt or dull bluish red when afterchromed. The dyeings have excellent fastness to light and wet treatments.

A more complex dye giving bluish grey or black shades was discovered by Schmidt and Tust in 1894. It is obtained by condensing purpurin with aniline in presence of boric acid, sulphonating the product and converting it into the sodium salt; the product may have a structure of the type [104]. Dyes made by such processes

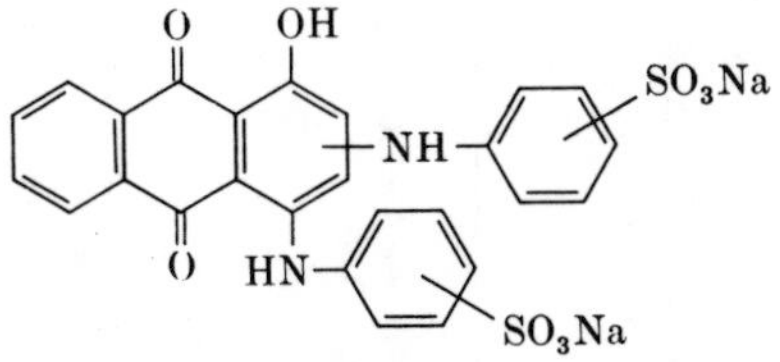

[104]

are sold by many firms under names such as *Alizarine Blue Black B* (CI Mordant Black 13; CI 63615). They are applied to wool by any of the chroming processes, or to nylon by the afterchrome method.

Table 9-1 Anthraquinone disperse dyes

CI Ref. Nos.	Structure and process refs.	Name of typical dye	Hue	Chief applications
CI Disperse Orange 11 CI 60700	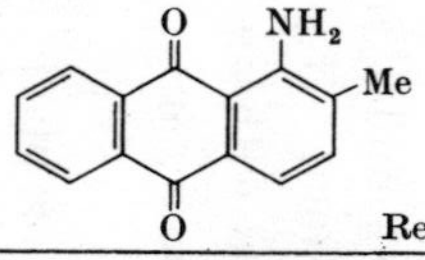 [anthraquinone structure: NH$_2$, Me] Ref. 11	Duranol Orange G (ICI)	Bright orange (acetate); bright yellowish red (nylon)	Acetate, nylon, acrylic, polyester, PVC fibres
CI Disperse Red 11 CI 62015	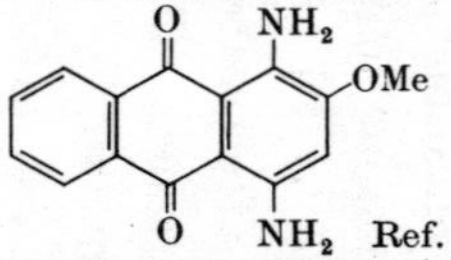 [anthraquinone structure: NH$_2$, OMe, NH$_2$] Ref. 12	Duranol Red X3B (ICI)	Bright bluish pink (acetate); reddish violet (nylon)	Acetate, nylon PVC fibres
CI Disperse Red 15 CI 60710	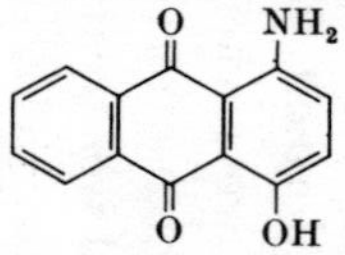 [anthraquinone structure: NH$_2$, OH] Ref. 11	Duranol Red 2B (ICI)	Bluish pink or red (acetate); reddish violet (nylon)	Acetate, nylon, acrylic, polyester fibres
CI Disperse Violet 1 CI 61100	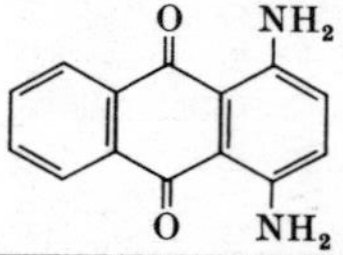 [anthraquinone structure: NH$_2$, NH$_2$] Refs. 11, 13	Duranol Violet 2R (ICI)	Bright violet (acetate); bluer violet (nylon)	Acetate, nylon, acrylic, polyester fibres
CI Disperse Violet 4 CI 61105	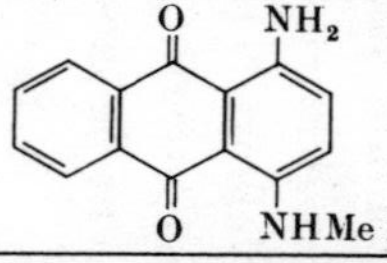 [anthraquinone structure: NH$_2$, NHMe] Ref. 14	Celliton Fast Violet 6B (BASF)	Bright bluish violet (acetate); bluer on nylon	Acetate, nylon, polyester, PVC fibres

CI Disperse Blue 1 CI Solvent Blue 18 CI 64500	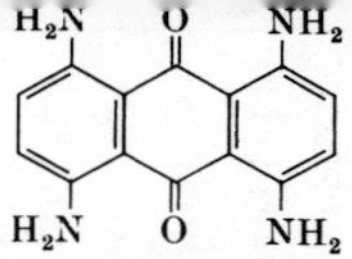 Ref. 15	Duranol Brilliant Blue CB (ICI)	Blue	Acetate, nylon, polyester fibres
CI Disperse Blue 3 CI 61505	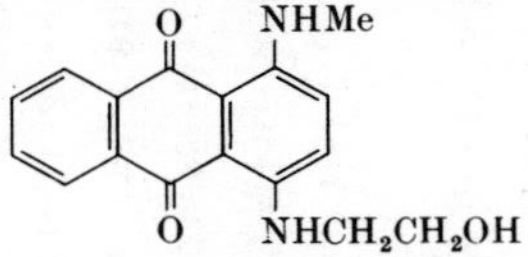 Ref. 16	Duranol Brilliant Blue B (ICI)	Bright blue (acetate); blue (nylon)	Acetate, nylon, acrylic, polyester fibres
CI Disperse Blue 6 CI 62050	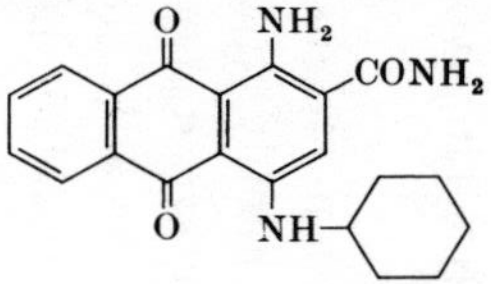 Ref. 17	Celliton Fast Blue FFG (BASF)	Bright blue	Acetate, nylon fibres

Fastness to light is good (grade 5 at normal depth or grade 6 at twice normal depth), and fastness to wet treatments is excellent.

9-3 Disperse dyes

An account has been given in Chapter 6 of the development by British Dyestuffs Corporation of azo disperse dyes for acetate fibre. At about the same date (1923) this firm also produced a series of anthraquinone disperse dyes, and these are still sold under the name *Duranol* for a similar application. Many other firms have manufactured dyes of the same type, mostly fairly simple 1-aminoanthraquinone derivatives carrying substituents such as alkyl, aryl, aralkyl or hydroxyalkyl groups. Table 9-1 gives the structures of some of these dyes, and in many cases manufacturing processes are described in the publications quoted in the second column. In the first place the dyes were marketed as aqueous dispersions, but re-dispersible powders or liquids are now generally preferred. The dispersing agents used include condensation products of alkylnaphthalenesulphonic acids with formaldehyde and of fatty alcohols with ethylene oxide.

Anthraquinone dyes were included in the *Ionamine* and *Solacet* ranges of water-soluble dyes for acetate fibre (see Section 6-1), but these ranges have now been withdrawn in favour of improved disperse dyes.

The light fastness of anthraquinone disperse dyes on acetate fibre is good, with SDC ratings mainly in the region 5–6—rather better than the average given by azo disperse dyes. Wet fastness properties of the two classes are broadly similar, with an average grading of about 4. A serious problem has often arisen in the storage of acetate goods in warehouses heated or lighted by gas, since fumes emitted by burnt gas have a marked reddening effect on most blue dyes of the anthraquinone class. It has been shown that this result is due to the action of oxides of nitrogen on amino or substituted amino groups in the dye molecules.[9] Various inhibitors have been applied to the dyed fibre to protect it from such attack; examples are *N,N*-diphenylethylenediamine and diphenylacetamidine. This subject has been reviewed by Giles.[10]

Many anthraquinone disperse dyes are suitable for application to synthetic polyamide fibres, but in some cases light-fastness is a little lower than on acetate. Selected dyes are used on triacetate, polyacrylonitrile, polyester and polyvinyl chloride fibres. In recent years application of disperse dyes to polyester fibres has received an impetus from the general introduction of high pressure dyeing equipment which enables such fibres to be dyed in heavy shades at a temperature of 120°C or more.

In this field the patent literature is growing rapidly, and it is clear that most manufacturers are devoting a great part of their research effort to the subject. Recent work cannot be reviewed satisfactorily within the scope of the present book, but it is described in the publications listed in the Bibliography.

10 Vat dyes

The term *vat dyes* relates to dyes of any chemical class that are applied by the vat process. The dyes are insoluble in water and cannot be used directly for dyeing, but on reduction to a *leuco* form they become soluble in presence of an alkali and acquire affinity for cellulosic fibres; a solution of a leuco compound can be applied by dyeing or printing and on reoxidation (usually by exposure to air) the original insoluble dye is formed within the structure of the fibre. A final treatment with hot soap or other detergent brings about aggregation or crystallisation so that the particles of pigment become firmly fixed and the shade is fully developed.

One of the earliest vat dyes was *indigo*, which has been used in India from time immemorial. Another was *Tyrian Purple*, obtained in Mediterranean countries from certain shell-fish, and known at the time of Moses. It may be conjectured that the vat process was developed as a result of observation of the effect of accidental fermentation on these natural dyes, the colour being destroyed by reduction during the process but restored on exposure to air. The name *leuco compound* (Greek λευκός, white) is somewhat misleading, since although indigoid reduction products are usually colourless they are applied as sodium salts which are yellow, and in the anthraquinone series the reduction products are coloured (but usually differing in hue from the oxidised dyes). All vat dyes contain a quinonoid system based on carbonyl groups, and in the vatting operation these are reduced to $\diagup$C-OH; since an alkaline medium is used salts of the type $\diagup$C-O$^{\ominus}$Na$^{\oplus}$ are formed. On reduction anthraquinone forms a series of products,[1] and vat dyes containing several anthraquinone residues give rise to a still more complex series. In the preparation of a vat reduction proceeds only to the hydroquinone stage, and in complex dyes it may be unnecessary to reduce all of the keto groups present.

All vat dyes can be applied to cellulosic fibres, and some of them also to wool, silk, nylon and acetate fibres. The need for alkaline application restricts their use on wool and acetate fibres, and in the case of many anthraquinone dyes the necessary conditions are unduly severe. Protective agents such as glue are customarily used to minimise damage to wool. Most vat dyes have low affinity for nylon, and on that fibre their fastness to light is often lower than on wool. Dyes of high molecular weight cannot usually be applied satisfactorily to acetate fibre. Air oxidation of leuco compounds is sometimes augmented by the use of acid dichromate, especially if the goods are in the form of loose cotton, cops, cheeses or pieces dyed on a 'jigger', when access of air is restricted. An aftertreatment with soap or another detergent is necessary for removal of loose pigment and promotion of crystallinity; it often results in a marked change in shade and improvement in fastness properties.[2]

Some important vat dyes representing the chief chemical classes will now be described.

10-1 Indigoid dyes

10-1-1 Indigo

Many plants of the genus *Indigofera* have been cultivated for production of indigo in India, China, Japan, Central America, West Indies, Brazil, South and Central Africa, Madagascar, Java and the Philippine Islands. The colouring principle is present as a glucoside of indoxyl known as *indican*, and this was hydrolysed to free indoxyl by enzyme action; indigo (also known as *indigotin*) was obtained by oxidation of indoxyl:

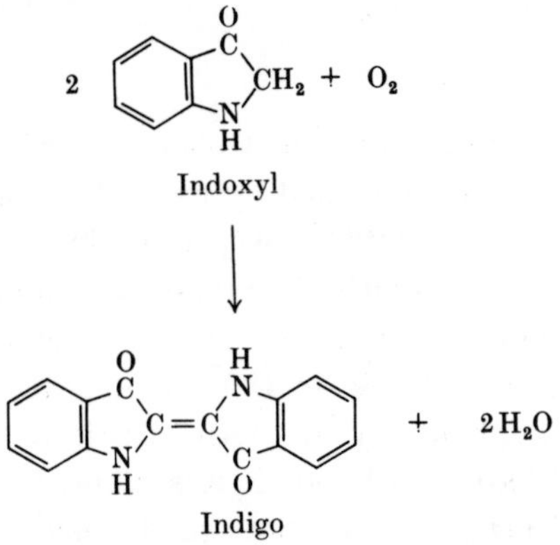

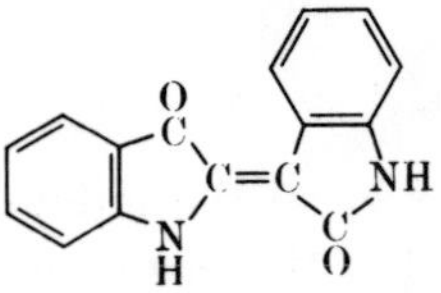

Indoxyl

Indirubin

Indigo

Natural indigo contains a red isomer of indigo known as *indirubin* and other impurities in varying proportions. These constituents facilitate preparation of the vat, and were considered to have a desirable effect on the dyed shade, but the variable properties were a nuisance to the dyer. Woad, which was extracted from the plant *Isatis tinctoria*, and used in Western Europe over many centuries for colouring yarns, fabrics and the bodies of the inhabitants, contains a small amount of indigo.

After many years' work Adolf Baeyer[3] determined the structure of indigo in 1883. The ethylene linkage in its molecule (see structure shown on p. 151) leads to the possibility of stereoisomerism. It has been shown by X-ray crystallography that indigo normally exists in the *trans* form, but both *cis* and *trans* forms have been isolated;[4] the *cis* rapidly reverts to the *trans* form during storage, however.[5]

Many attempts have been made to explain the deep hue of indigo, which appears inconsistent with the absence of a long conjugated chain in Baeyer's structure. Kuhn[6] has pointed out that a tetrapolar structure [105] would be more highly conjugated. On

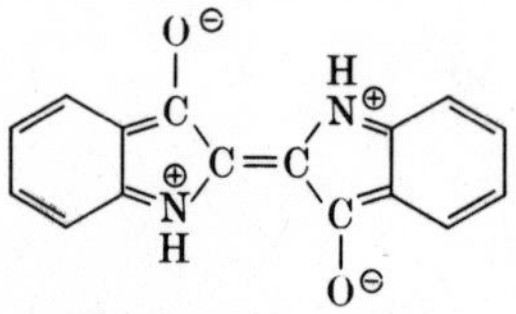

[105] 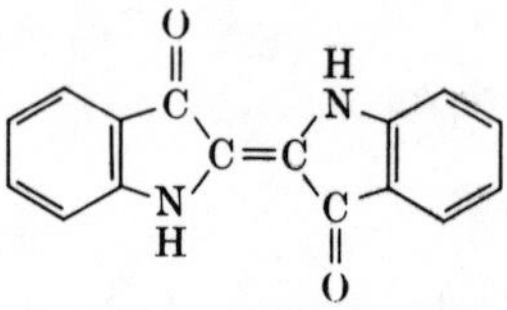   [106]

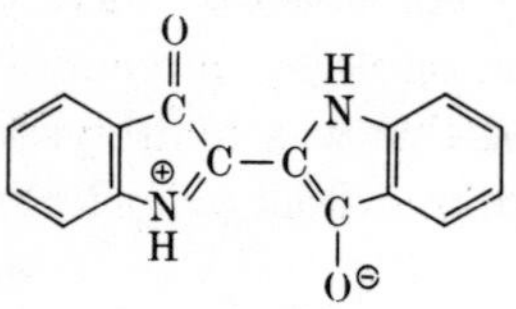

[107] 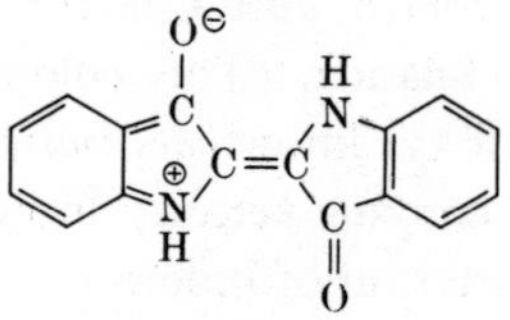   [108]

the other hand the independent studies of van Alphen and Knott[7] suggest that the phenomenon may be explained by regarding indigo as a resonance hybrid of the structures, [106], [107], and [108].

Early processes for manufacturing synthetic indigo were devised by Baeyer, Sandmeyer and Heumann, but the first commercially successful operation was achieved by BASF in 1897 using a process based on the fusion of *o*-carboxyphenylglycine with caustic potash and oxidation of the resulting indoxyl. In 1901 it was found by the Deutsche Gold- und Silber-Scheideanstalt that good yields are obtained at a lower temperature by using a fusion mixture containing sodamide, caustic potash and caustic soda.[8] Originally phenylglycine was obtained by condensing aniline with chloroacetic acid, but in consequence of a shortage of acetic acid during World War I another route was introduced, and it is still generally preferred. The whole process is represented as follows:

$$\text{C}_6\text{H}_5\text{-NH}_2 \xrightarrow[\text{NaHSO}_3]{\text{CH}_2\text{O}+} \text{C}_6\text{H}_5\text{-NHCH}_2\text{SO}_3\text{Na} \xrightarrow{\text{NaCN}} \text{C}_6\text{H}_5\text{-NHCH}_2\text{CN}$$

$$\xrightarrow{\text{NaOH}+\text{H}_2\text{O}}$$

$$\xleftarrow[\substack{\text{NaNH}_2+ \\ \text{NaOH}+\text{KOH}}]{\text{fusion with}} \text{C}_6\text{H}_5\text{-NHCH}_2\text{COONa} \;+\; \text{NH}_3$$

oxidation

Indigo

After the introduction of synthetic indigo, cultivation of the natural product declined rapidly and is now negligible. The synthetic product was produced in vast quantities for many years and is still extensively used, but it has lost much of its former importance.

For application of indigo to cellulosic fibres vats of various types have been used. The hydrosulphite process is now the most important, and the others (zinc–lime, ferrous sulphate, bisulphite–zinc–lime and the traditional fermentation process) are chiefly of historical interest. The hydrosulphite process has advantages over the others in simplicity, speed and ease of control. It depends on the use of sodium hydrosulphite ($Na_2S_2O_4$) in conjunction with caustic soda. Indigo is easily reduced at room temperature, giving a yellow alkaline solution of the leuco compound. Cellulosic materials are treated in the resulting vat either cold or at about 50°C, salt being added to improve exhaustion. Since the leuco compound has low affinity for cellulose several impregnations (each followed by air oxidation) may be needed for deep shades. The dyed material is rinsed, treated with acid, rinsed again, then soaped at the boil. The dyed shade is often modified by 'bottoming' or 'topping' with dyes of other application classes.

Indigo is applied to wool by a broadly similar process, using mildly alkaline conditions with an addition of glue or other suitable colloid to protect the fibre. Since the affinity of reduced indigo is low wool is usually dyed at 40°–60°C. Several makers have marketed ready-reduced indigo, which can be applied to wool from a bath containing ammonia and glue.

Many textile printing processes are available for application of indigo to natural or synthetic fibres by means of direct, discharge or resist styles.

Attempts to simplify the application of indigo were made by several workers, and these culminated in the introduction of a stable disulphuric ester of leuco indigo by Bader and Sunder[9] in 1921. This product, having the structure [109], was placed on the market by

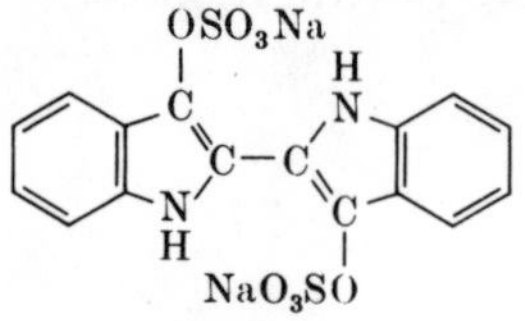

[109]

Durand and Huguenin under the name *Indigosol O*; equivalents are now made by many other firms and sold under different names. Indigosol O was originally obtained by treating leuco indigo in pyridine solution with chlorosulphonic acid, and converting the disulphuric ester into its disodium salt. An improved process was later discovered by Morton Sundour Fabrics Ltd,[10] whereby *unreduced* vat dyes, including indigo and its derivatives, are treated with sulphur trioxide, chlorosulphonic acid or methyl chlorosulphonate in presence of pyridine and a metal such as copper, iron or zinc; an intermediate compound of the type

$$\left[\geqslant C-OSO_3 \right]_2 Cu \cdot C_5 H_5 N$$

is formed, and on reaction with caustic soda the disodium salt of the disulphuric ester is obtained.

Indigosol O is readily soluble in water, has affinity for cellulose and can be rapidly and quantitatively oxidised on the fibre with formation of indigo. Since the affinity is somewhat low and the cost relatively high this product is used mainly for pale shades; it is also especially suitable for wool since it has good affinity for that fibre and can be applied from a weakly acid bath. Development of dyed cellulose or wool is carried out either by means of sodium nitrite (often added to the dyebath) followed by acid treatment, or by an aftertreatment with acid dichromate. Indigosol O can be applied to acetate fibre from a strongly acid bath and developed by the nitrite method.

Although indigo has only moderately good fastness to light (approximately grade 4 on cotton, or 4–5 on wool) it has a great advantage over many other dyes in that as fading proceeds there is little or no change in hue.

10-1-2   Other indigoid dyes

Since indigo is blue the range of shades obtainable by substitution of its molecule cannot be great, and in fact all commercial indigoid dyes are blues. Apart from indigo itself only halogeno derivatives are of technical interest. The indigo molecule is numbered as follows:

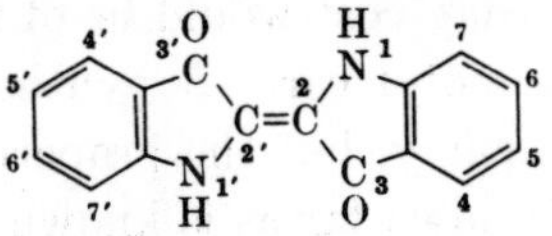

The first derivative to be mentioned is *Tyrian Purple*, although it is solely of historical interest. Its discovery was later than that of indigo, but it is believed to have been known in 1600 BC. The dye was obtained from various molluscs, especially *Murex brandaris* and *Murex trunculus*, which flourished on Mediterranean shores. Since

Table 10-1   Halogenated indigoid vat dyes

CI Constitution No.	CI Generic Name	Constitution	Hue
CI 73040	CI Vat Blue 41	5,5′,7,7′-Tetrachloroindigo	Reddish blue
CI 73041	CI Solubilised Vat Blue 41	5,5′,7,7′-tetra-chloroindigo disulphuric ester (disodium salt)	Reddish blue
CI 73045	CI Vat Blue 2	5,5′-Dibromo-4,4′-dichloroindigo	Greenish blue
CI 73046	CI Solubilised Vat Blue 2	5,5′-Dibromo-4,4′-dichloroindigo disulphuric ester (disodium salt)	Greenish blue
CI 73060	CI Vat Blue 35	5,5′-Dibromoindigo	Dull blue
CI 73065	CI Vat Blue 5	5,5′,7,7′-Tetra-bromoindigo	Blue
CI 73066	CI Solubilised Vat Blue 5	5,5′,7,7′-Tetra-bromoindigo disulphuric ester (disodium salt)	Blue

Note: The solubilised vat dyes are all represented above as disodium salts, but potassium, lithium or calcium salts may also be used.

the dye content is very small and much labour was needed to extract it the cost was so great that only royalty and the highest religious dignitaries were able to afford it. Friedländer[11] succeeded in extracting 1·4 g of dye from about 12,000 molluscs, and identified its main component as 6,6'-dibromoindigo. In 1920 Mason[12] quoted a calculation of the cost of preparing 1 kg of the dye from shell-fish as about £2,500; on that basis the present-day cost would be of the same order as that of the world's best motor-car. A synthetic equivalent could now be produced quite cheaply, but the properties of the dye are poor by modern standards, and so far as is known no such manufacture has ever been carried out.

The commercial halogeno derivatives of indigo do not match the parent dye in importance. Some of the more useful members of the series are listed in Table 10-1; details of the halogenation processes are available in publications quoted in the Colour Index under the Constitution Numbers. Some of the dyes are produced also in the form of water-soluble salts of disulphuric esters by processes corresponding to that described for Indigosol O (Section 10-1-1). The applications of halogenated indigoid dyes are similar to those of indigo.

10-2 Thioindigoid dyes

Thioindigoid dyes are analogues of indigo and its derivatives in which the two —NH— groups are replaced by sulphur atoms. The first of these, *Thioindigo Red B* [110], was discovered by Friedländer[13]

[110]

in 1906. As indicated by its name, this dye gives bluish red shades. Derivatives with a very much wider range of shades than those available in the indigoid series can be obtained by suitable substitution. The effect of substituents may be either hypsochromic or bathochromic, and examples quoted later include dyes giving orange, red, violet and brown shades. The dyes have good fastness properties, and on account of their versatility they have surpassed those of the indigoid class (except indigo itself) in importance. It will be seen from the following account of their manufacture, however, that the processes required are somewhat complex, and the resulting high cost has caused these dyes to lose favour as cheaper products with comparable fastness properties have been introduced.

It is not practicable to include a full account of the chemistry of the thioindigoid dyes here, but the following examples illustrate two of the more important industrial processes.

10-2-1   Manufacture of Thioindigo Red B

Thioindigo Red B (CI Vat Red 41; CI 73300) is made by many firms and sold under various names. The following reaction scheme represents the stages of a typical manufacturing process:[14]

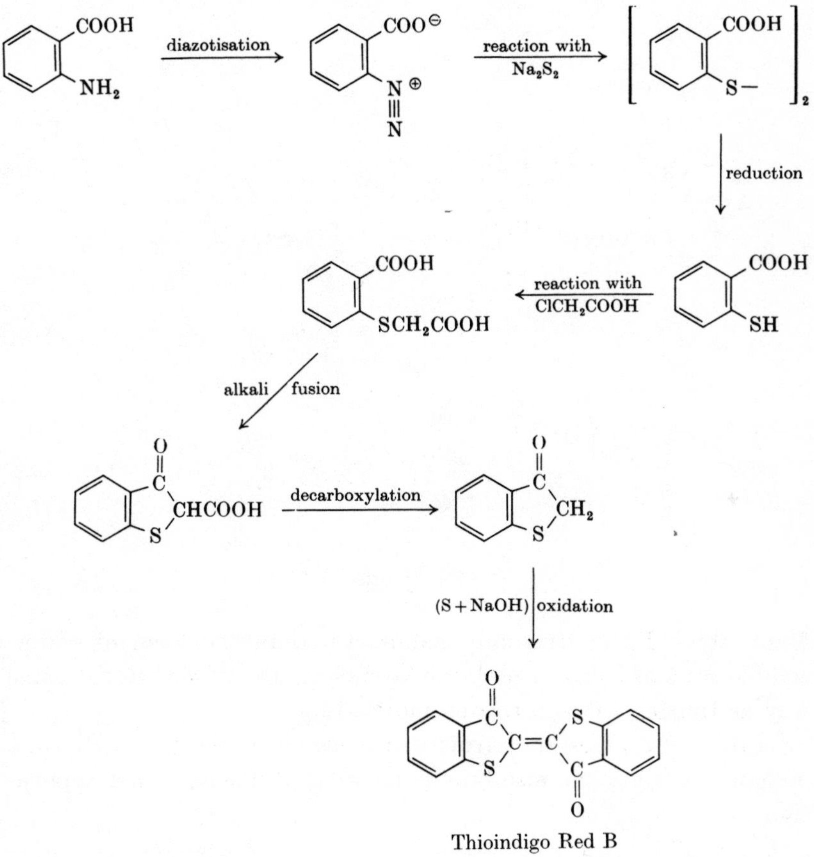

Thioindigo Red B

10-2-2   Manufacture of Hydron Pink FF

Hydron Pink FF (CI Vat Red 1; CI 73360), formerly manufactured by IG and since produced by over twenty firms under their own brand names, is obtained by the following series of reactions:[15]

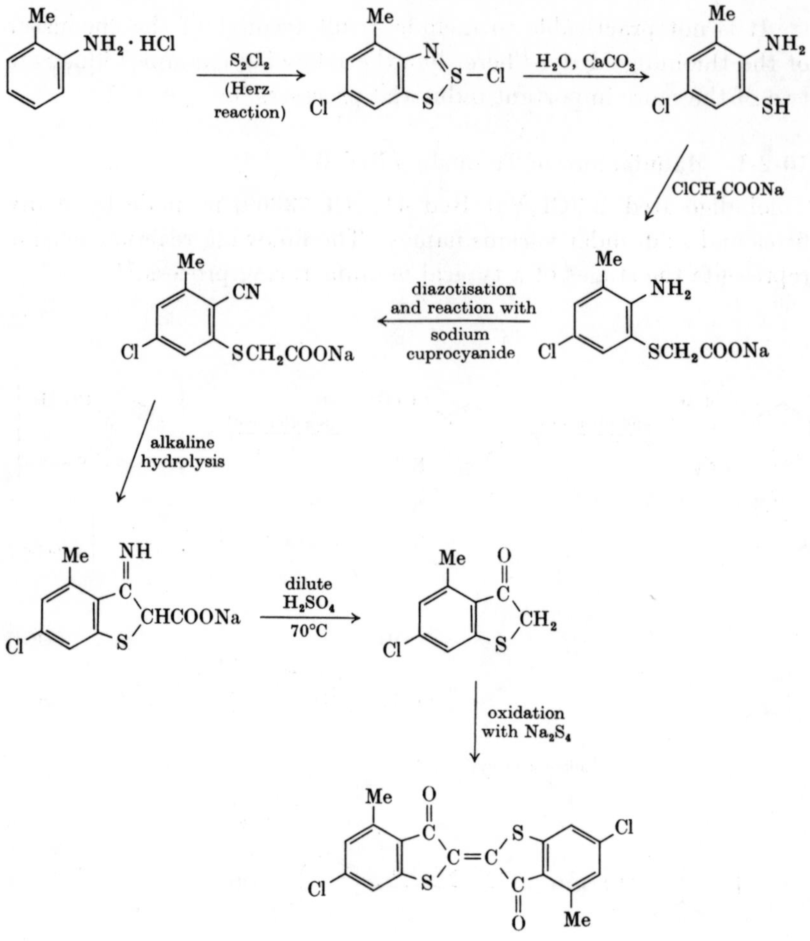

Many thioindigoid dyes are manufactured in the form of water-soluble salts of leuco disulphuric esters and are applied in the same way as Indigosol O and related indigoid dyes.

Table 10-2 gives the structures of some of the principal thioindigoid vat dyes and also brief particulars of hue and chief applications.

10-3 Dyes with mixed indigoid-thioindigoid structures

By condensing isatin α-chloride or anilide, or a derivative of one of these compounds, with thioindoxyl or one of its derivatives unsymmetrical dyes having an indigoid residue at one end of the molecule and a thioindigoid residue at the other are readily obtained. These dyes serve mainly to provide violet, brown, grey and black hues. The following examples illustrate dyes of this type.

Anthrasol Violet ARR (FH) (CI Solubilised Vat Violet 8; CI 73601), with the structure [111], is obtained by condensing 5,7-dichloroisatin α-chloride with 6-chloro-4-methylthioindoxyl followed

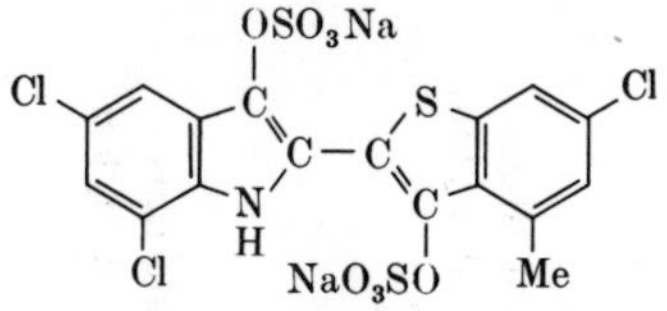

[111]

by conversion into the disulphuric ester.[16] It gives bright violet shades, and is applied to cellulosic fibres, silk and wool.

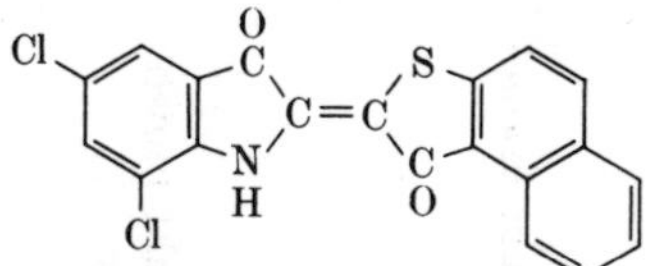

[112]

Indanthren Printing Brown R (FH) (CI Vat Brown 42; CI 73665) is obtained by condensing 5,7-dichloroisatin chloride with 4,5-benzothioindoxyl, and has the structure [112].[17] It gives brown shades, and is applied to cellulosic fibres, silk and wool.

Indanthren Printing Black BL (FH) (CI Vat Black 1; CI 73670), obtained by condensing 5-bromoisatin chloride with the appropriate chloro derivative of 6,7-benzothioindoxyl, has a structure [113], which is related to that of the preceding example.[18]

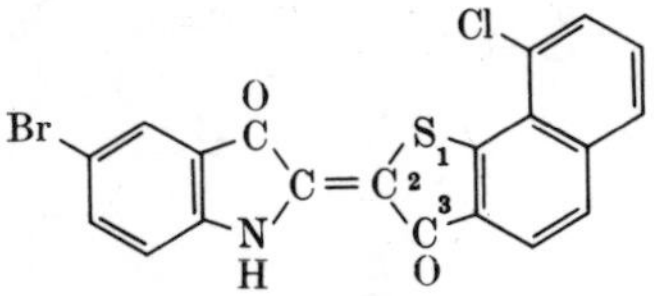

[113]

It gives bluish black shades, and is suitable for application to cellulosic fibres, silk, wool or acetate. The disulphuric ester (CI Solubilised Vat Black 1; CI 73671) manufactured by several firms is used for production of bluish grey shades.

10-4   Miscellaneous vat dyes containing indigoid or thioindigoid residues

A few vat dyes are obtained by condensing indoxyl or thioindoxyl (or a derivative of these compounds) with quinones of various types. Two examples of such dyes are illustrated on p. 162. CI Vat Blue 8 (CI 73800) gives blue or navy shades, and is applied to cellulosic fibres, silk and wool.

Table 10-2   Some important thioindigoid dyes

CI Ref. Nos.	*Structure*	*Hue*	*Application: chief substrates*
CI Vat Red 41 CI 73300		Bluish red	Cellulosic fibres, silk, wool
CI Vat Orange 5 CI 73335		Bright orange	Cellulosic fibres, silk, wool, nylon
CI Solubilised Vat Orange 5		Bright orange	Cellulosic fibres, silk, wool, nylon, acetate
CI Vat Red 1 CI 73360		Bright bluish pink	Cellulosic fibres silk, wool, nylon

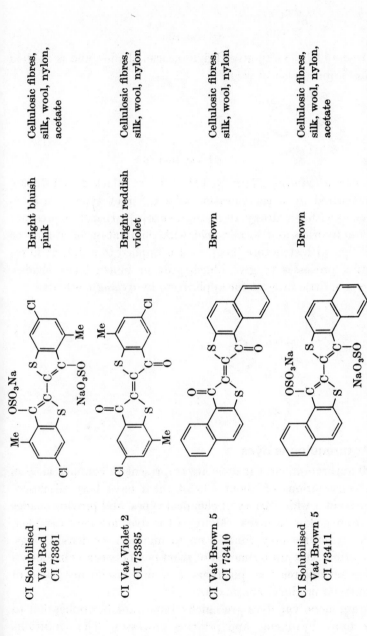

CI name		Colour	Fibres
CI Solubilised Vat Red 1 CI 73361		Bright bluish pink	Cellulosic fibres, silk, wool, nylon, acetate
CI Vat Violet 2 CI 73385		Bright reddish violet	Cellulosic fibres, silk, wool, nylon
CI Vat Brown 5 CI 73410		Brown	Cellulosic fibres, silk, wool, nylon
CI Solubilised Vat Brown 5 CI 73411		Brown	Cellulosic fibres, silk, wool, nylon, acetate

Note: The solubilised vat dyes are all represented above as disodium salts, but potassium, lithium or calcium salts may also be used.

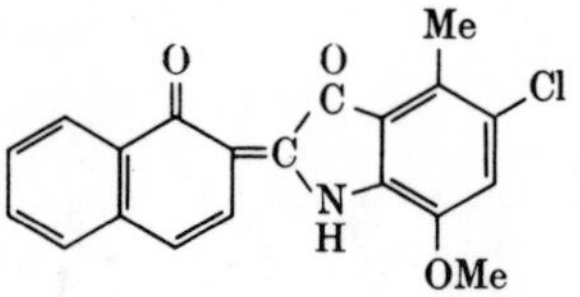

CI Vat Blue 8

CI Vat Red 45 (CI 73860) gives bright scarlet shades, and is applied to cellulosic fibres, also to wool.

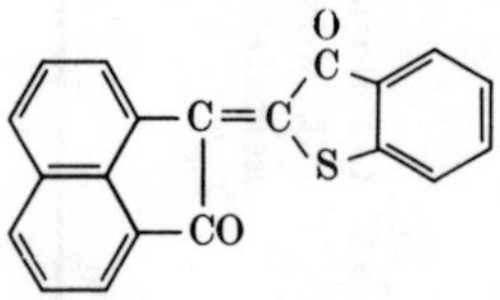

CI Vat Red 45

Indanthren Printing Black B (FH) (CI Vat Black 2; CI 73830) is manufactured by a condensation of a different type. Isatin α-anilide reacts with 4-hydroxy-10-methylbenzo[a]carbazole in presence of acetic anhydride and formic acid with elimination of aniline to yield the dye with structure [114].[19] It is applied to cellulosic fibres by printing processes to give bluish grey or bluish black shades. This dye is of little interest for application by dyeing methods.

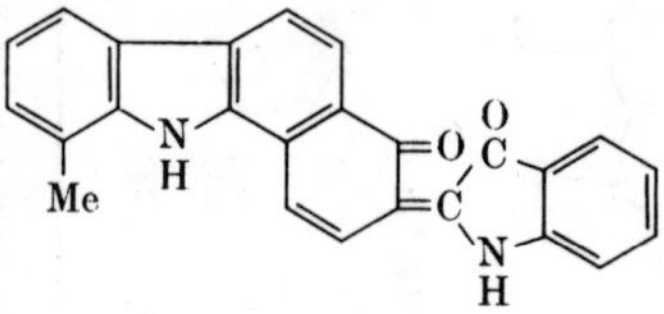

[114]

10-5 Anthraquinone dyes

Over 200 anthraquinone vat dyes are at present in commercial use, and the constitutions of about 130 of them have been disclosed. They represent a wide variety of chemical types, and provide shades ranging from yellow to black. Many of the dyes are very complex, and their structures may contain up to nineteen condensed rings. They are often built up by means of reactions between components containing several reactive positions, and in consequence some of the commercial products are mixtures.

Anthraquinone vat dyes are chiefly important in application to cellulosic fibres by dyeing and printing processes. The conditions used for vatting vary considerably but the only reducing agent of practical importance is alkaline sodium hydrosulphite.

The first anthraquinone vat dye was obtained by R. Bohn in 1901 in the course of an attempt to prepare an analogue of indigo by caustic fusion of 2-anthraquinonylglycine. The expected reaction did not take place, but a blue vat dye was formed which proved to have the structure [115]. The same product was obtained by caustic,

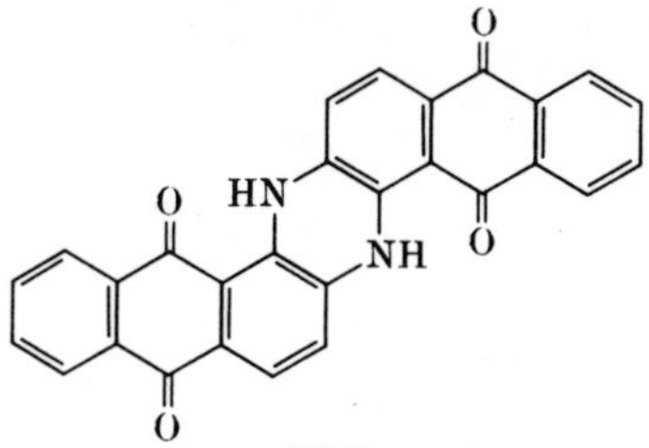

[115]

fusion of 2-aminoanthraquinone. Bohn called his product *Indanthren* (the name being derived from *indigo* and *anthracene*), and later it was marketed by BASF as *Indanthren Blue R*. It will be seen that the dye is a dihydrodianthraquinonylazine, and it was later given the chemical name *indanthrone*, thereby avoiding the trade name and at the same time indicating the quinonoid structure.

The excellent fastness properties of Indanthren Blue R encouraged further research, and many other vat dyes were developed and sold as members of the Indanthren range. Other makers have marketed comparable products under their own brand names; these include the *Algol* (FBy), *Alizanthrene* (British Alizarine Co., later ICI), *Calcoid* (ACY), *Caledon* (ICI), Carbanthrene (NAC), *Cibanone* (CIBA), *Paradone* (LBH), *Ponsol* (DuP), *Sandothrene* (S), and *Tinon* (Gy) ranges of vat dyes.

The following account of the chemistry of these dyes covers some of the chief commercial products. More comprehensive information is available in the Colour Index and other major works.

10-5-1 Carbocyclic dyes

Acylaminoanthraquinones. These are among the dyes with simpler structures. An example is *Indanthren Yellow GK* (CI Vat Yellow 3; CI 61725), introduced by Bayer in 1909, which is obtained by dibenzoylating 1,5-diaminoanthraquinone. It gives yellow shades of good all-round fastness properties, and is used mainly on cellulosic fibres. Greener yellow shades are given by *Indanthren Yellow 5GK* (FBy) (CI Vat Yellow 26; CI 65410), obtained by reaction of 1-aminoanthraquinone with isophthaloyl chloride.

If hydroxyl groups are introduced into the molecule of Indanthren Yellow GK in positions 4 and 8 the shade becomes violet; this product is manufactured as *Indanthren Brilliant Violet BBK* (FBy) (CI Vat Violet 15; CI 63355). If the benzoylamino groups are then

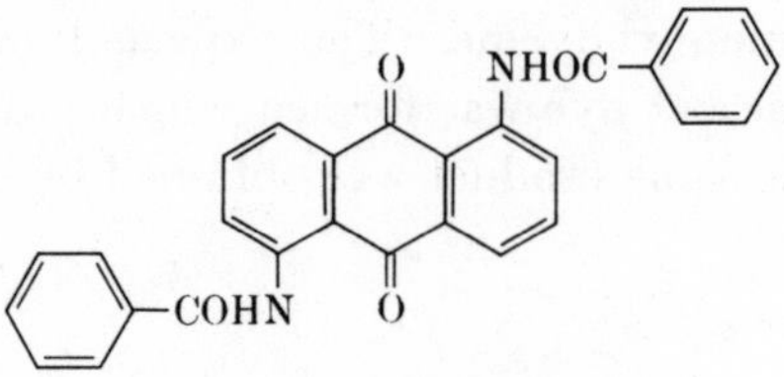

Indanthren Yellow GK (FBy)

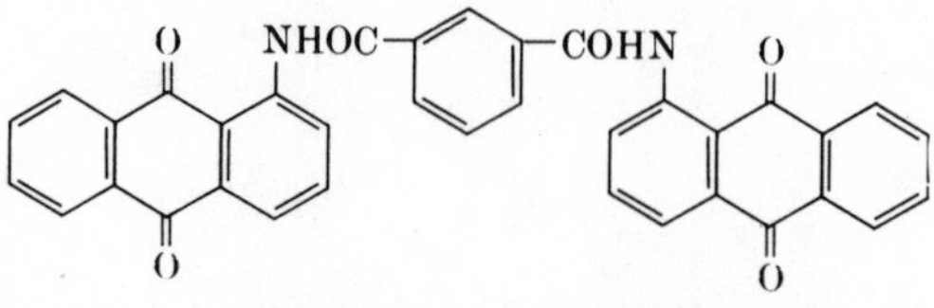

Indanthren Yellow 5GK (FBy)

replaced by *p*-anisoylamino groups a dye giving somewhat redder shades is obtained, and this is of importance because of its excellent fastness to light; it is marketed as *Indanthren Brilliant Violet RK* (FBy) (CI Vat Violet 17; CI 63365).

Triazinylaminoanthraquinones. As a vat dye containing a reactive chlorine atom, discovered as long ago as 1921, *Cibanone Orange 6R* (CIBA) (CI Vat Orange 18; CI 65705) [**116**] is of some interest; it is

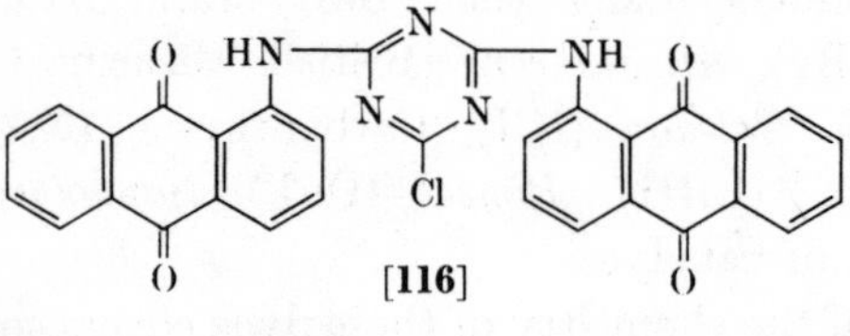

[**116**]

not clear, however, to what extent the reactive atom is removed during vatting. This dye gives bright reddish orange shades on cellulosic fibres, and it can also be applied to silk. The capacity of structures of this type for reaction with the fibre was not appreciated before the development of the *Procion* dyes by ICI in 1954–6 (see Chapter 13); recent work on reactive vat dyes is described in Section 10-7. *Cibanone Red G* (CIBA) (CI Vat Red 28; CI 65710) has a structure corresponding to that of Cibanone Orange 6R with an amino group in place of the chlorine atom. It gives yellowish red shades which are dischargeable.

Anthrimides. A typical dye of the anthrimide type is *Indanthren Orange 7RK* (FBy) (CI Vat Red 48; CI 65205), which is manufactured by condensing 2,6-dichloroanthraquinone with 1-aminoanthraquinone (2 mol.) in nitrobenzene medium in presence of cuprous chloride and sodium acetate.[20] Another example is *Indanthren Corinth RK* (FBy) (CI Vat Violet 16; CI 65020), obtained by

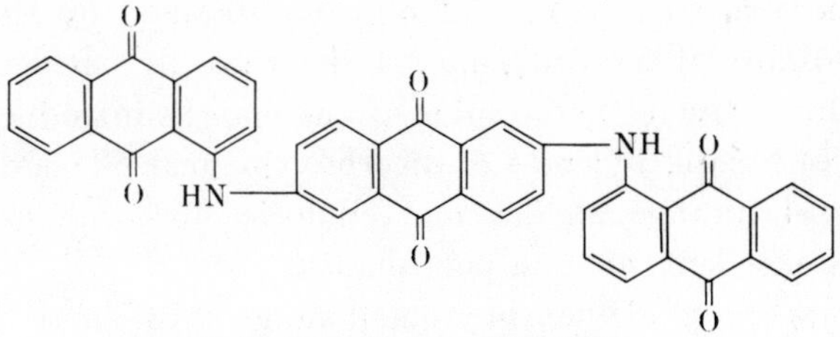

Indanthren Orange 7RK (FBy)

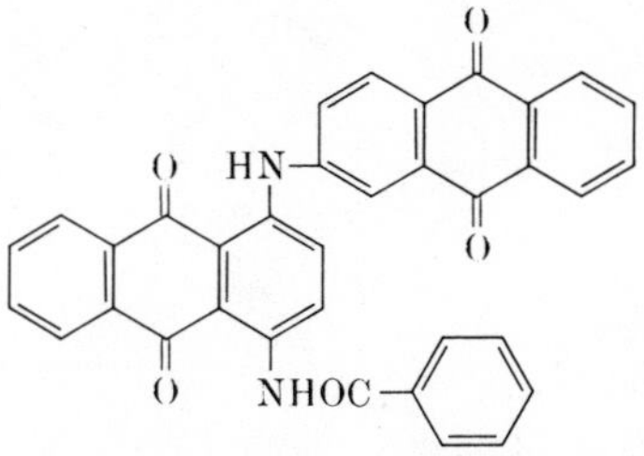

Indanthren Corinth RK (FBy)

condensing 1-amino-4-benzamidoanthraquinone with 2-chloroanthra-quinone under similar conditions but in molten naphthalene medium.[21] These dyes give dull yellowish red and dull violet shades respectively on cellulosic fibres, the latter having exceptionally high fastness to light (SDC grade 7–8 at normal depth).

The anthrimides are not of major importance as vat dyes, but they are valuable intermediates for the manufacture of anthraquinonecarbazole dyes (Section 10-5-2).

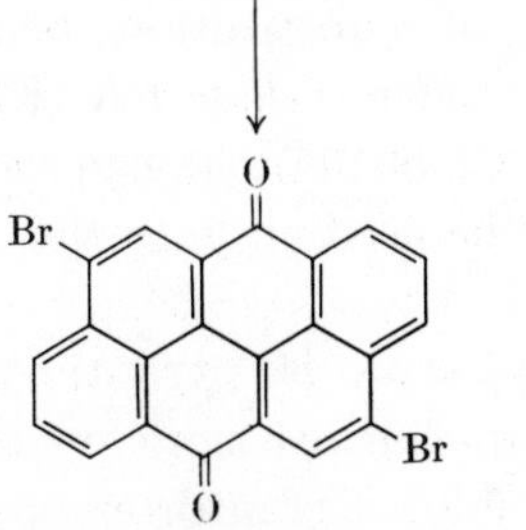

[117]

Anthanthrones. The chief dye of this type is *Indanthren Brilliant Orange RK* (CI Vat Orange 3; CI 59300), formerly sold under this name by IG and now produced by many firms under their own brand names. It has the structure [117], and may be obtained by ring-closure of 8,8′-dibromobinaphthylene-8,8′-dicàrboxylic acid in sulphuric acid; alternatively the bromine atoms may be introduced after ring-closure of binaphthylene-8,8′-dicarboxylic acid. This dye gives bright reddish orange shades on cellulosic fibres or silk; fastness to light is excellent, even in pale shades.

Dibenzopyrenequinones. Dibenzopyrenequinone [118] may be

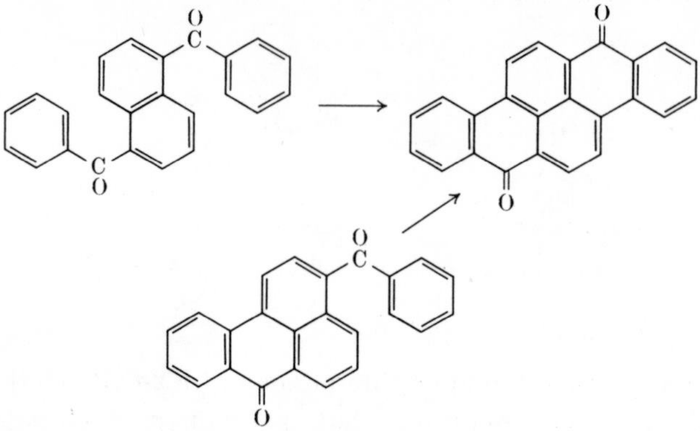

[118]

obtained either from 1,5-dibenzoylnaphthalene by ring-closure in a sodium chloride–aluminium chloride melt supplied with oxygen, or from 3-benzoylbenzanthrone by fusion with aluminium chloride and a hydrogen acceptor such as sodium *m*-nitrobenzenesulphonate.[22] Dibenzopyrenequinone was introduced as a vat dye by MLB in 1922 under the name *Indanthren Golden Yellow GK* (CI Vat Yellow 4; CI 59100), and equivalent products are marketed by many makers. Reddish yellow shades are obtained on cellulosic fibres and on silk or nylon; fastness to washing and light is good, but resistance to bleaching is poor.

A valuable bright yellowish orange dye is obtained by dibrominating dibenzopyrenequinone (the positions of substitution being unknown). This is marketed as *Indanthren Golden Yellow RK* (FH) and equivalent brands (CI Vat Orange 1; CI 59105); it has very good all-round fastness properties, and may be used on yarn that is to be bleached.

Pyranthrones. The parent dye of this class is pyranthrone [119], discovered by R. H. Scholl in 1905 during his work on the constitution of flavanthrone (see Section 10-5-3). Pyranthrone may be obtained (among other ways) by the reactions shown on p. 167.[23] This dye was first marketed by BASF as *Indanthren Gold Orange G* (CI Vat Orange 9; CI 59700), and there are now many equivalent products. The shade is yellowish orange, and general fastness

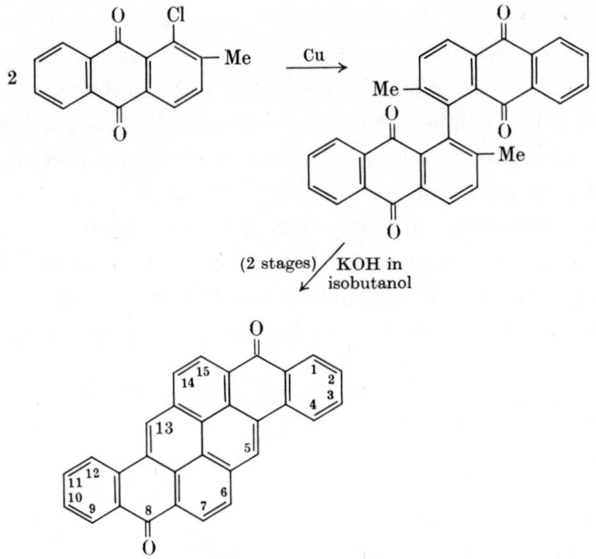

[119]

properties are good. Fastness to light is not of the highest order (SDC grade 5-6 at normal depth), but resistance to bleaching is good; these properties are suitable for applications such as towellings. A drawback of Indanthren Gold Orange G and its equivalents arises from its influence in promoting the tendering of cellulosic fibres on exposure to light; this characteristic, however, is shared with many other yellow and orange vat dyes.[24]

A dibromopyranthrone is manufactured as *Indanthren Orange RRT* (BASF) and its equivalents (CI Vat Orange 2; CI 59705). IG records show a structure with the bromine atoms in positions 4 and 12. This dye gives bright reddish orange shades and has good general fastness properties. A tribromo derivative giving reddish orange shades is available as *Indanthren Orange 4R* (BASF) and its equivalents (CI Vat Orange 4; CI 59710). The bromine atoms were shown by IG in positions 1, 4 and 12.

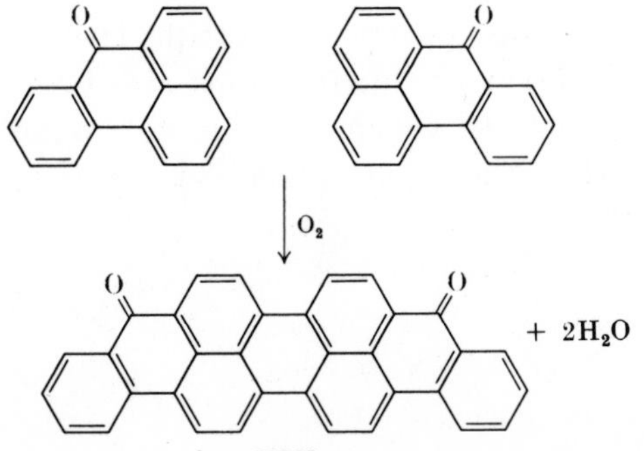

[120]

Dibenzanthrones. The dibenzanthrone series provides a number of important violet, blue and green dyes. They include structures of two types based on dibenzanthrone [120] and isodibenzanthrone [121], respectively. Dibenzanthrone (also called violanthrone) is obtained by condensation of two molecules of benzanthrone in a caustic fusion process, oxidation resulting in union in the 3,3' and 4,4' positions. Isodibenzanthrone (or isoviolanthrone) is also formed in the fusion by union at the 3,4' and 3',4 positions, and there are other by-products. The original manufacturing process for isodibenzanthrone consisted in heating 3-chlorobenzanthrone in

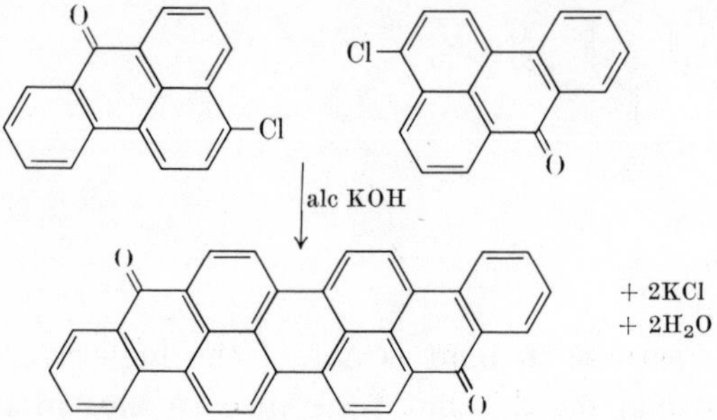

[121]

alcoholic potash at 150°C.[25] In later processes 3,3'-dibenzanthronyl sulphide or selenide is first produced as an intermediate compound.[26]

Dibenzanthrone was introduced by BASF in 1904 as a vat dye under the name *Indanthren Dark Blue BO* (later BOA) (CI Vat Blue 20; CI 59800). It gives dark blue shades on cellulosic fibres or silk, and has good fastness to light. The dyeings are sensitive to heat and are temporarily reddened by water-spotting. This dye is still very extensively used. A trichloro derivative of dibenzanthrone was introduced by the British Alizarine Co. in 1925 under the name *Alizanthrene Navy Blue R* (CI Vat Blue 18; CI 59815), and this is much less sensitive to water-spotting than the unsubstituted dye; it is still of importance, and is marketed by ICI and many other makers.

An outstanding discovery was made by Scottish Dyes Ltd (later part of ICI) in 1920 when they produced *Caledon Jade Green X* (now *XBN*, ICI) (CI Vat Green 1; CI 59825). This is 16,17-dimethoxydibenzanthrone [122]. It has a bright green shade and good

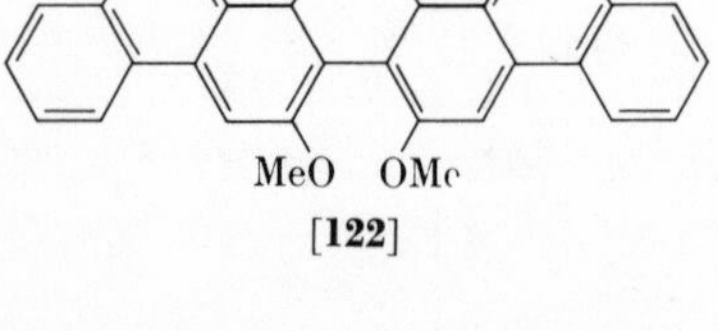

[122]

all-round fastness properties. The dye is obtained by oxidising dibenzanthrone with manganese dioxide and sulphuric acid and dimethylating the resulting dihydroxy derivative.[27] The effect of the two methoxy groups in transforming the blue colour of dibenzanthrone into a bright green has been attributed to steric hindrance and consequent distortion of the molecule. The energy required to preserve planarity is provided at the expense of resonance energy and the wavelength of maximum absorption is therefore raised.

By dibrominating the dimethoxydibenzanthrone a dye giving a yellower shade of green is obtained. Bromination is carried out in sulphuric acid monohydrate in presence of sodium nitrite at 40°C; under these conditions demethylation is avoided.[28] The resulting product is marketed as *Indanthren Brilliant Green GG* (BASF) and numerous equivalent brands (CI Vat Green 2; CI 59830).

A dinitrated dibenzanthrone is sold as *Indanthren Black BB* (or *BGA*) (BASF) (CI Vat Green 9; CI 59850). Since the nitro groups are reduced in the vat the shade produced is that of the diamine; it is a bottle green of good fastness to light, but sensitive to chlorine. On oxidation of deep dyeings with chlorine or other suitable agent black shades of high fastness to light are obtained, and the product is chiefly used in this way.

The ethylene ether of 16,17-dihydroxydibenzanthrone [**123**] was first prepared by Scottish Dyes Ltd in 1921 and sold by them and later by ICI as *Caledon Dark Blue G* (CI Vat Blue 16; CI 71200).[29] It gives navy shades with good fastness properties on cellulosic fibres or silk. It is of interest to compare the shade of this dye with

[**123**]

that of the corresponding dimethoxy derivative (Caledon Jade Green X) [**122**]. The cyclic ether structure prevents the distortion caused by steric hindrance in the dimethoxy derivative and the shade is consequently not greatly different from that of the unsubstituted dibenzanthrone.

Commercial isodibenzanthrone dyes are not numerous. Isodibenzanthrone itself yields a vat with some difficulty but is reduced at a temperature of 50°–60°C. The Colour Index records only two makers, who sell it as *Benzadone Violet B* (YDC) and *Paradone*

Violet B New (LBH) (CI Vat Violet 10; CI 60000). It gives bluish violet shades on cotton, which are developed only by thorough soaping, and markedly redder shades on viscose. Isodibenzanthrone has been largely superseded as a vat dye by halogenated derivatives with better dyeing properties. Various brominated derivatives are manufactured by many firms who sell them under their own brand names; the earliest of these was *Indanthren Brilliant Violet 3B* (BASF) (CI Vat Violet 9; CI 60005), introduced in 1909. Deep bright bluish violet shades are obtained on cellulosic fibres; the shades on silk are redder. Dichlorinated isodibenzanthrones are extensively used and are marketed by many makers. An example is *Indanthren Brilliant Violet RR* (BASF) (CI Vat Violet 1; CI 60010), which gives a bright bluish violet shade with good general fastness properties and is applied to cellulosic fibres, wool, silk and nylon. Like other violet dibenzanthrone dyes it is reddened by water spotting.

10-5-2 Five-membered heterocyclic dyes

Anthraquinonecarbazoles. Many anthraquinone vat dyes contain carbazole nuclei, and these provide a wide range of hues. Three isomeric dyes illustrating the effect on shade of varying the positions of benzoylamino substituents are *Indanthren Olive R* (FBy) (CI Vat Black 27; CI 69005), *Indanthren Brown R* (FBy) (CI Vat Brown 3; CI 69015) and *Indanthren Golden Orange 3G* (FBy) (CI Vat Orange 15; CI 69025):

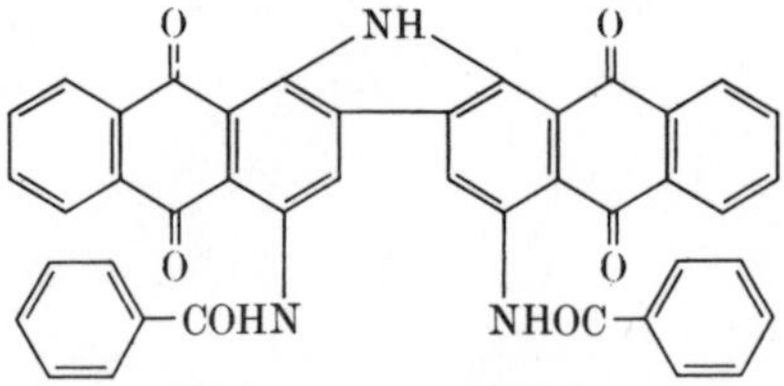

Indanthren Olive R (FBy)

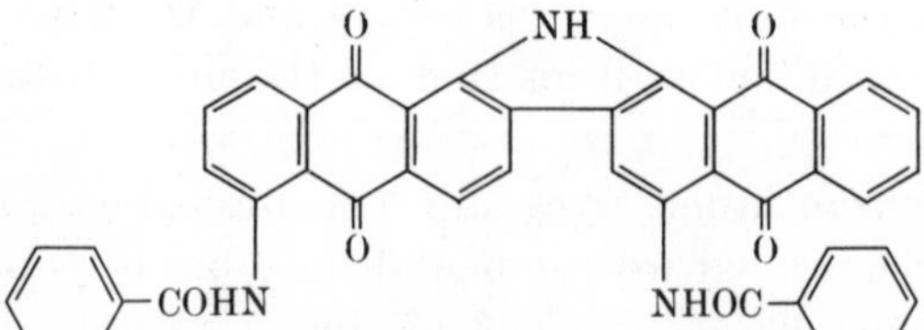

Indanthren Brown R (FBy)

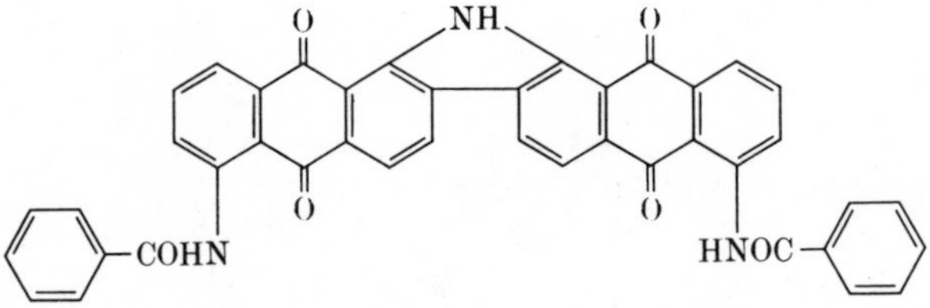

Indanthren Golden Orange 3G (FBy)

Indanthren Olive R is made by condensing together 1-amino-anthraquinone and 1-chloroanthraquinone to form 1,1'-dianthri-mide, dinitrating this, reducing to the diamine, dibenzoylating, then cyclising the product by treating it with sulphuric acid and finally oxidising with sodium chlorate.[30] Indanthren Brown R is obtained by condensing 1-amino-5-benzoylaminoanthraquinone with 4-benzoylamino-1-chloroanthraquinone, then cyclising the product as in the previous example.[31] Similar reactions are used in the manu-facture of Indanthren Golden Orange 3G, the starting materials being 1-amino-5-benzoylaminoanthraquinone and 5-benzoylamino-1-chloroanthraquinone.[32] These dyes give brownish grey, reddish brown and yellowish orange shades, respectively. All have good fastness properties, and they are applied to cellulosic fibres, wool, silk, and sometimes to nylon.

Other isomeric dyes showing a marked difference in hue are *Indanthren Brown BR* (FBy) (CI Vat Brown 1; CI 70800) [**124**] and *Indanthren Yellow 3R* (FH) (CI Vat Orange 11; CI 70805) [**125**]. The first of these is obtained by condensing two molecules of 1-chloro-anthraquinone with one molecule of 1,4-diaminoanthraquinone, then cyclising by means of aluminium chloride, and the second dye by condensing two molecules of 1-aminoanthraquinone with one molecule of 1,5-dichloroanthraquinone, then cyclising as before.[33,34] Both dyes have very good fastness to light and are widely used;

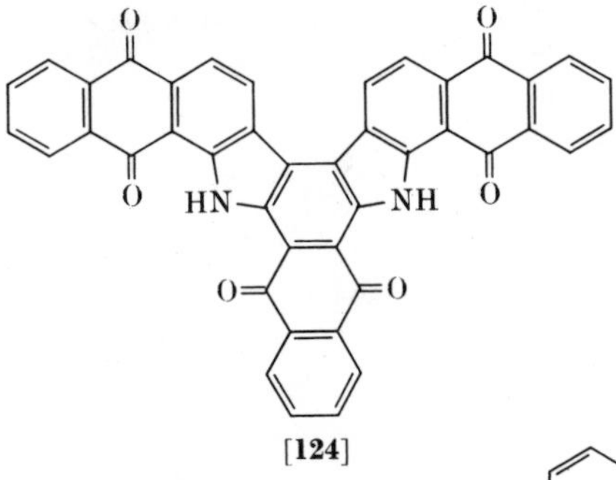

[**124**]

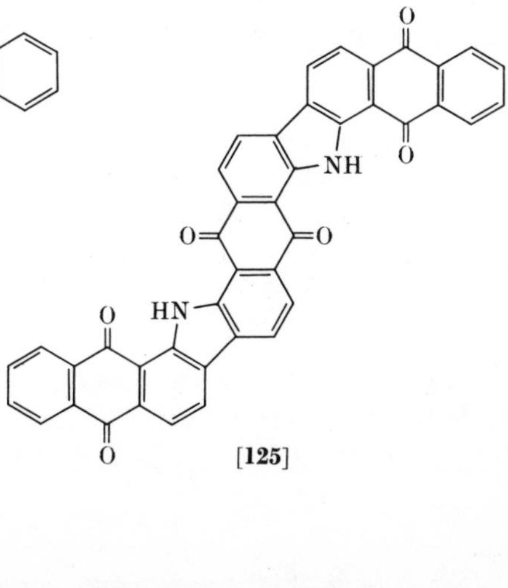

[**125**]

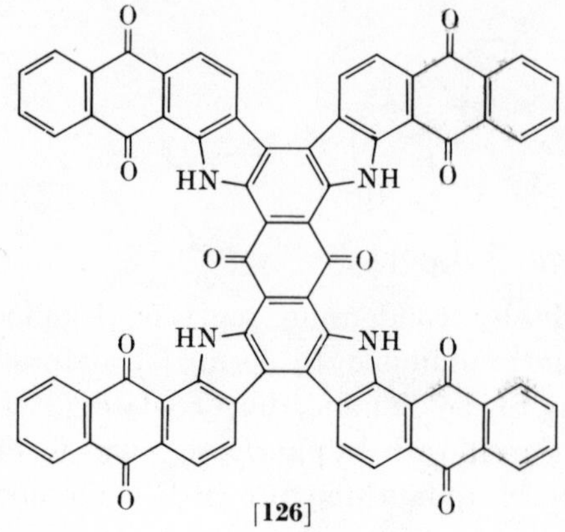

[126]

they give reddish brown and yellowish orange shades, respectively.

Indanthren Khaki GG (FH) (CI Vat Green 8; CI 71050) is remarkable in that it is a large molecule (said to contain 19 rings) and has a molecular weight of about 1084, yet it can be made from 1-aminoanthraquinone in only two operations. The process consists in condensing this amine (4 mol.) with 1,4,5,8-tetrachloroanthraquinone (1 mol.) in nitrobenzene medium in presence of copper and soda ash, then cyclising the resulting pentanthrimide by means of aluminium chloride.[35] The product is said to have the structure [126], but there is much doubt about the formation of four carbazole rings.[36] Khaki shades of good fastness properties are obtained on cotton, viscose and silk.

Pyrazoloanthrones. A few dyes of this class are of commercial interest. One of the simplest is *Indanthren Rubine R* (Cassella) (CI Vat Red 13; CI 70320), obtained by heating 1-hydrazino-anthraquinone with alcoholic potash and ethylating the resulting pyrazolodianthronyl in alkaline conditions.[37] The dye probably has the structure [127]. It gives bluish red shades of good fastness to light, washing and bleaching.

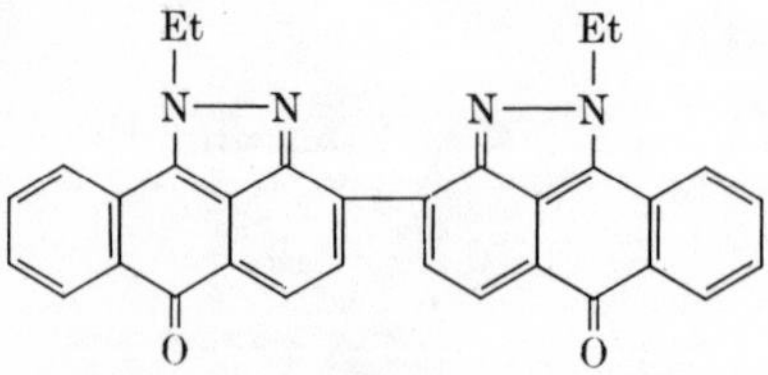

[127]

A more complex dye, said to contain residues of carbazole, acridine and benzanthrone in addition to pyrazole, is *Indanthren Grey M* (FH) (CI Vat Black 8; CI 71000). The main component

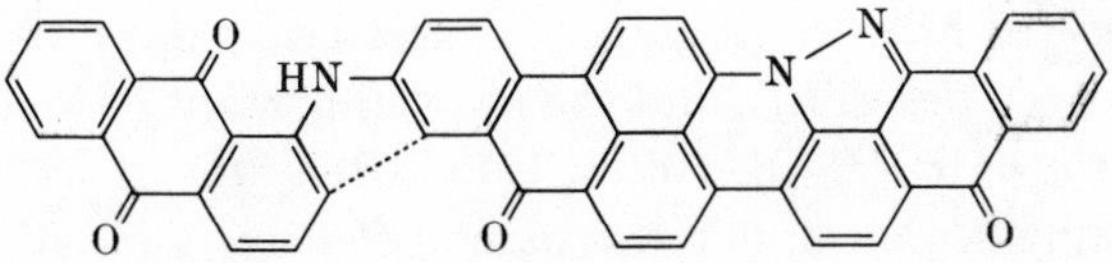

[128]

has been accorded the structure [128], but the existence of the
bond shown by a dotted line appears improbable.

Indanthren Grey M is manufactured by condensing 3,9-dibromo-
benzanthrone first with pyrazoloanthrone then with 1-amino-
anthraquinone, cyclising the product by means of alcoholic potash
then oxidising with air.[38] This dye gives bluish grey shades and has
good fastness properties.

Anthraquinone-oxazoles and -thiazoles. A useful dye of the
anthraquinoneoxazole class is *Indanthren Red FBB* (BASF) (CI
Vat Red 10; CI 67000), with the structure [129]. It is obtained by

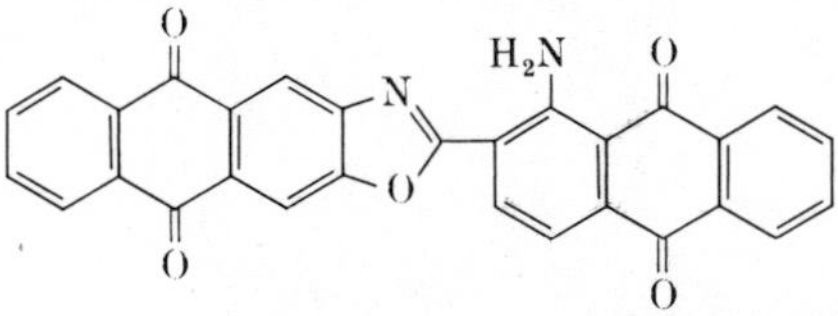

[129]

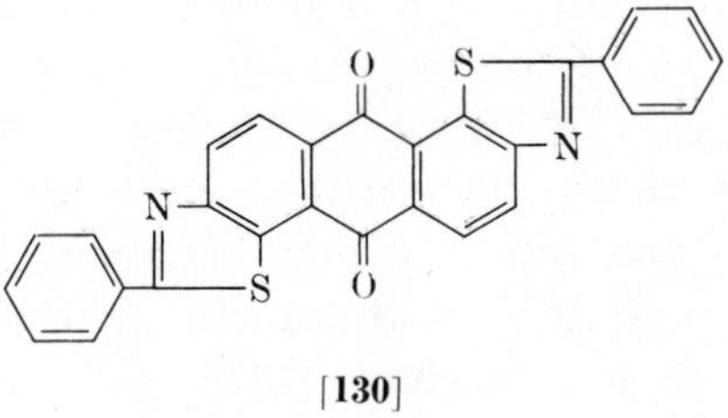

[130]

condensing 1-nitroanthraquinone-2-carbonyl chloride with 2-amino-
3-hydroxyanthraquinone, cyclising to the oxazole by means of
concentrated sulphuric acid and converting into the amine by reaction
with ammonia under pressure.[39] This dye gives bluish red shades
with good fastness properties.

The symmetrical bisthiazole derivative [130] is marketed as *Anthra
Yellow GC* (BASF) and many equivalent brands (CI Vat Yellow 2;
CI 67300). A convenient manufacturing process consists in condensing 2,6-diaminoanthraquinone with benzotrichloride and sulphur in
molten naphthalene in presence of cuprous chloride.[40] The dye gives
greenish yellow shades, but fastness to light is only moderately good
and exposure leads to marked tendering of the fibre. In spite of these
defects the product is extensively used, especially for bright greens
obtained in conjunction with Caledon Jade Green.

Other five-membered heterocyclic dyes. Several other dyes of this general type have been described, and the most important of them is *Indanthren Blue Green FFB* (BASF) (CI Vat Blue 7; CI 70305). This was first manufactured under the name *Cibanone Blue 3G* by SCI Basle in 1908 using a process depending on sulphurisation of 4-methylbenzanthrone. An improved process was later devised by IG in which benzanthrone-3-sulphinylacetic acid (obtained by oxidising the thioglycollic acid obtained from 3-bromobenzanthrone via the thiophenol) is heated with aqueous caustic potash, then oxidised with sodium hypochlorite. The dye has the structure [131].[41] It is chiefly used in textile printing, and gives dull greenish blue shades with good fastness to light but poor resistance to soda boiling and bleaching.

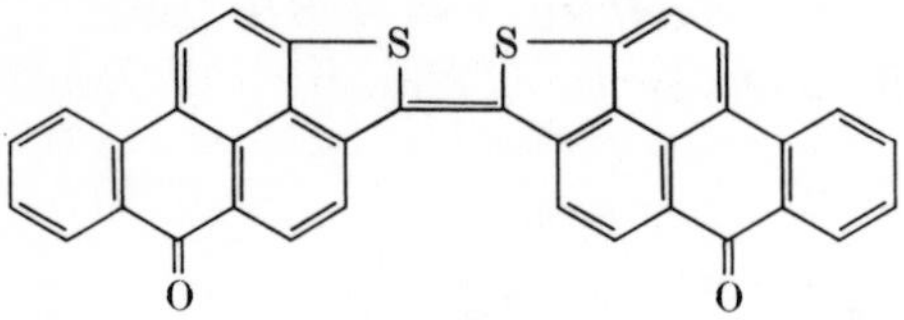

[131]

10-5-3 Six-membered heterocyclic dyes

Benzanthroneacridines. An important dye containing benzanthrone, anthraquinone and acridine residues is *Indanthren Olive Green B* (BASF) and its equivalents (CI Vat Green 3; CI 69500). It is made by condensing 3-bromobenzanthrone with 1-aminoanthraquinone in boiling naphthalene in presence of sodium carbonate and copper oxide, then cyclising by heating with caustic potash in isobutanol.[42] The product, with the structure [132], gives olive

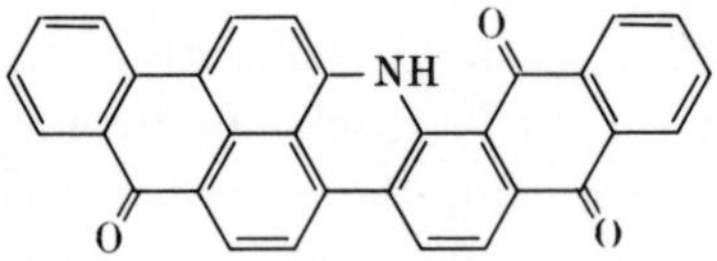

[132]

green shades with excellent all-round fastness properties and outstanding fastness to light (SDC grade 8 at standard depth).

A derivative of the dye just described containing a further anthraquinone residue is obtained by condensing 3,9-dibromodibenzanthrone with two molecular proportions of 1-aminoanthraquinone and then cyclising as before.[43] The resulting dye is *Indanthren Olive T* (CI Vat Black 25; CI 69525), with the structure [133]. Brownish grey shades are produced with outstandingly good fastness to light, and also good fastness to soda-boiling and chlorine.

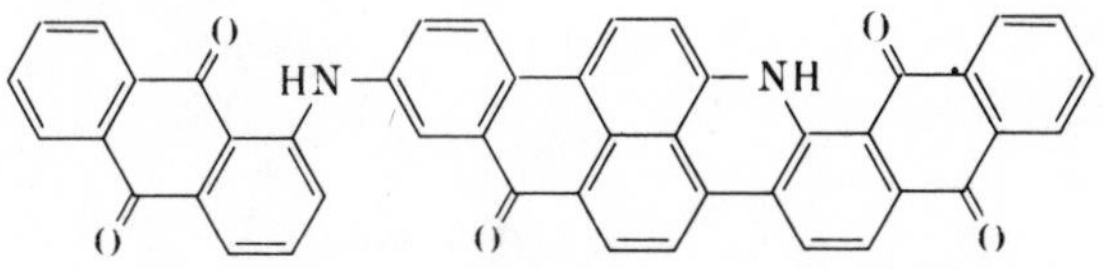

[133]

Anthraquinoneazines. The discovery of indanthrone by Bohn in 1901 has already been mentioned (Section 10-5), and this dye continues to be extensively used. It is marketed by BASF under the name *Indanthren Blue RS* (CI Vat Blue 4; CI 69800) and also by many other firms under their own brand names. The process used by Bohn is slightly modified in modern manufacture, and 2-amino-anthraquinone is usually fused with a mixture of caustic potash, caustic soda, sodium acetate and an oxidising agent such as sodium nitrate.[44] The product gives an attractive bright reddish blue shade with excellent fastness to light and washing; unfortunately resistance to bleaching is poor. This defect is avoided by dichlorinating the molecule, and the resulting dye, with the structure [**134**], is marketed as *Indanthren Blue BC* (BASF) (CI Vat Blue 6; CI 69825) and many equivalent brands. It gives a bright blue shade and has good all-round fastness properties, including fastness to hypochlorite.

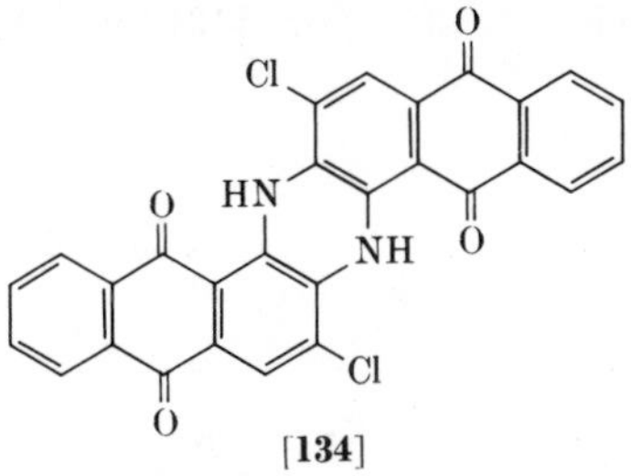

[134]

A monochloroindanthrone is sold as *Indanthren Blue GCD* (BASF), and there are many equivalent products (CI Vat Blue 14; CI 69810). It gives a bright blue shade with good fastness to light and washing, but poor fastness to bleaching; the dye is applied chiefly in textile printing (which is not followed by bleaching).

A dye of uncertain structure is manufactured by treating indanthrone with 100% sulphuric acid in presence of boric acid at 95°C;[45] it is believed to consist mainly of a hydroxyindanthrone. This product is sold as *Indanthren Brilliant Blue 3G* (BASF) and various equivalents (CI Vat Blue 12; CI 69840). It gives bright blue shades with good fastness to light but not to washing or bleaching, and is used chiefly for furnishing fabrics.

Pyrazinoanthraquinones. Dyes of this type were introduced by IG in 1936, and are exemplified by *Indanthren Brilliant Scarlet RK* (BASF) (CI Vat Red 40; CI 68300), with the structure [**135**].

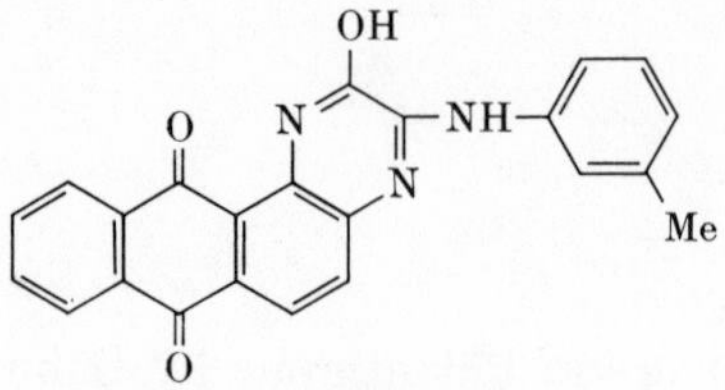

[135]

This dye is manufactured from 1,2-diaminoanthraquinone by heating it with oxalic acid at 150°C to form the dihydroxy-1,2-pyrazino-anthraquinone, purifying this and then condensing it with *m*-toluidine in presence of zinc chloride.[46] The shades obtained are bright red and have excellent fastness to light; the dyeings resist bleaching and are moderately fast to soda-boiling.

Flavanthrone. In the course of his work on the production of indanthrone by fusion of 2-aminoanthraquinone with caustic potash Bohn observed that if the reaction is carried out at 300°–350°C instead of the usual 220°–225°C, a yellow dye is formed in addition to the blue indanthrone. The yellow dye was produced commercially by heating 2-aminoanthraquinone with antimony pentachloride in nitrobenzene solution,[47] and was sold under the name *Flavanthrene*, and later *Indanthren Yellow G* (BASF). It structure [136] was later

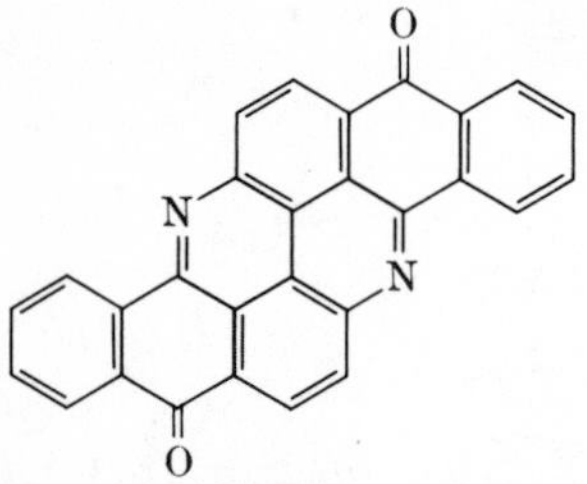

[136]

established by Scholl,[48] and it has been accorded the chemical name *flavanthrone*. Various processes have been devised for its production, and that used by IG consisted in (1) condensing 2-amino-1-chloro-anthraquinone with phthalic anhydride in trichlorobenzene medium in presence of a small quantity of ferric chloride, (2) refluxing the resulting 1-chloro-2-phthalimidoanthraquinone in dry trichloroben-zene in presence of copper powder to form 2,2′-diphthalimido-1,1′-dianthraquinonyl and (3) removing residual copper, then hydrolysing and cyclising in a single operation by boiling with aqueous caustic soda solution.[49] Flavanthrone is now sold under many brand names (CI Vat Yellow 1; CI 70600). It gives reddish yellow shades, and is extensively used in dyeing and printing applications. When used alone it is phototropic, but in mixtures with certain other vat dyes this characteristic is no longer apparent, and fastness to light is good. Flavanthrone is very easily reduced, but re-oxidation of the leuco compound is slow, and is usually brought about by use of acid dichromate or a peroxide. The dye has poor fastness to soda-boiling as a result of reduction by cellulose in alkaline medium. It differs from many other vat dyes, however, in that it does not promote tendering of cellulosic fibres on exposure to light.

In preparation of a flavanthrone vat it is necessary to reduce only one keto group, and this yields a blue leuco compound; further reduction gives a brown solution. The great ease of reduction has led to the use of filter-paper impregnated with flavanthrone as a general test for the condition of a vat, presence of free hydrosulphite being shown by the production of a blue colour when a drop of the solution is placed upon the paper.

Anthraquinoneacridones. About a dozen anthraquinone vat dyes containing an acridone ring are known. One of the more important of these is *Indanthren Red Violet RRK* (BASF) (CI Vat Violet 14; CI 67895), which consists mainly of the trichloro compound [**137**]. It may be obtained, for example, by chlorinating

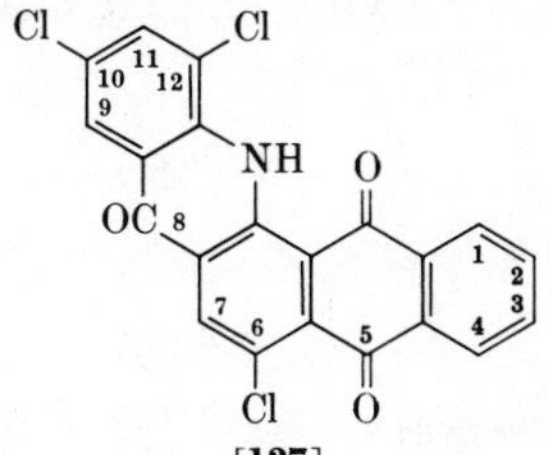

[**137**]

anthraquinone-1-(2′-carboxy)anilide with sulphuryl chloride in nitrobenzene medium in presence of iodine; chlorination and cyclisation take place in the same operation.[50] This dye gives reddish violet shades with exceptionally good fastness to light, but resistance to soda-boiling is poor; these properties render it suitable for furnishing fabrics. Various substituted derivatives of the structure are or have been used commercially. The effect on shade of introducing chlorine atoms in different positions in the benzene ring is remarkable, as shown by the following non-commercial examples:[51]

Positions of Cl	Shade
12 　,	Bluish red
9 and 12	Scarlet
9 and 11	Orange
10 and 11	Violet
9, 10 and 12	Scarlet
9, 11 and 12	Orange

A derivative of anthraquinone containing two acridone residues is *Indanthren Violet FFBN* (BASF) (CI Vat Violet 13; CI 68700) with the structure [138]. This is manufactured by condensing

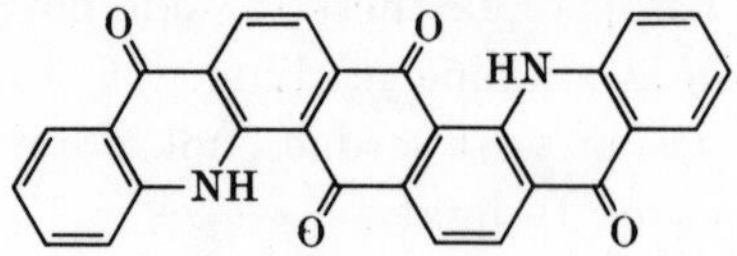

[138]

1,5-dichloroanthraquinone (1 mol.) with anthranilic acid (2 mol.) in aqueous isobutanol in presence of caustic potash, magnesium oxide and cupric oxide under pressure at 150°C, then cyclising the product by dissolving it in sulphuric acid monohydrate and stirring with chlorosulphonic acid at 20°–28°C.[52] The dye gives bluish violet shades, and is used for curtains, awnings, etc., also as a shading colour.

Anthrapyrimidines. Commercial dyes of this class (also known as pyrimidoanthrones) are not numerous and all give yellow shades. Examples are *Indanthren Yellows 7GK, 4GK* and *4GF* (BASF) (CI Vat Yellows 29, 31 and 20; CI 68400, CI 68405 and CI 68420 respectively), with the structures shown:

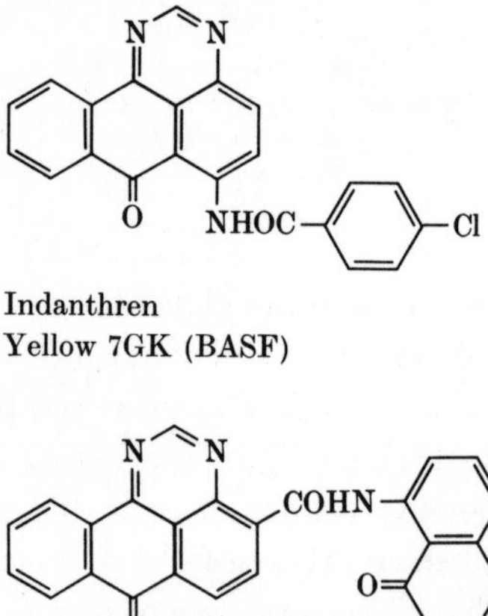

Indanthren
Yellow 7GK (BASF)

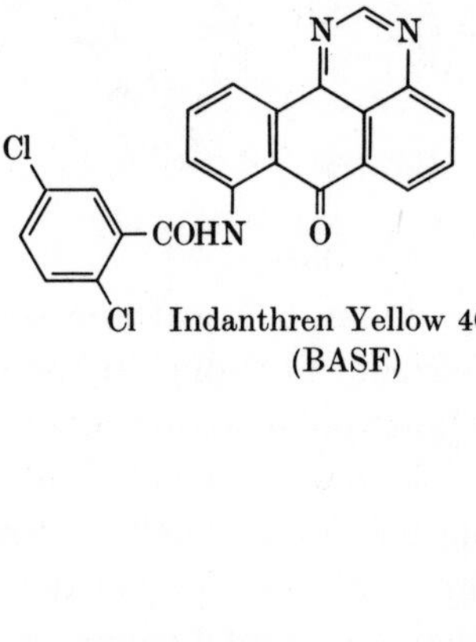

Indanthren Yellow 4GK
(BASF)

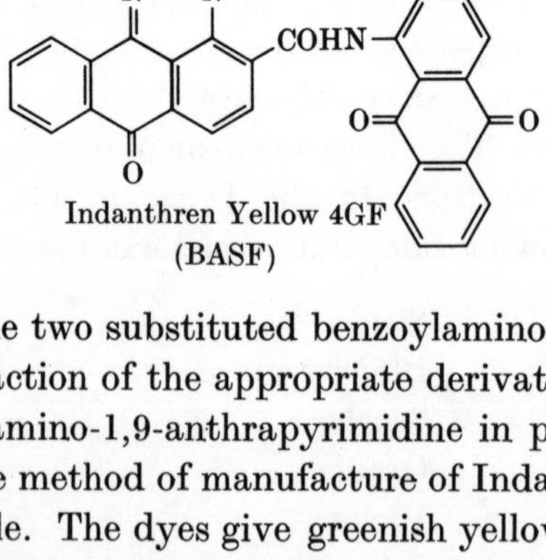

Indanthren Yellow 4GF
(BASF)

The two substituted benzoylamino derivatives are manufactured by reaction of the appropriate derivative of benzoyl chloride with 4- or 5-amino-1,9-anthrapyrimidine in presence of pyridine.[53] Details of the method of manufacture of Indanthren Yellow 4GF are not available. The dyes give greenish yellow shades of good fastness to light and bleaching, and are of value in that they do not cause tendering of cellulosic fibres on exposure to light.

10-5-4 Solubilised anthraquinone vat dyes

Solubilised forms of indigoid vat dyes have already been described in Section 10-1, and the important process devised by Morton Sundour Fabrics Ltd whereby the unreduced dyes are converted into sulphuric ester derivatives of their leuco compounds has been mentioned. This work, carried out in 1924, was primarily directed towards production of solubilised derivatives of anthraquinone dyes in which the firm was mainly interested. The process consists in treating the dye with a tertiary base such as pyridine, a metal such as copper, iron or zinc and sulphur trioxide or a suitable derivative such as chlorosulphonic acid or an alkyl chlorosulphonate; an intermediate compound is formed which yields the desired sodium salt of the disulphuric ester on treatment with caustic soda solution.[54] The reations may be represented as follows:

(1) $2 \left[\bigcirc C{=}O \right] + Cu + 2SO_3 + 2C_5H_5N \rightarrow$

$$\left[\bigcirc C{-}OSO_3 \right]_2 Cu \cdot C_5H_5N$$

(2) $\left[\bigcirc C{-}OSO_3 \right]_2 Cu \cdot C_5H_5N + 2NaOH \rightarrow 2 \left[\bigcirc C{-}OSO_3Na \right]$

$$+ CuO + 2C_5H_5N + H_2O$$

The water-soluble sulphuric ester salts were marketed as *Soledon* dyes by Scottish Dyes Ltd, and are now produced under the same name by ICI; many similar products are manufactured by other firms. The technical value of Soledon dyes depends largely on their low affinity for cellulose, which enables them to be applied by padding to give level pale shades.

The range of solubilised vat dyes is restricted to products for which the additional cost can be justified. Fewer than half of the dyes mentioned in this chapter are manufactured in solubilised form; these include CI Vat Yellows 2, 3, 4, CI Vat Oranges 1, 2, 3, 4, 9, 11, CI Vat Red 10, CI Vat Violet 1, CI Vat Blues 4, 6, 7, CI Vat Greens 1, 2, 3, CI Vat Browns 1, 3 and CI Vat Black 25. A typical example is CI Vat Green 1, with the structure [**139**].

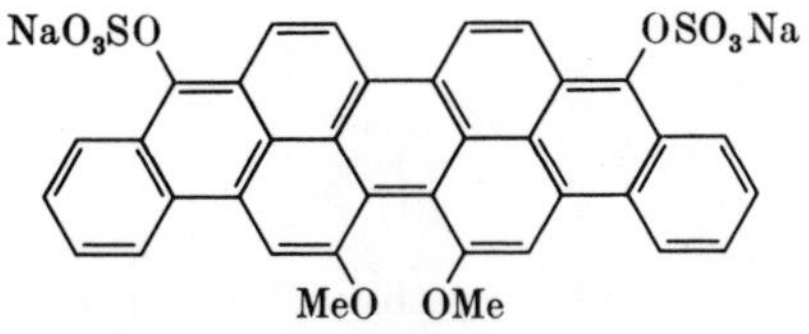

MeO   OMe

[**139**]

The dyes are applied to cellulosic fibres, and some of them are used to a small extent on wool, silk, nylon and acetate. Methods of application are in general similar to those already described for the Indigosol series (Section 10-1-1).

10-6 Other vat dyes

A few vat dyes not included in the chemical classes already referred to have attained commercial importance, and some examples of these are now described.

By condensing naphthalene-1,4,5,8-tetracarboxylic acid with o-phenylenediamine in acetic acid medium a mixture of isomeric perinone dyes with the structures [140] and [141] is obtained. The

[140]   [141]

mixture is marketed as *Indanthren Scarlet GG* (FH) (CI Vat Red 14; CI 71110), and gives dull yellowish red shades of good fastness to light. By heating the mixture with alcoholic potash the components can be separated, the potassium salt of [141] remaining in suspension whilst that of [140] passes into solution. The undissolved fraction is easily hydrolysed with water, and the resulting *trans* isomer is sold as *Indanthren Brilliant Orange GR* (FH) (CI Vat Orange 7; CI 71105).[55] It gives bright reddish orange shades with good fastness to light (SDC grade 6 at standard depth). The *cis* isomer recovered from the filtrate and hydrolysed with dilute acid is sold as *Indanthren Bordeaux RR* (FH) (CI Vat Red 15; CI 71100). It gives deep red shades, and although it is less important than the orange isomer this dye is of some interest for application to furnishing fabrics, awnings and the like.

Several imides of perylene-3,4,9,10-tetracarboxylic acid are manufactured as vat dyes. An example is *Indanthren Red GG* (BASF) (CI Vat Red 23; CI 71130), with the structure [142].

[142]

This dye is obtained by caustic fusion of *N*-methylnaphthalimide.[56] It gives dull yellowish red shades, and is used for furnishing fabrics.

10-7 Recent developments

Many new vat dyes have been described in the patent literature, but additions to manufactured ranges are now rather infrequent. New dyes are often built from structures of known types, and in the absence of commercial examples appraisal of the technical merits of such products is a speculative exercise for which space cannot be devoted here. However, mention may be made of a few publications describing the application of new principles.

A polymeric vat dye has been obtained by condensation of 5,5'-bi-isatyl with thiophene. It has been assigned the structure [143], and gives deep blue shades on cotton or linen.[57] It is not clear whether any technical advantage is shown.

[143]

Many vat dyes containing a system capable of reaction with cellulosic fibres have been described by CIBA.[58] The reactive groups include mono- and di-chlorotriazinyl types, also many sulphur-linked structures such as $-SO_2NH(CH_2)_4OSO_3Na$, $-SO_2NHCH_2CH_2Cl$, $-SO_2NHCH_2CH_2SSO_3Na$, $-SO_2NHCH_2CH_2-OSO_3Na$, $-SCH_2CH=CH_2$, $-SO_2CH_2CH=CH_2$ and $-SO_2-CH_2CH_2Cl$. These systems were originally developed for the anionic dyes described in Chapter 13, and an account of their chemistry is given there. It will be noticed that some of the systems contain solubilising groups which are lost on reaction with the fibre; these promote ease of vatting. As evidence of fibre-reaction it has been shown in many cases that the dyes are not removed from the fibre by means of hot dimethylformamide, whereas non-reactive vat dyes are readily extracted. Apparently the reactive groups are not removed in the vat. It might be thought that since conventional vat dyes have in general excellent wet-fastness properties there is not much to be gained by introducing fibre-reactivity. It is stated, however, that an improvement in resistance to dry-cleaning results.

In the application of reactive dyes a small proportion of the dye reacts with water instead of the substrate, and this unfixed dye must be removed for maximum wet-fastness. In the case of the usual insoluble vat dyes this is difficult, but sulphonated reactive vat dyes such as [144] have been described,[59] and presumably hydrolysed portions of these can be washed out of the fibre.

In recent years certain firms have devoted much attention to the study of non-reactive anthraquinone vat dyes containing sulphonic acid groups.[60] Many of these dyes are readily soluble in water, and can indeed by applied by direct dyeing, but the vat process is preferred. Sulphonic acid groups are sometimes eliminated during vatting, and when this is so their main function is to facilitate the preparation of the vat. The sulphonated dyes are said to have

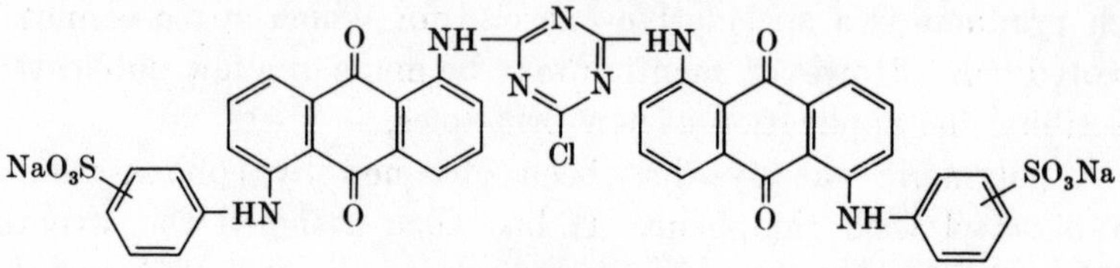

[144]

advantages in ease of penetration and good levelling properties, and wet-fastness properties on the fibre are described as excellent. If sulphonic acid groups remain after application the advantage of the vat process in providing temporary solubilisation appears to have been partially abandoned, but the system may be valuable as a means of temporarily increasing the solubility of sparingly soluble dyes, of promoting resistance to dry-cleaning solvents or of providing dyes for application to union fabrics.

The technical merits of sulphonated vat dyes remain at present in some doubt. So far as is known neither reactive vat dyes nor sulphonated vat dyes have yet been produced commercially.

Sulphur dyes

Although dyes of the sulphur class are used in substantial quantities, there appears to be no justification for providing more than a brief description here. In spite of their long history little is known about the chemical structure of these dyes. In recent years their importance has declined, and little needs to be added to the excellent accounts published during the period 1950–1958 (see Bibliography).

The first commercial sulphur dye was made in France by Croissant and Bretonnière in 1873. These workers prepared brown dyes for cotton by heating a variety of organic materials of animal or vegetable origin with aqueous sodium sulphide or polysulphide. They also used slightly more complex processes in which the initial products were baked at temperatures above 200°C; the shade obtained could often be varied by adjusting the temperature and duration of heating.[1] Of the many dyes examined the only one that attained importance was *Cachou de Laval*, obtained by heating sawdust with sodium sulphide. It was manufactured by several firms for many years, and is still included in the Colour Index (CI Sulphur Brown 1; CI 53000). It may be applied to cotton from a sodium sulphide bath and fixed on the fibre by aftertreatment with aqueous potassium dichromate; the resulting shades vary from yellowish brown to brownish olive.

It was not until 1893 that a sulphur dye was made from intermediates of known structure. The sulphurisation process was then applied by Vidal to a great variety of organic substances, and dyes were obtained that could be fixed on cotton by oxidation.[2] The most important of these was *Vidal Black* (CI Sulphur Black 3; CI 53180), obtained from *p*-aminophenol or *p*-phenylenediamine by means of a sulphur melt. In 1897 a better black sulphur dye was manufactured by heating 4-hydroxy-2′,4′-dinitrodiphenylamine with sodium polysulphide, and this was marketed by Cassella as *Immedial Black V* (CI Sulphur Black 9; CI 53230). Two years later a further improvement was obtained by sulphurisation of the cheap intermediate 2,4-dinitrophenol, and the resulting dye was produced by AGFA as *Sulphur Black T* (CI Sulphur Black 1;

183

Table 11-1   Examples of important commercial sulphur dyes

CI Generic Name	CI Constitution No.	Commercial name	Intermediates	Outline of manufacturing process
CI Sulphur Yellow 2	CI 53120	Eclipse Yellow G (Gy)	N,N'-Diformyl-m-tolylene-diamine + benzidine	Heat with sulphur at 140°–150°C and raise during 15 hr to 218°–220°C (ref. 3)
CI Sulphur Yellow 4	CI 53160	Immedial Yellow GG (Cassella)	2-(p-Amino-phenyl)-6-methylbenzo-thiazole + benzidine	Heat with sulphur at 190°–220°C then reflux with aq. NaOH and oxidise with air. (ref. 4)
CI Sulphur Orange 1	CI 53050	Immedial Orange C Extra (Cassella)	m-Tolylene-diamine	Heat with sulphur at 215°–220°C, then treat with NaOH (ref. 5)
CI Sulphur Red 6	CI 53720	Immedial Red Brown 3B Extra (Cassella)	3-Amino-2-methyl-6-hydroxy-phenazine	Heat with sodium polysulphide at 115°–116°C (ref. 6)
CI Sulphur Blue 7	CI 53440	Immedial Indone RR Extra (Cassella)	4-Amino-4'-hydroxy-3-methyldi-phenylamine	Heat with aq. sodium poly-sulphide at 106°–112°C, then oxidise with air (ref. 7)
CI Sulphur Green 3	CI 53570	Thional Brilliant Green 3G (S)	8-Phenylamino-5-p-hydroxy-phenylamino-naphthalene-1-sulphonic acid	Reflux with aq. sodium poly-sulphide in presence of $CuSO_4$, then oxidise with air (ref. 8)
CI Sulphur Brown 10	CI 53055	Immedial Yellow Brown G (Cassella)	m-Tolylene-diamine	Heat with sulphur at 210° rising to 250°C. Dissolve the product in aq. Na_2S + NaOH, heat at 240° and evaporate (ref. 9)
CI Sulphur Black 1	CI 53185	Immedial Black AT (Cassella) and many other brands	2,4-Dinitro-phenol or 2,4-dichloronitro-benzene	Heat with aq. sodium poly-sulphide under reflux (110°–120°C), dilute and oxidise with air (ref. 10)

CI 53185). Many equivalent products were made by other firms, and the dye is still of importance. It gives blacks of good fastness to washing and light.

During the years 1897–1902 a great deal of experimental work was carried out on sulphur dyes, and every available intermediate was subjected to sulphurisation. This work led to an extensive patent literature and the manufacture of many competing ranges of dyes. An almost complete range of shades was produced, lacking a true red, however. After 1902 the rate of expansion of this field slackened, but the occasional introduction of new dyes continued until the 1950s. Table 11-1 gives details of some of the more important sulphur dyes.

Since so little is known of their structures, sulphur dyes are usually classified according to the chemistry of their starting materials. The manufacturing processes are chiefly of three types:

1 A dry mixture of the organic starting material (or materials) with sulphur is heated (the temperature usually exceeding 200°C).
2 As 1, but using sodium polysulphide instead of sulphur. The baking temperature varies widely.
3 The starting material is heated with aqueous sodium polysulphide, either under reflux or in a closed vessel under pressure. Some or all of the water may be replaced by butanol.

The shade and properties of the resulting dyes may vary considerably with the reaction temperature and duration of heating. In all cases hydrogen sulphide is evolved during reaction and it is absorbed in aqueous caustic soda. The dyes are usually isolated from alkaline solution by air oxidation. Many of them are subject to deterioration during prolonged storage.

The chemistry of sulphur dyes has been studied by many workers, and although it has not been possible to assign definite structures the presence in certain dyes of chromophoric systems of the thiazole

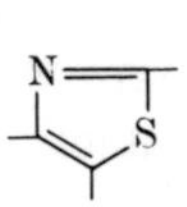

[145] 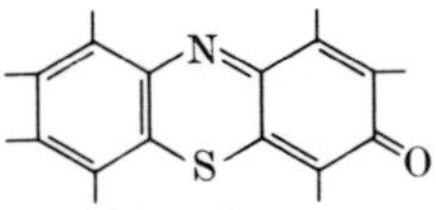   [146] 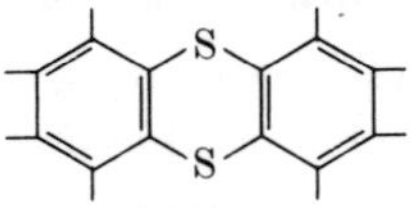   [147]

[145], thiazone [146] and thianthrene [147] types has been established.[11] These and other aromatic nuclei are linked by disulphide or disulphoxide bridges which are broken on treatment with sodium sulphide with formation of —SNa groups, and on reoxidation the disulphide bridges are re-formed on the fibre.

The properties of sulphur dyes are intermediate between those of direct dyes and vat dyes. As already stated, reds are poorly represented, only dull bordeaux shades being available. Other hues are plentiful, but almost all sulphur dyes are somewhat dull. Wet-fastness properties are usually good, but resistance to bleaching is poor. With some notable exceptions, as in Sulphur Black T and its equivalents, light-fastness is only fair or moderate (rarely exceeding SDC grade 5). The great demand for sulphur dyes is due to their moderately good properties and low cost. They are applied almost exclusively to cellulosic fibres, the alkaline bath required being unsuitable for wool and silk. The process consists in dissolving the dye in a solution of sodium sulphide, whereby it is reduced to a leuco compound with affinity for the fibre, carrying out dyeing just below the boil, then exposing the dyed material to air so that oxidation and development of the shade take place. Sometimes the dyeings are aftertreated with a mixture of a dichromate and copper sulphate for improvement in fastness to light and wet treatments, but this is liable to result in tendering of the fibre by slow liberation of sulphuric acid. Cotton dyed with sulphur colours acquires affinity for basic dyes, and these are sometimes applied as 'topping' colours in order to brighten the shades. Sulphur blacks can also be topped with Aniline Black (see Section 8-8) to give very deep black shades with increased fastness to milling.

A bright green sulphur dye with excellent fastness properties was formerly included in the ICI range under the name *Thionol Ultra Green B* (CI Sulphur Green 14). It was a derivative of copper phthalocyanine containing thiocyano groups which gave a water-soluble mercaptide on reduction with sodium sulphide.[12] Cotton dyed with this leuco compound is grey, but oxidation in air yields a bright green shade with very good fastness to light, washing and chlorine. With the advent of green reactive dyes (see Chapter 13) this product has been superseded.

11-1 Sulphurised vat dyes

The sulphurised vat dyes form a small but important group of products which resemble sulphur dyes in that they are manufactured by sulphurisation processes but they are applied from a hydro-sulphite vat in the manner of vat dyes. The first of these was introduced by Cassella in 1909 under the name *Hydron Blue R* (CI Vat Blue 43; CI 53630). It is obtained by condensing *p*-nitrosophenol with carbazole in sulphuric acid medium to form the indophenol

[148]

[148] and refluxing this (or its leuco compound) with sodium polysulphide in butanol.[13] This dye gives reddish blue shades, and is valuable in that it has better fastness properties than most blue sulphur dyes and is used as an inexpensive substitute for indigo. It cannot be completely reduced by sodium sulphide, and a vat is usually prepared by using a mixture of sodium sulphide and hydrosulphite.

A greener blue is manufactured similarly by sulphurisation of the indophenol obtained from *N*-ethylcarbazole and *p*-nitrosophenol; this is *Hydron Blue G* (Cassella) (CI Vat Blue 42; CI 53640). Several related dyes have been made by modified processes and by using mixtures of indophenols.

Attempts have been made to assign a constitution to Hydron Blue R but its structure has not been firmly established.[14]

11-2   Ready-reduced and solubilised sulphur dyes

Many sulphur dyes have been manufactured in a reduced or partly reduced form and supplied either as solutions or powders which easily dissolve in the dyebath with a small amount of sodium sulphide.

Sulphur dyes are also solubilised in the unreduced state by introducing thiosulphonic acid groups, and the resulting derivatives give clear stable aqueous solutions. They lack substantivity for cellulose until they have been reduced, but show advantages in freedom from insoluble matter (especially important in package dyeing), better control during application and superior levelling properties. By application of such products to the fibre from a sodium sulphide bath and exposure to air dyeings are obtained with the same properties as those of the corresponding conventional sulphur dyes.

11-3   Recent developments

The *Inthion* (FH) and *Dykolite* (Southern Dyestuff Co.) ranges are sometimes regarded as sulphur dyes, but as their properties differ in several respects from those of sulphur dyes they are treated separately (Chapter 14).

12 Miscellaneous dyes

Dyes of the chemical classes to which this chapter is devoted are not numerous, but they include some products of commercial importance.

12-1 Amino- and hydroxy-ketone dyes

These dyes contain a chromophoric system based on the carbonyl group with an amino, substituted amino or hydroxyl group as auxochrome. They are mostly vat dyes but include some acid, mordant and disperse dyes. An example is *Helindon Yellow CG* (FH) (CI Vat Yellow 5; CI 56005) [149], which is obtained by condensation

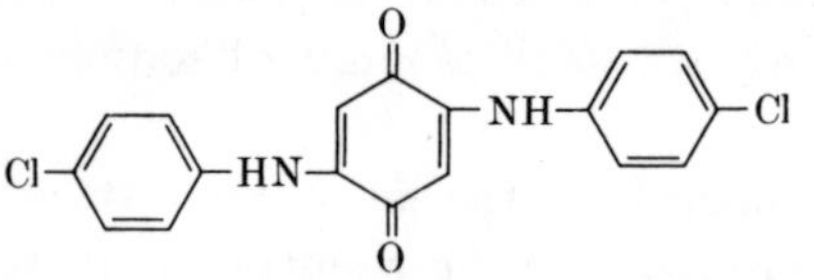

[149]

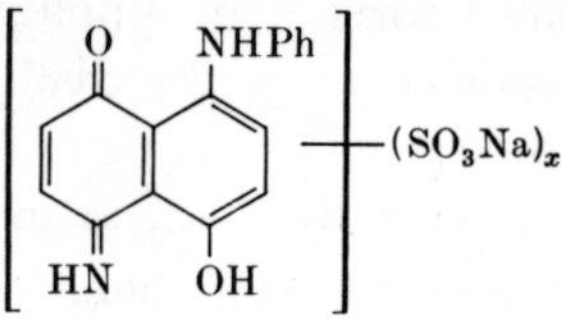

[150]

of benzoquinone with *p*-chloroaniline in presence of manganese acetate and oxidation with a dichromate.[1] It gives dull brownish yellow shades with good fastness properties, and is used in the dyeing of woollen material for military uniforms.

An example of an acid dye of this class is *Acid Alizarine Grey G* (FH) (CI Acid Black 47; CI 56055), with the structure [150]. It is obtained by condensing 8-amino-5-hydroxy-1,4-naphthoquinone imine with aniline and sulphonating the product.[2] Bluish grey shades are produced on wool, silk or nylon by dyeing or printing

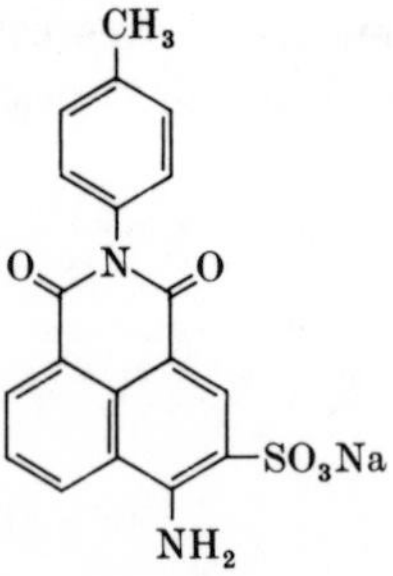

[151]

methods. Several aminophthalimide dyes are in commercial use, for example *Brilliant Sulpho Flavine FF* (FH) CI Acid Yellow 7; CI 56205). This is manufactured by condensing 4-amino-3-sulpho-naphthalic anhydride with *p*-toluidine,[3] and has the structure [**151**]. It gives bright greenish yellow fluorescent shades on wool, silk or nylon, but its use is restricted by poor fastness to light and wet treatments.

Several hydroxyketone dyes were formerly manufactured, but only one now remains, and it is produced on the fibre by applying the colourless intermediate chromotropic acid (1,8-dihydroxynaph-thalene-3,6-disulphonic acid) to wool and aftertreating with a dichromate. According to the Colour Index, 8-hydroxy-1,4-naphthoquinone-6-sulphonic acid is formed on the fibre and this is converted into a chromium derivative. Reddish brown shades are obtained with good fastness to light and wet treatments. The intermediate is marketed under various names (CI Mordant Brown 7; CI 57030).

Logwood is included in this chemical class, and is one of the few natural dyes still widely used (see Section 1-3).

12-2   Indamine and indophenol dyes

This class consists of derivatives of benzoquinone mono- or di-imine:

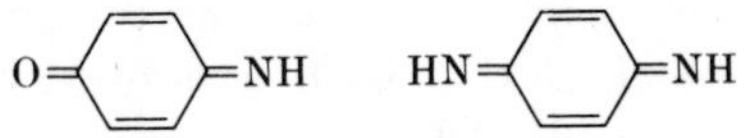

or corresponding naphthalene compounds. An early example was *Bindschedler's Green* (CI 49405):

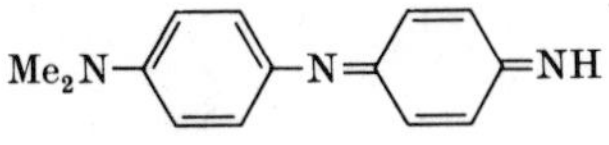

Bindschedler's Green

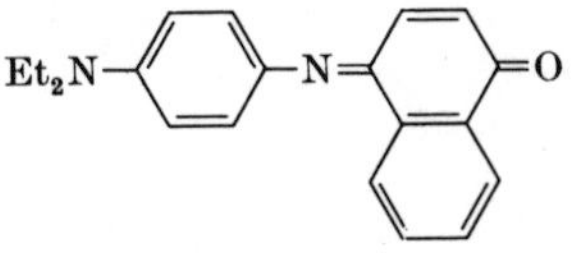

[**152**]

but this is no longer in use. Dyes of these classes are not now used for textile coloration, but they are applied in colour photography and also serve as intermediates for sulphur dyes (Chapter 11). *Fat Blue Z* (FH) (CI Solvent Blue 22; CI 49705), with the structure [**152**], is used for colouring spirit lacquers, fats and waxes. It is obtained by oxidising a mixture of *N,N*-diethyl-*p*-phenylenediamine and α-naphthol in alkaline solution.

12-3 Methine and polymethine dyes

Methine and Polymethine dyes are characterised by the presence of a chromophoric system containing an acyclic link or chain with a structure $-\overset{|}{C}(=\overset{|}{C}-\overset{|}{C})_n=$ (where $n=0$ or an integer) or $(-\overset{|}{C}=\overset{|}{C}-)_n$ (where n is an integer). The *cyanine* dyes form an important class of methine dyes with links or chains of the first type containing an odd number of carbon atoms attached to two basic heterocyclic residues.

The first cyanine dye was discovered by Greville Williams in 1856 (the year in which W. H. Perkin discovered mauveine, the first commercial synthetic dye). Williams heated crude quinoline, containing lepidine, with isoamyl iodide and caustic soda and obtained a blue dye which he called *Cyanine*.[4] It was later shown to have the structure [153].[5] The fastness properties of cyanine are

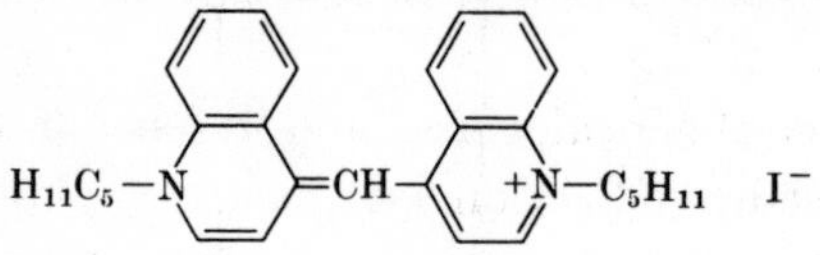

$$H_{11}C_5-N \bigg\rangle\!\!=\!\!CH- \bigg\langle\; ^+N-C_5H_{11} \quad I^-$$

[153]

poor, but in 1875 Vogel found that it has photosensitising properties. Whereas his photographic plates in the undyed state were sensitive to blue light only, after treatment with cyanine the plates became sensitive also to green light.[6] Unfortunately cyanine caused fogging of the plates, but later isocyanines such as that with structure [154] were found to be of practical value.[7] In 1905 König discovered *Pinacyanol* [155], and this blue dye was the first sensitiser to red

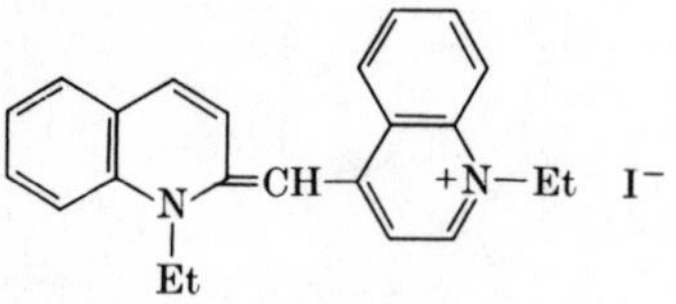

$$\underset{Et}{N}\!\!=\!\!CH- \;^+N-Et \quad I^-$$

[154]

$$\underset{Et}{N}\!\!=\!\!CH-CH\!\!=\!\!CH- \;^+\underset{Et}{N} \quad I^-$$

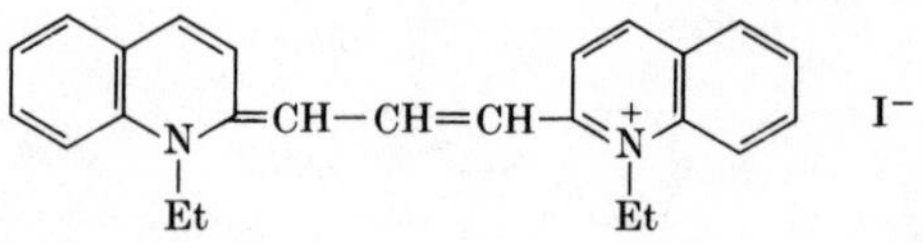

[155]

light; it is obtained by condensing quinaldine ethiodide with formaldehyde[8] or with ethyl orthoformate in acetic anhydride solution.[9]

As a result of their photosensitising properties, the cyanine dyes attracted much interest, and a rough measure of the amount of work devoted to them is given by the 790 pages contained in the principal reference work in which it is described.[10] It is not possible to provide an adequate summary in the space available here.

For many years methine dyes were considered of no interest for textile application. In 1935, however, IG introduced several disperse dyes of this class, obtained by condensing p-substituted benzaldehyde derivatives with ethyl cyanoacetate in presence of piperidine.[11] One of the best of these was *Celliton Fast Yellow 7G* (IG) [**156**],

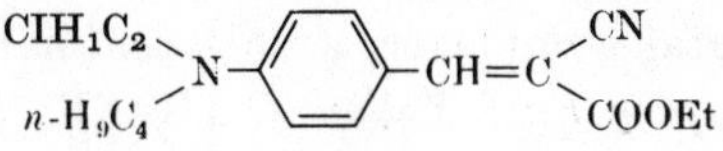

[**156**]

now manufactured by other firms under their own brand names (CI Disperse Yellow 31; CI 48000). This dye is applied to acetate or nylon and gives greenish yellow shades with good fastness to light, burnt gas fumes and hot pressing. Afterwards the *Astrazon* range was introduced by IG for application to acetate, and a similarly named range was later marketed by Bayer, mainly for polyacryloni-trile fibres. The structures of some members of this range are given in Table 8–1 (p. 134). It will be seen that the range includes poly-methine dyes of various types and also representatives of other chemical classes.

12-4   Azamethine dyes

Azamethine dyes correspond to methine dyes in which at least one —CH= group is replaced by —N=. Azacyanine dyes in which two heterocyclic nuclei were linked by nitrogen were first prepared by Diepolder and his co-workers[12] in 1923, and shortly afterwards similar dyes were described by Hamer.[13] In the azamethincyanine dye [**157**] replacement of —CH= by —N= has resulted in a hypso-chromic effect. $\alpha:\beta$-Diazatrimethincyanine dyes such as [**158**]

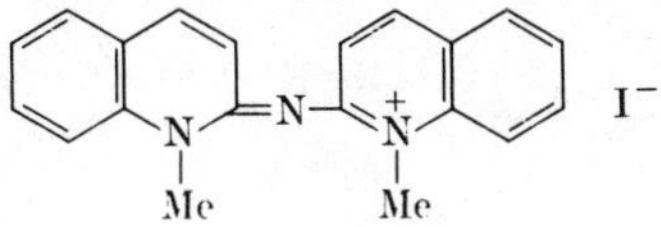

[**157**] 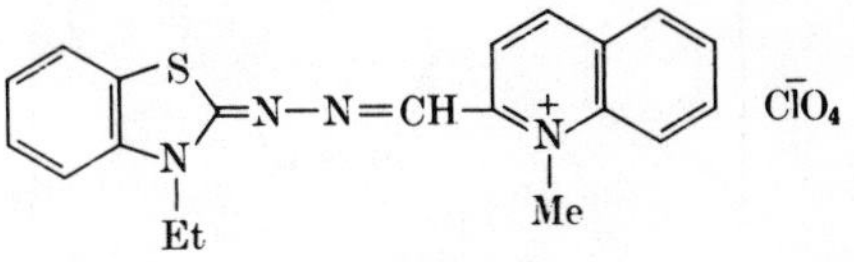   [**158**]

were described by Fuchs and Grauaug[14] in 1928, and related com-pounds were examined by Fisher and Hamer in 1937; some of these dyes are photographic desensitisers. Fisher and Hamer found that when =CH—CH=CH— is replaced by =N—CH=N— or =N—N=CH— in analogues of the dye [**159**] a hypsochromic shift results; it is much greater in the $\alpha:\gamma$ than in the $\alpha:\beta$ iosomer.[15] $\alpha:\gamma$-Diazatrimethincyanines, such as [**160**], were prepared by Kendall, and were found to have a sensitising action on silver chloride emulsions to about 4,200 Å.[16]

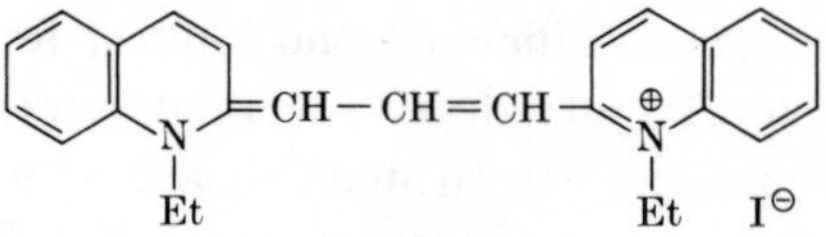

[159]

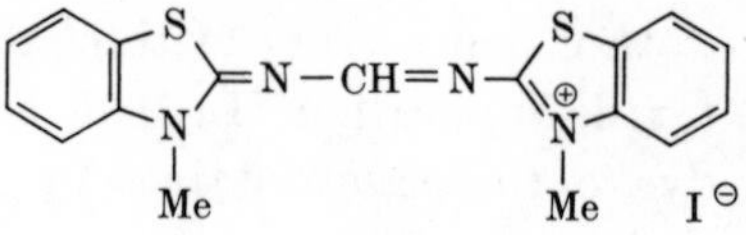

[160]

Interest in azamethine dyes was initially confined to their photographic applications, but metal complexes were later manufactured as colouring matters. *Zapon Fast Yellow G* (BASF) (CI Solvent Yellow 32; CI 48045) has the structure [161], and is obtained by condensing salicylaldehyde with 4-nitro 2-aminophenol-6-sulphonic acid and converting the product into its chromium complex.[17] It gives bright greenish yellow shades in nitrocellulose lacquers and has various uses as a colorant for solvents and stereo inks. A range of *Perlon Fast* dyes planned by IG included *Perlon Fast Yellow RS* (CI 48050),* which was the 1:2 chromium complex of the dye [162] (obtained by condensing 3,5-dichlorosalicylaldehyde with 2-amino-phenol-4-sulphonamide).[18]

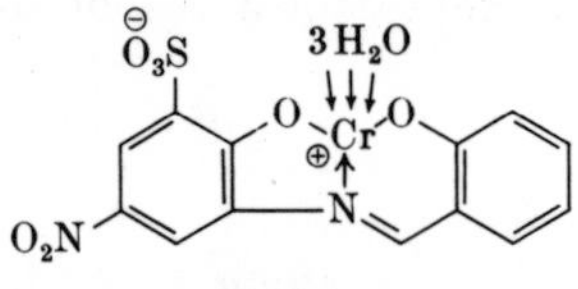

[161]

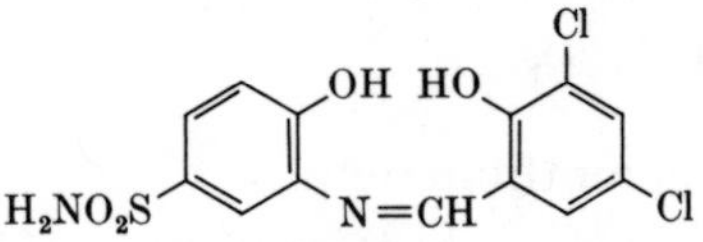

[162]

Unsymmetrical α:β-diazatrimethine dyes suitable for application to polyacrylonitrile fibres have been described in numerous patent specifications. Thus dyes with structures [163] and [164] are said to

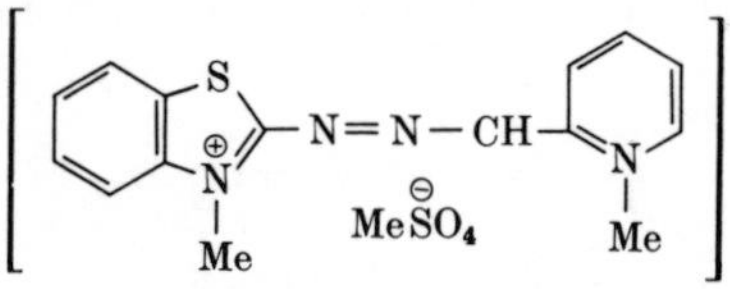

[163]

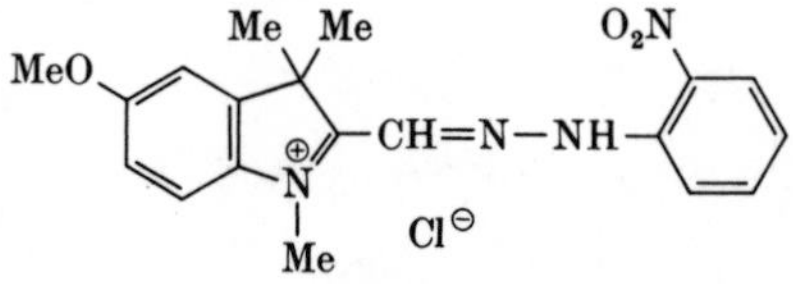

[164]

give reddish yellow shades upon such fibres.[19] An interesting study of the application of azatrimethincyanine dyes to polyacrylonitrile fibres has been reported by Voltz[20] in which it was observed that symmetrical dyes containing heterocyclic nuclei linked by azamethine chains —N=CH—CH=, —CH=N—CH=, —CH=N—N=, —N=CH—N= and —N=N—N= showed improved light-fastness with increasing substitution of methine groups by nitrogen atoms.

---

* Perlon is a German trademark relating to Nylon 6.

12-5   Nitro dyes

A nitro group may be present in dyes of almost any chemical class and is not usually an essential part of the main chromophoric system. In a few dyes, however, the nitro group is the only chromophore. A hydroxyl or amino group is then invariably present as auxochrome, and resonance between two or more tautomeric forms gives rise to colour; o-nitrophenol serves as a simple model of such a system, its salts being strongly coloured:

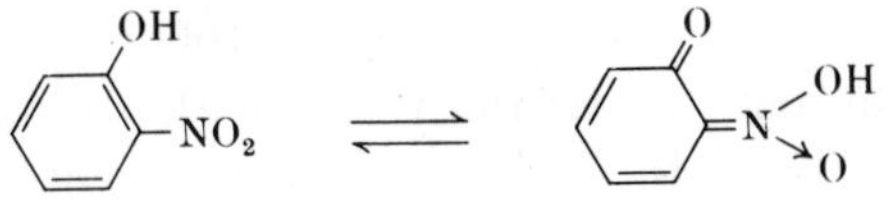

The first commercial nitro dye was picric acid (CI 10305), formerly used as an acid dye giving greenish yellow shades on silk. It was abandoned many years ago because of its toxicity and low fastness properties. Another early nitro dye was *Martius Yellow* (CI Acid Yellow 24; CI 10315); it is an ammonium, sodium or calcium salt of 2,4-dinitro-1-naphthol, but is now seldom used. *Naphthol Yellow S* (CI Acid Yellow 1; CI 10316), discovered by Caro in 1879, however, is still used in spite of very poor fastness properties. It consists of the sodium or potassium salt of 2,4-dinitro-1-naphthol-7-sulphonic acid. An acid dye of a different type is *Amido Yellow E* (CI Acid Orange 3; CI 10385), introduced by MLB in 1911 and now made by many firms. This has the structure [165], and is obtained by

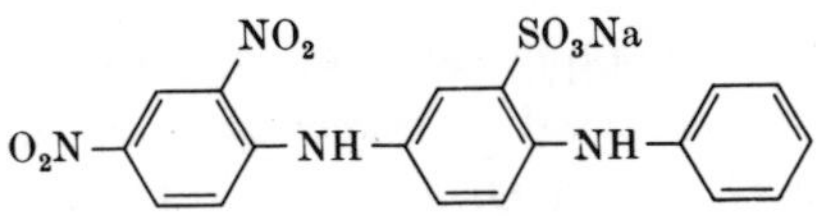

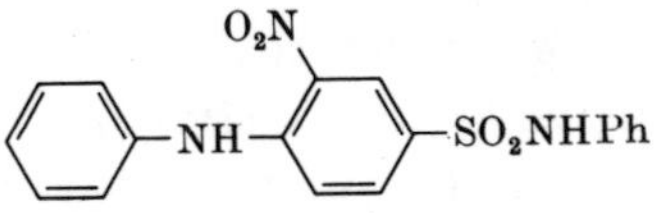

condensing 1-chloro-2,4-dinitrobenzene with 4-aminodiphenylamine-2-sulphonic acid.[21] It gives dull yellowish orange shades with good fastness to light but poor fastness to washing.

A disperse dye of the diphenylamine series which was one of the early acetate dyes introduced by British Celanese Ltd in 1923 and now made by many firms is CI Disperse Yellow 1 (CI 10345). It has the constitution 4-hydroxy-2',4'-dinitrodiphenylamine, and is obtained by condensing 1-chloro-2,4-dinitrobenzene with p-amino-phenol.[22] Reddish yellow shades are produced on acetate, nylon or acrylic fibres. A disperse dye introduced more recently (but long known as a compound) is *Dispersol Fast Yellow T* (ICI) (CI Disperse Yellow 42; CI 10338). This has the structure [166] and is obtained by condensing 4-chloro-3-nitrobenzene-1-sulphonyl chloride with two molecular proportions of aniline.[23] It gives greenish yellow shades on acetate or polyamide fibres, or bright yellow on polyester, with good fastness to light and wet treatments.

12-6   Nitroso dyes

A few green dyes of the nitroso class are of importance. A mordant dye discovered by Fuchs[24] in 1875 is obtained by nitrosating β-naphthol in the 1 position and converting the product into its bisulphite derivative. This dye, sold as *Fast Printing Green S* (ICI) and also under other names (CI Mordant Green 4; CI 10005), gives brownish olive shades on a chromium mordant or yellowish green on iron; it is dyed on cotton or applied by printing on cotton, wool and silk. By treating the dye just described with ferrous sulphate, then with caustic soda, a complex derivative with the structure [167] is obtained.[25] This is an important pigment sold as *Pigment Green B* (BASF) and also under other names (CI Pigment Green 8; CI 10006). It gives yellowish green shades and has good general fastness properties; the applications of this product are diverse.

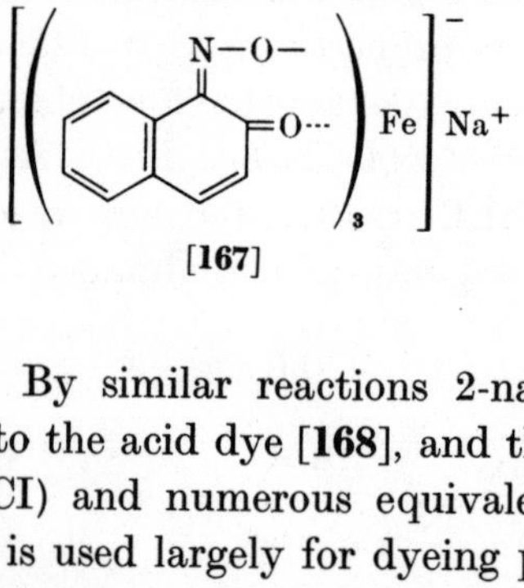

[167] 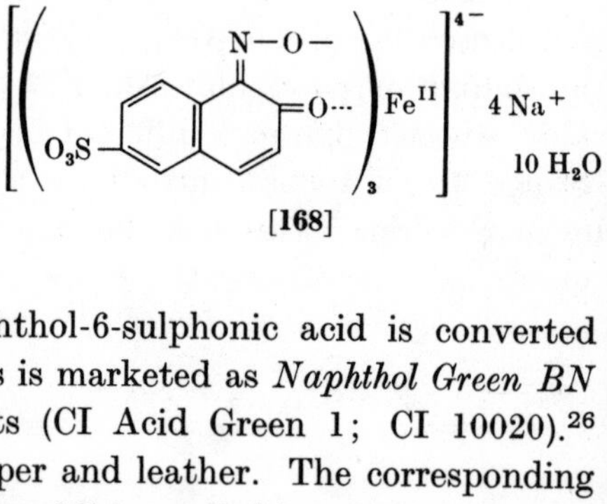   [168]

By similar reactions 2-naphthol-6-sulphonic acid is converted into the acid dye [168], and this is marketed as *Naphthol Green BN* (ICI) and numerous equivalents (CI Acid Green 1; CI 10020).[26] It is used largely for dyeing paper and leather. The corresponding barium iron salt (CI Pigment Green 12) is applied in printing inks and lacquers.

12-7   Quinoline dyes

The quinoline dyes form a small class containing various derivatives of quinophthalone [2-(2-quinolyl)-1,3-indandione]. The parent compound [169] (R = H) is obtained by condensing quinaldine with

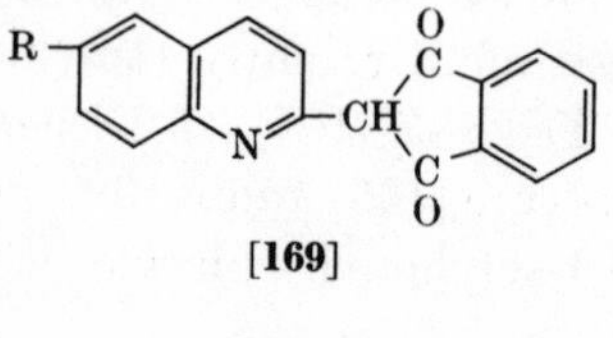

[169] 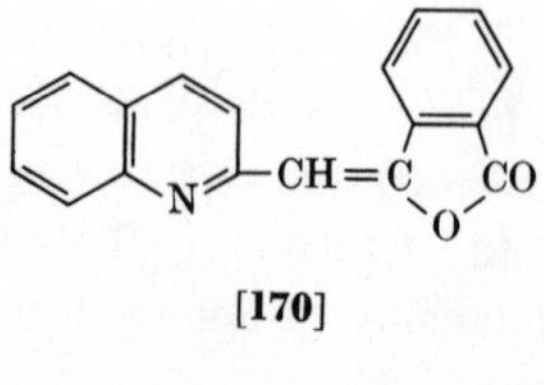   [170]

phthalic anhydride (the product containing a small amount of the isomeric phthalyl derivative [170]). Commercial dyes are often made from mixtures of quinaldine and 6-methylquinaldine and then contain a considerable proportion of the homologue [169] (R = Me).[27] The resulting mixtures are sold under names such as *Quinoline Yellow A Spirit Soluble* (BASF) (CI Solvent Yellow 33; CI 47000), and are used in spirit lacquers and cosmetic products.

Various sulphonated derivatives containing 1–3 sulphonic acid groups are marketed as *Quinoline Yellow A Extra* (BASF) and equivalents (CI Acid Yellow 3; CI 47005). They have poor fastness properties, but are of interest because of their bright greenish yellow shade. These dyes are often used with suitable blues for dyeing billiard cloth and for other purposes not requiring high fastness properties.

12-8   Stilbene dyes

The stilbene dyes are characterised by presence in their structures of the stilbene residue:

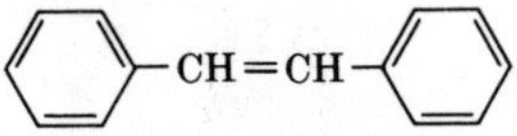

but the chromophoric system is based on azo or azoxy groups, or both. Most of the dyes are obtained from 4-nitrotoluene-2-sulphonic acid by a series of reactions, but the precise structures of the products are unknown, and in most cases they are mixtures. In this starting material the methyl group is activated by the two electronegative groups and is easily oxidised. On heating 4-nitrotoluene-2-sulphonic acid with caustic soda self-condensation takes place with formation

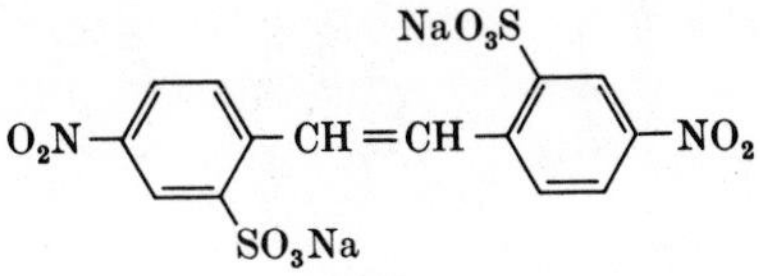

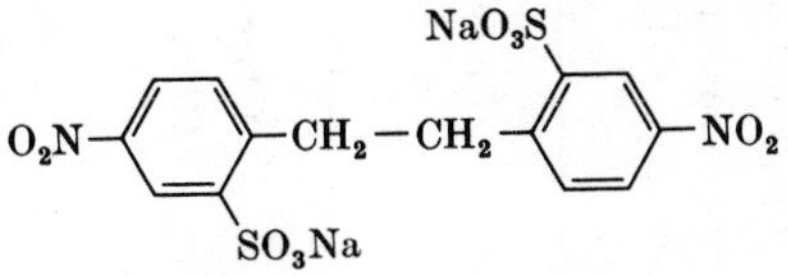

of 4,4'-dinitrostilbene-2,2'-disulphonic acid [171] and 4,4'-dinitro-dibenzyl-2,2'-disulphonic acid [172]. The course of further reactions varies according to the concentration of alkali, the temperature and duration of heating, and leads to the production of yellow stilbene derivatives containing azo and azoxy groups. The first of the stilbene dyes was discovered in 1883 by J. Walter and is still manufactured by many firms under various brand names such as *Curcumine S* (FBy) (CI Direct Yellow 11; CI 40000). It gives reddish yellow shades of somewhat low fastness to light, and is widely used for dyeing paper.

Table 12-1 Examples of stilbene-azo condensation products

These dyes are manufactured by heating the azo compound shown in the third column with 4,4′-dinitrostilbene-2,2′-disulphonic acid and caustic soda

CI Constitution No.	CI Generic Name	Azo compound	Dyed shade
CI 40215	CI Direct Orange 34	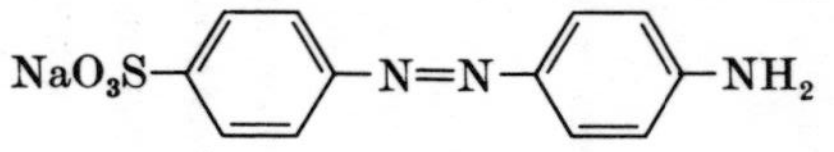 NaO$_3$S—⟨ ⟩—N=N—⟨ ⟩—NH$_2$	Yellowish orange
CI 40215	CI Direct Orange 39	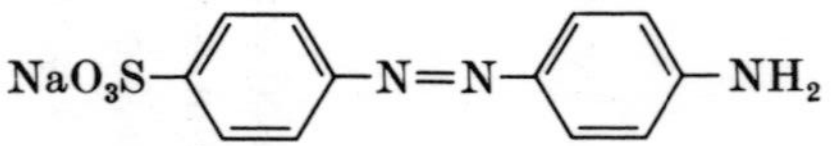 NaO$_3$S—⟨ ⟩—N=N—⟨ ⟩—NH$_2$	Reddish Orange
CI 40215	CI Direct Orange 46	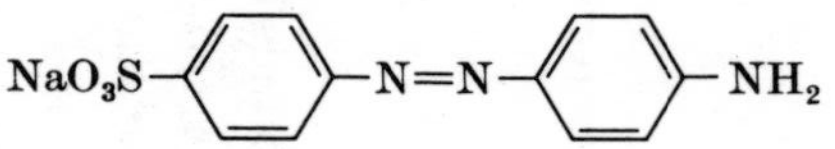 NaO$_3$S—⟨ ⟩—N=N—⟨ ⟩—NH$_2$	Bright orange
CI 40220	CI Direct Orange 34	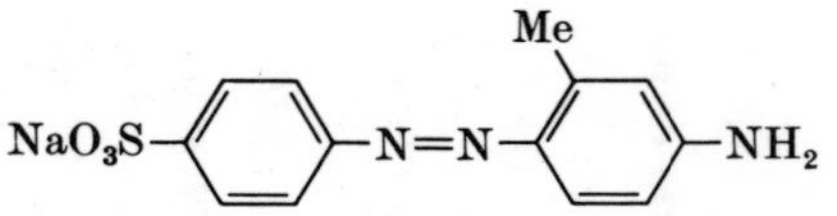 NaO$_3$S—⟨ ⟩—N=N—⟨Me⟩—NH$_2$	Yellowish orange
CI 40270	CI Direct Red 76	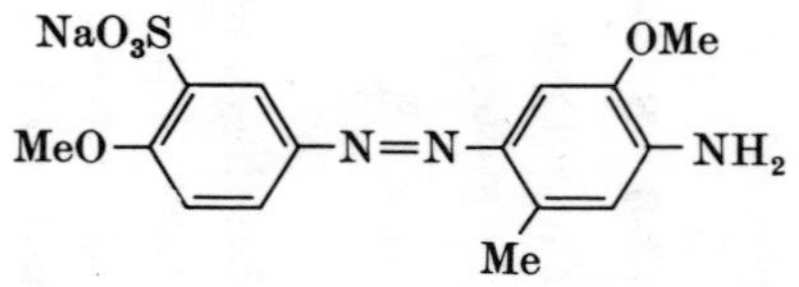 MeO, NaO$_3$S—⟨ ⟩—N=N—⟨OMe, Me⟩—NH$_2$	Yellowish red

CI 40290	CI Direct Red 111	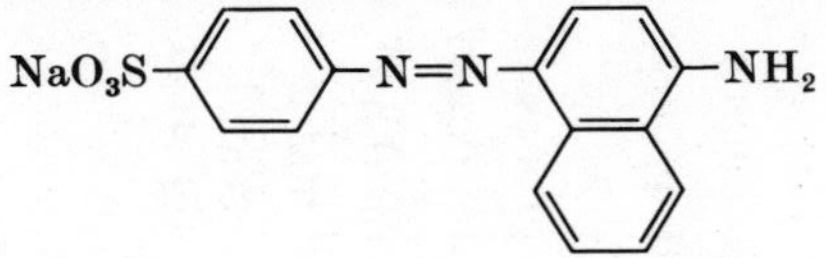	Dull yellowish red
CI 40290	CI Direct Red 112	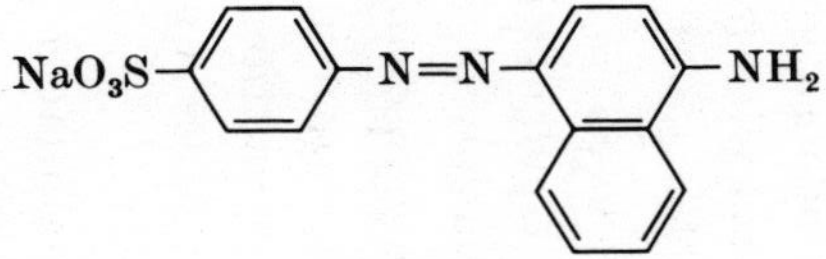	Dull yellowish red
CI 40290	CI Direct Brown 78	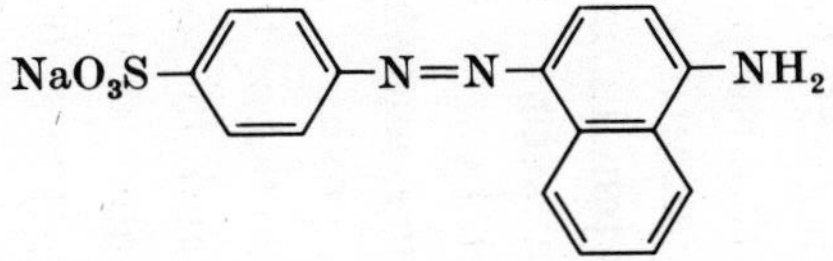	Dull reddish orange or brown

Much work on this subject was carried out by Green and his collaborators,[28] and several constitutions were proposed by them and by later workers; none of these is free from objection, however, and the structural problem remains.

Many variations have been introduced into the basic process. Reducing agents such as glucose or sodium sulphide may be added to the reaction mixture, and as a result of reduction of azoxy to azo groups the product then has a redder shade; CI Direct Orange 15 (CI 40002 and CI 40003) includes numerous dyes made in this way and widely used on cellulosic fibres, paper and leather. Alternatively the dyes obtained from the alkaline condensation may be oxidised with hypochlorite with increase in brightness and fastness to light (CI Direct Yellow 6; CI 40006). Certain dyes included in CI Direct Yellow 6 are obtained by carrying out the condensation in presence of formaldehyde or by aftertreating the product with formaldehyde; these have been assigned CI Constitution No. 40001, but process details relating to many brands remain undisclosed.

Many stilbene dyes are manufactured by condensation processes of the type described modified by the inclusion of an aminoazo compound in the reaction mixture, and these give orange, brown or red shades. Examples of such products are shown in Table 12-1. The properties of the dyes are affected by the proportions of reactants and other process variables, and in some cases quite different products are derived from the same components.

It will be seen that the processes for manufacture of stilbene dyes often contain an element of cookery, and this is reflected in marked differences between products covered by the same CI Generic Name. Nevertheless stilbene dyes are of importance because of their bright shades, fairly good fastness properties and modest cost.

Azo dyes have been manufactured by coupling tetrazotised 4,4'-diaminostilbene-2,2'-disulphonic acid with arylamines, phenols or naphthols, but few of them remain in use. A classical example is *Brilliant Yellow* (CI Direct Yellow 4; CI 42890), obtained by coupling the tetrazo compound with two molecular proportions of phenol. This dye is well known as a laboratory indicator. Because of its sensitivity to alkali it has no significant textile application, but it is used for dyeing paper. By ethylating the two hydroxyl groups *Chrysophenine* (CI Direct Yellow 12; CI 24895) is obtained. This derivative is not sensitive to alkali and is widely used as a general-purpose dye for cellulosic fibres, and also for leather and paper.

The stilbene group includes one product which (although not of major importance) is noteworthy in that it contains no chromophoric system. This is *Benzamin Fast Yellow GS* (FBy) (CI Direct Yellow 62; CI 36900), with the structure [173]. When applied to cotton it gives only a weak tint, but by diazotising on the fibre and developing with 3-methyl-1phenylpyrazol-5-one a bright yellow shade is obtained.

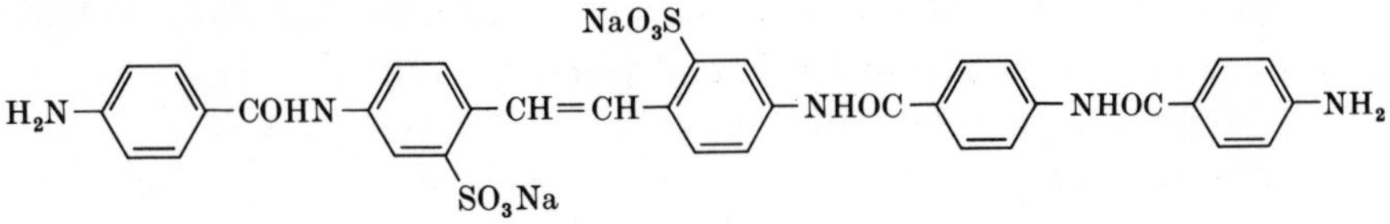

$$H_2N-\langle\ \rangle-COHN-\langle\ \rangle-CH=CH-\langle\ \rangle-NHOC-\langle\ \rangle-NHOC-\langle\ \rangle-NH_2$$

NaO₃S (top), SO₃Na (bottom)

[173]

12-9   Thiazole dyes

One of the earliest cotton dyes was *Primuline* (CI Direct Yellow 59; CI 49000), discovered by A. G. Green in 1887.[29] He prepared it by heating *p*-toluidine with sulphur and sulphonating the product. In the sulphur melt dehydrothiotoluidine [174] is obtained first, and this condenses further to yield a mixture consisting mainly of [175] together with some of [176]. Primuline is obtained by sulphonating this mixture, one sulphonic acid group entering each of the

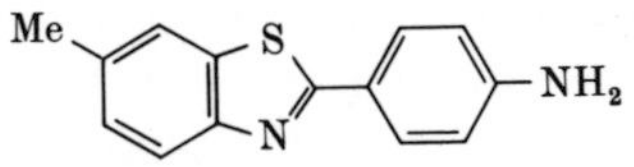

[174] 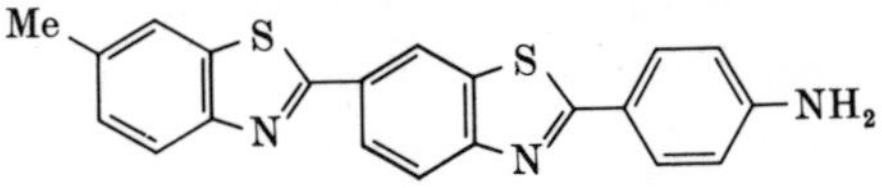   [175]

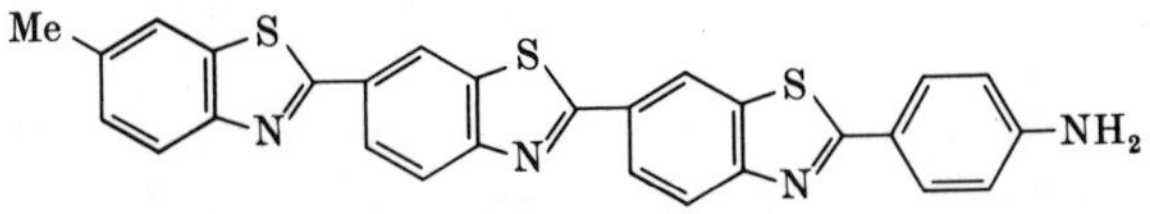

[176]

methyl-substituted benzene rings. The dye gives greenish yellow shades on cellulosic fibres, but the direct shade is of no interest because of its low fastness properties. It can be diazotised on the fibre, however, and developed with a solution of a coupling component such as β-naphthol, phenol, resorcinol, *m*-phenylenediamine or 3-methyl-1-phenylpyrazol-5-one, giving shades varying from reddish yellow to red with good fastness to wet treatments; light-fastness is poor or fair. Aftertreatment of Primuline with sodium hypochlorite gives a yellowish orange shade with good fastness to light. The azo derivatives were the first developed dyes, and were described by Green as *Ingrain* dyes. It is regrettable that the term has since been diverted from its original significance and is now used to describe dyes of other types produced on the fibre such as azoic, oxidation and temporarily solubilised phthalocyanine dyes.

One of the earliest Diazotype processes for reproduction of designs on paper or cotton fabric was based on the light-sensitivity of diazotised Primuline. Dyed material was treated with nitrous acid, dried in darkness, exposed to light under a stencil or other original, then the undecomposed diazo compound remaining in the shielded portions of the design was developed with a suitable coupling component, thus giving a coloured print.[30]

Trimethylated dehydrothiotoluidine [**177**] is manufactured as a basic dye for bast fibres, tanned cotton and silk, and is marketed as

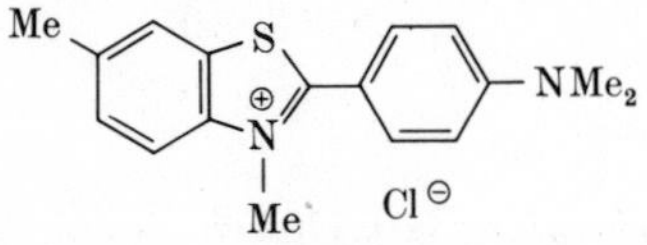

[**177**]

Acronol Yellow T (ICI) (CI Basic Yellow 1; CI 49005) and other equivalent brands. It is also produced as a phosphotungstomolyb-date and supplied as a pigment (CI Pigment Yellow 18). In this form it has good fastness to light, and is used in printing inks for many applications.

A greenish yellow derivative of Primuline is manufactured by methylation and sulphonation (or these reactions in the reverse order), and the product is sold as *Thioflavine S* (Cassella)[31] and various equivalents (CI Direct Yellow 7; CI 49010); its exact structure is uncertain. This dye is applied to cellulosic and union fibres, but its fastness properties are poor.

Recently a valuable greenish yellow direct dye has been introduced by DuPont under the name *Pontamine Brilliant Yellow 5G* (CI Direct Yellow 119). Its structure has not been disclosed but is probably identical with that of a dye [**178**] with corresponding

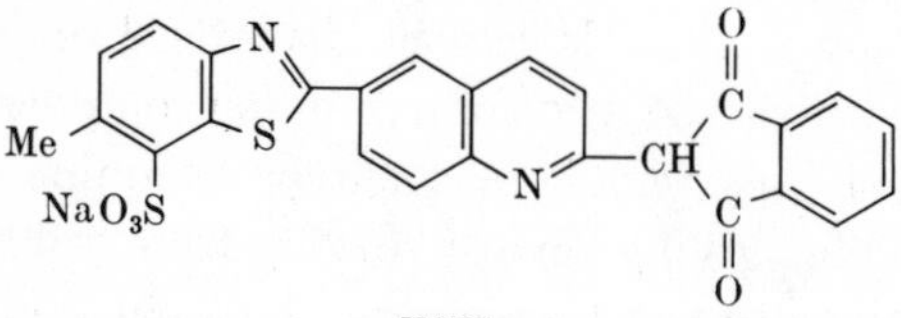

[**178**]

properties which has been described in the patent literature.[32] This is obtained from dehydrothio-*p*-toluidinesulphonic acid by a reaction of the Skraup type with paraldehyde and condensation of the resulting quinaldine derivative with phthalic anhydride. The dye is especially suitable for application to paper pulp and gives good exhaustion over a wide pH range.

Reactive dyes

13-1 Dyes for cellulosic fibres

13-1-1 Introduction

The molecules of which natural fibres are composed abound in reactive groups. Cellulosic fibres are polymers consisting of chains of D-glucose units each containing three hydroxyl groups, and protein fibres are built from a variety of amino acid residues. Hydroxyl groups in cellulose and amino or carboxylic acid groups in wool undoubtedly play a part in the attachment of dyes of the direct, acid and basic classes to the fibres concerned, but the dyes are fairly easily removed by suitable solvents, and are evidently not attached by covalent linkages. Cellulose was benzoylated by Cross and Bevan in 1895 and many derivatives have been prepared since then. During the past 50 years there have been numerous attempts to attach dyes to cellulosic fibres by means of covalent bonds. Several of these did indeed bring about chemical union, but in all of the early work the conditions employed were so drastic that serious degradation of the fibre occurred. It seems not to have been appreciated that in order to effect dyeing by such means it is necessary to bring about reaction with only a few of the many hydroxyl groups available in the fibre molecule, and that mild conditions are suitable.

The first practical success was achieved by Rattee and Stephen of ICI in about the year 1954 when they discovered a means whereby dyes containing dichlorotriazinyl groups react with cellulosic fibres in alkaline conditions to give dyeings with very high fastness to wet treatments without significant weakening of the fibre.[1] Since dichlorotriazinyl derivatives behave as acid chlorides the reaction may be regarded as an esterification of the Schotten–Baumann type. The essential novelty of this work lay in the use of mild conditions, for CIBA had acylated cellulose with cyanuric chloride in 1931 (using rather severe conditions), and many dichlorotriazinyl dyes had been examined previously without discovery of their fibre reactivity. The work of Rattee and Stephen led to the introduction of the *Procion* range of reactive dyes by ICI in 1956. These were based on various chromophores and contained dichlorotriazinyl groups attached to the dye molecules through —NH— links. Under suitable conditions both chlorine atoms can be replaced, but the second reacts much less readily than the first. Some reaction takes place with water, and there are therefore five possible products, shown in the following scheme:

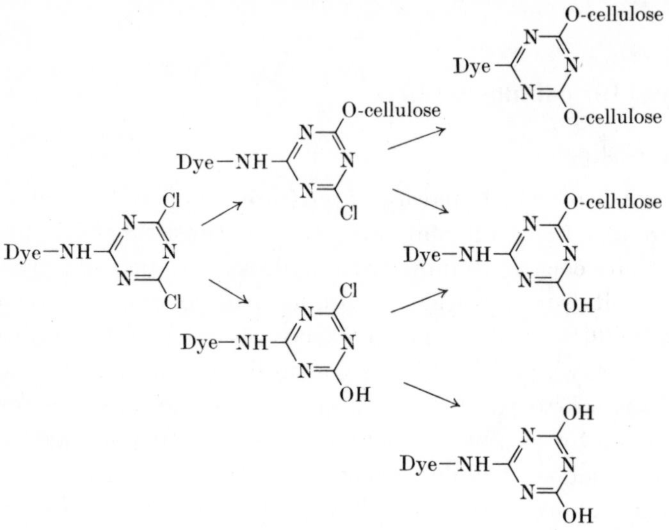

The proportions of the products vary according to the characteristics of the dye concerned and application conditions, but in the commercial dyes a high degree of bonding with the fibre can be achieved. Procion dyes of this type are so reactive that they can be applied in cold conditions by means of a variety of dyeing processes. For application by printing the high reactivity of these products is disadvantageous since in long runs the loss by hydrolysis in the alkaline printing paste causes progressive weakening of the printed shade. A new range of *Procion H* dyes was therefore introduced by ICI in 1957 consisting of monochlorotriazinyl derivatives which are more stable in cold alkaline conditions and suitable for application by printing as well as dyeing processes. For reaction with the fibre more strongly alkaline conditions and a temperature of at least 60°C are necessary, and in printing practice fixation is conveniently brought about by steaming. Thickening agents based on starch or other reactive carbohydrates must be avoided, but sodium alginate (containing only secondary hydroxyl groups) or a hydrocarbon emulsion can be used satisfactorily.

The original cold-developing Procion range has been considerably extended and has been re-named *Procion M.*

The loss by hydrolysis of dichlorotriazinyl dyes during dyeing varies over a range of about 15–40%. At first sight it appears remarkable that heterogeneous reaction with the fibre predominates in competition with the homogeneous reaction with water molecules present in great excess. Since the dye molecules are rapidly adsorbed by the fibre, however, the reactive groups in the dye and fibre are brought into proximity and the concentration of dye in the solid cellulose substrate is then much greater than that in aqueous solution. A further favourable factor lies in the lower pK value for cellulose (pK 13·7) in comparison with that of water (pK 15·7).[2]

There is an optimum value for the cellulose substantivity of reactive dyes intended for application by dyeing methods. It must be sufficient to ensure adsorption by the fibre but not so high as to cause difficulty in washing the hydrolysed portion out of the fibre, since the presence of unfixed dye with inferior fastness properties would result in bleeding and staining of undyed fibre during subsequent wet treatments. For printing applications, in which the dye is applied mechanically at a suitable concentration, the necessary substantivity is of a much lower order.

The discovery of reactive dyes for cellulosic fibres undoubtedly ranks as one of the greatest in the field of synthetic colouring matters, and it has had far-reaching effects. With increase in the use of these dyes there has been a falling off in the demand for dyes of other classes, and in consequence many ranges of direct, vat, sulphur and azoic dyes have been curtailed. It must be remembered, however, that high wet-fastness properties are unnecessary in dyes for paper and some furnishing fabrics, and in such applications the older dyes have held their ground.

13-1-2   Reactive systems based on nucleophilic substitution

Triazinyl Derivatives. The use of the triazinyl ring as a chromophoric block in manufacture of direct dyes has been mentioned in Chapter 5. These dyes are obtained by reaction of cyanuric chloride with two or three molecules of amino-substituted dyes in succession.[3] The manufacture of chloro- and dichlorotriazinyl dyes for reactive ranges depends on similar condensations but not more than two stages are required since at least one reactive chlorine atom must remain in the final product.

Dichlorotriazinyl derivatives are readily obtained from dyes containing a primary or secondary amino group by reaction with an equimolecular proportion of cyanuric chloride. Commercial dyes are derived mainly from the azo, anthraquinone and phthalocyanine classes (discussed in Chapters 3, 9 and 15). Anthraquinone dyes provide chiefly bright blue and phthalocyanines bright turquoise shades. Greens are derived from structures containing mixed chromophores of the anthraquinone–stilbene, anthraquinone–azo or phthalocyanine–azo classes, and the remainder of the shade range mainly from the azo class. For deep brown or black shades metal complexes of o,o'-dihydroxyazo or o-carboxy-o'-hydroxyazo dyes are often used; structures of this type also provide rubine, violet and blue shades.

Although many disazo and polyazo reactive dyes have been described in the patent literature their substantivity is often undesirably high, and most commercial dyes therefore contain only one azo group. The reactive group in azo dyes may be attached to either the diazo or the coupling component, and it is sometimes preferable that it should be introduced into the component concerned before azo coupling is carried out.

Monochlorotriazinyl dyes of the type [179] are of little interest as reactive dyes because their cellulose-substantivity is in general too

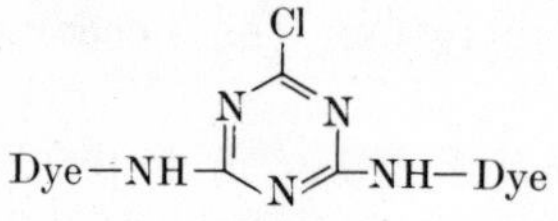

$$\text{Dye}-\text{NH}-\underset{\underset{\text{N}}{\big\Vert}}{\overset{\overset{\text{Cl}}{\big\vert}}{\text{N}}}-\text{NH}-\text{Dye}$$

[179]

high. Suitable dyes can be obtained from dichlorotriazinyl dyes, however, by replacing one of the chlorine atoms by a non-labile substituent such as an alkoxy, aryloxy, amino, arylamino or other substituted amino group; m- or p-sulphoanilino derivatives are often used as a convenient means of introducing an additional solubilising group. Alternatively the non-labile substituent may be introduced into the triazine ring first and the resulting dichlorotriazinyl derivative then condensed with the dye concerned; this procedure is often preferred. The two general methods may be represented thus:

Method 1

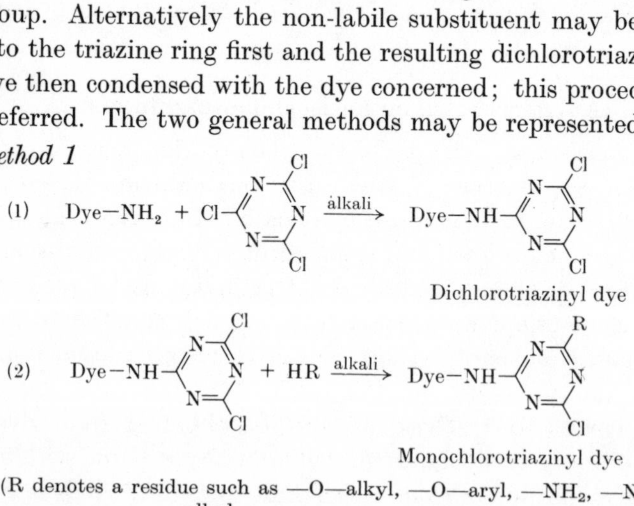

(1) Dye—NH$_2$ + Cl—[triazine-Cl,Cl] $\xrightarrow{\text{alkali}}$ Dye—NH—[triazine-Cl,Cl]

Dichlorotriazinyl dye

(2) Dye—NH—[triazine-Cl,Cl] + HR $\xrightarrow{\text{alkali}}$ Dye—NH—[triazine-R,Cl]

Monochlorotriazinyl dye

(R denotes a residue such as —O—alkyl, —O—aryl, —NH$_2$, —NH—alkyl, —N(alkyl)$_2$, —N⟨alkyl,aryl, —NH—aryl or —NH—arylsulphonic acid)

Method 2

(1) 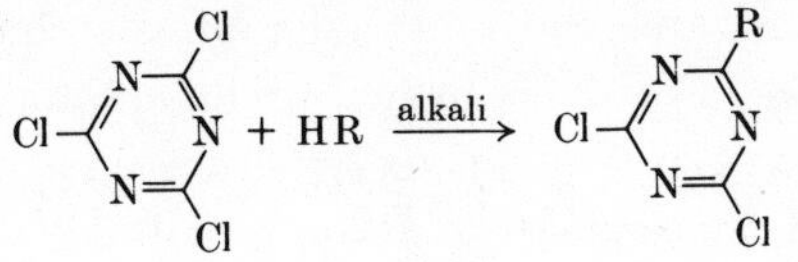 Cyanuric chloride + HR $\xrightarrow{\text{alkali}}$ monochloro-substituted triazine (R replacing one Cl)

(2) 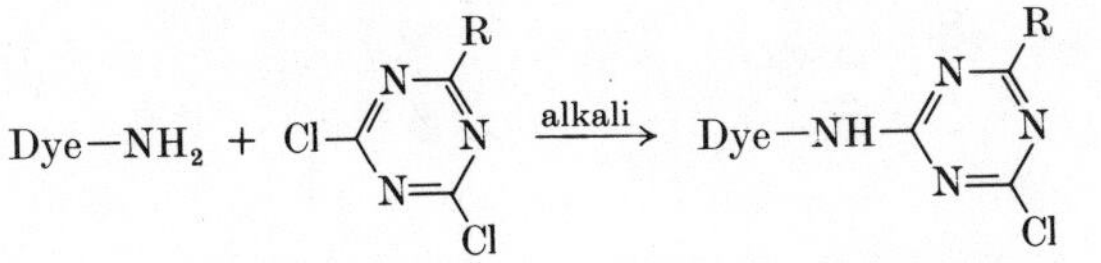 Dye—NH$_2$ + dichlorotriazinyl compound $\xrightarrow{\text{alkali}}$ Dye—NH—triazinyl (R)

Monochlorotriazinyl dye

(R denotes a radical as above)

One of the chief advantages arising from dye-fibre reaction is freedom from the necessity of using dyes with structures conferring affinity for cellulose. Smaller and simpler dye molecules can be used and in consequence the shades are in general much brighter than those given by direct dyes. Simple dye structures have a further advantage in that they diffuse rapidly through the fibre and application can therefore be completed in a short time.

Procion dyes provide a complete range of shades in both the M and H series. In consequence of their earlier work on direct dyes containing triazinyl residues CIBA had built up a strong patent position by 1956 and this enabled them to manufacture a competing range of reactive monochlorotriazinyl dyes; these were marketed under the name *Cibacron*. Tables 13-1 and 13-2 give a selection of dyes from these two ranges. Since not many constitutions of commercial dyes have been made public some examples from the patent literature (not necessarily used commercially) are included in order that the range of structures and shades available may be more fully illustrated.

Dichlorotriazinyl dyes are manufactured by condensing amino-substituted dye bases with cyanuric chloride in aqueous medium. Since cyanuric chloride is insoluble in water it must be used in the form of a fine suspension, usually obtained either by slow addition of a solution in a water-miscible solvent such as acetone to a well

Table 13-1 Examples of reactive dichlorotriazinyl dyes

Structure	Shade on cotton	Commercial name and CI Generic Name	References
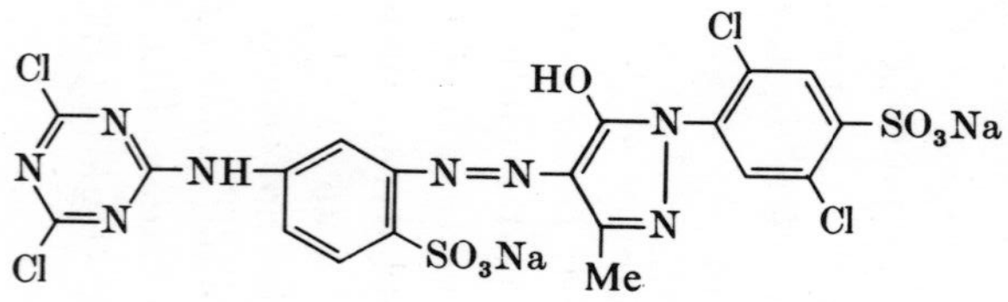	Bright greenish yellow	Procion Brilliant Yellow M-6G (ICI) CI Reactive Yellow 1	4
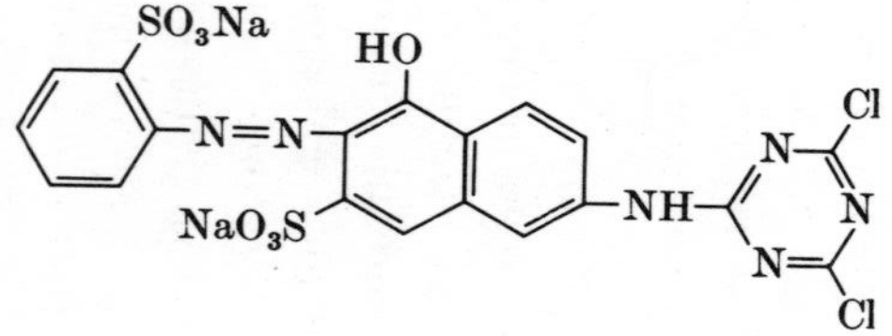	Bright yellowish orange	Procion Brilliant Orange M-G (ICI) CI Reactive Orange 1	5
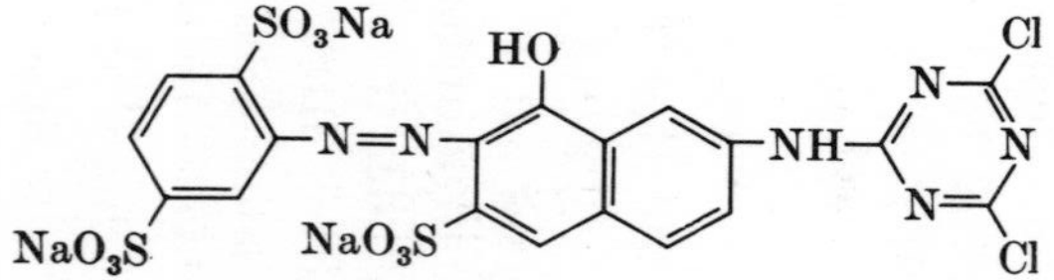	Bright scarlet	—	6

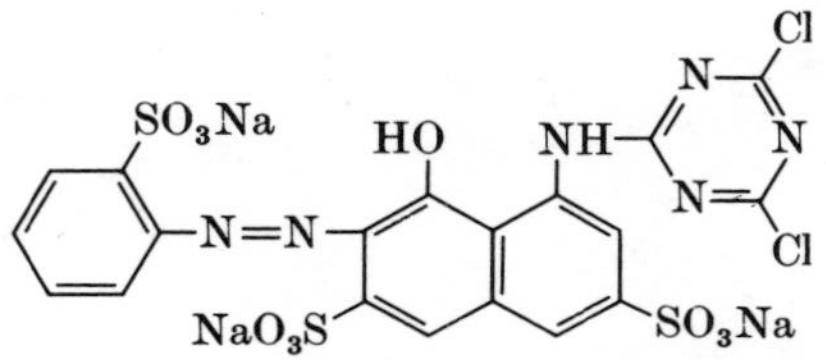 7	Procion Brilliant Red M-2B (ICI) CI Reactive Red 1	Bright bluish red
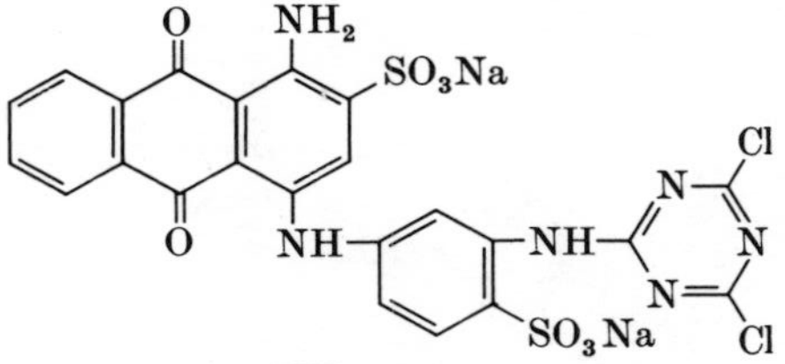 8	Procion Brilliant Blue M-R (ICI) CI Reactive Blue 4	Bright reddish blue
9	—	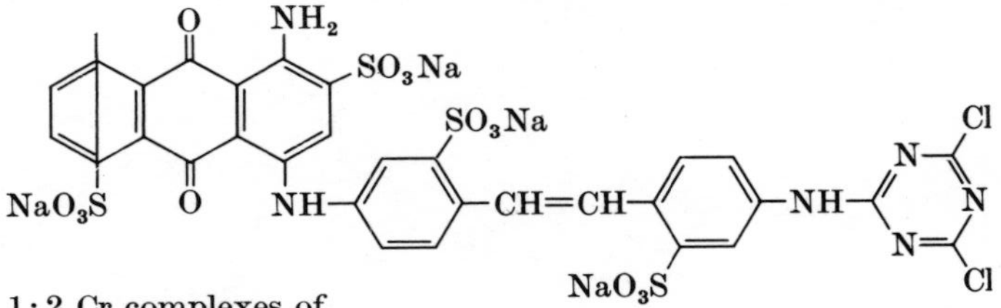 Bright bluish green
10	—	Brown

1 : 2 Cr complexes of

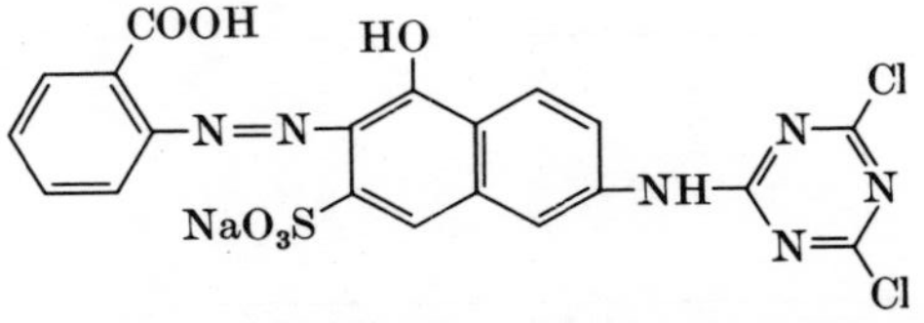

Table 13-2 Examples of reactive monochlorotriazinyl dyes

Structure	Shade on cotton	Commercial name and CI Generic Name	References
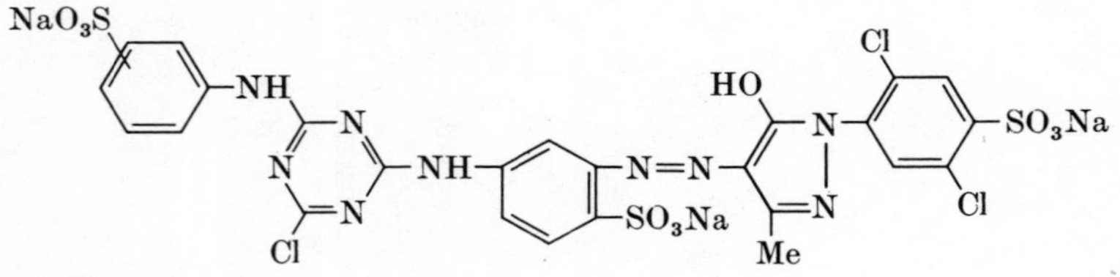	Bright greenish yellow	Procion Brilliant Yellow H-5G (ICI) Cibacron Brilliant Yellow 3G (CIBA) CI Reactive Yellow 2	11
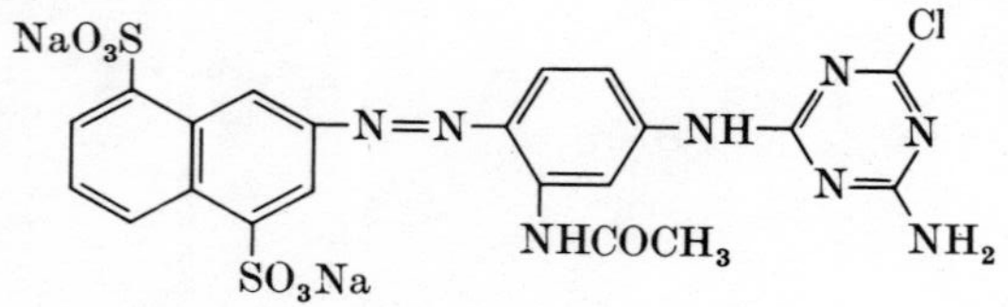	Bright yellow	Procion Yellow H-A (ICI) Cibacron Yellow R (CIBA) CI Reactive Yellow 3	11
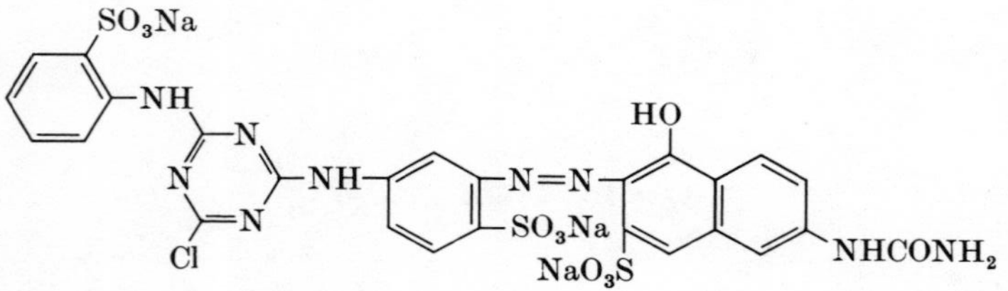	Bright orange	Procion Brilliant Orange H-GR (ICI) Cibacron Brilliant Orange G (CIBA) CI Reactive Orange 2	11

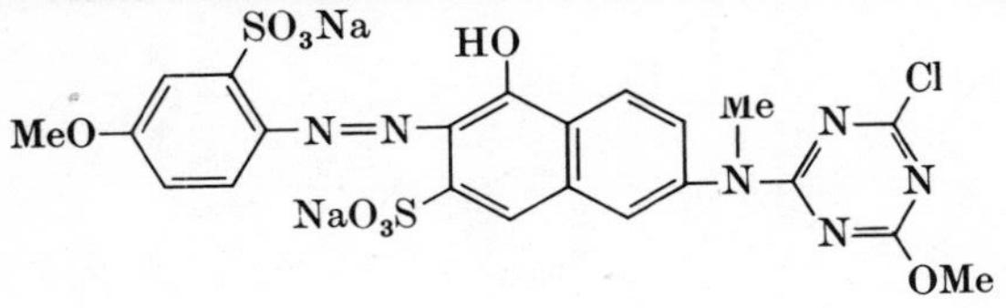 12	Procion Scarlet H-R (ICI) Cibacron Scarlet RP (CIBA) CI Reactive Red 13	Scarlet
4	Procion Brilliant Red H-3B (ICI) CI Reactive Red 3	Bright bluish red
11	Procion Brilliant Red H-7B (ICI) Cibacron Brilliant Red 3B (CIBA) CI Reactive Red 4	Bright bluish red
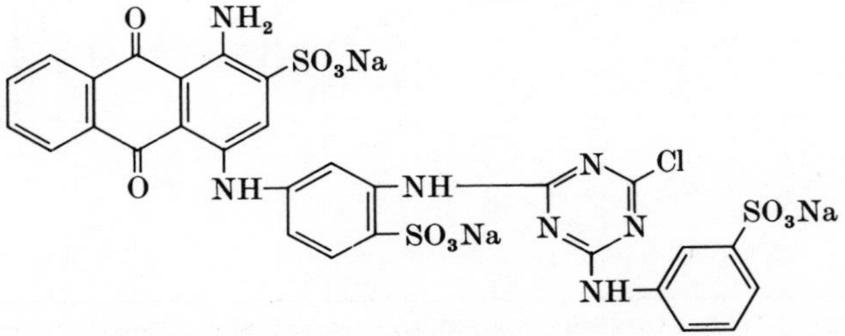 11	Cibacron Brilliant Blue BR (CIBA) CI Reactive Blue 5	Bright greenish blue

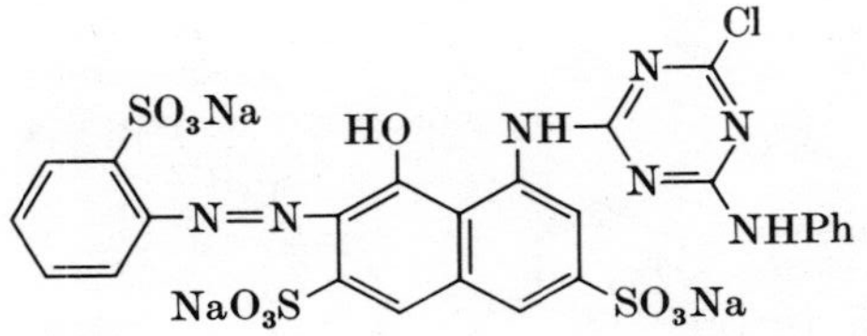

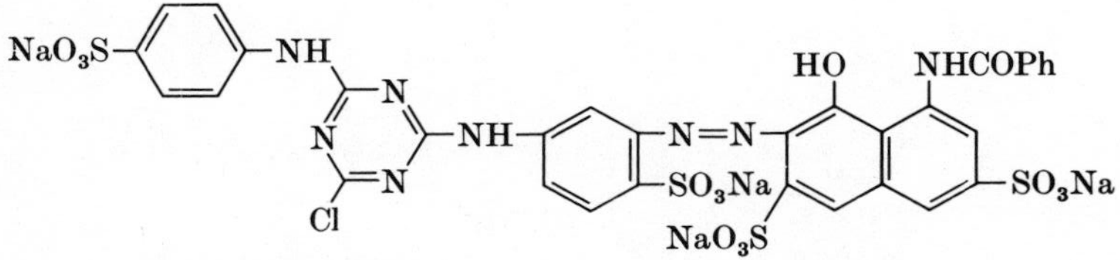

Table 13-2 Examples of reactive monochlorotriazinyl dyes *(Contd.)*

Structure	Shade on cotton	Commercial name and CI Generic Name	References
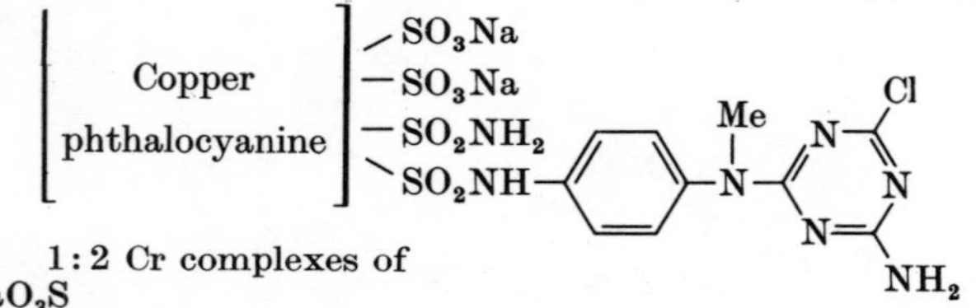 Copper phthalocyanine with —SO₃Na, —SO₃Na, —SO₂NH₂, —SO₂NH— substituents linked to NH—phenyl—N(Me)—triazine(Cl)(NH₂); NaO_3S ... 1:2 Cr complexes of (naphthol azo structure with NH-triazine-Cl and NH-phenyl-SO₃H)	Greenish blue	—	13
Mixture of 1:2 Cr and Co complexes of (naphthol azo structures with NaO₃S, NO₂, OH groups) 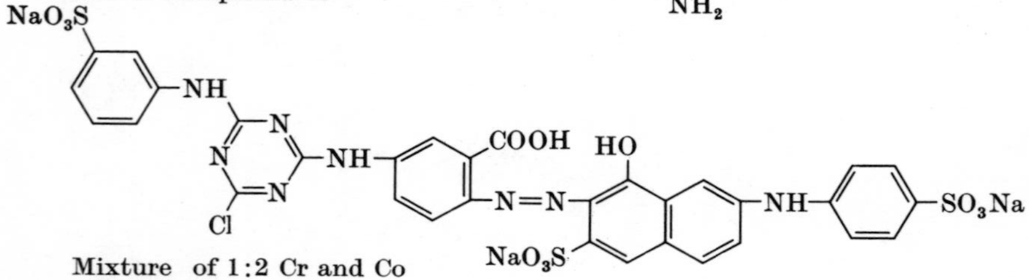	Dark brown	—	14
(azo naphthol structure with NH-triazine(Cl)(NH₂), OH, NaO₃S, O₂N groups)	Black or grey	Procion Black H-G (ICI) Cibacron Black BG (CIBA) CI Reactive Black 1	11

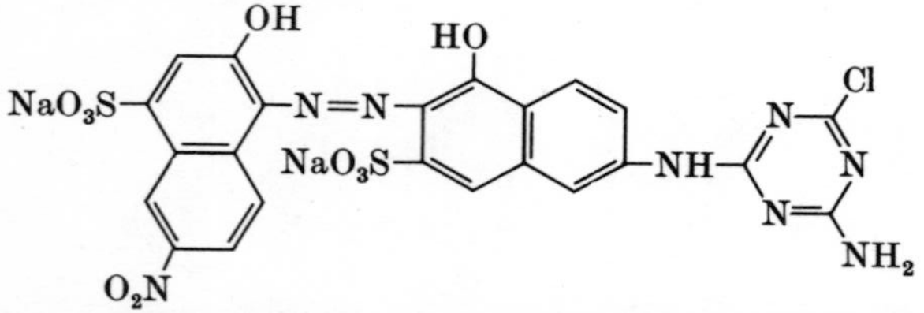

stirred mixture of ice and water, or by stirring a suspension of cyanuric chloride with ice-water in presence of a surfactant such as a sulphonated methyl oleate. Condensation is brought about by stirring the dye base with the cyanuric chloride suspension in slight excess at 0°–5°C and adding an aqueous solution of caustic soda or sodium carbonate at such a rate that the pH value is maintained at approximately 6·0. Completion of the reaction is normally shown by a sharp rise in pH as alkali absorption ceases. The product may then be isolated by salting in the usual way. If, however, a further condensation is required to give a monochlorotriazinyl dye the intermediate product is not usually isolated. An addition of the appropriate reagent is made and the mixture is heated slowly until a fall in pH shows that reaction is taking place. The temperature is maintained at that point and alkali is added as before to maintain pH 6·0 until the second reaction stage is complete. The product is then isolated by salting as required.

Monochlorotriazinyl dyes are sufficiently stable to withstand long periods of storage, but dichlorotriazinyl dyes are liable to hydrolyse with loss of hydrogen chloride. Storage tests carried out with selected dyes in solution showed the rate of hydrolysis to be a minimum at pH 6·4.[1] It was found that the stability of dichlorotriazinyl dyes in dry storage can be greatly improved by addition of a buffer such as a mixture of potassium dihydrogen phosphate and disodium hydrogen phosphate; hydrolysis is evidently accelerated by presence of acid.[15]

Triazinylamino derivatives of dyes may carry reactive substituents other than chlorine. Bromine and fluorine have been mentioned in many patent examples but are not known to have been used commercially. Cyanuric iodide has been described but is difficult to obtain in a pure state and has not been used as a dye intermediate.[16] Dichlorotriazinyl dyes readily react with sodium sulphite or sodium bisulphite to yield the corresponding s-triazinedisulphonic acids; these derivatives can be used as reactive dyes[17] but have no advantages over dichlorotriazines and are less versatile. Phthalocyanine dyes have been described, however, in which a triazine ring is substituted by one sulpho group together with a non-labile group such as amino, alkylamino, dialkylamino or alkoxy, and these give high fixation on cellulosic fibres.[18] Thiocyano, thiosulphuric acid and many other sulphur-linked groups have served as a basis for reactive dyes.[19] Methoxy and phenoxy groups can take part in fibre-reaction by transesterification, and the presence of one or more electronegative groups in a phenoxy substituent greatly enhances reactivity.[20]

A marked increase in the reactivity of monochlorotriazinyl dyes can be obtained by adding certain tertiary amines to the dyebath, and this effect is no doubt attributable to the formation of highly reactive quaternary salts. Pyridine, trimethylamine, N,N-dimethylhydrazine and 1,4-diazabicyclo-2,2,2-octane (DABCO) [180] are

$$\begin{array}{c} \quad\;\; \overset{\displaystyle CH_2CH_2}{} \\ N-CH_2CH_2-N \\ \quad\;\; CH_2CH_2 \end{array}$$

[180]

especially effective auxiliary compounds in this respect.[21] The value of this device is restricted, however, by a lack of consistency in the conditions required by individual dyes and the consequent need for care in selecting compatible dyes for use together. The disagreeable odour of many of the tertiary amines is an adverse factor in some application processes, and although DABCO is free from this objection it is a somewhat expensive agent. Quaternary salts of these types can be isolated, and many examples have been described, but it has not been disclosed whether commercial use has been made of such products.

Other heterocyclic structures. The success of the ICI Procion dyes brought about a revolution in dye chemistry. Every major manufacturer immediately began an extensive programme of research with the object of producing marketable equivalent products. In view of the long history of investigation without practical results the rapid success that was then achieved in many different ways is astonishing. Few chemists had believed in the practicability of fibre reaction, but once it had been demonstrated and the general principles had been established a great amount of experimental work quickly produced a variety of reactive systems suitable for industrial use. Over 200 reactive systems have been examined by ICI alone and the more useful ones have been patented. Many of these and others examined elsewhere are of only academic interest, and relatively few systems have found commercial application.

The use of polyhalogeno heterocyclic structures other than triazine derivatives was an obvious approach to the problem, and several firms filed patent applications relating to 2,4-dichloropyrimidinyl dyes containing the group [181]. These, however, were

[181]   [182]

claimed in an earlier ICI patent.[22] Subsequently dyes containing 2,4,5-trichloropyrimidinyl groups [182] were introduced by Geigy and Sandoz under the respective names *Reactone* and *Drimarene*.[23] Whereas in dichloropyrimidinyl dyes only one of the chlorine atoms is replaceable, in 2,4,5-trichloropyrimidinyl dyes the chlorine atoms in positions 2 and 4 are both replaceable under suitable conditions. There is therefore a possibility of cross-linking between cellulose molecules as in the case of dichlorotriazinyl dyes. Reactivity is lower than that of the dichlorotriazinyl dyes and cold application methods are unsuitable. Good results are obtained by printing and hot continuous dyeing methods, however.

If the 2,4-dichloropyrimidine residue is linked to the chromophore by a carbonyl group in the 5 position the resulting dyes have cold-dyeing properties and approach dichlorotriazinyl dyes in this respect.[24] Commercial use of this system has not been reported.

The systems so far considered all depend on substitution reactions giving cellulose derivatives of the ester type. Others depending on addition reactions giving ether derivatives were introduced at about the same time, and these are described in Section 13–1–3. Later several commercial ranges based on further halogeno hetero-cyclic structures appeared. In 1962 Bayer produced the *Levafix E* dyes containing a reactive system depending on the 2,3-dichloroquin-oxaline residue linked to the chromophore via a carbonyl group in the 6 position.[25] The dye [183] is an example of such a structure.

[183]

The Levafix E dyes have a reactivity intermediate between that of mono- and di-chlorotriazinyl dyes. They can be applied at about 40°C, but show good stability in cold alkaline solution and are there-fore suitable for printing methods. When applied by a pad-batch process (Section 13-1-5) at 25°C only one of the chlorine atoms reacts, but on steaming at 103°C or baking at 140°C the second chlorine atom is largely replaced. Some of the *Cavalite* (DuPont) dyes are also based on this system.[26]

An attempt to use 3,4,5-trichloropyridazine in the same way as cyanuric chloride was unsuccessful since stepwise reaction did not take place.[27] However, BASF later introduced a range of *Primazin P* dyes containing a reactive system based on 4,5-dichloro-6-pyrida-zone, usually linked to the chromophore by means of a group

—NHCOCH$_2$CH$_2$—. An example of a red dye of this type with the structure [184] has been quoted.[28] The chlorine atom at position 4 is

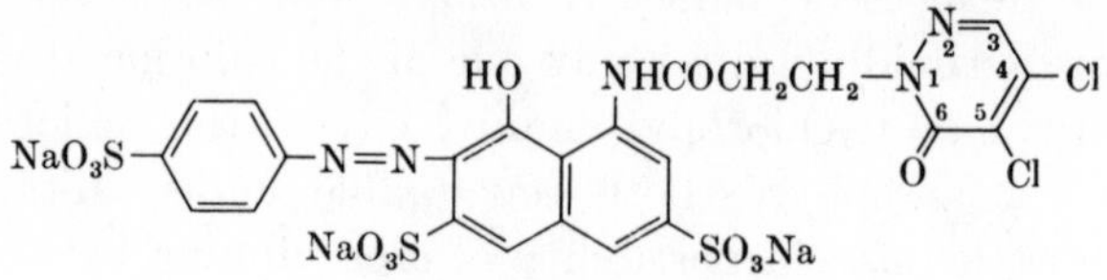

[184]

labile, and fixation is brought about by steaming in alkaline conditions. These dyes are especially suitable for printing applications because of their low substantivity and high stability in printing paste.

A reactive system depending on a labile alkylsulphonyl substituent attached to a pyrimidine ring has been devised by Bayer.[29] If, for example, 4,5-dichloro-6-methyl-2-methysulphonylpyrimidine is condensed with a suitable amino-substituted dye base in neutral conditions the 4 chlorine atom is replaced with formation of a reactive dye which can be fixed on cellulosic fibres by replacement of the methylsulphonyl group.[30] This system is used in Bayer's *Levafix P* range; an example from UK 1,120,761 has the structure [185] and gives bluish red shades on cotton by dyeing or printing processes.

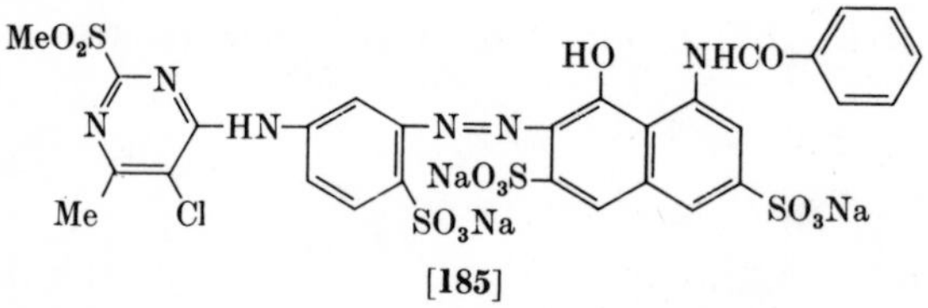

[185]

Dyes containing dichlorophthalazine residues have been used in commercial ranges. Although the chlorine atoms in 1,4-dichlorophthalazine are not easily replaced the system becomes activated when this residue is linked to a chromophore via a carbonyl group in position 6 and the resulting dye is reactive. Only one of the chlorine atoms is labile in dyebath conditions. It has been stated that this system is used in some members of the *Reatex* (Fran), *Elisiane* (Fran) and *Solidazol* (Cassella) ranges.[26,31] An example of a blue dye of this type selected from the patent literature[32] is shown on p. 215 [186].

Reactive dyes based on the chlorobenzothiazole residue linked with the chromophore via —CONH—, —SO$_2$NH—, —NH— or azo groups have been described by five firms.[33] The reddish yellow dye [187] is a typical example of these. A labile methylsulphonyl group

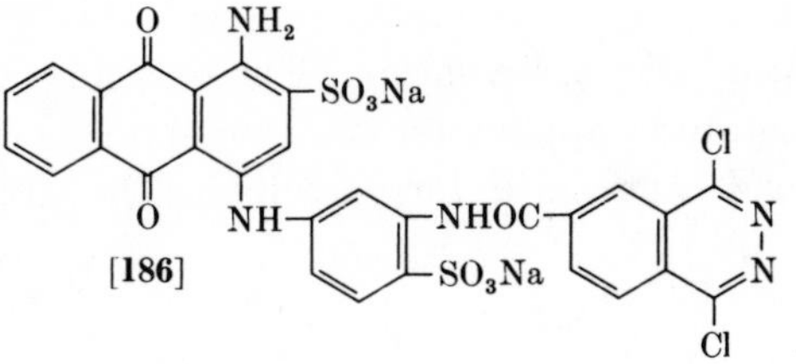

[186]

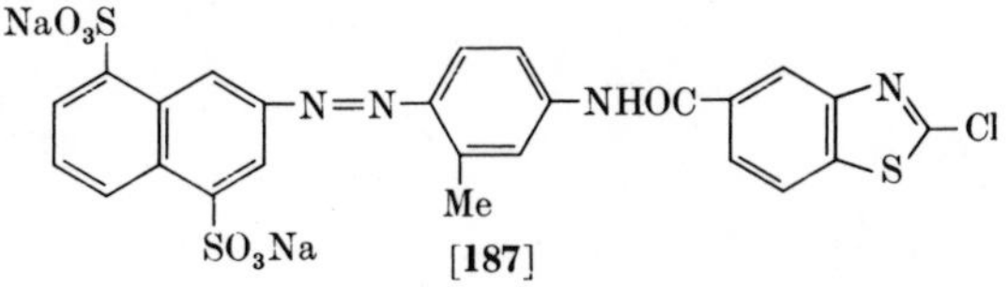

[187]

may take the place of the usual chlorine atom. According to Wegmann[26] some of the Reatex dyes (Fran) contain reactive chlorobenzothiazole groups.

One of the newer reactive systems depends on a polyfluorocyclo-butyl residue, usually linked to the remainder of the dye molecule via a —CONH— or —CH=CH·CONH— group.[34] In many of the dyes that have been described two adjacent carbon atoms of the cyclobutyl ring each carry two fluorine atoms, but in some examples one of these carbon atoms is substituted by two fluorine and the other by two chlorine atoms.[35] Structures selected from patents[36] are reproduced below; at present there is no evidence to suggest that such dyes have been used commercially:

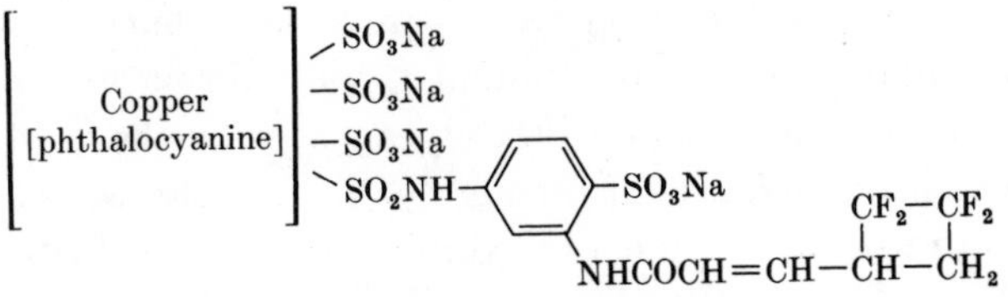

(greenish blue)

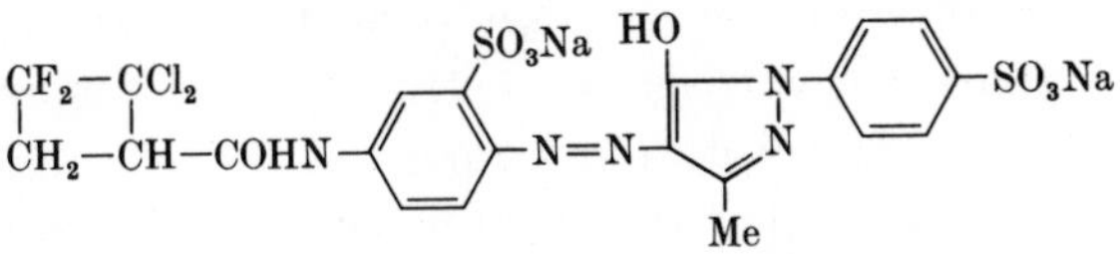

(reddish yellow)

13-1-3   Reactive systems based on nucleophilic addition

In 1949–50 Farbwerke Hoechst applied for patents relating to the manufacture of dyes containing vinyl sulphone, sulphatoethyl sulphone or β-chloroethyl sulphone groups.[37] The possibility of reaction with unspecified fibres was mentioned, but this was not treated as a major feature of the invention. The examples quoted in the patents relate mainly to application on wool and it is evident that the dyes were intended primarily for that fibre. The structures

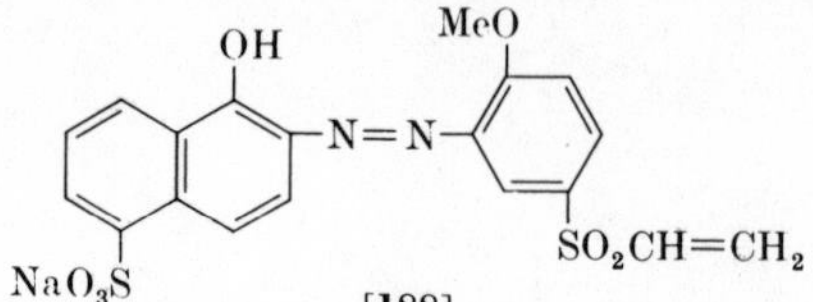

[188]

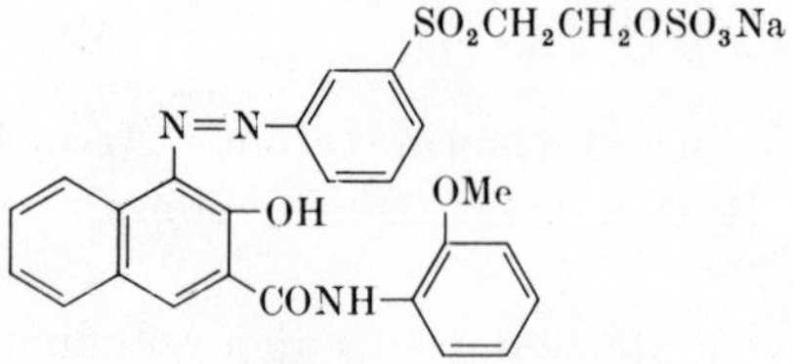

[189]

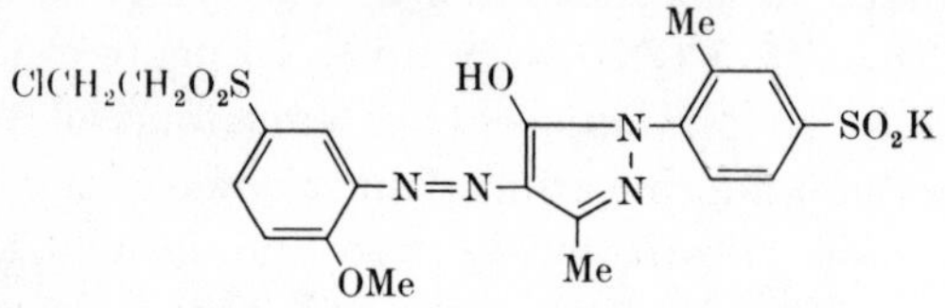

[190]

[188], [189] and [190] are examples of the three types. The sulphatoethylsulphonyl derivatives are dyes of the temporarily solubilised type (when other solubilising groups are absent) since during application the sulphato group is eliminated with formation of a vinyl sulphone group. The *Remalan* (FH) dyes placed on the market in the early 1950s are based on one or more of these systems. They are used mainly on wool and nylon and exhibit excellent wet-fastness properties on these fibres; their reactive character was not mentioned, however, in the technical literature issued when they were introduced.

After the appearance of the Procion dyes the possibility of applying vinyl sulphone derivatives as reactive dyes for cotton was examined by Farbwerke Hoechst, and a range of *Remazol* dyes for this purpose based on the sulphatoethyl sulphone group was quickly produced. They react with cellulose in alkaline conditions in two stages:

(1) Dye—$SO_2CH_2CH_2OSO_3Na \rightarrow$

Dye—SO_2CH=$CH_2 + Na_2SO_4 + H_2O$

(2) Dye—SO_2CH=$CH_2 + HO$—cellulose $\rightarrow$

Dye—$SO_2CH_2CH_2O$—cellulose

It is possible that direct substitution of the sulphuric ester group by cellulose also takes place.[38] In 1964 the same firm introduced a range of *Remazol D* dyes with structures of the general type:

$$\text{Dye—N—SO}_2\text{CH}_2\text{CH}_2\text{OSO}_3\text{Na}$$

with CH_3 on the N.

The methylimino link causes a lowering of reactivity and in consequence the dyes are especially suitable for printing applications.[30]

The earlier reactive dyes included the *Permafix* range introduced by Bayer, but the name was soon changed to *Levafix*. These dyes contain sulphatoethylaminosulphonyl groups, and are believed to react with cellulose in two stages, as follows:

(1) $\text{Dye—SO}_2\text{NHCH}_2\text{CH}_2\text{OSO}_3\text{Na} + \text{NaOH} \rightarrow$

$$\text{Dye—SO}_2\text{—N}\begin{smallmatrix}\text{CH}_2\\ |\\ \text{CH}_2\end{smallmatrix} + \text{Na}_2\text{SO}_4 + \text{H}_2\text{O}$$

(2) $\text{Dye—SO}_2\text{N}\begin{smallmatrix}\text{CH}_2\\ |\\ \text{CH}_2\end{smallmatrix} + \text{HO — cellulose} \rightarrow$

$$\text{Dye—SO}_2\text{NHCH}_2\text{CH}_2\text{O — cellulose}$$

Since the dyes are solubilised only by the sulphuric ester group which is removed by hydrolysis fixation might be attributed to temporary solubilisation. It is also possible for the molecules to react together to form more complex structures such as:

$$\text{Dye—SO}_2\text{NHCH}_2\text{CH}_2\text{N}\begin{smallmatrix}\text{SO}_2\text{—Dye}\\ \\ \text{CH}_2\text{CH}_2\text{OSO}_3\text{Na}\end{smallmatrix}$$

Levafix dyes may therefore be attached to the fibre in several ways, and this probably accounts for their high degree of fixation.[39]

The *Primazin* dyes (BASF) have structures of the general type $\text{Dye—NHCOCH}_2\text{CH}_2\text{OSO}_3\text{Na}$, and their reactive system is similar to those of the Remazol and Levafix ranges except in the nature of the link with the chromophore. The Primazin dyes (to be distinguished from the chemically different Primazin P dyes already described) react with cellulose in alkaline conditions in the following steps:

(1) $\text{Dye—NHCOCH}_2\text{CH}_2\text{OSO}_3\text{Na} + \text{NaOH} \rightarrow$
$\qquad \text{Dye—NHCOCH}=\text{CH}_2 + \text{Na}_2\text{SO}_4 + \text{H}_2\text{O}$

(2) $\text{Dye—NHCOCH}=\text{CH}_2 + \text{HO—cellulose} \rightarrow$
$\qquad \text{Dye—NHCOCH}_2\text{CH}_2\text{O—cellulose}$

The reactions thus correspond to those of the Remazol series.

Dyes that combine with cellulose by addition reactions form ether-type derivatives which in general withstand acid better than alkaline conditions. A rigid classification into structures of ether and ester types should be avoided, however.

13-1-4 Reactive systems based on the use of a cross-linking agent

In 1965 BASF introduced the *Basazol* dyes, which are applied to cellulosic fibres with the aid of a polyfunctional cross-linking agent. The dyes contain nucleophilic groups such as $-NH_2$, $-NHalkyl$, $-SO_2NH_2$, $-OH$, $-SH$ or $-COCH_2COCH_3$ which react neither with cellulose nor with water. Cross-linking agents of many types can be used, suitable compounds being those containing two or more positively charged carbon atoms; one of the preferred compounds is 1,3,5-triacryloylhexahydro-*s*-triazine [191], and this is sold as

$$COCH{=}CH_2$$

$$H_2C{=}HCOC \overset{\displaystyle H_2C \overset{\displaystyle N}{\diagup} \overset{\displaystyle \diagdown}{CH_2}}{\underset{\displaystyle \underset{H_2}{C}}{\diagup} \overset{\displaystyle N}{\diagdown}} COCH{=}CH_2$$

[191]

Fixing Agent P (BASF). Basazol dyes are designed for application by printing. On applying a thickened paste containing a suitable dye, a cross-linking agent and a small amount of alkali to cellulosic textile material, then developing by steaming or by the Thermofix baking process, the cross-linking agent reacts with molecules of dye, cellulose and water. A trifunctional cross-linking agent and a monofunctional dye may yield up to ten products, three of which provide indirect links between dye and fibre; under suitable conditions a high degree of fixation occurs. This system has advantages in that the dyes concerned are not subject to hydrolysis and that losses of cross-linking agent by hydrolysis during application can be counterbalanced by using this relatively inexpensive component in suitable excess. The presence of multiple linkages between dye and cellulose results in good wet-fastness properties. Suitably substituted dyes of any chemical class can be used as described, but the Basazol range consists mainly of 1:2 metal complexes.[40]

Wegmann found that Basazol dyes are extracted from the fibre almost quantitatively by means of a solution of cadoxen (a complex derived from cadmium hydroxide and ethylenediamine), and he concluded that they are fixed by 'co-polyreaction'—a process in which dye molecules become united with each other via the cross-linking agent.[26] Baumgarte[41] has since published evidence of the existence of dye-fibre bonds in Basazol dyeings. It therefore appears probable that the cadoxen reagent is capable of rupturing such bonds.

13-1-5 Application of reactive dyes to cellulosic fibres

Reactive dyes are applied to cellulosic fibres by a variety of dyeing processes, but these fall broadly into three main types.

Batchwise dyeing processes. In these processes the fibre is dyed in a bath containing salt at a temperature varying according to the reactivity of the dyes concerned; thus Procion M dyes are applied from a cold bath, but Procion H dyes from a bath at 60°–90°C. Dyeing is usually complete in half to three quarters of an hour, and at this stage sodium carbonate is added to bring about fixation. This requires a further half to one hour. In all cases hydrolysed dye is removed in a final treatment with soap or other detergent.

Semi-continuous dyeing processes. These processes, also known as pad-batch processes, offer many of the advantages of continuous handling without the need for expensive plant. The fibre to be dyed is padded with a solution of the dye, alkali and a wetting agent at 20°–30°C, and is then allowed to stand until fixation is complete (1–24 hours). The alkali used may be caustic soda, sodium meta-silicate, carbonate or bicarbonate.

Continuous dyeing processes. Continuous dyeing can be carried out by padding cloth with a neutral solution of a reactive dye, drying, then passing it successively through a bath of caustic soda solution, a steamer, soap bath, rinsing bath and dryer. In the case of dyes of fairly low reactivity the alkali may be applied together with the dye, and even with highly reactive dyes this can be done if the pad-trough is fed separately with solutions of dye and alkali. For light shades decomposition can be minimised by using sodium bicarbonate instead of caustic soda, carbonate being formed on steaming. Many continuous processes are in use and are essentially similar to the semi-continuous processes, except in that the reaction time is reduced to a few minutes by the use of a higher temperature. They are usually preferred where suitable equipment is available.

The Procion Resin process. Crease-resist processes are extensively applied to fabrics of cotton or viscose by padding with a mixture of a resin pre-condensate, wetting and softening agents, then drying and heating to bring about polymerisation to form the resin.[42] The Procion Resin process enables Procion dyes to be applied together with certain crease-resist finishes, the dye being added to the padding liquor. The dye then reacts with basic groups in the resin pre-condensate and becomes attached to the fibre via the resin. In this

way almost 100% fixation can be attained, but the fastness properties are limited by the durability of the resin finish. This defect can
be avoided by padding with a solution of the dye and bicarbonate,
drying and then applying the resin pre-condensate; unfixed dye is
held by the resin so that good colour value is obtained, but fixation
is due mainly to reaction with the fibre. This modified process has
the advantage that it can be applied with resin finishes of all types.

Application by printing. There are several direct printing processes
for application of reactive dyes to cellulosic fibres. For example, the
fabric can be printed with a solution of the dye containing sodium
carbonate or bicarbonate, urea and a thickener such as sodium
alginate, then dried, steamed, washed off and dried again. Alternatively fixation may be brought about by baking at 140°C (or 100°C for
Procion M dyes) instead of steaming. In another process Procion
M dyes are printed with or without sodium bicarbonate, then the
fabric is dried, padded with sodium carbonate or bicarbonate,
dried on a cylinder, washed off and dried. Printers with little
equipment sometimes make use of a very simple process in which
alkali-prepared cloth is printed with Procion M dyes, then hung in
air for several hours until fixation is complete, washed off and finally
dried.

In addition to the direct printing processes various resist and
discharge styles are in use, also more complex procedures whereby
reactive dyes are applied in conjunction with azoic or solubilised
vat dyes or with pigment printing compositions.

General comparison of reactive systems. The many reactive systems
in commercial use provide a wide range of properties, and the marketed dyes vary in reactivity, stability in solution, stability of the
dye-fibre bond, efficiency of fixation and ease with which the hydrolysed dye is removed from the fibre. Fowler and Marshall[43] have
published a diagram showing the relative reactivity of various
systems in the increasing order: acryloylamino, chloropyrimidine,
monochlorotriazine, vinyl sulphone, dichloroquinoxaline, dichloro-
triazine. The halogenopyrimidinyl dyes form links with the fibre
that are highly resistant to alkaline hydrolysis, and their substantivity is lower than that of the corresponding halogenotriazinyl
dyes. In practice the latter factor is not important, since by suitable
selection ranges of both chemical types are manufactured with
substantivities within the required limits. The fibre bonds formed
by dyes of the vinylsulphone type are fairly easily ruptured by
alkaline treatments;[44] the Levafix and Primazin dyes in which the
$-CH_2CH_2OSO_3Na$ group is linked to the chromophore by sulphonamide and carbonamide groups, respectively, form more stable

links with the fibre but their reactivity is lower than that of the sulphone-linked Remazol dyes. More detailed information concerning the stability of the dye-fibre bond i given in a paper by Rattee.[45]

The mono- and di-chlorotriazinyl dyes have great advantages in simplicity of manufacture and cheapness of the cyanuric chloride from which the reactive system is derived. The commercial position will soon be affected by the expiry of the earlier patents relating to reactive dyes of these types, and it will then be interesting to observe the reassessment of the various systems now in use.

Evidence for the existence of a covalent bond between reactive dyes and cellulosic fibres. Evidence of the chemical union between Procion and other reactive dyes and cellulosic fibres[46] may be summarised as follows:

1 If cotton is dyed with a Procion M dye from a neutral bath and then washed with water most of the colour is removed; if, however, the dyed fabric is treated with alkali most of the dye becomes fixed and is not removed in a boiling soap bath.

2 Procion dyes are not removed from dyed cotton by extraction with boiling pyridine, *o*-chlorophenol or chloroform. On the other hand direct, vat and azoic dyes are stripped by these solvents.

3 Cellulose dyed with Procion M dyes is insoluble in cuprammonium solution, but similar fibres dyed with direct dyes dissolve completely.

4 When cotton dyed with the monoazo dye Procion Yellow M-R is treated with sodium hydrosulphite the dye is split into two colourless amino-substituted components. The component containing the reactive group remains anchored to the fibre and can be diazotised and coupled with an amine or phenol to give a new dye.

5 Zollinger and his co-workers subjected cellulose dyed with a Remazol dye to microbiological degradation, purified the water-soluble coloured products chromatographically and hydrolysed the main fraction; they identified glucose in the product. Since the glucose must have been derived from cellulose its presence is evidence of a dye-fibre chemical union. Later, however, Stamm showed that Remazol and Procion dyes yield mainly glucosides with glucose or cellulose in alkaline solution and pointed out that the deductions from the microbiological degradation work were therefore not entirely reliable.

6 Wegmann treated dyed cotton with a solution of cadoxen of such a concentration that cellulose is swollen by it but not dissolved. No bleeding of Cibacron, Reactone or other reactive dyes of the imide—chloride type occurred but there was partial removal of Remazol dyes. This work was believed to show that Cibacron and Reactone dyes are covalently linked with the fibre and that Remazol dyes are fixed partly by self-condensation. The limitations of the cadoxen technique have already been discussed in Section 13-1-4.

Reactive dyes with high-fixation properties. Most of the reactive dyes so far described have been subject to fairly heavy losses by hydrolysis during application. Wastage often exceeds 30%, and this adds appreciably to the cost of the dyeing operation. In recent years many patent specifications have been published describing dyes with high fixation efficiency. Most of these depend on the presence of two reactive groups. The dichlorotriazinyl and other polyhalogeno heterocyclic systems contain two reactive halogen atoms, but the two differ markedly in reactivity. In seeking dyes with high fixation properties, manufacturers have examined dyes with two reactive groups attached to the molecule at a distance from each other and usually with reactivity of a similar order although they are sometimes chemically different.

No systematic study of these dyes has yet been published, but the presence of an additional reactive group clearly ensures that more of the dye molecules become attached to the fibre by at least one chemical linkage. If, for example, 30% of each reactive group is hydrolysed, probably only 9% of the dye molecules will be wasted by hydrolysis of both groups; similarly 20% hydrolysis will lead to a wastage of only 4%. However, by no means all dyes with two reactive groups are technologically useful, and in order to provide a commercial range a selection must be made from the many possible structures in order to obtain the desired shades, fastness properties, water-solubility, diffusibility and substantivity.

A great many high-fixation dyes have been described in the patent literature.[47] To select but one example, the bluish red dye [**192**] is said to be fixed on cellulosic fibres to the extent of at least

[**192**]

95%.* A range of high-fixation dyes for printing applications has been placed on the market by ICI under the name *Procion Supra*. In comparison with older reactive dyes they are economical in use, not only because losses are low but also as a result of savings in water, steam and detergents.

13-2 Dyes for wool

The arrival of reactive dyes for cellulosic fibres made a considerable impact because durable shades on these substrates had previously been obtained chiefly from vat dyes, which are often costly and lacking in brightness, or from azoic dyes applied by rather complex processes. For wool, however, high fastness properties have long been available in the chrome dyes, and bright shades of reasonably good fastness properties are provided by many acid dyes. When reactive dyes for this fibre appeared they were accepted as useful additions to the marketed fast dyes, but the new feature of fibre-reactivity was not immediately noticed. Probably the first of them was *Supramine Orange R* (IG, later marketed by Bayer) (CI Acid Orange 30; CI 17770). This dye has the structure aniline → N-chlooacetyl J acid; its wet-fastness properties are not particularly good and it is doubtful whether extensive reaction with the wool fibre occurs under the conditions of application. The *Remalan* dyes (FH) already mentioned (Section 13-1-3) were introduced in the early 1950s, but although the possibility of reaction with unspecified fibres was mentioned in patents[48] this aspect was not stressed by the manufacturers until later. The first specifically reactive dyes for wool were produced by ICI in the *Procilan* range (1963), and according to the makers' pattern card they are mainly 1:2 metal complexes containing a reactive group differing from that used in other ICI reactive ranges in that it is not subject to hydrolysis in the dyebath. Wegmann[26] states that the acrylamide group is used in the Procilan dyes.

Dyes containing reactive acrylamido, other unsaturated aliphatic acylamido groups and also halogenated aliphatic acylamido groups are described in an extensive patent literature. Many such products are stated to be suitable for application to natural or synthetic polyamide fibres and also to cellulosic fibres, but in general their reactivity is somewhat inadequate for use on cellulosic fibres. An example of such a dye giving reddish grey shades on wool has the structure [193].[49]

* UK 1,104,911 (ICI).

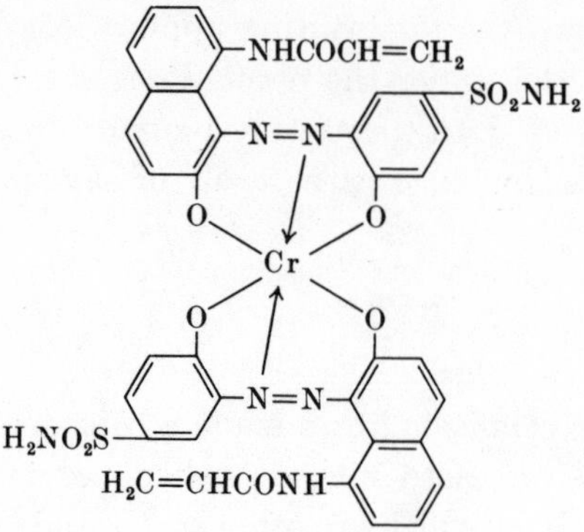

[193]

Procilan dyes are applied to wool from neutral or weakly acid baths and in these conditions combination with the fibre occurs and dyeings with very good wet-fastness and light-fastness properties are obtained. Reaction is usually incomplete, however, and if maximum fastness to wet treatments is required further reaction can be brought about by prolonged boiling, use of pressure equipment or dyeing at pH 8–8·5. In view of the possibility of damage to the fibre, for most purposes these conditions are not recommended.

13-3 Dyes for synthetic polyamides

It might be expected that synthetic fibres would have an advantage over natural fibres in uniformity, but in practice it is extremely difficult to produce synthetic polyamide fibres with uniform dyeing properties. Nylon fibres are manufactured by extruding the molten polyamide through spinnerets, and when cold they are drawn out to between 400 and 600% of their original length. The stretching process brings about partial crystallisation, and during the later textile operations of weaving or knitting variations in tension further affect the distribution of crystalline regions in the fibre. Affinity for dyes tends to be lower in the crystalline than in the amorphous regions, and this gives rise to uneven coloration (the so-called *barré* effect) in dyed fabric. As already stated in Chapter 6, disperse dyes are relatively insensitive to variations in the fibre, but their washing fastness leaves something to be desired. Acid dyes have much better wet-fastness properties but they reveal fibre irregularities.

A range of reactive *Procinyl* dyes introduced by ICI in 1959 successfully combines the application properties of disperse dyes with the outstanding wet-fastness properties associated with fibre-reaction. These dyes are applied to nylon in weakly acid conditions which prevent reaction with the fibre, and level dyeing is readily attained. When the dyebath is exhausted it is made alkaline, and reaction with the fibre then takes place so that the resulting dyeings are not only level but also resistant to wet treatments. In another method the dyes are applied from a bath containing sodium bicarbonate; on raising the temperature gradually from 40° to 90°–100°C the pH value rises as the bicarbonate is decomposed. Wegmann[26] states that Procinyl dyes contain reactive chlorohydrin groups. Many dyes based on the reactivity of such groups are described in the patent literature, examples being the yellow azo dye [194][50] and the blue anthraquinone derivative [195].[51] It is possible that more

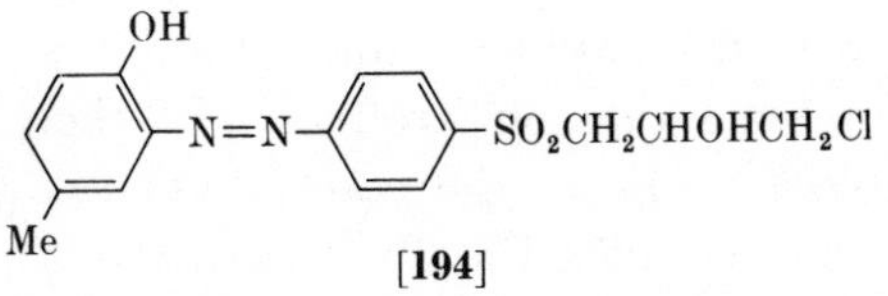

[194]

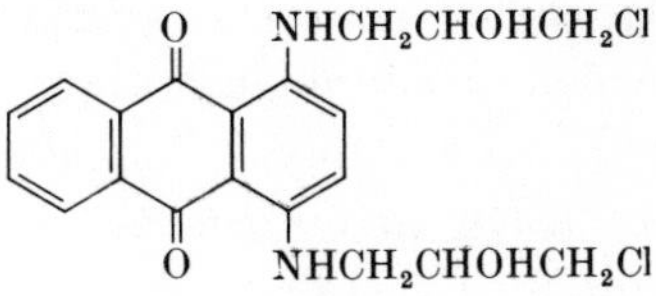

[195]

than one reactive system is employed in the Procinyl range; no information regarding the structure of individual members is available.

Elöd and Einsele[52] established by means of chromatographic and other techniques that Procinyl dyes form bonds with polyamide fibres. Reaction takes place primarily with free amino groups in the fibre, but there are not enough of these to account for the observed extent of fixation. Scott and Vickerstaff[53] suggested that reaction occurs partly with amide groups, and although substitution of such groups usually takes place only in extreme conditions Elöd and Einsele (loc. cit.) established that Procinyl dyes can be fixed on substrates such as urea-formaldehyde resins or polyurethanes containing no amino groups. The possibility that fixation is due to physical inclusion in the fibre rather than reaction was examined. Dyeings obtained in alkaline conditions resisted extraction with isopropanol, but when the dyes were applied in neutral or weakly alkaline conditions (under which reaction with the fibre does not occur) they were quantitatively removed by the solvent. Dyes applied by the normal procedure to secondary acetate fibre containing no reactive groups were easily extracted. It therefore appears probable that Procinyl dyes are fixed to polyamide fibres by chemical bonds attached to both amino and amide groups. A possibility remains, however, that fixation is partly due to the formation of a polymeric dye anchored to the fibre by reaction between an end-molecule and an amino group.

14 Polycondensation and related dyes

In earlier chapters several classes of dyes have been described in which insoluble colouring matters are produced upon the fibre, either by applying an alkali-soluble reduction product and then oxidising to re-form the insoluble dye (as in the case of vat and sulphur dyes) or by forming an azo dye upon the fibre (azoic dyes). In recent years another class of temporarily solubilised dyes has appeared, consisting of dyes the molecules of which react together upon the fibre to form polymers or other condensation products of fairly high molecular weight with elimination of the solubilising groups. Various names have been proposed for this class, including Polycondensation, Thiocondensation, Polyreaction and Condense dyes, but none of them has yet been generally accepted. The Colour Index Editorial Board is provisionally using the term Condense dyes, and has defined the class as 'dyes which during or after application react covalently with themselves or other compounds (other than the substrate) to form molecules of much increased size'.

Experimental work with dyes of this type was described by Milligan and Swan[1] in 1961. They found that dyes containing groups such as —NHCOCH$_2$SSO$_3$Na when applied to wool from an acetic acid bath formed insoluble disulphides of the type [Dye—NHCOCH$_2$ S—]$_2$ that were resistant to washing but could be removed by extraction with acetone. Some reaction with the fibre also occurred, disulphides probably being formed with thiol groups in the wool:

$$\text{Wool—SH} + \text{Dye—NHCOCH}_2\text{SSO}_3\text{Na} \rightarrow$$
$$\text{Wool—S—S—CH}_2\text{CONH—Dye}$$

Self-condensing dyes containing thiosulphate groups were first used commercially by Farbwerke Hoechst in their *Inthion* range introduced in 1960.[2] The reactive groups are linked with the dye molecule via —CH$_2$— groups, and the alkali metal salts of such derivatives (often called *Bunte* salts) are soluble in water.[3] The aliphatic disulphides formed by condensation are stable towards sodium sulphide, and differ in this respect from aromatic disulphides and the sulphur dyes.[4] Thiosulphate groups can be introduced by reaction of halogenoalkyl compounds with sodium thiosulphate, or by reaction of dyes containing sulphonyl or carbonyl halide groups with compounds such as β-aminoethyl thiosulphate. Inthion dyes usually contain more than one thiosulphate group.[2] Condensation on the fibre is brought about by treatment with sodium sulphide, and the reaction is believed to take place in two stages, a trisulphide being formed first which then loses one atom of sulphur:[5]

(1) $2 \text{ Dye—SSO}_3\text{Na} + \text{Na}_2\text{S} \rightarrow \text{Dye—S}_3\text{—Dye} + 2\text{Na}_2\text{SO}_3$

(2) $\text{Dye—S}_3\text{—Dye} + \text{Na}_2\text{SO}_3 \xrightarrow{\text{Na}_2\text{S}} \text{Dye—S—S—Dye} + \text{Na}_2\text{S}_2\text{O}_3$

The first dye of the Inthion range was *Inthion Brilliant Blue 5GL*, later re-named *Inthion Brilliant Blue I 5G* (CI Condense Blue 1). It is a phthalocyanine derivative giving bright turquoise shades with excellent fastness to light and wet treatments. The constitution has not been disclosed, but Hoechst patents[6] include several references to the condensation products of copper phthalocyanine trisulphonyl chloride with three and the tetrasulphonyl chloride with four molecular proportions of 2-aminoethylthiosulphonic acid; it seems likely that the commercial product has a structure of one of these types. (The structure of copper phthalocyanine is given on p. 232.)

Inthion dyes may be applied to cellulosic fibres by padding, drying, passing the treated fibre through a solution of sodium sulphide or hydrosulphide, exposing to air, rinsing and soaping. Various printing processes are also in use. The dyes can be applied to wool or nylon, and even to polypropylene, but on the last-named fibre fastness to washing is for some reason impaired on exposure to light.[2]

In 1966 a range of polycondensation dyes was introduced under the name *Dykolite* by Southern Dyestuff Company (a division of Martin-Marietta Corporation, Charlotte, N. Carolina, USA). Few details are available, but it is known that these dyes contain thiosulphate groups attached to aryl nuclei. The range provides yellow, orange, orange-brown, scarlet and turquoise shades, many of which are bright. Probably most of the dyes are azo derivatives, but the blues are of the phthalocyanine class. Many of Martin-Marietta's patent specifications[7] apparently relate to the Dykolite dyes, and products specifically claimed include [**196**], [**197**] and [**198**]. The Dykolite dyes are soluble in water but lack substantivity for cellulosic fibres. They may be applied to such fibres in continuous

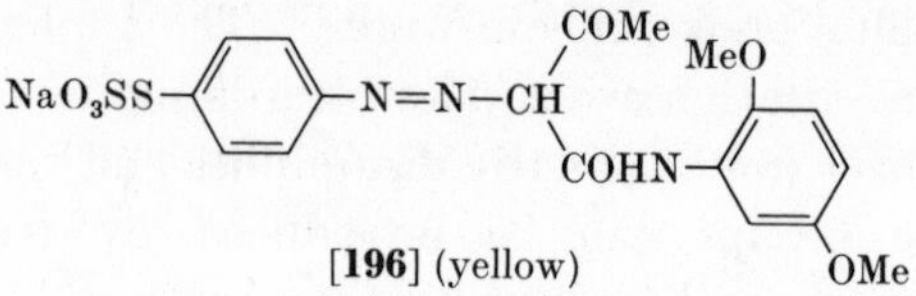

$$NaO_3SS-\langle\!\!\!\!\!\!\!\!\!\bigcirc\!\!\!\!\!\!\!\!\!\rangle-N=N-CH\begin{array}{c}COMe\\\\COHN\end{array}$$

[196] (yellow)

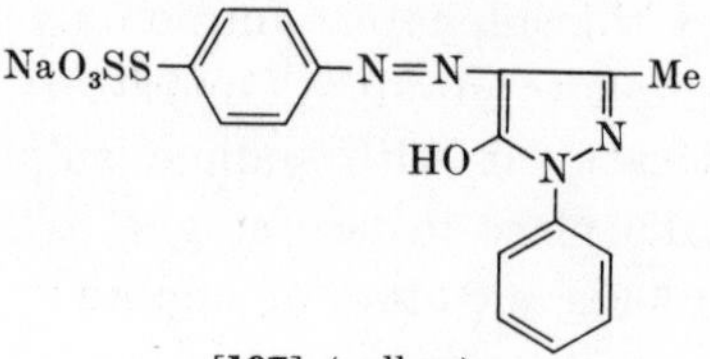

[197] (yellow)

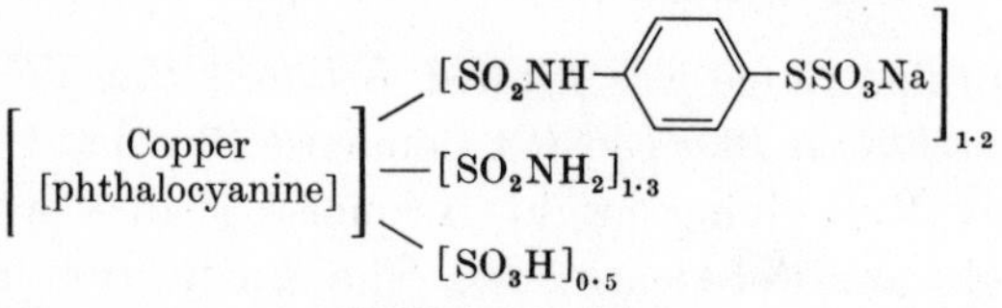

$$\begin{bmatrix}Copper\\[phthalocyanine]\end{bmatrix}\begin{cases}[SO_2NH-\langle\!\!\bigcirc\!\!\rangle-SSO_3Na]_{1\cdot2}\\-[SO_2NH_2]_{1\cdot3}\\[SO_3H]_{0\cdot5}\end{cases}$$

[198] (bright blue)

processes by padding with an aqueous solution of the dye and urea, drying, padding with a solution containing an auxiliary agent *Sodyefide F-40* and salt, rinsing, soaping, rinsing again and drying. The auxiliary agent brings about condensation with formation of an insoluble dye within the fibre, dye residues apparently becoming linked by disulphide or polysulphide chains. Alternatively the fibre may be padded with a solution of the dye, urea and thiourea, dried and heated for 1 min at 200°C to bring about fixation (Thermo-fix method). Processes have been devised whereby members of this range can be applied in conjunction with solubilised or pre-reduced sulphur dyes (see Chapter 11); they may also be applied together with disperse dyes to cotton/polyester blends.[8] The fact that Dykolite dyes are stripped by sodium sulphide solution is claimed as an advantage in that it affords a means of dealing with faulty dyeings.

Numerous azo disulphide dyes which can be applied by usual reduction-oxidation methods have been described by Martin-Marietta.[9] On the fibre they yield structures identical with or similar to those of Dykolite dyes, but they differ in that the disulphide bond is introduced in manufacture rather than application. An example of such a dye has the constitution 4,4′-diaminodiphenyl disulphide $\rightrightarrows$ (3-methyl-1-phenylpyrazol-5-one)$_2$; it gives a bright golden yellow shade on cotton fabric.

A range of dyes marketed by American Cyanamid Co. (ACY) under the name *Calcobond* may probably be classed as polycondensation dyes although it has been suggested that they react with cellulose.[10] These dyes contain a methylolated amino group similar to that used in many textile finishing agents. Wegmann[11] has shown that Calcobond Turquoise Blue B (ACY) can be fixed on inert polyester fibre just as well as on cotton, and this supports the view that fixation depends on self-condensation rather than reaction with the fibre. Calcobond dyes are applied by padding or printing, and are 'cured' by dry heat in presence of an acid catalyst such as ammonium chloride. The rather severe conditions necessary cause some degradation of the fibre with loss of tensile strength of the order of 10–20%, but there are advantages in high fixation efficiency (90% or more) and the possibility of combining dyeing with acid-catalysed finishing processes.

Numerous self-condensing or polymerising dyes are described in the patent literature. A system resembling that of the Calcobond dyes has been devised by CIBA, and is based on the use of dyes containing triazinyl rings substituted by amino and hydroxyalkyl-amino groups; these are applied to the fibre with a resin pre-condensate and a catalyst such as ammonium chloride, and fixation is brought about by brief heating at 150°C.[12] A Japanese firm has described the use of polymerisable dyes obtained by reaction of dyes containing amino, hydroxyl or carboxy groups with a vinyl compound such as glycidyl methacrylate:

$$CH_2{=}\overset{\overset{\displaystyle CH_3}{|}}{C}{-}COOCH_2CHOHCH_2OH$$

which can be applied to textile material and then treated with a catalyst such as azoisobutyronitrile at temperatures up to 120°C to bring about polymerisation.[13] Another system uses dyes containing sulphonylurea groups which are fixed by heat treatment to give very good wet-fastness properties.[14] Co-polymers formed from dyes containing unsaturated groups such as acryloylamino groups together with suitable colourless monomers have been proposed for the simultaneous dyeing and finishing of textile fibres.[15]

Instead of introducing polymerisable groups into a dye molecule several investigators have introduced a chromophoric system within a polymeric structure. In one such process polymers containing epoxy groups are combined first with an aromatic amine and then with a diazonium salt so that a coloured product is obtained which can be incorporated into polyacrylonitrile fibre by a wet spinning process.[16] In another system co-polymers derived from a mixture of monomers including a phenolic compound (such as 3-acryloyl-aminophenol) are coupled with a diazonium salt, and the resulting coloured resins are applied to textile materials and fixed by heat treatment.[17] Another device makes use of diazonium salts such as that derived from copper tetra(4-amino)phthalocyanine as polymerisation initiators, enabling coloured products to be obtained from suitable monomers (such as mixtures of acrylamide and methyl acrylate), and these also can be fixed on textile fibres by means of heat.[18]

It is not yet clear whether systems such as those described are likely to attain commercial importance.

Phthalocyanine pigments and dyes

In 1928 chemists of Scottish Dyes Ltd (now part of ICI) were called upon to investigate the cause of a discoloration affecting certain batches of phthalimide, a vat dye intermediate manufactured by passing ammonia gas into molten phthalic anhydride. The presence of a blue pigment was detected, and this was isolated and examined. It proved to be an extremely stable crystalline substance containing iron (the metal evidently having originated in the reaction vessel), and the iron content was not affected by treatment with concentrated sulphuric acid. The chemists concerned, A. G. Dandridge, H. A. E. Drescher, S. W. Dunworth and J. Thomas, perceived the possible importance of the new pigment, and they succeeded in preparing it by passing ammonia into molten phthalic anhydride containing iron filings. After removal of alkali-soluble components the product was purified either by vatting or by fractional precipitation from solution in concentrated sulphuric acid. It gave a blue shade on cotton when applied from a vat. A similar preparation in which iron was replaced by cuprous chloride gave a blue pigment which could not be vatted, and another non-vattable product was obtained by using a nickel salt. Patent protection was obtained for the manufacture of these pigments.[1]

Since the new products appeared to belong to a new chemical class they were clearly of academic interest. An invitation to investigate their structure was accepted by Dr R. P. (later Sir Patrick) Linstead of the Imperial College of Science and Technology, London, and whilst his work was in progress the properties of the pigments were more closely examined by ICI. It became clear that the discovery was of major importance, and that the copper compound in particular was a pigment with outstanding properties.

Linstead came to the conclusion that the pigments have a structure derived from four isoindole units connected by four nitrogen atoms to form a strainless 16-membered ring with a central metal atom. In recording his work[2] he acknowledged the help of Professor

231

I. M. (later Sir Ian) Heilbron and Dr F. Irving, who pointed out that the copper pigment had undoubtedly been prepared previously from phthalonitrile by de Diesbach and von der Weid.[3] Earlier still an analogous metal-free pigment had been obtained by Braun and Tcherniak[4] by heating o-cyanobenzamide. These authors failed to appreciate the importance of their observations, and did not identify or study the pigments further. Linstead represented the copper derivative as [199], and assigned the name *phthalocyanine* to the new

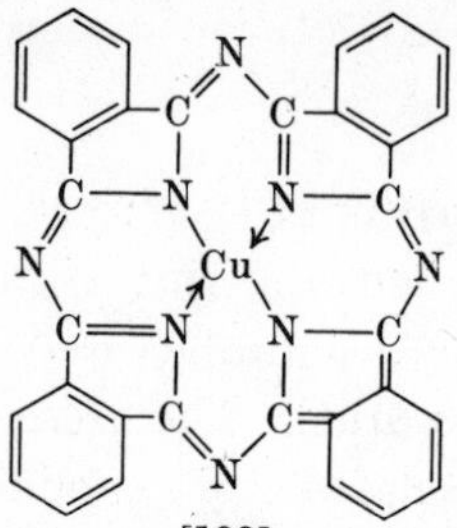

[199]

class of colouring matters. His structure was soon confirmed by Dr J. M. Robertson of the Royal Institution, who published an X-ray contour diagram showing the position of every atom in the molecule.[5] This was one of the earliest applications of X-ray analysis. Robertson pointed out that the system is continuously conjugated and that the o-quinonoid ring in Linstead's structure has no definite location. The structure is a perfect example of resonance, and the high stability and tinctorial value may be attributed to this fact.

The phthalocyanines are structurally related to the natural porphin pigments. Chlorophyll and the blood pigment hemin are well known members of this class.

Linstead found that many metallic phthalocyanine derivatives can be prepared conveniently by heating o-cyanobenzamide with the metal concerned, or its oxide, sulphide or carbonate, at a temperature of about 250°C.[6] Later he used phthalonitrile similarly, and this compound reacts readily with copper or a copper salt at 190°–210°C. Cuprous chloride (2CuCl) reacts with phthalonitrile (4 mol.) at 170°C to give copper phthalocyanine, leaving half of the copper behind as cupric chloride; on the other hand cupric chloride reacts only above 200°C with formation of copper monochlorophthalocyanine.[7]

15-1 Manufacture of phthalocyanine pigments

The first manufacturing process developed by ICI was based on the reaction of phthalonitrile with cuprous chloride.[8] The course of the reaction is not as simple as might be supposed, and Lecher, Lacey and Orem found that the presence of either air or a little cupric chloride is essential for successful operation.[9]

Before this process was fully established a much cheaper route was discovered by the late Dr Max Wyler. After a long career devoted to the manufacture of dyes at the ICI Blackley Works instead of retiring at the usual age he turned his attention to research. In one of many projects he studied the manufacture of copper phthalocyanine, and found that it can be obtained by fusion of phthalamide or diammonium phthalate with the ammonium salt of sulphamic acid in presence of a copper salt.[10] It then occurred to him that urea might serve as a cheap source of the necessary nitrogen, and in experiments carried out in collaboration with R. L. M. Allen the pigment was obtained by melting together phthalic anhydride, urea and cupric chloride.[11] Although the yield then obtained was inferior to that from phthalonitrile the process showed a considerable economic advantage because of the cheapness of the starting materials. Wyler later found that inclusion of a small quantity of boric acid resulted in an improvement in yield.[12] A further improvement was effected by Riley by including in the melt a catalyst such as ammonium molybdate, ammonium phosphate, or an element of Periodic Group V or VI.[13] Many further modifications of the process have been described, and a summary of the literature is given by Moser and Thomas.[14]

According to Wolf, Degener and Peterson,[15] the synthesis of copper phthalocyanine from phthalic anhydride and urea takes a course that may be represented as shown, involving compounds [**200**]–[**207**] (p. 234).

Because of the difficulty of dealing with the hard cake given by the early fusion processes, the operation was later carried out by baking in iron trays or by heating in solvents such as trichlorobenzene; laboratory yields of 97% are said to have been obtained by the latter method.[16] Purification of the crude product is carried out in various ways. Unreacted materials and by-products may be removed by extraction with dilute alkali, then with dilute acid, but such treatment is often omitted when a solvent is used, the product being simply filtered off, washed and dried (with recovery of solvent). In all cases, however, conversion into a suitable pigmentary form is essential. This is often brought about by dissolving the pigment in cold concentrated sulphuric acid, then running the solution slowly into hot water (which may contain a dispersing agent) with good stirring. The resulting pigment particles are small and fairly uniform in size (0.01–$0.5\,\mu$, and mainly at the smaller end of this range). Another common method consists in milling the pigment with a crystalline inorganic substance such as sodium chloride or sulphate, and improved processes have been devised in which the inorganic agent is accompanied by an organic solvent such as acetone or trichlorobenzene.[17] The milling agents are easily removed by suitable extraction processes, and the concentrated pigment remains in the desired finely divided form.

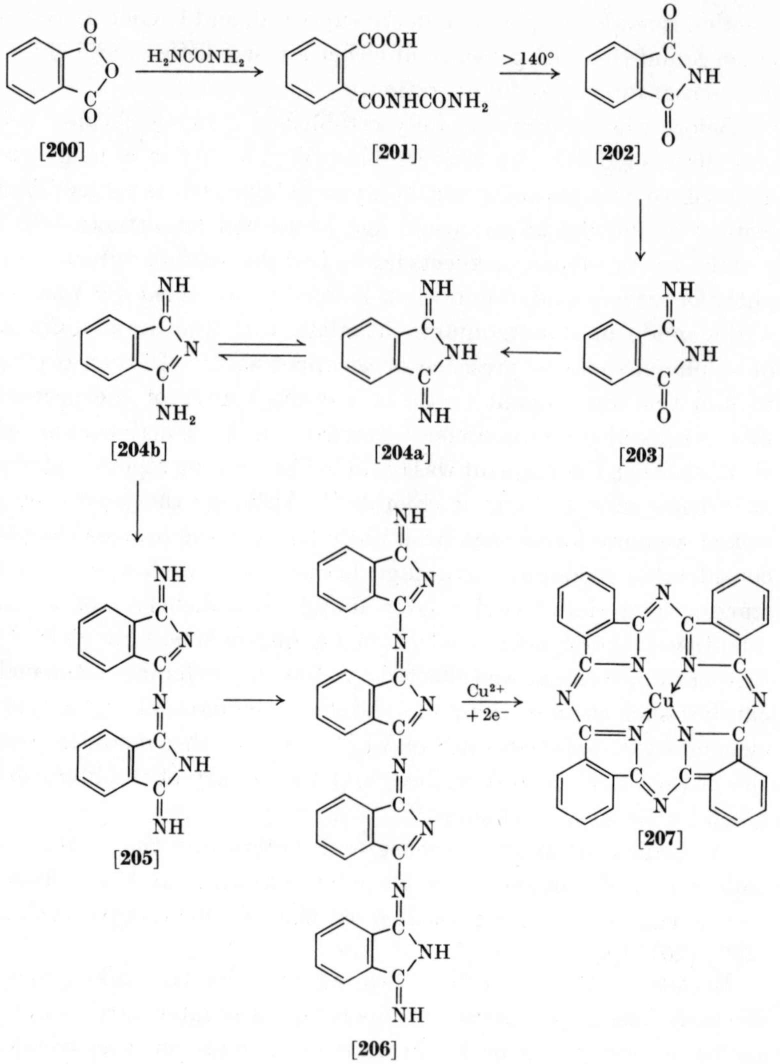

Physical treatments of the kind described bring about not only a reduction in particle size but also a polymorphic change. Copper phthalocyanine is known in at least four crystalline forms, and it is unfortunate that there is some confusion in the nomenclature that has been applied to them. The form given by the melt or solvent process is generally known as the β form, and it appears under the microscope as long needles.[14] Conversion into the α form is effected by reprecipitation from concentrated sulphuric acid solution or one of the milling processes described above. On heating with solvents such as o-chlorophenol in which the small α form crystals are slightly soluble reconversion into the β form takes place. Both of these polymorphs are used commercially (see Section 15-4). Other polymorphs (the γ and δ forms) have been described, but so far commercial applications for them have not been found.[18]

15-2 Metal-free phthalocyanine

Metal-free phthalocyanine is a bright greenish blue pigment. It is formed when phthalonitrile is heated in a sealed glass vessel at 350°–360°C, either alone[19] or with an acid amide, a phenol, naphthol or an aliphatic hydroxy compound or with triethanolamine.[20] The origin of the two atoms of hydrogen which take the place of the metal atom is not clear, but they are apparently liberated by decomposition of one or more of the substances present. Metal-free phthalocyanine can also be obtained by eliminating metal from phthalocyanine complexes with labile metals such as magnesium or calcium by reaction with a strong acid,[21] or even more easily by treatment of disodium phthalocyanine (see below) with cold methanol.[22] It is not obtainable by fusion of phthalic anhydride with urea.

15-3 Phthalocyanine complexes from metals other than copper

Phthalocyanine derivatives have been prepared from metals of every group in the Periodic Table. All are blue or green in hue, the copper compound being the reddest and others greener in the order: nickel, cobalt, zinc, aluminium, beryllium, tin, lead. Several metal derivatives have been obtained by double decomposition between dilithium phthalocyanine and suitable metal salts.[23]

Disodium phthalocyanine is a dull greenish blue powder, and may be obtained by refluxing phthalonitrile with sodium amyloxide in amyl alcohol or by melting together phthalonitrile and metallic sodium.[24] The metal is very easily displaced.

Numerous substituted derivatives of copper phthalocyanine and other metallic complexes have been prepared, but only the halogenated copper derivatives are of commercial importance. These are described later. A copper tetraphenylphthalocyanine has found limited use for textile application (see Section 15-5).

15-4   Application of phthalocyanine pigments

The copper derivative is by far the most important of the phthalocyanine pigments. It is manufactured by ICI as *Monastral Fast
Blue B* (CI Pigment Blue 15; CI 74160) and now also by many
other firms; the world production is measured in millions of pounds
annually. The outstandingly good properties of this pigment
include a bright blue shade, high tinctorial strength, resistance to
acid, alkali, oxidising and reducing agents and to most organic
solvents, and high fastness to light and heat. Copper phthalocyanine
sublimes unchanged at 580°C.[25] The product is largely used in printing inks, also in lacquers, emulsion paints, distempers, rubber,
plastics, leathercloth and paper; further applications are found in
textile printing and mass pigmentation processes. An ingenious
method for colouring motor-car bodies or other large metal surfaces
has been described, in which a solution of phthalonitrile in acetone
is applied, and after the solvent has evaporated the metal is heated
to bring about pigment formation.[26] The shade varies according to
the metal concerned, but adhesion is said to be excellent. For
paints containing an aromatic solvent Monastral Fast Blue B is
unsuitable, since such solvents promote change of the crystal form
and consequent loss of strength. *Monastral Fast Blue LB* has been
developed for such applications, and is a modified form of copper
phthalocyanine free from this defect (see below).

    Metal-free phthalocyanine is manufactured as *Monastral Fast
Blue G* (ICI) (CI Pigment Blue 16; CI 74100). It is used in printing
inks, emulsion paints, paper, bookcloth, linoleum, artists' colours and
numerous other products. Like Monastral Fast Blue B it is subject
to change in shade on contact with certain organic solvents. The
unmetallised pigment is relatively unimportant since its shade is
greener and less bright than that of the copper derivative, and its
fastness properties are somewhat lower.

    Copper monochlorophthalocyanine, obtained either by reaction
of phthalonitrile with cupric chloride (see p. 232) or of a mixture
of phthalic anhydride (3 mol.) and 4-chlorophthalic anhydride
(1 mol.) with urea and cupric chloride, is manufactured under
various names. The product is classified in the Colour Index under
Constitution No. CI 74250, but at present the commercial pigments
are included with unchlorinated copper phthalocyanine under CI
Pigment Blue 15; since the properties are markedly affected by the
presence of chlorine it seems likely that the two types will be separated when the classification is reviewed. The chlorinated pigments
are slightly greener than copper phthalocyanine, but they have a

great advantage in that the halogen atom has a steric effect preventing growth of β form crystals, so that the pigment is stable in presence of aromatic solvents.[27]

Whereas β copper phthalocyanine formerly existed only in relatively large crystals with poor tinctorial value, it can now be produced in a pigmentary form with much smaller crystals. Salt grinding converts the β into the α form, as already stated, but by grinding with salt in presence of a crystallising solvent either the α or the β form can be converted into β form with pigmentary properties. Alternatively the α form obtained by salt grinding can be treated with solvent to yield pigmentary β form provided that the initial grinding has not been continued too long; sufficient β form crystals must remain to serve as seeds to bring about phase change without crystal growth.[27] These operations require careful control. The products give a greener shade than that of the α form.

In common with pigments of other classes the phthalocyanines are affected by a tendency to *flocculate* in paint medium. The phenomenon is due to aggregation of particles with loss of colour value, followed by redispersion under the influence of shearing forces applied in application by spraying or brushing. Numerous agents have been used as anti-flocculants, and the subject has been reviewed by Moser and Thomas.[14]

Many polyhalogenophthalocyanines have been manufactured. In general chlorination yields a progressively greener product up to a content of about 14 chlorine atoms in the molecule, and the effect continues in less marked fashion as the remaining two hydrogen atoms are substituted. By direct halogenation under pressure it is difficult to introduce more than 12 atoms of chlorine or 13 of bromine into the pthalocyanine molecule,[28] but in a molten eutectic mixture of aluminium chloride and sodium chloride between 15 and 16 atoms of halogen can be introduced. *Monastral Fast Green GBS* (ICI) is a bright green copper polychlorophthalocyanine pigment with excellent general fastness properties. Highly halogenated pigments have been manufactured by using mixtures of chlorine and bromine,[29] but the pattern of distribution of the halogen atoms corresponds to that of a statistical mixture, so that a precise structure cannot be assigned to these products. *Monastral Fast Greens 3Y* and *6Y* (ICI) (CI Pigment Greens 43, 41) are important polyhalogeno derivatives containing both chlorine and bromine; they are very bright yellowish green pigments with excellent fastness properties, and are suitable for application in paint, printing inks and many other media.

15-5   Phthalocyanine dyes for textile materials

The sulphonation of copper phthalocyanine was described in the first patent specification relating to dyes of this class,[1] but the name 'phthalocyanine' was then unknown. The water-soluble sodium salt of the disulphonic acid was introduced by ICI as a direct dye under the name *Durazol Blue 8G* (CI Direct Blue 86; CI 74180), and has since been manufactured by many firms. It is applied to cellulosic fibres, wool and nylon, and gives a bright greenish blue shade with very good fastness to light. Its wet-fastness properties are poor, but can be improved by aftertreatment with a resin finish. The dye is used for colouring paper—an application for which high wet-fastness properties are not required. The corresponding trisulphonic acid is manufactured as *Durazol Blue 10G* (ICI) (CI Direct Blue 87; CI 74200). This dye has wet-fastness properties inferior to those of the disulphonic acid, but again it is of value for application to paper.

In 1944 Haddock and Wood of ICI developed processes whereby temporarily solubilised derivatives of copper phthalocyanine can be applied to cellulosic fibres.[30] A chloromethyl group is introduced into each of the four benzene rings in the molecule by reaction of copper phthalocyanine with dichlorodimethyl ether in an aluminium chloride melt in presence of a base such as triethylamine. From the resulting reactive intermediate compound water-soluble onium derivatives are obtained by reaction with a tertiary base such as pyridine or triethylamine, or with thiourea. In another method the tetra(chloromethyl)phthalocyanine is treated with a metal salt of an alkyl, aralkyl or aryl mercaptan, and by further reaction with dimethyl sulphate or methyl *p*-toluenesulphonate the product is converted into a ternary sulphonium salt. The water-soluble dyes so obtained can be applied to cellulosic fibres by dyeing or printing, and are fixed by steaming and aftertreatment with dichromate and acetic acid. The solubilising group is thereby removed and an insoluble phthalocyanine dye is formed within the fibre. The *Alcian* dyes introduced by ICI in 1948 are dyes of the phthalocyanine and other chemical classes based on one or more of the systems described. The range includes blue, green and yellow dyes (CI Ingrain Blues 1, 3, 4 and 8, Greens 1 and 2 and Yellow 1).

The possibility of applying certain phthalocyanine dyes from a vat has already been mentioned (p. 231), but in many cases the reduction products are unstable. Cobalt phthalocyanine, however, is an exception, and forms a stable yellow-brown reduction product with good affinity for cellulosic fibres from an alkaline bath. The reduction-oxidation system may be represented as follows:

$$\xrightarrow[\text{O}_2]{2\text{H}}$$

The ease of reduction and solubility of the reduction product are greatly improved by the introduction of one sulphonic acid group. *Indanthren Brilliant Blue 4G* (FBy) (CI Vat Blue 29; CI 74140) is a vat dye of this kind. By dyeing or printing it gives greenish blue shades on cellulosic fibres with high fastness to light and washing. Its application is limited, however, by its sensitivity to chlorine.[31]

Most of the processes so far described for production of phthalocyanine dyes on the fibre yield water-insoluble derivatives, but substituents remain in the dye molecules and these usually have an adverse effect on fastness properties. Means of producing an unsubstituted metal phthalocyanine on the fibre have therefore been sought. Wyler[11] showed that iminophthalimidine ([**203**], p. 234) is formed as an intermediate in the production of copper phthalocyanine by the urea route, but it cannot be converted into the phthalocyanine under conditions suitable for textile application. Later, however, Baumann and others[32] discovered that diiminoisoindoline [**204a**], the next intermediate in the series, can be isolated in good yield from the melt as its sparingly soluble nitrate if ammonium nitrate is included in the reaction mixture. They further found that on treatment with a salt of copper or nickel and a suitable solvent 1-amino-3-iminoisoindolenine [**204b**], which is a tautomeric form of [**204a**], readily yields the metal phthalocyanine at a temperature of about 100°C. This base therefore serves as a convenient building block from which the pigments can be formed upon textile fibres, and it was marketed by Bayer in 1951 under the name *Phthalogen Brilliant Blue IF3B* (CI Ingrain Blue 2; CI 74160). It may be applied by printing with a thickened solution containing a copper or nickel salt and a special solvent (*Levasol P*, FBy), drying the printed material, then developing in acid steam. A method for dyeing application was also developed. The solvent is said to consist of a dihydric alcohol such as ethyleneglycol and an amide such as formamide.[33]

Compounds such as 1-amino-3-iminoisoindolenine which by appropriate treatment yield phthalocyanines on the fibre are called *phthalocyanine precursors.* A phenyl derivative [208] is marketed as

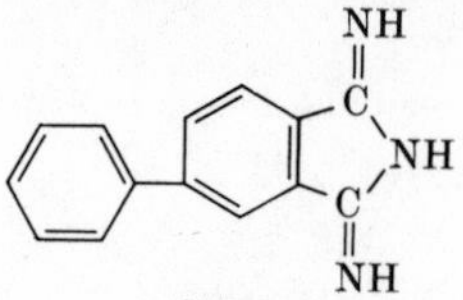

[208]

Phthalogen Brilliant Green IFFB (FBy) (CI Ingrain Green 3; CI 74280), and although somewhat expensive this has found use for shading purposes. Physical mixtures of 1-amino-3-iminoisoindolenine with organic complexes of copper or nickel have been marketed as a means of simplifying the application process, and later still a further improvement resulted from the production of metal complexes of polyisoindolines. Such products are available as *Phthalogen Brilliant Blue IF3GK* (copper complex) and *Phthalogen Turquoise IFBK* (FBy) (nickel complex). These products (both listed as CI Ingrain Blue 2; CI 74160) can be applied by dyeing or printing, and give bright blue and greenish blue shades, respectively.[34]

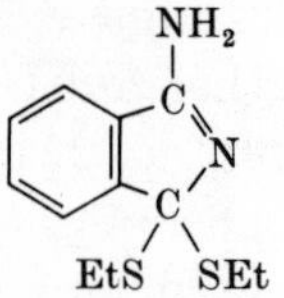

EtS   SEt
[209]

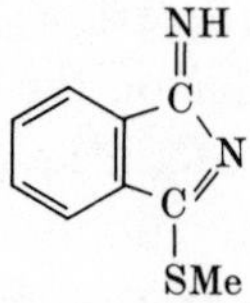

SMe
[210]

Precursors such as 1-amino-3,3-bis(ethylmercapto)isoindolenine [209] and 1-imino-3-methylmercaptoisoindolenine [210] have been developed by N. H. Haddock and his collaborators (ICI),[35] and others by DuPont chemists.[36]

Pigments other than phthalocyanines

Pigments are solid decorative materials in the form of small discrete particles, insoluble in the medium in which they are applied. The term 'pigment' includes white, black and coloured materials. Applications are diverse, and include surface coatings, mass coloration and dispersion in air (smokes). For surface coating the media include water (containing a binder such as glue or an emulsion of drying oil), drying oils (usually in admixture with one or more organic solvents), synthetic resins and nitrocellulose (with a plasticiser). Mass coloration is applied to plastic materials of all kinds (including rubber), and also to synthetic fibres.

Since pigments are used in suspension the physical condition of their particles is of major importance. Many pigments are polymorphic, and manufacturing conditions must be arranged so that the desired crystalline form is produced. The particle size must be small and fall within a fairly narrow range. In order that a standard product may be obtained production conditions are rigidly controlled to ensure uniformity; small changes are liable to affect the shade and strength adversely, and correction may be impracticable.

The earliest pigments were inorganic and of natural origin. Examples are white lead (basic lead carbonate), red lead (lead tetroxide, Pb_3O_4), lapis lazuli (a complex sodium aluminosilicate), malachite (basic copper carbonate), cinnabar (mercuric sulphide) and various oxides of iron. The oldest synthetic pigment is *Egyptian Blue* (CI Pigment Blue 31; CI 77437), a mixed silicate of copper and calcium, found in murals dating from about 1000 BC. Vegetable pigments were also used in ancient times, but as these are less durable than mineral products not much evidence of them remains; an alumina lake of madder has been identified, however, among pigments found in a collection of refuse at Corinth, believed to be associated with the destruction of that city in 146 BC.[1]

The introduction of new pigments took place very slowly until the synthetic dyestuffs industry was founded by W. H. Perkin in 1856, and even then for several decades the new synthetic pigments were simply insoluble salts derived from textile dyes by precipitation in various ways. It was not until the 20th century that synthetic organic pigments were specially developed for use in paints and printing inks. These products are now of major importance, but some of the old inorganic pigments which are cheap and durable and also many of the earlier organic pigments continue to be manufactured on a large scale.

16-1   Inorganic pigments

White pigments now in commercial use include titanium dioxide, zinc oxide, zinc sulphide and white lead. These differ considerably in properties, and a useful account has been published by the Oil and Colour Chemists' Association.[2]

The lead chromes form a series of pigments which are among the most important of the inorganic pigments now used. Lead chromate forms crystals of three types, tetragonal, orthorhombic and monoclinic, and this fact together with its property of forming mixed crystals with lead sulphate enables it to be used in conjunction with the latter substance to produce a range of pigments with shades varying from pale primrose to scarlet. If lead chromate and sulphate are co-precipitated by adding a solution containing sodium chromate and sodium sulphate to a solution of lead nitrate the lead chromate is initially obtained in orthorhombic crystals, and the presence of 30–50% of lead sulphate results in a product with a pale primrose shade. This form can be stabilised by adding tartaric acid, but in absence of such an agent the lead chromate crystals change during washing and drying to the monoclinic system and the shade becomes stronger and redder (primrose or pale lemon). Lead chromate alone in monoclinic crystals (Middle Chrome) has a golden yellow shade. Basic lead chromate crystallises in the tetragonal system and provides an orange shade. In presence of lead molybdate and lead sulphate lead chromate forms tetragonal crystals and the product is scarlet.

Lead chrome pigments are widely used in paints, printing inks and linoleum. They have very good fastness to light, but tend to darken on exposure; all of them are sensitive to alkali. The use of some of the lead chromes is restricted by the provisions of the *Lead Paint (Protection against Poisoning) Act*, 1926 and subsequent orders. Table 16-1 shows the composition, shade and CI reference numbers of the pigments.

Table 16-1   Details of lead chrome pigments

CI Ref. Nos.	Shade	Composition	Crystal system
CI Pigment Yellow 34 CI 77603	Pale primrose	Lead chromate Lead sulphate (30–55%) Tartaric acid	Orthorhombic
CI Pigment Yellow 34 CI 77603	Primrose or pale lemon	Lead chromate Lead sulphate (45–55%)	Monoclinic
CI Pigment Yellow 34 CI 77603	Lemon	Lead chromate Lead sulphate (20–45%)	Monoclinic
CI Pigment Yellow 34 CI 77603	Middle	Lead chromate	Monoclinic
CI Pigment Orange 21 CI 77601	Orange	Basic lead chromate	Tetragonal
CI Pigment Red 104 CI 77605	Scarlet	Lead chromate Lead sulphate Lead molybdate	Tetragonal

Various basic zinc chromates and basic zinc potassium chromates are used in priming paints as corrosion inhibitors (CI Pigment Yellow 36; CI 77955).

The *Prussian Blue* series of pigments, of which the first example was made by Diesbach in 1704, are still of importance. Much experimental work has been carried out to determine their structure, and they are now usually represented by the formula $MFe . Fe(CN)_6 . xH_2O$, where M is the ion of an alkali metal or ammonium. They may be regarded equally correctly as alkali metal ferric ferrocyanides or ferro-ferricyanides.[3] The potassium compounds are generally preferred, but sodium ammonium blues are often used because of their lower cost. Although they contain carbon, these pigments are usually classed as inorganic.

Prussian blues are manufactured by reaction of ferrous sulphate with potassium ferrocyanide to give a 'white paste', and this is then oxidised by acid potassium dichromate to give the blue pigment:

$$FeSO_4 + K_4Fe(CN)_6 \rightarrow K_2Fe . Fe(CN)_6 + K_2SO_4$$
$$K_2Fe . Fe(CN)_6 + H_2SO_4 + O \rightarrow 2KFe . Fe(CN)_6$$
$$+ K_2SO_4 + H_2O$$

There are many commercial brands (CI Pigment Blue 27; CI 77510, CI 77520), giving clear blue shades with a bronze effect in full shades. They have excellent fastness to light, and withstand temperatures up to 120°C, but are sensitive to alkali. Prussian blues are used in paints, printing inks, lacquers, linoleum and leathercloth; a 'soluble' version, which is actually a fine dispersion, is used for colouring paper.

A green pigment (CI Pigment Green 17; CI 77288) consisting of chromic oxide, Cr_2O_3, is obtained by burning a mixture of sodium dichromate and sulphur, or recovered from dichromate oxidation processes. It is fast to light, heat, acids and alkalis, but has a dull shade. This product is used in distempers and for colouring cement on account of its resistance to alkali, and also in ceramic products. A hydrated chromic oxide $Cr_2O(OH)_4$ is also used as a green pigment (CI Pigment Green 18; CI 77289). It has a much brighter shade than that of the anhydrous oxide but cannot be used satisfactorily in ceramic products and is somewhat sensitive to acids.

Many natural iron oxides are in use as pigments, giving yellow, red, brown and black shades. The ores are dried, ground, purified by various washing and sedimentation processes and sometimes calcined to remove combined water and deepen the shade. Synthetic oxides and hydrated oxides of iron are manufactured mainly from ferrous chloride (pickle liquor) and ferrous sulphate (copperas), which are by-products from the treatment of iron and steel in preparation for galvanising processes. Details of the natural and synthetic iron oxide pigments are available in *Paint Technology Manuals* published by the Oil and Colour Chemists' Association[2] and in the Colour Index under the numbers CI Pigment Yellows 42, 43 (CI 77492), CI Pigment Reds 101, 102 (CI 77491), CI Pigment Browns 6, 7 (CI 77491, 77492) and CI Pigment Black 11 (CI 77499).

The iron oxides are widely used because of their durability, chemical inertness and low cost. Natural micaceous iron oxide functions as an absorber of ultra-violet light and thus affords some protection to a polymerised oil film containing it. Some of the yellow and brown hydrated oxides tend to redden on exposure to heat.

Ultramarine (CI Pigment Blue 29; CI 77007) is an ancient pigment still used to a small extent at the present time. It is equivalent to the pigment derived from the mineral lapis lazuli, and is now made by prolonged heating at $800°C$ of a mixture of calcined kaolin, sodium carbonate, sulphur, silica and resin. The pigment is a polysulphide of sodium (or potassium, lithium or silver) alumino-silicate, but its structure is unknown. By varying the proportions of the raw materials the shade of the pigment can be varied from bright violet to bluish green.[4] The ultramarines are fast to light, heat and alkali, but are decolorised by acids. They are easily dispersed in water and have long been used as laundry blues; other applications include paints, lacquers, distempers, plastics, paper, soap, linoleum and artists' colours.

Several cadmium pigments are of technical interest. *Cadmium Yellow* (CI Pigment Yellow 37; CI 77199) consists of cadmium sulphide, and although this occurs to a small extent as a mineral it is manufactured from cadmium salts by reaction with hydrogen sulphide or sodium sulphide. *Cadmium Red* (CI Pigment Red 108; CI 77202) is cadmium sulphoselenide (CdS . xCdSe), and gives a range of yellowish red to bordeaux pigments (the redder shades being obtained by increasing the proportion of selenide). These pigments have good fastness to light, heat and alkali; they are used in stoving enamels and other heat-resisting finishes, also in artists' colours.

The mineral *cinnabar*, consisting of mercury sulphide, has been used as a pigment from early times, and was the original *vermilion* (CI Pigment Red 106; CI 77766). Synthetic vermilion is now manufactured by treating mercury with sulphur or an alkali sulphide and distilling the resulting mercury sulphide. It is a bright red pigment with good fastness properties. The importance of this product has now declined, but it is still used in rubber, printing inks and artists' colours.

Cobalt Blue (CI Pigment Blue 28; CI 77346) is a cobalt aluminate of variable composition and provides a brilliant blue pigment used in ceramics, coloured glass and artists' colours. It has outstanding fastness to heat and is unaffected by a temperature of 900°–1000°C.

Red lead (Pb_3O_4) (CI Pigment Red 105; CI 77578) is worthy of mention, but its colour is of secondary interest, and its main use is as a protective agent for iron and steel. It combines with linseed oil to form a tough elastic film.

Several metals are used in the form of finely divided powders or flakes and applied as pigments in a paint medium. Aluminium, copper, tin and zinc are used in this way both in protective coatings and for purposes of decoration. Lead powder is sometimes used in protective paint, and gold is used in decorative gilding.

16-2 Organic pigments

16-2-1 Carbon pigments

The simplest of the organic pigments is carbon itself, although in its various pigmentary forms it is often classed with inorganic pigments. It is manufactured as *Lamp Black* by collecting the soot from incomplete combustion of vegetable oils, *Carbon* (or *Gas*) *Black* by a similar process from natural gas, *Acetylene Black* from acetylene derived from waste calcium carbide, *Thermatomic Black* by cracking natural gases under pressure and *Bone Black* by calcination of bones. *Mineral Black* is obtained from carbonaceous earths (the principal British deposit being at Bideford, Devon), and *graphite* is obtained from mineral deposits in various parts of the world. The properties of these forms of carbon vary widely; they are classified in the Colour Index as CI Pigment Blacks 6, 7 (CI 77266), 8 (CI 77268), 9 (CI 77267) and 10 (CI 77265). The manufactured carbons are used in paints, printing inks (especially newsprint), carbon papers and plastics. Mineral blacks are now little used in paint but are sometimes incorporated in cement; graphite is used in stove polishes, stoving blacks and anti-corrosive paints.

16-2-2   Lakes

The early development of the synthetic dyestuffs industry in the nineteenth century was concerned mainly with dyes for textile purposes, but pigments were obtained by converting anionic dyes into sparingly soluble or insoluble barium, calcium or manganese salts. In this process precipitation is carried out in presence of an inorganic substrate such as alumina–blanc fixe, and this can be prepared *in situ* from a solution of aluminium sulphate by adding first soda ash to form aluminium hydroxide then barium chloride to form barium sulphate (blanc fixe). When a barium or other salt of a water-soluble dye is precipitated in presence of a substrate the substrate forms an integral part of the product and the resulting pigment is called a *lake*. In some cases the dye salt can be precipitated satisfactorily without a substrate, and the pigment is then known as a *toner*.*

Salt-type pigments have good resistance to hydrocarbon solvents, but they are somewhat sensitive to acids and alkalis. Many of the early pigments have been superseded, but some are still manufactured on a large scale.

A selection of the more important anionic pigments and their main uses are listed in Table 16-2.

Pigments were also manufactured from cationic dyes by converting them into insoluble tannates, but the serviceability of these products was restricted by their low light fastness. Just before the first World War, however, the Badische Company discovered a new means whereby pigments of greatly improved light fastness were obtained from cationic dyes. Their precipitants were complex acids such as phosphotungstic and phosphomolybdic acids or their salts.[5]

---

* In the USA the term 'toner' is often applied to all full-strength pigments.

After the war these methods were developed further and even better properties were secured by the use of more complex precipitants derived from phosphotungstomolybdic acid.[6] The *Fanal* (BASF) series of pigments are lakes produced by means of agents of this type, and corresponding products are manufactured by other firms.

Table 16-3 lists a few important cationic pigments of the xanthene and triphenylmethane classes.

16-2-3 Non-ionic organic pigments

Azo pigments. Non-ionic pigments are now of greater general importance than lakes, but so far as application is concerned the distinction between them has little or no significance. Azo pigments predominate, and provide mainly yellow, orange, red and brown hues. Violet, blue and green hues are mostly derived from other chemical classes, and the choice available to the user is less plentiful than that in the azo class. An account of phthalocyanine pigments has been given in Chapter 15, and those of other classes are now described.

Most of the azo pigments contain only one azo group, but there are some important yellow, orange and red pigments of the type $D \rightleftarrows E_2$; commercial products with more than two azo groups are virtually unknown.

Yellow pigments are derived almost entirely from acetoacetarylamides. The monoazo derivatives CI Pigment Yellows 1 (CI 11680) and 3 (CI 11710) give bright yellow and bright greenish yellow

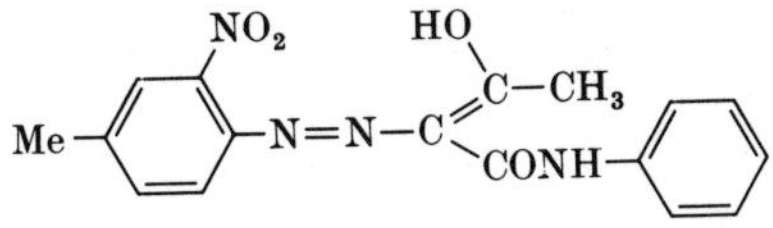

CI Pigment Yellow 1

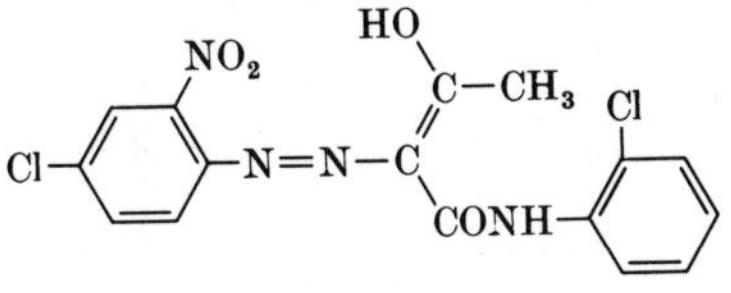

CI Pigment Yellow 3

shades, respectively, and have very good fastness to light but only fair resistance to organic solvents such as xylene. They are used largely in paints and printing inks. In contrast with these several disazo compounds obtained by coupling tetrazotised 3,3'-dichlorobenzidine with two molecular proportions of an acetoacetarylamide

Table 16-2 Anionic pigments of the Lake type

CI Ref. Nos.	Structure (as free acid)	Metal salts used	Shade	Chief uses
CI Pigment Red 48 CI 15865	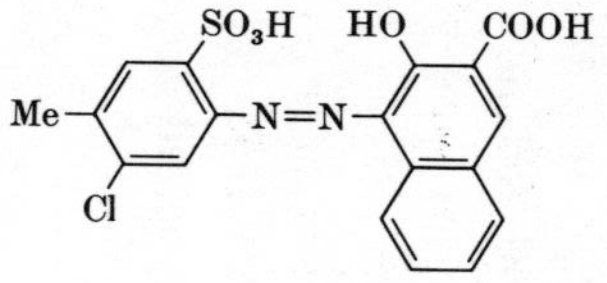	Barium Calcium Manganese	Bright yellowish red Bright red Red	Printing inks, paints, alkyd resin enamels, lacquers, rubber, paper
CI Pigment Red 49 CI 15830	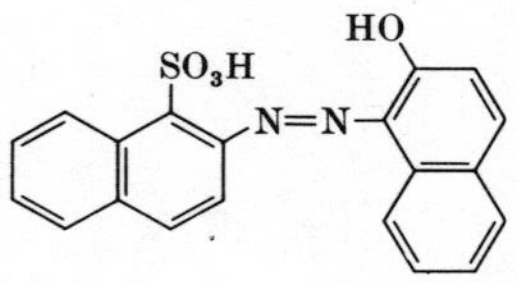	Barium Calcium Strontium	Yellowish red Yellowish red Yellowish red	Printing inks, paints, alkyd resin enamels, lacquers, rubber, paper
CI Pigment Red 53 CI 15855	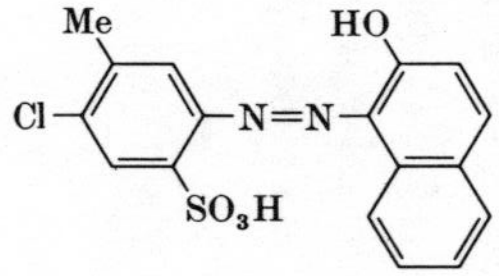	Barium Calcium	Yellowish red Yellowish red	Printing inks, rubber, PVC and other plastics, stoving finishes, paper

CI Pigment Red 57 CI 15850	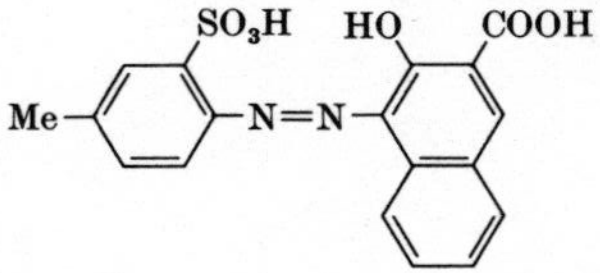	Barium Calcium	Red Red	Printing inks, paints, alkyd resin enamels, lacquers, rubber, paper
CI Pigment Red 60 CI 16105	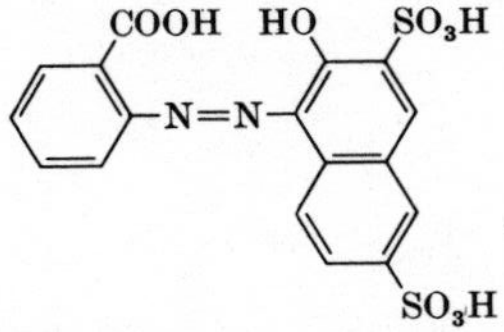	Barium	Bright red	Printing inks, paints, alkyd resin enamels, lacquers, rubber, paper

Table 16-3 Cationic pigments of the Lake type

CI Ref. Nos.	Structure of cation	Laking agent	Shade	Chief applications
CI Pigment Red 81 CI 45160	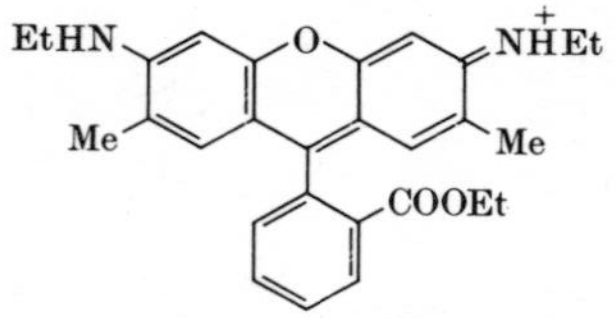 (Rhodamine 6G)	PTMA*	Bright bluish red	Printing inks, paints
CI Pigment Red 90 CI 45380	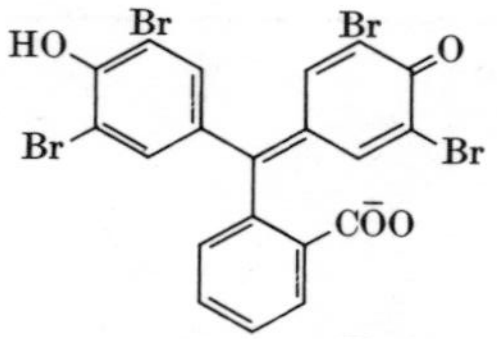 (Eosine)	Lead or aluminium salt	Bright red	Printing inks, (Al salt is used in cosmetics)
CI Pigment Violet 1 CI 45170	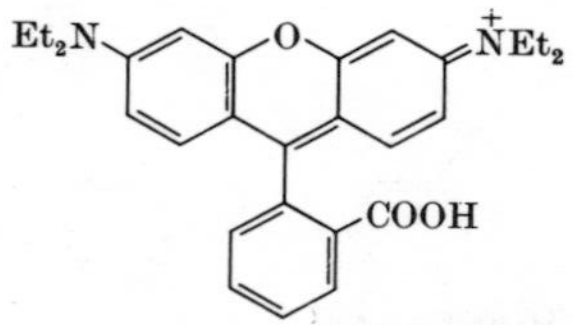 (Rhodamine B)	PTMA*	Bright reddish violet	Printing inks, paints

CI Pigment Violet 3
CI 42535

Mainly the *N*-tetra, penta- and hexomethyl derivatives of:

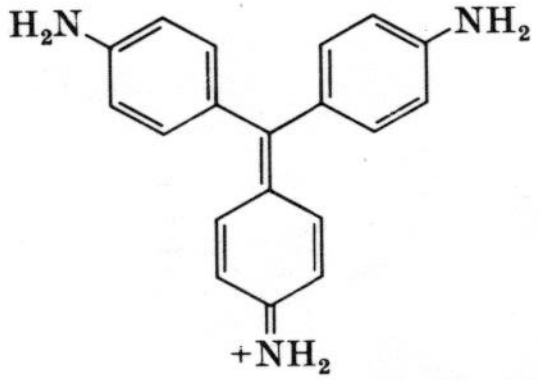

H_2N — — NH_2

$+NH_2$

(Methyl Violet)

PTMA*

Bright bluish violet

Printing inks, paints

CI Pigment Blue 1
CI 42595

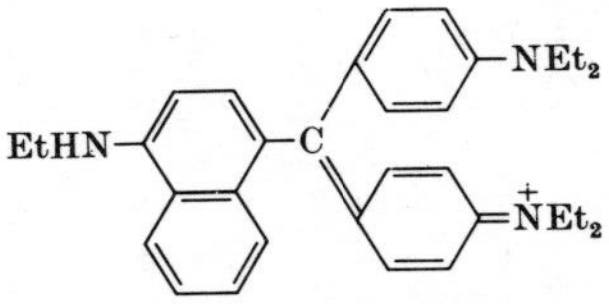

NEt_2

$+NEt_2$

EtHN

(Victoria Pure Blue BO)

PTMA*

Bright reddish blue

Printings inks, paper, leather

CI Pigment Green 1
CI 42040

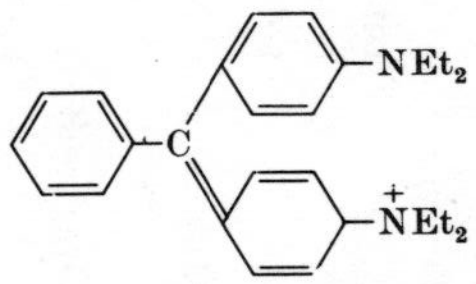

NEt_2

$+NEt_2$

(Brilliant Green)

PTMA*

Bright bluish green

Printing inks, paints, alkyd resin enamels, paper, plastics

* PTMA = phosphotungstomolybdic acid; in some brands phosphotungstic or phosphomolybdic acid may be used.

Table 16-4   Examples of yellow and orange azo pigments

CI Ref. Nos.	Structure	Fastness to light	Fastness to organic solvents
CI Pigment Yellow 1 CI 11680	4-Methyl-2-nitroaniline → acetoacetanilide	Very good	Fair
CI Pigment Yellow 3 CI 11710	4-Chloro-2-nitroaniline → acetoacet-o-chloroanilide	Very good	Poor
CI Pigment Yellow 12 CI 21090	3,3′-Dichlorobenzidine ⇉ (acetoacetanilide)$_2$	Fair	Good
CI Pigment Yellow 13 CI 21000	3,3′-Dichlorobenzidine ⇉ (acetoacet-2,4-dimethylanilide)$_2$	Good	Fair
CI Pigment Yellow 14 CI 21095	3,3′-Dichlorobenzidine ⇉ (acetoacet-o-toluidide)$_2$	Good	Very good
CI Pigment Orange 1 CI 11725	4-Methoxy-2-nitroaniline → acetoacet-o-toluidide	Very good	Fair
CI Pigment Orange 2 CI 12060	o-Nitroaniline → β-naphthol	Good	Poor
CI Pigment Orange 3 CI 12105	2-Methyl-5-nitroaniline → β-naphthol	Good	Fair
CI Pigment Orange 15 CI 12075	2,4-Dinitroaniline → β-naphthol	Excellent	Poor
CI Pigment Orange 6 CI 12730	4-Methyl-2-nitroaniline → 3-methyl-1-phenyl-pyrazol-5-one	Very good	Poor
CI Pigment Orange 13 CI 21110	3,3′-Dichlorobenzidine ⇉ (3-methyl-1-phenyl-pyrazol-5-one)$_2$	Good–Very good	Fair
CI Pigment Orange 14 CI 21165	Dianisidine ⇉ (acetoacet-2,4-dimethylanilide)$_2$	Very good	Very good
CI Pigment Orange 15 CI 21130	o-Tolidine ⇉ (acetoacetanilide)$_2$	Fair	Poor
CI Pigment Orange 16 CI 21160	Dianisidine ⇉ (acetoacetanilide)$_2$	Fair	Poor

give pigments with somewhat lower fastness to light but improved resistance to solvents. Examples of these are CI Pigment Yellows 12, 13 and 14 (see Table 16-4), used for yellow shades in printing inks, lacquers, rubber and plastics.

In orange pigments the chemical structures are more diverse and their effects on properties more complex. Some generalisations can be made, relating to both the yellow and orange pigments. The highest light fastness is found in monoazo and the best solvent fastness in disazo structures. Introduction of methyl groups in positions 2 and 4 of the acetoacetanilide molecule has a beneficial effect on light fastness, and derivatives of 3-methyl-1-phenylpyrazol-5-one tend to have poor fastness to solvents. An anomaly is noticeable in that if tetrazotised dianisidine is coupled with acetoacet-2,4-dimethylanilide instead of acetoacetanilide there is an improvement in the fastness to both light and solvents, but a corresponding change in pigments derived from 3,3'-dichlorobenzidine leads to improvement in light fastness but a worsening of solvent fastness.

The yellow and orange pigments shown in Table 16-4 are made by many firms. Most of them are used in printing inks, some in paints, plastics and rubber, and there are diverse minor applications.

A few red azo pigments are obtained from variously substituted aniline derivatives by diazotisation and coupling with β-naphthol, but the coupling components chiefly used are 2,3-hydroxynaphthoic arylamides. The initial development of these pigments took place alongside that of the azoic dyes produced on cotton fibre (see Chapter 7), and most of the diazo and coupling components are also used as Fast Bases or Naphthols. In general the products give bright shades, have high fastness to light and can withstand a temperature of 140°C or higher, but their fastness to solvents is only moderately good. They are manufactured by many firms, and applications include paints, lacquers, printing inks, rubber, plastics, paper and textile printing; properties vary considerably and the applications of a given pigment are selected accordingly.

Examples of commercial red and brown pigments are shown in Table 16-5.

Manufacture of azo pigments. The conditions for manufacture of azo colouring matters are chosen to favour coupling rather than diazo decomposition (see Section 3-5). The optimum pH value varies according to the components concerned, but for pigments usually weakly acid or weakly alkaline conditions are required. Most coupling components used for non-ionic pigments are then out of solution, but provided that their particles are small coupling with the diazo

Table 16-5   Examples of red and brown azo pigments

CI Ref. Nos.	Structure	Shade
CI Pigment Red 1 CI 12070	p-Nitroaniline → β-naphthol	Dull red
CI Pigment Red 3 CI 12120	4-Methyl-2-nitroaniline → β-naphthol	Yellowish red
CI Pigment Red 4 CI 12085	2-Chloro-4-nitroaniline → β-naphthol	Yellowish red
CI Pigment Red 5 CI 12490	2-Methoxyaniline-5-sulphondi- ethylamide → 2,3-hydroxy- naphthoic 5'-chloro-2',4'- dimethoxyanilide	Bright red
CI Pigment Red 7 CI 12420	4-Chloro-2-methylaniline → 2,3-hydroxynaphthoic 4'chloro- 2'-methylanilide	Red
CI Pigment Red 11 CI 12430	5-Chloro-2-methylaniline → 2,3-hydroxynaphthoic 5'- chloro-2'-methylanilide	Bright bluish red
CI Pigment Red 12 CI 12385	2-Methyl-4-nitroaniline → 2,3-hydroxynaphthoic o-toluidide	Bluish red
CI Pigment Red 22 CI 12315	2-Methyl-5-nitroaniline → 2,3-hydroxynaphthoic anilide	Red
CI Pigment Red 23 CI 12355	2-Methoxy-5-nitroaniline → 2,3-hydroxynaphthoic 3'-nitroanilide	Bluish red
CI Pigment Red 38 CI 21120	3,3'-Dichlorobenzidine ⇄ (3-carboethoxy-1- phenylpyrazol-5-one)$_2$	Red
CI Pigment Brown 1 CI 12480	2,5-Dichloroaniline → 2,3-hydroxynaphthoic 2',5'- dimethoxyanilide	Reddish brown
CI Pigment Brown 2 CI 12071	Copper complex of 4-Nitroaniline → β-naphthol	Reddish brown

compound usually proceeds quite rapidly. Acetoacetarylamides, pyrazolones and naphthols are usually dissolved with an excess of caustic
alkali and reprecipitated by addition of an acid such as acetic acid in
presence of a dispersing agent, with good agitation, and the resulting

fine dispersion is coupled under the required conditions of pH and temperature. When pigment formation is complete it is usually advisable to warm the suspension to a temperature of at least 70°C to bring about a degree of aggregation and so facilitate filtration. The isolated product is well washed, and may either be supplied in the form of aqueous paste or dried and ground. Drying tends to result in aggregation of particles, with a marked effect on shade and colour value, and must therefore be carefully controlled. Sometimes the dry pigment is so hard that it is difficult to obtain a satisfactory dispersibility in oil by normal grinding processes. This problem is often avoided by using a *flushing* process in which the pigment is transferred directly from aqueous suspension into an oily medium by mixing with the oil in suitable equipment. Many pigments are preferentially wetted by oil so that migration of particles takes place across the interface; the globules of oil then coalesce and eventually most of the aqueous phase can be run off. The remaining water can then be removed by evaporation.

Azo condensation pigments. In the manufacture of a disazo pigment the first coupling gives an intermediate compound that is very sparingly soluble in water and has low coupling energy, and because of this it is often difficult to bring the second coupling to completion. This partly explains the small number of disazo pigments marketed. Pigments of high molecular weight include many valuable products with good resistance to solvents and heat, however. A method has been developed by CIBA whereby disazo pigments are obtained from monoazo derivatives of 2,3-hydroxynaphthoic acid (or another coupling component containing a carboxylic acid group) by converting them into acid chlorides and then condensing with diamines of the benzidine type. In this way the final condensation can be carried out in an inert solvent at a high temperature. The simplest example of such a process is illustrated thus:

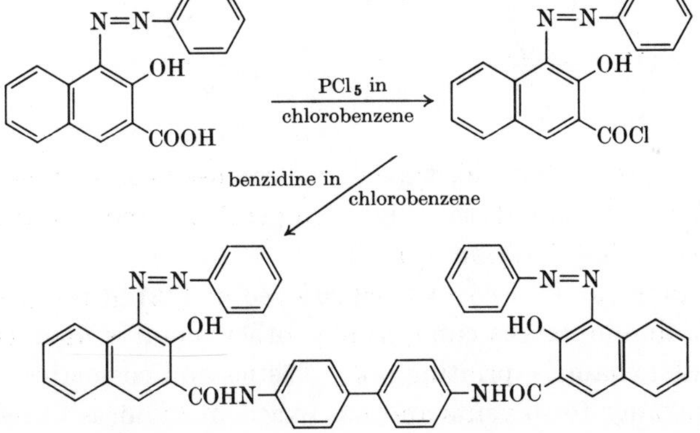

The condensation is said to give yields of up to 95%. Over 10,000 different azo condensation pigments have been examined, some having molecular weights of the order of 1,500. Many of these products have good fastness to light, outdoor exposure, heat and dry-cleaning. Some members of the *Cromophthal* (CIBA) range are believed to be azo condensation products of this type.[7]

Metallised azo pigments. A yellowish green pigment with excellent fastness properties consisting of the nickel complex of the azo compound p-chloroaniline → 2,4-dihydroxyquinoline was introduced by DuPont in 1946 and is marketed as *Green Gold*, or *Lithosol Fast Yellow 3GD* (DuP) (CI Pigment Green 10; CI 12775).[8] It has good fastness to light and heat, and is practically insoluble in most organic solvents. It appears surprising that apart from CI Pigment Brown 2 (see Table 16-5) no other commercial pigment of this type has been reported.

Non-azo pigments. Probably every known vat dye has been examined as a pigment, but the requirements of the two applications differ widely and many excellent vat dyes are useless as pigments. Some products, however, are valuable in both fields. One of these is *Flavanthrone* (CI Vat Yellow 1; CI 70600; see p. 176), and it is used in alkyd resins and lacquers, for pigmentation of paper pulp and sometimes in printing inks. In paint it shows very good fastness to weathering.

The two isomeric perinone dyes [**140**] and [**141**] (p. 180) (CI Vat Orange 7, CI Vat Red 15; CI 71105, CI 71100) have been developed as pigments in recent years, and are used in mass coloration of viscose and paper.

Several substituted imides of perylene-3,4,9,10-tetracarboxylic acid such as [**211**], where R = hydrogen, p-ethoxyphenyl or 3,5-dimethylphenyl, have been described by Farbwerke Hoechst,[9] and

[**211**]

it is believed that products of this type have been used commercially. They are said to withstand the high temperature and reducing conditions in the melt coloration of nylon.[10]

Alizarin (CI Pigment Red 83; CI 58000; see p. 143) in the form of its lake with aluminium, calcium, iron or other metal is used as a pigment in paints, enamels, printing inks, plastics and cosmetics. It shows good resistance to solvents and has excellent fastness to light

The hue varies from yellowish red to bordeaux according to the metal used.

Several red and violet pigments have been obtained from halogenated thioindigo derivatives, examples being as follows:

CI Pigment Red 87 (CI 73310) 7,7'-dichlorothioindigo
CI Vat Red 1 (CI 73360) 6,6'-dichloro-4,4'-dimethylthioindigo
CI Vat Red 2 (CI 73365) 5',6,7'-trichloro-4,4'-dimethylthioindigo
CI Vat Violet 2 (CI 73385) 5,5'-dichloro-7,7'-dimethylthioindigo
CI Vat Violet 3 (CI 73395) 5,5'-dichloro-4,4',7,7'-tetramethyl-thioindigo

Valuable bordeaux and maroon pigments have also been obtained from 4,4',7,7'-tetrachloro- and 4,4'-dichloro-7,7'dimethylthioindigo, respectively.[10] Applications of individual pigments are varied, but in general the thioindigoid pigments are used in paints, alkyd resin enamels, lacquers, printing inks, plastics, and for mass coloration of viscose.

An interesting discovery was made by DuPont in their quinacridone pigments, introduced in 1958. Linear quinacridone [**212**] was first described by Liebermann[11] in 1935, but its practical value was not then apparent. The DuPont synthesis consists in condensing a dialkyl succinylosuccinate with aniline (2 mol.) in 'Dowtherm A' (Dow Chemical Co.) in presence of hydrogen chloride to give a dialkyl 2,5-dianilino-3,6-dihydroterephthalate, cyclising without isolation by heating to about 250°C to give the dihydroquinacridone and oxidising this with sodium m-nitrobenzenesulphonate in presence of caustic alkali.[12]

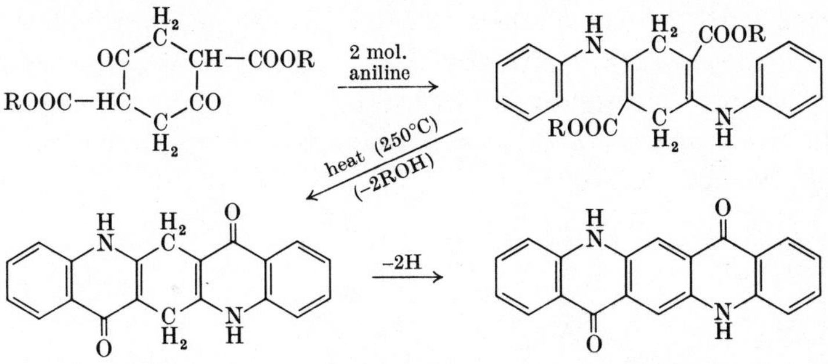

[**212**]

Linear quinacridone is known in three crystalline forms, and by various physical treatments all have been produced with a pigmentary character. The α and γ forms are bluish red and the β form is violet, but only the β and γ forms are technically important, both of these having outstanding general fastness properties.[10] They are sold as

Cinquasia Red B, Red Y (both the γ form, differing in crystal size) and *Violet R* (β form) (DuP), also under other names; all are classed under CI Pigment Violet 19 and CI 46500. The application of these pigments is somewhat restricted by their high cost, but they are extensively used in motor-car finishes.

A bright violet triphendioxazine pigment was introduced by Farbwerke Hoechst in 1952 under the name *Permanent Violet RL* (CI Pigment Violet 23; CI 51319). It is obtained by condensing 3-amino-9-ethylcarbazole with chloranil in presence of anhydrous sodium acetate in a solvent such as trichlorobenzene,[13] and has the following structure:

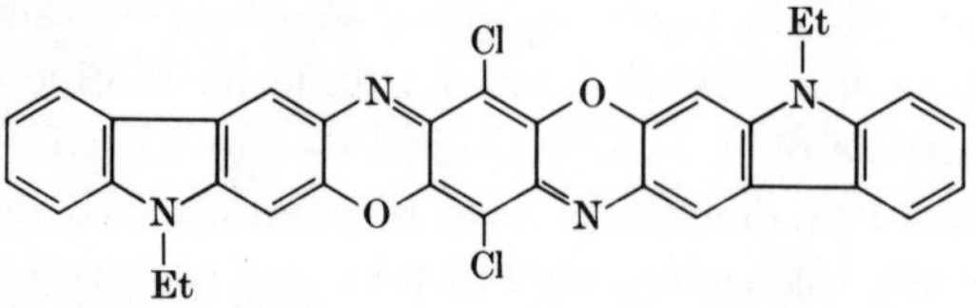

This pigment has high tinctorial strength and very good fastness properties. It is used in paints, printing inks, plastics and paper laminates, also as a shading component for phthalocyanine pigments.

The bright reddish blue vat dye Indanthrone (see p. 163) is widely used as a pigment for a great variety of purposes. In a medium such as a synthetic stoving enamel it has high weathering fastness. Indigo (see p. 151) also has application as a pigment, especially for colouring rubber and paper, and for mass pigmentation of viscose.

Pigment Green B (BASF) (CI Pigment Green 8; CI 10006), introduced in 1921, is now made by many firms and widely used. It is obtained by treating the bisulphite compound of 1-nitroso-β-naphthol with ferrous sulphate, then with sodium hydroxide, and has the structure [**213**].[14] This product gives yellowish green shades, rather lacking in brightness, withstands alkali (and is therefore suitable for application to new plaster) and has good weathering fastness in emulsion paints.

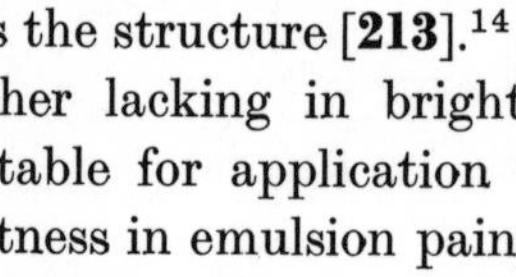

[**213**]

Pigments recently marketed by Geigy under the name *Irgazine* have outstanding fastness to light, weathering and solvents. They are believed to be obtained by condensation of two molecular proportions of 4,5,6,7-tetrachloroisoindolin-1-one (or its 3,3-dichloride) with aromatic amines. The preparation of a typical example from tetrachlorophthalimide is represented thus:

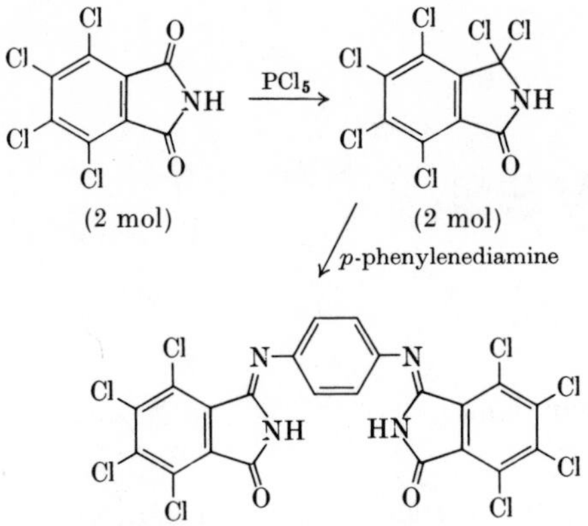

By varying the aromatic diamine yellow, orange, red and brown pigments are obtained.[15]

The only black organic pigment of importance (apart from carbon blacks) is *Aniline Black* (CI Pigment Black 1; CI 50440; see p. 127). This is manufactured as a pigment by oxidation of aniline in presence of a catalyst such as a copper or vanadium salt. It has very good fastness to light and is resistant to acids, alkalis and most organic solvents. Aniline Black is used in lacquers, emulsion paints and distempers, leathercloth, plastics, paper, carbon paper and typewriter ribbons.

17 Solvent dyes

17-1 Solvent dyes and their uses

There are many applications for which dyes are required to be soluble in an organic solvent. Materials coloured by such dyes vary widely and include wood stains, varnishes, lacquers based on nitrocellulose, cellulose acetate or a synthetic resin, polishes for floors or leather, candles, printing inks of certain types, ball-pen inks, carbon papers, typewriter ribbons, petroleum, soap and foodstuffs. Solvent dyes are also used in moulding powders, for mass coloration of various plastic materials and in coloured smokes used for military signals. Sometimes the dye is simply dissolved in the substrate, as in the colouring of wax for candles, but an organic solvent may be used as a vehicle, as in the application of spirit stains to wood.

Solvent dyes resemble pigments in that they are usually insoluble in water, but since they are used in solution their properties are not greatly affected by their physical condition. In order that a dye may be readily soluble in an organic solvent its molecule must be fairly small. The presence of a strongly acid substituent, such as a sulphonic acid group is in general undesirable, but metal complex dyes used as components of spirit-soluble dyes (discussed later) may be sulphonated. Solubility in alcohol and hydrocarbon solvents is promoted by the presence of higher alkyl groups. When maximum solubility is needed dyes are often used in mixtures, since each component then tends to have a solubilising effect on the others; an advantage is also obtained by using a mixture of solvents.

Solvent dyes are derived mainly from the various cationic classes (especially triarylmethanes), azo and anthraquinone classes, but phthalocyanines are also represented. In general the azo class supplies yellow, orange and red, cationic dyes orange to green, anthraquinone dyes violet to green and phthalocyanines blue hues.

The cationic dyes are usually free bases corresponding to well known dyes of the Basic application class, and most of the important products are described in Chapter 8. Table 17-1 gives examples representing the various chemical classes.

Several anionic dyes are used in solvent applications. These are mainly xanthenes, and most of them are polyhalogeno derivatives of fluorescein. An example is *Eosine* (Section 8-6), which is used extensively in cosmetics.

Most of the azo solvent dyes contain only one azo group, but disazo dyes provide a few red and brown shades. The $1:1$ and $1:2$ chromium and cobalt complexes of certain acid dyes are readily soluble in alcohol, acetone, ethyl acetate and 'Cellosolve', but usually not in hydrocarbon solvents. Introduction of a metal atom into dyes of suitable structure leads to improved fastness properties and enables the shade range to be extended into the violet region. Examples of azo solvent dyes are given in Table 17-2.

Several commercial solvent dyes consist of salts formed between a cationic dye and an acid dye, the latter being usually in the form of a chromium complex. Products of this type have generally good fastness to light and thus show a great advantage over cationic dyes used alone. CI Solvent Red 35, consisting of the salt of Rhodamine B (CI 45170) with the chromium complex of 2-amino-4-chlorophenol → 2-napthol-6,8-disulphonic acid (CI 16260) is an example. It gives bright bluish red shades with good fastness to light, and is used in lacquers, wood stains and printing inks, also for the dyeing of anodised aluminium.

Solvent dyes of the anthraquinone series include various N-alkyl, N-aryl, N-alkyl-N'-aryl, N,N'-dialkyl, and N,N'-diaryl derivatives of 1,4-diaminoanthraquinone, for example CI Solvent Green 3 (CI 61565), which is 1,4-di-p-toluidinoanthraquinone. This dye gives bluish green shades with good fastness to light, and is used in wood stains, polishes, soap and plastics; as a solution in oleic or stearic acid it finds application in rotogravure printing inks. The acid dye Alizarine Cyanine Green G (Section 9-1-1) is a corresponding disulphonated derivative.

If anthraquinone is substituted in the 1 and 4 positions by n-amylamino groups a dye is obtained with greatly increased solubility in hydrocarbon solvents in comparison with the dyes referred to above. The resulting dye is *Calcogas Blue NA* (CCC) (CI Solvent Blue 14; CI 61555), and is used to impart a greenish blue colour to petroleum and other hydrocarbons; in such applications its poor fastness to light is of no consequence.

The effectiveness of long alkyl chains in promoting solubility in organic solvents is shown by the fact that even copper phthalocyanine, which has outstanding solvent resistance, can be converted into a solvent dye by introduction of four isohexylamine residues.

Table 17-1 Solvent dyes of various cationic classes

Chemical class	CI Ref. Nos.	Common name of dye	Structure	Hue and chief uses
Quinoline	CI Solvent Yellow 33 CI 47000	Quinoline Yellow A	See Section 12-7	Bright greenish yellow. Used in spirit lacquers, cosmetics and coloured smokes
Diphenylmethane	CI Solvent Yellow 34 CI 41000B	Auramine 0	See Section 8-1	Bright greenish yellow. Used in oils, fats, waxes and spirit stains
Acridine	CI Solvent Orange 15 CI 46005B	Acridine Orange	See Section 8-7	Bright orange. Used in oils, fats and waxes
Xanthene	CI Solvent Red 49 CI 45170B	Rhodamine B	See Section 8-6	Bright bluish red. Used in ball-pen inks, rotogravure printing inks and carbon papers
Triarylmethane	CI Solvent Red 41 CI 42510B	Magenta	See Section 8-2-2	Bright bluish red. Used in oils, fats and waxes
Triarylmethane	CI Solvent Violet 8 CI 42535B	Methyl Violet	See Section 8-2-3	* Bright bluish violet. Used in typewriter ribbons, copying papers, printing inks and ball-pen inks. The stearate is used in rotogravure inks
Triarylmethane	CI Solvent Violet 9 CI 42555B	Crystal Violet	See Section 8-2-2	* Bright bluish violet. Uses as for Methyl Violet (above)
Triarylmethane	CI Solvent Blue 3 CI 42775	Spirit Blue	Mixture of phenylated Pararosaniline and Rosaniline (hydrochloride, sulphate or acetate)	Blue. Used in oils, fats, waxes and spirit stains

Class	CI Solvent	Colour Name	Reference	Description
Triarylmethane	CI Solvent Blue 4 CI 44045B	Victoria Blue B	See Section 8-3	* Bright blue. Used in printing inks, carbon papers, typewriter ribbons, stamping inks and ball-pen inks. The stearate is used for rotogravure inks
Triarylmethane	CI Solvent Green 1 CI 42000B	Malachite Green	See Section 8-2-1	Yellowish green. Used in oils, fats and waxes
Thiazine	CI Solvent Blue 8 CI 52015B	Methylene Blue	See Section 8-10	* Greenish grey. Used in oils, fats and waxes
Indophenol	CI Solvent Blue 22 CI 49705	Fat Blue Z	See Section 12-2	Blue. Used in oils, fats, waxes and spirit stains
Induline	CI Solvent Blue 7 CI 50400	Induline	See Section 8-8	* Reddish blue. Used in printing inks, carbon papers, typewriter ribbons, stamping inks, spirit varnishes, oils, fats and waxes
Nigrosine	CI Solvent Black 5 CI 50415	Nigrosine Spirit Soluble	See Section 8-8	Bluish black. Used in spirit stains, varnishes, lacquers, marking inks, leather finishes and printing inks
Nigrosine	CI Solvent Black 7 CI 50415B	Nigrosine Base	See Section 8-8	* Bluish black. Used in shoe polishes, oils, fats, waxes, typewriter ribbons, carbon papers, stamping inks and leather finishes

* Dissolved in oleic, stearic or other fatty acid for use.

Note: In most cases the dyes are used in the form of free base.

Table 17-2   Solvent dyes of the azo class

CI Ref. Nos.	Structure	Hue	Chief uses
CI Solvent Yellow 1 CI 11000	4-Aminoazobenzene (Aniline Yellow; see (p. 21)	Reddish yellow	Spirit lacquers and varnishes, candles, shoe and floor polishes, oil stains and styrene resins
CI Solvent Yellow 2 CI 11020	4-(Dimethylamino)- azobenzene	Reddish yellow	Oils, fats, waxes, polishes, petroleum, soap and polystyrene resins
CI Solvent Yellow 14 CI 12055	Aniline → β-naphthol	Bright reddish yellow	Wax polishes, candles, varnishes, petroleum, soap, polystyrene resins and coloured smokes
CI Solvent Orange 1 CI Food Orange 3 CI 11920	Aniline → resorcinol	Yellowish orange	Wax polishes, moulding powders
CI Solvent Orange 2 CI 12100	o-Toluidine → β-naphthol	Reddish orange	Varnishes, oils, fats, waxes, drugs, cosmetics
CI Solvent Orange 3 CI 11270B	Aniline → m-phenylenediamine (Chrysoidine; see (p. 22)	Dull yellowish orange	Wax polishes
CI Solvent Orange 7 CI 12140	2,4-Xylidine → β-naphthol	Reddish orange	Wax polishes, candles, polystyrene resins
CI Solvent Red 4 CI 12170	α-Naphthylamine → β-naphthol	Yellowish red	Oil, fats, waxes, 'carbolic' soap
CI Solvent Red 23 CI 26100	4-Aminoazobenzene → β-naphthol	Yellowish red	Oils, fats, waxes, stains, cosmetics
CI Solvent Red 24 CI 26105	4-Amino-2,3'-dimethyl- azobenzene → β-naphthol	Red	Wax polishes, wood stains, petroleum, soap, polystyrene resins
CI Solvent Brown 1 CI 11285	α-Naphthylamine → m-phenylenediamine	Reddish orange to brown	Spirit lacquers, wax polishes and photo- gravure printing inks
CI Solvent Brown 5 CI 12020	α-Naphthylamine → α-naphthol	Dull brown	Wax polishes, cellulosic and synthetic resin lacquers
CI Solvent Brown 12 CI 21010B	Mainly m-tolylenediamine ⇉ (m-tolylenediamine)$_2$	Dull yellowish red to brown	Wood stains, varnishes, fats, and waxes
CI Solvent Red 8 CI 12715	1:2 Chromium complex of 2-amino-5- nitrophenol → 3-methyl-1-phenyl- pyrazol-5-one	Bright bluish red	Nitrocellulose, spirit and synthetic resin lacquers, printing inks, wood stains and anodised aluminium
CI Solvent Violet 1 CI 12196	1:2 Cobalt complex of 2-amino-5-nitrophenol → β-naphthol	Dull bluish violet	Nitrocellulose, spirit and synthetic resin lacquers, printing inks and wood stains

Zapon Fast Blue HFL (BASF) (CI Solvent Blue 25; CI 74350) is obtained by reaction of copper phthalocyanine with chlorosulphonic acid to give the 3,3′,3″,3‴-tetrasulphonyl chloride and then treating this with four molecular proportions of isohexylamine. The product contains the di- and trisulphonisohexylamides, the remaining acid chloride groups being hydrolysed to sulphonic acid groups, which then form isohexylamine salts.[1] This dye can be applied from mixed ester solvents, and has very good general fastness properties in lacquers, inks for rubber stereo printing and as a dye for anodised aluminium.

17-2 Application of dyes from solvent media

Much attention has been paid in recent years to the possibility of applying dyes to synthetic fibres from solution in an organic solvent or mixture of solvents. The method is not new, having been first proposed in 1908,[2] but as yet it has been operated only experimentally. Organic solvents are already in use for the scouring and finishing of textile materials, and equipment is available which could probably be adapted for dyeing. A possibility is therefore envisaged of carrying out finishing and dyeing operations in a single plant unit. Further advantages to be expected are avoidance of problems of water supply and effluent treatment, lower heating costs, increased output and the preservation of fabric dimensions and appearance (especially in knitted goods). The solvent must be available at low cost, free from fire-hazard and toxicity, and have adequate solvent power for a wide range of dyes. Trichloroethylene meets most of the requirements but is somewhat lacking in solvent power for many disperse dyes. An addition of about 10% of methanol gives an improvement in this respect but tends to cause 'tailing' of the dyebath and sometimes has an adverse effect on fibre strength. Perchloroethylene has been used and also requires a solubilising additive.

The *Vapocol* process devised in ICI laboratories enables acetate and triacetate fibres to be dyed with disperse dyes from trichloroethylene medium. Azoic components can be applied similarly from a chloroform medium and developed by subsequent treatment with nitrous acid.[3] In another process developed by Geigy disperse dyes or 1:2 metal complexes of azo dyes are applied to acetate, polyamide or polyester fibres from a solvent consisting mainly of trichloroethylene or perchloroethylene with a 10% content of methanol or dioxan, and dyeing is completed by 'thermofixing' at 180°–210°C.[4] Later it was reported that improved results were obtained by using perchloroethylene with a new additive, but its

identity has not been disclosed. The solubilising effect was still
insufficient to enable deep shades to be produced, however, and of
several hundred commercial dyes tested only 20–30 were successfully
applied to acetate fibre.[5]

Although solvent application processes offer a prospect of
technical and economic advantages further development is needed to
establish their practicability.

Oxidation bases

The oxidation bases are a group of dye intermediates applied to furs or textile fibres (especially cotton or viscose) and oxidised to form colouring matters on the fibre. The term 'base' is used somewhat loosely, and although most of the intermediates are aromatic amines, diamines or aminophenols several auxiliary compounds called 'Developers' which are in fact phenols are included in the commercial ranges.

Except in the case of Aniline Black and related products little is known of the structure of the oxidation products. The study of the subject is therefore largely concerned with application techniques the details of which are outside the scope of the present book. This chapter is restricted to a brief general account of the materials and processes used.

In 1834 Runge observed the formation of dark green and blue-black substances when aniline is oxidised by chromic acid. Twenty-two years later Perkin obtained Mauveine by oxidation of crude aniline (see Section 8-8), but his main product was a black pigment known as Aniline Black. Perkin was chiefly interested in the violet dye, but it was soon superseded. On the other hand Aniline Black became an important product within a few years and is still in use at the present time. It was first applied as a pigment in calico printing in 1862, and in the following year John Lightfoot of Accrington developed the first satisfactory process for producing it on cotton fibre.[1] His original process was based on the oxidation of aniline hydrochloride by means of potassium ferrocyanide and sodium chlorate, and was applied by a printing process. Traces of copper derived from the printing rollers served as a catalyst promoting oxidation, and later salts of copper or other metals were included for this purpose. Many modified processes have since been developed, and Aniline Black (CI 50440) is applied to cellulosic fibres and to silk by dyeing as well as printing methods. An outline of a typical dyeing process is given on p. 127. Since the oxidation takes place in presence of mineral acid great care is needed to avoid tendering of cotton. Application conditions must be regulated to ensure that the pigment is formed within the fibre and not merely upon its surface, otherwise the dyeing is liable to have poor fastness to rubbing and washing. When the process is skilfully operated it yields an intense black with excellent fastness to light, acids and alkalis. It is largely used for the dyeing of umbrella fabrics.

The chemistry of the process is discussed in Section 8-8.

In recent years Aniline Black has been largely superseded in printing applications by *Solanile Black* (Fran) and equivalent products (CI Oxidation Base 3). These are sulphamino derivatives of 4-aminodiphenylamine, with structures such as **[214]** or **[215]**,

[214]

[215]

which are soluble in neutral or alkaline conditions and more easily oxidised than aniline salt. The dyes can be developed on cellulosic fibres in neutral or acid steam, and give deep insoluble blacks with good fastness properties. These products have advantages in that they can be applied without serious risk of fibre degradation, and have good print paste stability, but the cost of the materials is somewhat higher than for Aniline Black.[2]

4-Aminodiphenylamine has long been used to produce intense blacks by oxidation on cellulosic fibres, and is known as *Diphenyl Black Base* (CI Oxidation Base 2; CI 76085). This base is also applied to fur, especially for grey shades.[3]

The use of organic bases for colouring fur or hair was first described by Erdmann[4] in 1888, and several years later The Berlin Aniline Company marketed a range of bases for such purposes under the name *Ursol*. When applied to fur and oxidised with hydrogen peroxide these compounds yield strongly coloured products which are insoluble in water. In many cases deep hues can be produced with the aid of a mordant such as a salt of iron, chromium, copper or aluminium. Ranges of such fur bases are now manufactured by several firms. Since most aromatic bases are liable to cause dermatitis it is essential when they are used as dyes to ensure that no unoxidised base remains in the fur and that any loose dye is removed.

Table 18-1 shows the constitution of some of the more important oxidation bases and their chief uses. Several 'Developers' which are used only in conjunction with other bases are included. Most of them have little value when used alone, and their shade effect in admixture with other bases is sometimes additive and sometimes quite anomalous.

Table 18-1   Structure and applications of typical oxidation bases

CI Ref. Nos.	Structure of Base	Hue	Chief applications
CI Oxidation Base 1 CI 50440	Aniline hydrochloride	Black	Dyeing and printing of cellulosic fibres (Also used as pigment)
CI Oxidation Base 2, 2A, 2B CI 76085–7	4-Aminodiphenylamine (base, hydrochloride or oxalate)	Black or grey	Dyeing and printing of cellulosic fibres and acetate fibre for blacks. Dyeing of fur, unmordanted or with Fe, Cu or Cr mordant, for greys
CI Oxidation Base 3	N-sulphonic or N,N'-disulphonic derivatives of 4-aminodiphenylamine	Black	Printing of cellulosic fibres. Can be applied to mordanted or unmordanted fur
CI Oxidation Base 6, 6A CI 76550–1	p-Aminophenol (base or hydrochloride)	Browns (various)	Dyeing of fur mordanted with Cu, Fe or Cr. Can be applied to cellulosic fibres
CI Oxidation Base 7 CI 76545	m-Aminophenol	—	Applied to fur as Developer (variable shade effect)
CI Oxidation Base 8, 8A, 8B CI 76075–7	N,N-Dimethyl-p-phenylenediamine (base, sulphate or oxalate)	Grey (various)	Dyeing of fur with Cr or Cu mordant
CI Oxidation Base 9A CI 76021	4-Nitro-o-phenylene-diamine (dihydrochloride)	Yellows (various)	Applied as shading component (towards yellow) on fur unmordanted or mordanted with Fe, Cu or Cr
CI Oxidation Base 10, 10A CI 76060–1	p-Phenylenediamine (base or hydrochloride)	Black	Dyeing of fur mordanted with Cu, Cu/Fe or Cr
CI Oxidation Base 11 CI 76521	o-Aminophenol (copper salt)	Yellow or yellowish-brown	Dyeing of fur unmordanted or mordanted with Fe, Cu or Cr
CI Oxidation Base 12, 12A CI 76050–1	4-Methoxy-m-phenylenediamine (base or sulphate)	Grey	Applied to fur as Developer (variable shade effect)
CI Oxidation Base 31 CI 76505	Resorcinol	—	Applied to unmordanted or mordanted fur as Developer (variable shade effect)
CI Oxidation Base 33 CI 76605	α-Naphthol	—	Applied to unmordanted or mordanted fur as Developer (variable shade effect)

19 Retention of dyes in the fibre

Since scientific methods were first brought to bear upon the art of dyeing much study has been devoted to the forces that bring about transference of dyes from a solution (or suspension) in water to fibres immersed in it under appropriate conditions. The strength of the attachment between fibre and dye varies greatly, and it became clear quite early that there is more than one mechanism.

The mode of attachment of many dye classes is well established and has been discussed in the foregoing chapters. The purpose of this chapter is to provide a general review of the subject with special reference to dye application classes in which the association with the fibre still presents problems. In the space available it is only possible to comment on selected aspects of the subject, and the reader must be warned of the limitations of the present treatment. There is as yet no general agreement regarding either the means whereby direct dyes are attached to cellulosic fibres or the mechanism of certain processes for application of disperse dyes to polyester fibres. The state of knowledge in this field can be assessed only after fairly extensive reading, and attention is directed to the publications quoted in the reference list and Bibliography as a starting-point for further study.

19-1 Dyes attached by processes leading to pigmentation of the fibre

Dyes of several classes are formed within the fibre and are present as pigment particles in cavities in its structure. Since they are held mechanically and are insoluble in water the excellent fastness to wet treatments usually shown is readily understood. Azoic, sulphur, vat, *Alcian*, *Phthalogen* and polycondensation dyes applied chiefly to cellulosic fibres all yield pigments in the fibre by various reactions. The insoluble salts of basic dyes produced by dyeing cotton mordanted with tannic acid or a suitable synthetic agent are also supported mechanically. In mass coloration of synthetic fibres pigments are entrapped during formation of the fibre. In the case of sulphur, vat and most azoic dyes although the products are pigments they are derived from intermediates applied to the fibre by dyeing or printing processes.

19-2   Dyes attached wholly or partly by chemical union with the fibre

Mordant dyes such as alizarin (Section 9-2) are applied to cellulosic fibres together with metallic salts to give insoluble metal derivatives which are precipitated in the fibre. On the other hand the fixation of chrome dyes on wool is believed to depend partly on the formation of complexes in which the fibre is associated with the dye molecule and a metal atom (see Section 4-1-2). Such complexes may also be formed to some extent in the application of 1:1 chromium complexes of azo acid dyes to wool (Section 4-1-3). The high wet-fastness properties of mordant dyes may therefore be explained by the entrapment of insoluble dye particles or by the presence of a link with the fibre through the metal atom. The dye molecules may also be attached to the fibre by van der Waals forces.

The dyeing of wool with acid dyes of the levelling type (i.e., those with fairly simple structures) is due mainly to the formation of salt-type chemical links between dye anions and cationic groups in the fibre, and as these are easily broken the resulting dyeings have somewhat poor fastness to wet treatments. Acid dyes of the milling type have more complex structures or carry weighting groups and are more firmly attached to the fibre by van der Waals forces; because of their high affinity care is needed in application to avoid unlevelness, but the dyeings show better wet-fastness than those obtained from small and unweighted molecules.[1] The behaviour of acid dyes in application to nylon is broadly similar to that with wool, but since nylon contains fewer cationic sites it takes up a smaller amount of dye. It appears that van der Waals forces are effective only when the dye and fibre are brought into proximity by some means such as a salt-type link. Dyeings on the hydrophobic fibre nylon have in general better wet-fastness properties than on wool.

Basic dyes are attached to wool, silk or acrylic fibres containing anionic sites by salt-type linkages. Fastness to washing on wool and silk is in most cases rather poor (grade 1–2), but usually reaches a high standard (grade 4–5) on polyacrylonitrile fibres. This may be attributed partly to difference in the strength of salt bonds and partly to the hydrophobic nature of the synthetic fibre.

Among dyes that form chemical links with the fibre the Reactive dyes are of major importance. These are attached by means of covalent links of several types to cellulosic fibres, wool or nylon. Their stability to hydrolysis varies somewhat, but all yield dyeings with high fastness to wet treatments. The subject is discussed in Chapter 13 and therefore is not considered further here.

19-3 Cellulose-substantive dyes

After the discovery of the first direct dyes for cotton in 1884 an immense amount of experimental work was carried out and this led to the production of many direct dyes with widely varying properties. Whereas all anionic dyes can be applied to wool and silk only those with structures of certain types have substantivity for cotton (see Chapter 5). It was not until 1928 that an explanation for this was put forward by Meyer and Mark.[2] They pointed out that most direct dyes have long straight molecules and are similar in this respect to cellulose, so that it is possible for the fibre and dye to be held together by atomic interaction. Scale models of many substantive and non-substantive dyes were studied by Paine and Rose,[3] and they found that those of substantive dyes did indeed correspond closely in shape to others representing the cellulose structure. Further, the distance between azo groups in many substantive polyazo dyes was shown to be 10·8 Å, which is not greatly different from the distance between corresponding atoms in the cellulose polymer (10·3 Å). Since acetylation of cellulose results in a loss of affinity for direct dyes it is probable that cellulosic hydroxyl groups are concerned in the attachment of such dyes. It may be explained by the formation of hydrogen bonds between these hydroxyl groups and azo, amino, hydroxyl or amide groups in dye molecules,[4] which may be represented thus:

$$
\begin{array}{cccc}
\mathrm{Ar-N} & \mathrm{Ar-N-H} & & \mathrm{Ar-N-CO-Ar} \\
\quad\quad\diagdown\!\!\diagdown & \quad\mid & & \quad\quad\mid \\
\quad\mathrm{N-Ar} & \quad\mathrm{H} & \mathrm{Ar-O-H} & \quad\mathrm{H} \\
\mathrm{Cellulose\text{-}OH} & \mathrm{Cellulose\text{-}OH} & \mathrm{Cellulose\text{-}OH} & \mathrm{Cellulose\text{-}OH}
\end{array}
$$

It is believed that direct dyes with long molecules move into cavities in the cellulose structure and become attached by two or more hydrogen bonds. The presence of many cellulosic hydroxyl groups presents a great variety of possible bonding sites, and dyes in which bonding groups are distant from each other by more than 10·8 Å might be accommodated.

The substantivity of direct dyes is adversely affected if too many ionised solubilising groups are present. These increase affinity for the aqueous phase and their negative charge gives rise to electrical repulsion between the dye and the cellulose fibre which in aqueous medium is itself negatively charged. The number of solubilising groups should therefore be the minimum necessary for adequate solubility. It has been suggested that it is advantageous if the solubilising groups lie on one side of the dye molecule and hydrogen bonding groups are on the other side.[5]

Hodgson[6] pointed out in 1933 that for maximum substantivity it is not sufficient that dye molecules should be linear, but their benzene nuclei must also be capable of co-planarity. Substituents in the 2,2' positions in benzidine interfere with free rotation so that the derived disazo dyes cannot be co-planar, and a loss of substantivity results. If, however, the 2,2' positions are linked by a bridge such as —NH— or —SO$_2$— the two benzene rings must be co-planar and disazo dyes derived from such diamines are substantive. Substitution in the 3,3' positions does not prevent co-planarity, and accordingly 3,3'-benzidine derivatives yield substantive dyes.

Schirm suggested in 1935 that a conjugated chain containing at least eight double bonds is needed in the dye molecule if it is to exhibit cellulose-substantivity. He explained the lack of substantivity on the part of some dyes with longer conjugated chains as due to aggregation in solution.[7] However, many substantive dyes containing a urea link fail to conform to Schirm's proposed rule. Vickerstaff commented that Schirm's theory may be regarded as another form of Hodgson's co-planarity theory since it is now known that in absence of steric hindrance resonance in long conjugated chains forces the rings to assume a co-planar structure by virtue of the fact that one of the resonance forms has the quinonoid structure:

In most cases, therefore, Schirm's conditions imply that the aromatic nuclei are co-planar, and if this is in fact the essential condition the urea dyes are able to conform to it in spite of their shorter conjugated chains.[8]

It has long been known that at room temperature the molecules of substantive dyes are aggregated, but those of non-substantive acid dyes are not. This led to a theory that direct dyes are fixed by a process of aggregation within the fibre. Experimental work showed, however, that at the temperature at which cellulosic fibres are dyed (90°–100°C) the dye aggregates are dispersed.[9] Valkó has suggested that the observed association between substantivity and tendency to aggregate may signify only that the forces causing aggregation are of the same nature as those responsible for the attraction between fibre and dye.[10] Coates has recently expressed the opinion that with most dyes the aggregating forces are of the van der Waals type.[11]

Lead observed that some compounds such as stilbene-4-sulphonic acid containing no hydrogen-bond-forming group are nevertheless substantive. He suggested that in such cases bonding with cellulose is not necessarily solely due to the operation of van der Waals forces, and that it might be explained in part by interaction between π electrons of the conjugated system and hydrogen atoms of the cellulosic hydroxyl groups.[12] Shortly afterwards Giles and Hassan expressed the view that in aqueous medium cellulose molecules are surrounded by a layer of firmly bound water molecules which tend to prevent hydrogen bond formation with dyes or other organic solutes. These authors believed that vat dyes are adsorbed by the attraction of van der Waals forces alone, but they referred to the possibility of π electron–cellulose interaction.[13] Following this publication Lead pointed out that since van der Waals forces have an extremely short range it might be argued that they also would be rendered ineffective by a layer of water molecules. Further, if all that is required to account for substantivity is co-planarity of dye and fibre direct dyes should have affinity for linear polyethylene. Lead suggested that the extended π electron system of the dye molecule might form an intermediate layer between cellulose on one side and water molecules on the other, since interaction can occur between delocalized π electrons and the hydroxyl groups on each side.[14]

Whatever the explanation there is no doubt that the bonding of direct dyes with high molecular weight to cellulosic fibres is much less effective than that obtained by application of milling dyes to wool. Polyazo cotton dyes are comparable in complexity with wool dyes of the milling type, but the fastest dyeings on cotton do not approach the standard obtained on wool.

In considering cellulose-substantivity it should be borne in mind that the process of dyeing with direct dyes is reversible in every case, and all adsorbed dye can be removed by prolonged washing with water. In the application of vat dyes the purpose of the dyeing operation is merely to transfer the dye to the fibre; fastness to wet treatments is acquired in the following oxidation and soaping stages which render the dye insoluble in water and cause its particles to grow by crystallisation or aggregation.

The molecules of some reduced vat dyes and sulphonated phthalocyanines are not linear, but when hydrogen bonding groups are present the dyes may be attached by cross-linking between adjacent cellulose chains. The substantivity of sulphonated copper phthalocyanine is not very great (see Section 15-5). After a study of the affinities of a series of vat dyes Peters and Sumner put forward the view that attraction for the fibre depends partly on hydrogen bonding and partly on van der Waals forces.[15]

In spite of many years' work it cannot yet be said that the direct dyeing of cellulosic fibres is well understood.

19-4 Disperse dyes

When the first disperse dyes were manufactured for use on acetate fibre in 1923, it was recognised that the fibre serves as a solvent for the dyes.[16] Cellulose acetate has thermoplastic properties and was formerly considered to be a supercooled liquid. It is now usually regarded as a solid and the dyed fibre as a solid solution. A study by Vickerstaff and Waters of absorption isotherms cast some doubt upon the solution theory, since the concentrations of dye in the fibre and in the liquor failed to show the expected linear relationship.[17] Other workers reported observations showing a linear relationship, however, and Bird and Manchester pointed out that the anomalous results of Vickerstaff and Waters might be due to partial decomposition of the dispersing agent with liberation of sodium bisulphate which then formed a salt with the disperse dye.[18] The experimental evidence suggests that disperse dyes are not transferred directly into the fibre medium but are transmitted through aqueous solution. The highly dispersed particles have a small solubility in water and serve as a reservoir maintaining a saturated solution from which the dye passes into the fibre in a molecular state. In confirmation of this view Vickerstaff and Waters showed that acetate fibre can be dyed by a disperse dye enclosed in a seamless container of Cellophane suspended in the dyebath.

Vickerstaff and Waters showed that the dyeing of acetate fibre is a reversible process. At equilibrium, however, the distribution of dye between fibre and water is greatly in favour of the fibre so that in general fastness to wet treatments is fairly good.

Daruwalla, Rao and Tilak examined ten non-commercial quinonoid disperse dyes in application to acetate. These were selected to provide a comparison between dyes with co-planar molecules and others with generally similar but non-co-planar structures. Calculation of their affinities from the absorption isotherms at 80°C showed in each pair a significant difference in favour of the dye with a co-planar molecule. Since the dyes examined have average molecular dimensions of approximately 12–13 Å × 10 Å and were considered small enough to enter the pores of water-swollen acetate fibre, these authors suggested that the relatively low partition coefficients and affinities of the non-co-planar dyes are due to their inability to lie sufficiently close to the acetate molecules to allow inter-atomic forces to operate.[19] No evidence is available to show whether in these experiments the fibre was equally well penetrated by dyes of the two types.

The mechanism whereby nylon is dyed by disperse dyes has not been fully investigated but it is believed to be essentially similar to that of application to acetate. Hydrogen bonds may be formed between amino groups in the dye molecule and carbonyl groups in the fibre polymer.

Dyeing of polyester fibres is hindered by their hydrophobic character, tightly packed physical structure and lack of chemically active groups. The four main methods by which these fibres are dyed consist in the use of 'carriers', dyeing under pressure, the 'Thermosol' process and the application of azoic dyes; these are described in Chapters 6 and 7. Azoic dyes, as in their other applications, are pigments physically retained in the fibre.

In absence of a carrier diffusion of a disperse dye into polyester fibre from a dyebath at 85°–100°C is extremely slow, but in presence of an agent such as diphenyl or a hydroxydiphenyl dyeing can usually be completed at or below the boil within an hour. If o-hydroxydiphenyl is added as its sodium salt it dissolves in the dye-bath but the free phenol is liberated as an emulsified oil on addition of acetic acid during the dyeing operation. Several theories (varying in credibility) have been put forward to explain the mode of action of such carriers. At one time it was supposed that dye molecules become attached to the carrier and are drawn into the fibre with it as a result of the affinity of the fibre for the carrier. The action was also explained as a matter of simple lubrication. According to another view the carrier forms a film covering the surface of the fibre, the dye dissolves in it and is more easily transferred to the hydrophobic fibre from it than from aqueous medium.[20] This appears a reasonable explanation, since whether the fibre is surrounded in the dyebath (without carrier) by an envelope of air or a layer of molecules of a surface-active agent with hydrophobic heads and hydrophilic tails, a barrier is presented to the movement of dye molecules into the fibre. The carrier, however, is present in a liquid phase compatible with both fibre and water and can provide access between them. It does not appear to be necessary that the dye should be highly soluble in the carrier since its particles would probably pass from one phase to the other in much the same way as pigment particles are transferred from water into oil in the flushing process (Section 16-2-3).

There is evidence that most if not all commercial carriers cause swelling of polyester fibres, and it is widely believed that these function by causing the polymer chains to move apart so that dye molecules are more easily accommodated.[21] A possible difficulty arises in that if the chains are held apart by the interposition of carrier molecules, these would appear to block the entry of dye molecules. It is conceivable, however, that once the chains are forced apart the cohesive forces are sufficiently reduced to enable a mobile equilibrium to be established in which carrier molecules are partially replaced by dye molecules. Waters found that the practical effectiveness of carriers is not directly related to their swelling efficiency and concluded that the swelling action is not their sole function.[21] It appears possible that these agents provide a transfer phase and also promote fibre swelling, but until more experimental evidence becomes available their mode of action must remain largely a matter for conjecture.

In the pressure dyeing process the higher application temperature (120°–130°C) results in a great increase in the energy of dye molecules and in the mobility of polymer chains in the fibre. This process has advantages in that it enables a wide range of dyes to be used and heavy shades are obtainable. Suitable dyes can be applied to 'Terylene' in the vapour phase at 180°–210°C without use of increased pressure, but this process is not known to be used commercially.[22]

The 'Thermosol' process, developed by DuPont in 1949, has a wide range of uses and is of special importance in application of disperse dyes to polyester fibres. The fabric is padded with a dispersion of the dye, then dried and heated to 175°–200°C for a very short time, thereby bringing about rapid and even penetration of the fibre. The process is designed for continuous operation.

20 Fluorescent brighteners

It is a matter of everyday experience that white textile articles become yellowish long before they are worn out. There are three general methods whereby this undesired effect can be removed. The first involves the use of a chemical bleaching agent such as a hypochlorite or peroxide. Such compounds must be applied cautiously since they are liable to spoil coloured goods and damage the fibre. The second method consists in the application of a small amount of a blue colouring matter. This absorbs yellow light and so causes the yellowed fabric to appear white, but the real effect is an extension of the region of the spectrum over which light is absorbed so that the treated material becomes pale grey instead of yellowish. The third method is of more recent origin and depends on the application of a fluorescent compound which absorbs ultra-violet light and converts the energy thus acquired into visible light of higher wavelength. In this way a yellow appearance (which is due to the absorption of blue-violet light) can be corrected by the emission of a corresponding amount of blue-violet light by the fluorescent compound. The method therefore differs from that of the once-familiar blue bag treatment in that the amount of reflected light is increased rather than diminished and might be regarded as negative dyeing. The *visible* light reflected may indeed exceed the visible light received by the treated fabric, and in that case a brilliant white effect is produced with a slightly bluish cast. The effectiveness of fluorescent agents depends on the presence of ultra-violet light in the illuminant and is therefore much reduced in artificial light.

Fluorescent additives were first used in 1927 by the firm of Waterlow for treatment of banknote paper as a means of detecting forgeries; any chemical interference became apparent under ultra-violet light.[1] The process was later improved by ICI, who used fluorescent compounds such as disodium 4,4'-di(benzoylamino)-stilbene-2,2'-disulphonate having affinity for cellulose.[2]

The first use of a fluorescent compound to whiten textile materials was described by Krais[3] in 1929, but the principle was not adopted commercially until about 1940, and the practice of incorporating such brighteners in laundry and domestic detergents did not become common until after the second world war. For such a purpose an agent must be substantive, non-toxic, compatible with detergent action under all likely conditions and sufficiently fast to light to remain effective for a reasonable period. Apart from the absence of a chromophoric system structural requirements are as for a direct dye, and the molecules of most brighteners are · linear, contain long conjugated chains and have a co-planar configuration. It is important that coloured decomposition products should not be formed on prolonged exposure, but the shade of very pale dyed material is inevitably affected by fluorescence.

Very many brightening agents have been described in an extensive patent literature, and it has been estimated that 200–250 products are in commercial use. They are sold under names such as *Blankophor* (FBy), *Calcofluor* (ACY), *Fluolite* (ICI), *Leucophor* (S), *Photine* (HWL), *Pontamine White* (DuP), *Tinopal* (Gy) and *Uvitex* (CAC, CIBA). As a class they have been termed Fluorescent (or Optical) Whitening (or Brightening) Agents; for brevity 'Brighteners' seems preferable to 'Brightening Agents'.

Brighteners are now produced in many countries on a very large scale. They are applied to a great variety of substrates, but cellulosic materials account for the bulk of the market. Almost every commercial detergent now contains one or more of these agents, the amount present being usually 0·05 to 0·1% in British products but often 0·3% in American detergents.[4] Since most brighteners are by no means equally effective on all fibres detergents usually contain a mixture of agents. Apart from laundry uses brighteners are extensively applied in the manufacture of synthetic fibres of all types, also in paper and in conjunction with many textile finishing processes. For these widely varied purposes products must be carefully chosen to withstand the conditions encountered and to be compatible with the functions of other components.

20-1 Stilbene derivatives

Most water-soluble brighteners for the more hydrophilic textile materials are stilbene derivatives, and bistriazinyl derivatives of 4,4'-diaminostilbene-2,2'-disulphonic acid are of special importance. They are obtained by reaction of the diamine (1 mol.) with cyanuric chloride (2 mol.) and condensation of the product with suitable compounds in order to introduce groups such as amino, alkylamino, arylamino, hydroxy, alkoxy, aryloxy, etc. Examples of such products are CI Fluorescent Brightening Agent 1 (CI 40630) [**216**;

$X=Y=NH_2$; formaldehyde condensation product] and CI Fluorescent Brightening Agent 32 (CI 40620) [**216**; $X=OH$, $Y=NHPh$].

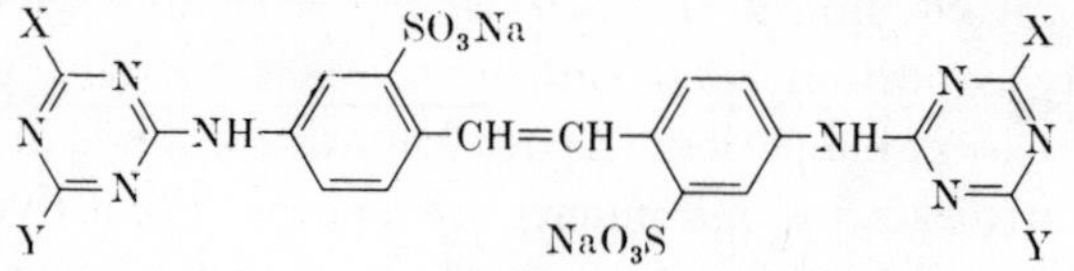

[**216**]

Compounds corresponding to structure [**216**] where X is arylamino and Y is morpholino:

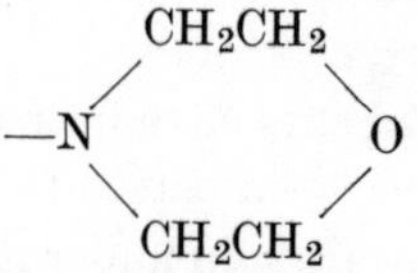

have proved especially valuable as brighteners.[5] These products are applied mainly to cellulosic substrates such as cotton or paper, but CI 40620 shows some affinity for nylon.

Unsymmetrical acyltriazinyl derivatives of 4,4'-diaminostilbene-2,2'-disulphonic acid have been described by Geigy, and are said to have good affinity for wool from a neutral bath.[6] An example has the structure [**217**].

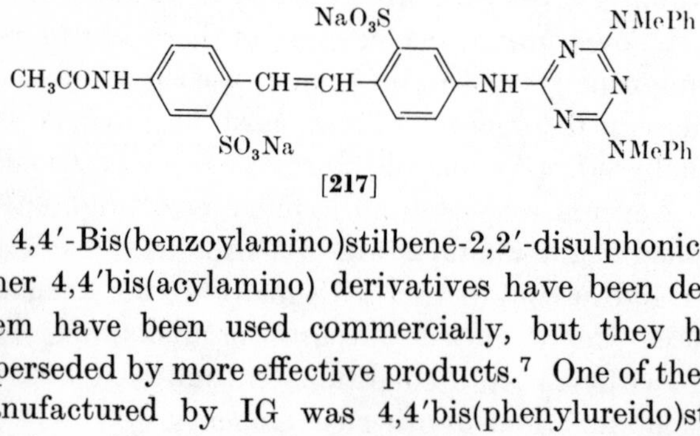

[**217**]

4,4'-Bis(benzoylamino)stilbene-2,2'-disulphonic acid and many other 4,4'bis(acylamino) derivatives have been described; some of them have been used commercially, but they have largely been superseded by more effective products.[7] One of the early brighteners manufactured by IG was 4,4'bis(phenylureido)stilbene-2,2'-disulphonic acid, obtained by reaction of 4,4'-diaminostilbene-2,2'-disulphonic acid with phenyl isocyanate in aqueous medium.[8] It was marketed as *Blankophor R* (CI Fluorescent Brightening Agent 30; CI 40600), and equivalents are still manufactured by several firms. The usefulness of this product is limited by its instability in a boiling bath.[9]

The colourless intermediate with structure [**173**] (see page 199), which is applied to cotton and then diazotised and developed to give a yellow dye on the fibre (CI Direct Yellow 62), is also used as a brightener (CI Fluorescent Brightening Agent 5; CI 36900) for paper.

With the object of obtaining an extended conjugated system Geigy prepared bis-stilbenes with structures such as [**218**] or [**219**].[10] These show intense fluorescence, give a pure white effect and have

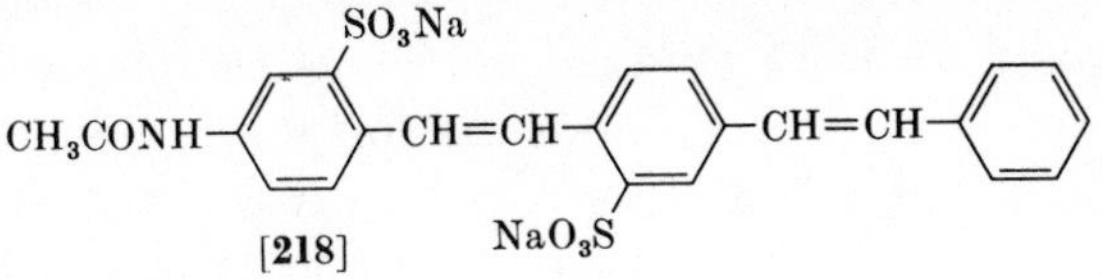

$$CH_3CONH - \underset{NaO_3S}{\overset{SO_3Na}{\bigcirc}} - CH{=}CH - \bigcirc - CH{=}CH - \bigcirc$$

[**218**]

$$CH_3CONH - \overset{SO_3Na}{\bigcirc} - CH{=}CH - \bigcirc - CH{=}CH - \overset{NaO_3S}{\bigcirc} - NHCOCH_3$$

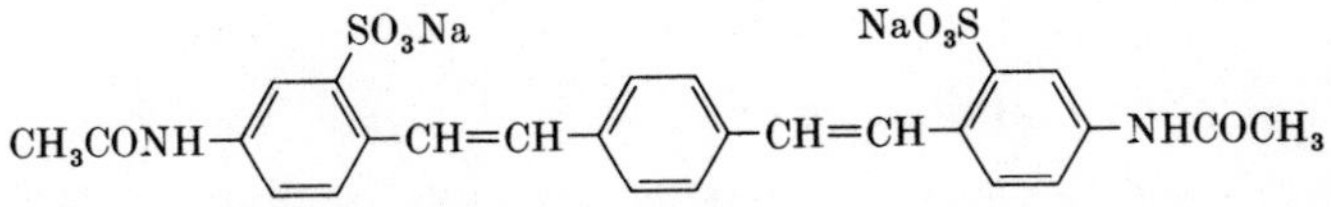

[**219**]

good fastness to washing. The same firm prepared unsymmetrical bis(triazinylamino)stilbene derivatives in which one benzene ring has a substituent sulphonic acid group as usual and the other has an alkyl, alkoxy or other group in the 2 position. These products are said to give a good neutral white effect.[11]

Numerous derivatives of stilbene containing a naphtho- or benzotriazole residue have valuable properties as brighteners. By coupling diazotised 4-aminostilbene-2-sulphonic acid with 2-aminonaphthalene-6-sulphonic acid and oxidising the product with alkaline hypochlorite a compound is obtained with structure [**220**; X=SO$_3$Na, Y=SO$_3$Na]; it can be added to a detergent as a

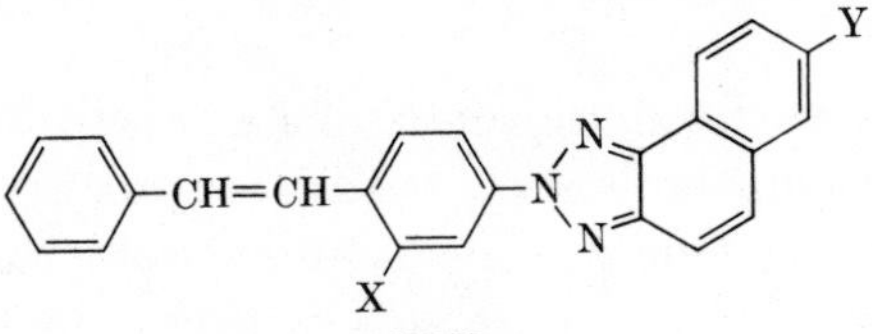

$$\bigcirc - CH{=}CH - \underset{X}{\bigcirc} - N{\overset{N}{\underset{N}{\big\langle}}}\text{(naphtho ring)}{-}Y$$

[**220**]

brightener and has an advantage over many other stilbene derivatives in that it remains effective in presence of bleaching agents.[12] Analogous products with similar properties are obtained by coupling the same diazo compound with a suitably substituted benzenoid amine such as 2-methoxy-4-methylaniline and then oxidising with copper sulphate and ammonia.[13] Unsulphonated agents such as [**220**; X=CN, Y=H] can be applied as brighteners for synthetic fibres or plastic materials;[14] others such as [**220**; X=SO$_2$OPh or SO$_2$N (alkyl)$_2$, Y=H] are said to be suitable for similar purposes and also for application to oils, fats and waxes.[15] Cationic groups such as —SO$_2$NHC$_2$H$_4$NMe$_2$ can be used to confer affinity for polyacrylonitrile fibres.[16]

Bistriazoles can be prepared similarly from tetrazotised diamines by coupling with two molecular proportions of a suitable arylamine and oxidising as before. The product obtained from 4,4'-diamino-stilbene-2,2'-disulphonic acid with 2-aminonaphthalene-5-sulphonic acid (2 mol.) and oxidising with ammoniacal copper sulphate has high substantivity for cotton and good fastness to washing, chlorine and light. When applied as a brightener it gives a slightly greenish white and can be used as a shading component with other brighteners giving a reddish cast.[17]

20-2 Other chemical classes

Fluorescent properties are found in compounds of many chemical classes. The present brief review is chiefly concerned with the non-stilbene structures that are of commercial interest. They are applied mainly to synthetic fibres and plastic materials.

20-2-1 Coumarin derivatives

The early experiments of Krais,[3] mentioned above, were made with the fluorescent compound aesculetin (6,7-dihydroxycoumarin). Later Lever Bros and others used the related compound β-methyl-umbelliferone [**221**],[18] and numerous other coumarin derivatives

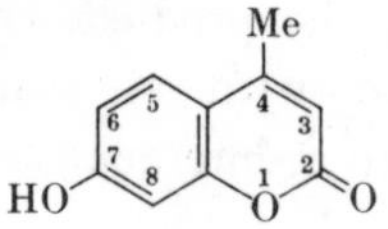

[**221**]

have been found of value, especially those containing a substituted amino group at position 7. Compounds such as the formaldehyde-bisulphite derivative of 7-ethylamino-4-methylcoumarin [**222**], the benzaldehydebisulphite derivative of 7-amino-4-methylcoumarin [**223**] or an acid salt of 7-diethylamino-4-methylcoumarin are of interest for application to wool or nylon.[19]

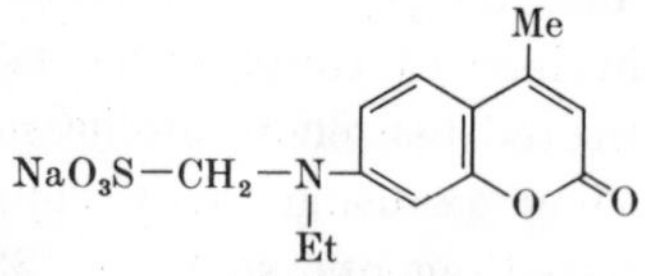

[**222**]

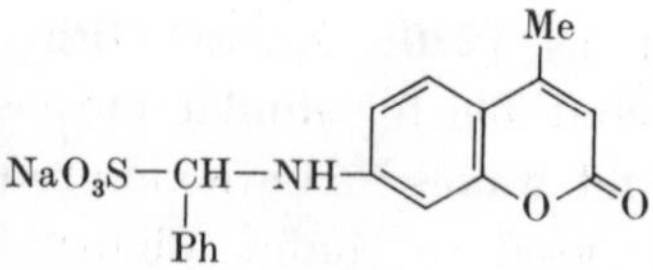

[**223**]

Coumarin derivatives substituted at position 3 by an aryl radical and at 7 by a group such as a ureido or a substituted triazinylamino group [**224**], [**225**] are of special interest in that they can be applied to fibres of cellulose, wool, polyamide, polyurethane, cellulose acetate or polyacrylonitrile by dyeing processes or to inert fibres such as polyesters by incorporation in the melt. They have good fastness to light and impart a neutral white appearance to treated fibres.[20]

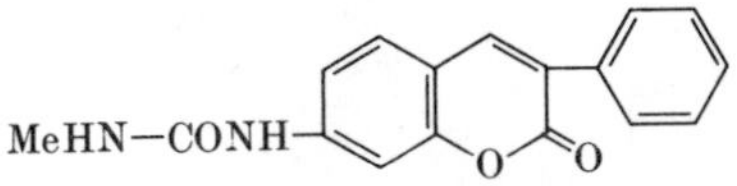

MeHN—CONH

[**224**]

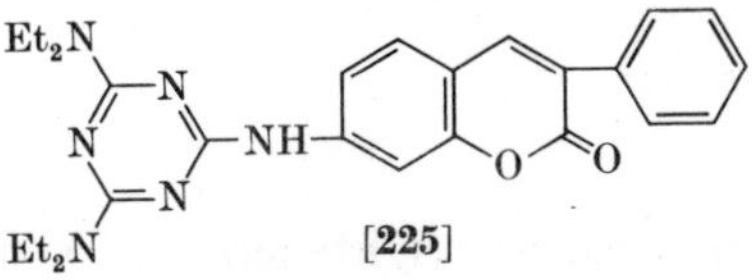

Et₂N

N—NH

Et₂N   [**225**]

20-2-2 Heterocyclic vinylene derivatives

Many fluorescent compounds have been described with structures in which two heterocyclic residues or one heterocyclic and one aromatic residue are united by a vinylene bridge. One of the earliest of these was 2-styrylbenzothiazole [**226**], first prepared by Hofmann in 1880 and obtained by condensing cinnamoyl chloride with *o*-aminothiophenol. It is marketed as *Uvitex RS* (CAC, CIBA) (CI Fluorescent Brightening Agent 41; CI 49015), and has the advantage of good fastness to chlorine.[21]

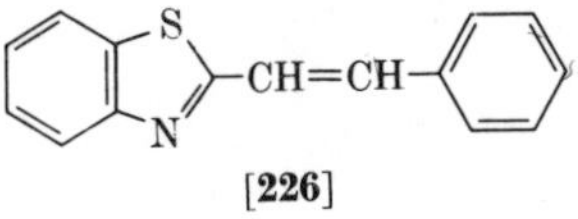

—CH=CH—

[**226**]

Symmetrical benzimidazole derivatives such as that with the structure [**227**] are said to be valuable brighteners for natural fibres or nylon.[22] Symmetrical oxazole compounds such as [**228**] have been applied to polyester fibres either by means of a detergent containing the agent or by incorporation in the polymer melt.[23] Unsymmetrical benzoxazole and benzothiazole derivatives of the general type [**229**] have been proposed as melt additives for polyester fibres.[24]

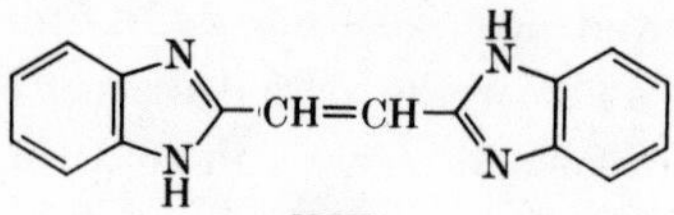

[227]

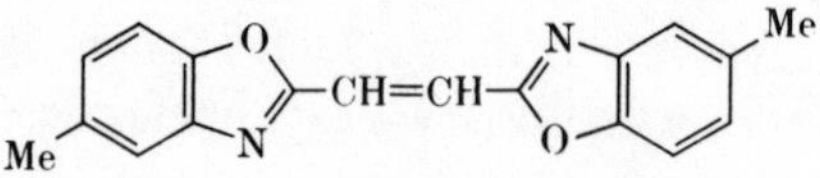

[228]

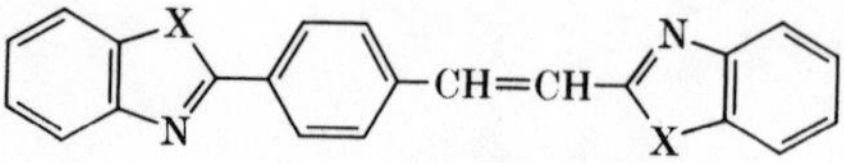

(X = O or S)

[229]

20-2-3 Diarylpyrazolines

Diarylpyrazolines form an important class of brighteners, and some of them are of commercial interest. They may be applied with detergents in the form of a dispersion or (when sulphonated) in solution; certain unsulphonated compounds are suitable for inclusion in polyamide melts. Typical structures are shown [230], but many other derivatives have been described. A chlorine atom in the *para* position of the 3-phenyl radical has an especially favourable effect on the intensity of fluorescence. Unfortunately the diarylpyrazolines are not resistant to hypochlorite treatments.[25]

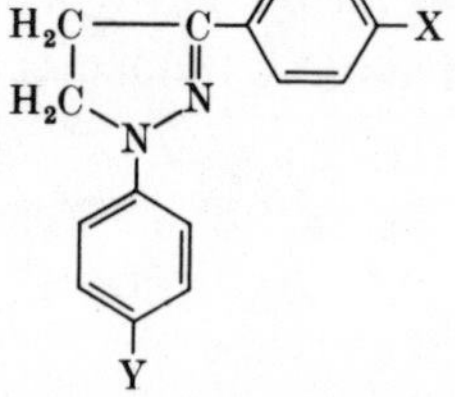

(X = H, Cl; Y = H, COOMe, SO$_2$NH$_2$ or SO$_3$H)

[230]

20-2-4 Naphthalic imides

Various substituted naphthalic imides have been described as effective brighteners, and it is believed that products of this type are manufactured in Japan. Preferred structures are illustrated [231]; fluorescence is greenish when Y is NHCOCH$_3$ and reddish when it is

O-alkyl. These compounds may be applied to polyesters, other synthetic fibres and plastic materials by incorporation during manufacture, and also added to detergents.[26]

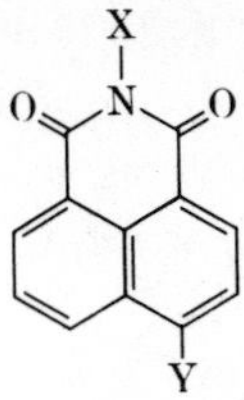

(X = alkyl or aryl; Y = O-alkyl, $NHCOCH_3$ or $NHCONH_2$)

[**231**]

20-2-5   Pyrene derivatives

Triazinyl derivatives of pyrene such as [**232**] have been described by ICI. These are highly effective brighteners for synthetic fibres, and

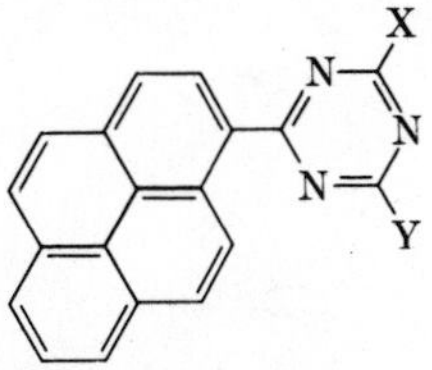

(X = substituted amino, alkoxy, substituted
      alkoxy, aryloxy, alkylthio, or substituted
      alkylthio;
Y = X or Cl)

[**232**]

can be applied from aqueous dispersion, as detergent additives or incorporated during fibre manufacture.[27] A similar product in which the pyrene residue carries a sulphonamide substituent is said to have some solubility in water and to show an advantage from this when applied in washing powders.[28]

20-2-6   Cyclic sulphones

Numerous derivatives of 3,7-diamino-2,8-disulphodibenzothiophene-5,5-dioxide are valuable brighteners for cellulosic fibres.[29] They appear to be somewhat less effective than most of the commercial stilbene derivatives but are fast to hypochlorite.[9] An example has the structure [**233**].

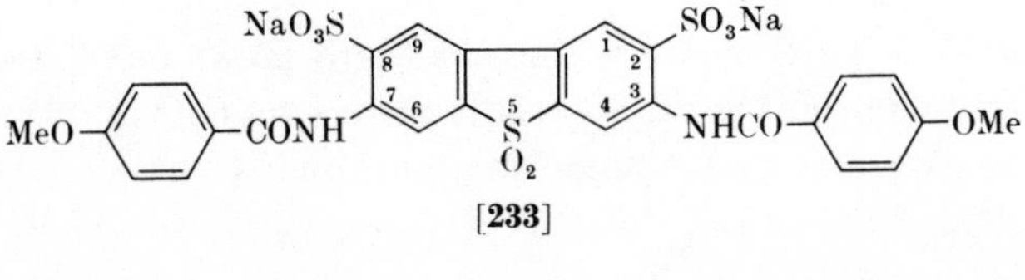

[**233**]

20-2-7   Miscellaneous chemical classes

One of the early brighteners made by IG was the diphenylimid-azolonedisulphonic acid [234], sold as *Blankophor WT* (CI Fluorescent Brightening Agent 48; CI 40640). It is obtained by condensation of benzoin with urea and disulphonation of the product.[30] This agent is now made by several firms under their own brand names and is chiefly suitable for application to wool.

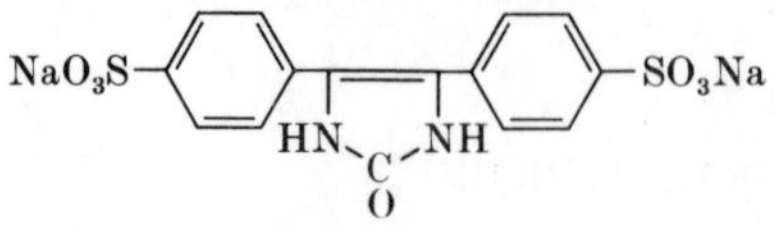

[234]

Many pyrazine derivatives have been found suitable as brighteners for wool and synthetic fibres of various types.[31] An example has the structure [235].

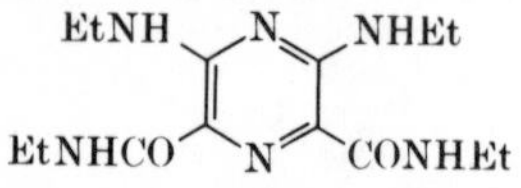

[235]

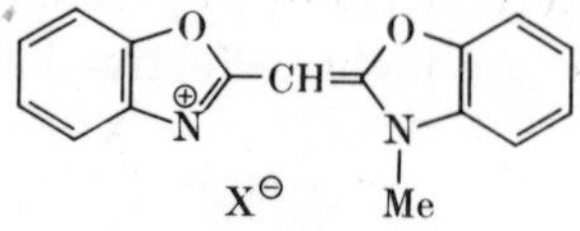

$(X^\ominus = \text{anion})$

[236]

Oxacyanines with structures such as [236] and its substituted derivatives were described by Ilford,[32] and subsequently related unsymmetrical cyanines in which one of the benzoxazole residues is replaced by a benzothiazole or indole residue were prepared by Geigy.[33] It is believed that cationic compounds of these and some of the other chemical classes mentioned have been used commercially. They are of special interest for application to acrylic fibres.

Agents containing both thiazole and triazole residues have been patented by DuPont. They are generally suitable for application to cellulosic fibres and to nylon, and have good fastness to chlorine.[34] An example of these is the compound with structure [237].

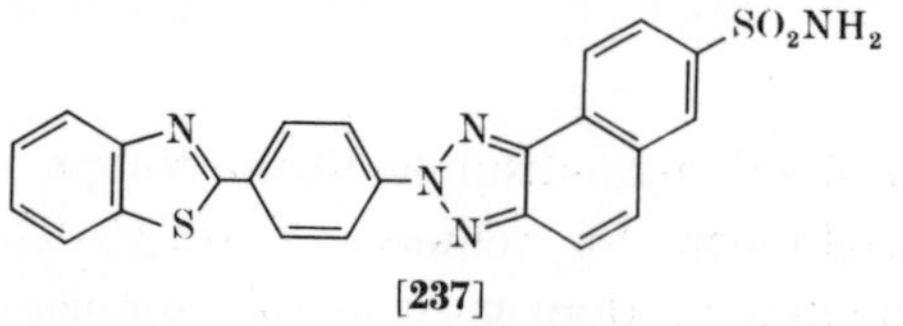

[237]

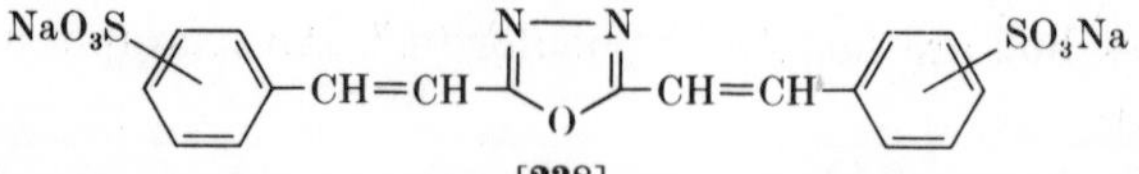

[238]

Oxadiazoles such as that with the structure [238] have been proposed by CIBA as brighteners, especially for use on cotton. They are said to have good fastness to chlorine and in many cases also to light.[35]

Colour photography

Although colour photography has been widely practised only in recent times the basic principles concerned have been understood for over a century. The first practical demonstration was made by Clerk Maxwell in 1861. He photographed a tartan silk bow through red, green and blue filters, prepared positive transparencies from the three negative images and then projected them upon a screen by means of three lanterns, each fitted with a coloured filter corresponding to that used in the original exposure so that the images were superimposed. It was reported that 'a coloured image was seen, which, if the red and green images had been as fully photographed as the blue, would have been a truly-coloured image of the ribbon'.[1] It has since been pointed out that some explanation of this result is necessary since photographic material available at the time was not sensitive to either green or red. An investigation by R. M. Evans has shown that it is just possible that a good green might be separated from blues and reds under the conditions used, but reds were quite beyond the limit of sensitivity. He found, however, that the reflectance curves obtained from materials dyed with almost any of the reds available in 1861 showed secondary reflectance in the ultra-violet region, and it appears probable that the red reproduced in Maxwell's experiment was actually recorded by ultra-violet light (the exposure having been made in daylight). Evans was able to reproduce this result and obtained fairly good colour photographs with reasonably good reds.[2]

Clerk Maxwell did not follow up his work in this field, but Ducos du Hauron and C. Cros carried out further studies independently, and in 1869 both set out in publications principles that are the basis of present-day practice. Application of these principles was prevented by the lack of suitable photographic materials.

In 1873 Vogel[3] observed that certain dry plates showed unusual sensitivity in the green region of the spectrum. He found that this was due to the presence of the yellow dye Coralline (the sodium salt of Aurine; see Section 8-2-4) which had been added to the emulsion to prevent halation (an undesired effect caused mainly by the scattering of light reflected from the rear surface of the plate). Further experiments showed that only certain dyes have a sensitising action. Vogel found that Cyanine (Section 12-3) was effective, and it was used as a sensitiser for some years notwithstanding a tendency to cause fogging. Nothing better was found until the isocyanines (see Section 12-3) were produced in 1901; four years later the discovery of Pinacyanol by König enabled satisfactory panchromatic plates to be produced and the way was opened for the development of processes of colour photography. Since then many other effective dyes have been discovered and the range of sensitisation has been greatly extended.

Sensitising dyes of practical value are obtained by linking heterocyclic residues such as quinoline, benzoxazole, benzothiazole, benzoselenazole, indoline, imidazole or their substituted derivatives by conjugated chains of varying length; the central carbon atom may carry an alkyl group. In general the sensitising maximum of a given dye approximates to the absorption maximum of its solution but often lies at a slightly higher wavelength.[4] As the length of the cyanine chain is increased both the absorption maximum and the sensitising range are displaced towards longer wavelengths.[4,5] The chemistry of this subject has been described in detail by Hamer.[6]

If the spectrum of white light is divided into blue, green and red regions the resulting bands (of wavelength ranges approximately 400–500, 500–600 and 600–700 mμ) can be used as *additive primaries*. By mixing light from these three bands in suitable proportions any colour within the visible range can be reproduced. This can be demonstrated by projecting light from three lanterns fitted with blue, green and red filters upon a screen. The combination of the three coloured beams yields white light, and the expected intermediate hues are obtained by combination of red and blue or blue and green; many people find it surprising, however, that a combination of red and green yields yellow light. If light is passed through such filters in series the results are quite different. Since each filter absorbs all except blue, green or red light no two of them have a common transmission band and a total barrier is therefore presented to the passage of light.

Artists and colourists are able to produce a wide range of hues by mixing pigments or dyes in suitable proportions, but in such applications *subtractive primaries* are used. They consist of:

Yellow (white minus blue = green + red)
Magenta (white minus green = blue + red)
Cyan (white minus red = blue + green)

Each of these primaries absorbs about one-third of the spectrum of white light so that any pair has a common transmission band. If a beam of white light is directed through pairs of subtractive filters light corresponding to the common part of the spectrum is transmitted, with results as follows:

yellow + magenta: red transmitted
yellow + cyan: green transmitted
magenta + cyan: blue transmitted.

Many processes of colour photography have been devised, and they may be classified into additive and substractive systems, the latter being the more important. Whereas additive processes can be used only for transparencies for direct viewing or projection, subtractive processes are suitable for these purposes and also for production of paper prints viewed by reflected light.

21-1   Additive processes

These are of three main types. The first is the *triple projection* process which is based on the method used by Clerk Maxwell in 1861 and already described. The second is the *screen unit* process, based on a proposal first put forward by du Hauron. A panchromatic emulsion is covered by a composite filter consisting of a mosaic of minute areas coloured red, green and blue. On exposure the image is broken up into a very large number of small components representing the colours of the subject. The resulting negative is then converted into a positive by a reversal process (consisting in removal of metallic silver by bleaching, exposure of remaining silver bromide to white light and redevelopment), and this is then viewed as a transparency through the original filter screen. The image is thus seen in its original colours. The *Dufaycolor* system was based on a process of this type. The third is the *lenticular process*. For this the film support is embossed on the side remote from the emulsion with a large number of minute cylindrical lenses. The camera lens is covered by a triple filter having red, green and blue strips side by side and parallel with the lenticular mouldings on the film base. The multiple image in the emulsion is thus split into three bands corresponding to the three filters. It is developed by reversal and the resulting positive is projected through a lens fitted with a three-colour filter corresponding to that used in the camera.

21-2   Subtractive processes

All modern systems produce colour photographs by means of the subtractive primaries yellow, magenta and cyan. The basic requirements are:

1. A means of recording separately the blue, green and red contents of the subject giving on development separation negative records in silver.

2. A means of converting the separation negative records by printing or otherwise into positive separation records and replacing the positive blue record by the subtractive primary yellow, the positive green record by the subtractive primary magenta and the positive red record by the subtractive primary cyan.

The general process is illustrated in Fig. 21-1.

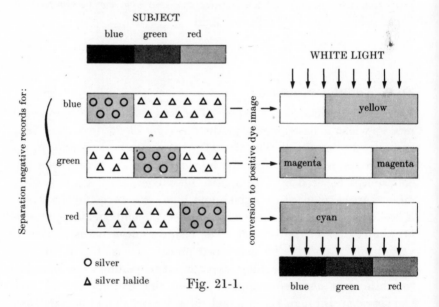

Fig. 21-1.

In certain processes such as the early *Technicolor* process, the three dye images are produced separately but simultaneously by means of a complex optical system containing only one lens, and they are then combined in exact register; this requires mechanical precision of a high order. In most modern processes, however, a single multi-layer film is exposed and processed so that perfect register is automatically obtained. The film carries three layers containing silver halide sensitised to respond respectively to blue, green and red regions of the spectrum. Since silver bromide is inherently sensitive to blue light the blue light record is placed at the top (facing incident light) with a yellow filter immediately below it to exclude blue light from the other layers which would otherwise also be affected by it. The sensitive layers are separated from each other by thin layers of clear gelatin to prevent migration of sensitising dyes, and there is a layer containing anti-halation dyes immediately below or above the film base. The anti-halation dyes and also the yellow colouring matter in the filter layer are removed during processing. An anti-stress layer provides general protection to the system and the whole structure is shown diagrammatically in Fig. 21-2.

| Anti-stress layer |
| Blue-sensitive silver halide emulsion |
| Yellow filter |
| Green-sensitive silver halide emulsion |
| Clear gelatin layer |
| Red-sensitive silver halide emulsion |
| Clear gelatin layer |
| FILM BASE |
| Anti-halation layer |

Fig. 21-2.

In spite of its many components the combined film may have a thickness of no more than 20 μ in addition to the supporting base.

On exposure and development of the film a negative record is obtained, and this can be converted into a positive either by printing upon a similar emulsion system or by a reversal process.

There are three main methods whereby the silver positive can be converted into subtractive colour, and these are now briefly described.

21-2-1 Dye transfer

In these processes the three positive silver records are produced on separate films. Development may be carried out by an agent such as catechol with a tanning action or the gelatin may be tanned by means of a dichromate after development. In either case the gelatin is hardened and its melting-point raised to an extent depending on the amount of silver present. Untanned gelatin can then be washed away with hot water, leaving a positive 'matrix' consisting of an image with a varying thickness of gelatin. The matrices for blue, green and red are dyed respectively yellow, magenta and cyan by means of acid or direct dyes, then the dyes are transferred successively by contact to a layer of film or paper impregnated with a suitable mordant. Combination of the three images in correct register presented a difficult mechanical problem, but it was satisfactorily solved. The process is well suited to the requirements of the cinematographic industry since many copies can be prepared from the matrices by re-dyeing and the cost of silver halide emulsions is avoided. The *Technicolor* process used for motion pictures and the *Kodak Dye Transfer* process are based on these principles.

21-2-2 Dye destruction

Subtractive primary colours can be introduced into the appropriate light-sensitive layers in manufacture, but they must then be removed from areas of the negative where they are not required, as can be seen from Fig. 21-1. In the blue-sensitive layer, which is to be dyed yellow in areas where blue light has not been received, the yellow dye must be removed in regions of the negative bearing a silver image. Similarly magenta dye must be removed from silver regions of the green-sensitive layer and cyan dye from silver regions of the red-sensitive layer. If azo dyes are used such removal can be effected by treating the film in an acid bath containing thiourea and a catalyst; reduction of the dyes takes place in proportion to the amount of silver present. This process was developed mainly by Gáspár, who suggested that the reaction could be expressed simply as:

$$Ag + H^{\oplus}X^{\ominus} \rightarrow Ag^{\oplus}X^{\ominus} + H$$

Thiourea probably serves to hinder the reverse reaction by forming with the silver salt a complex $Ag[CS(NH_2)_2]Cl$.

Many other reducing agents whose action is accelerated by the presence of silver have been used, and in some conditions it is possible to use oxidising agents for destruction of the dyes. The literature relating to these processes has been summarised (1952) by Collins and Giles.[7]

Dye destruction processes were used by Gáspár in the 1930s for production of cinema film prints, and have been applied more recently by Ilford and CIBA for preparing paper prints from colour transparencies. Since film speeds are low in consequence of the absorption of light by dyes in the emulsion these processes are restricted to printing applications.

21-2-3 Dye synthesis

In all photographic processes development of the silver image is normally carried out by means of a solution of an organic reducing agent which is itself oxidised in the course of the reaction. The oxidation products are usually removed as water-soluble derivatives formed by reaction with sodium sulphite present in the developer. It has long been known that the leuco compounds of certain dyes, such as indigo, can be used as developers, and that in absence of sulphite the developed image is coloured by the oxidised form of the dye employed; the silver image can be removed by treatment with a solution containing potassium ferricyanide and sodium thiosulphate leaving the dye intact. Although colour photographs can be produced in this way the process has not been used in practice. A related process, however, in which the oxidised developer reacts with a colour former to yield a dye, is the basis of the greater part of present-day colour photography.

It was shown by R. Fischer[8] in 1912 that if reactive methylene compounds were incorporated in suitably sensitised layers of the emulsion, on development with an N,N-dialkyl-p-phenylenediamine dyes were formed and deposited together with the silver image. It is clear from Fischer's publications that he envisaged a multi-layer system in which oxidative condensation of developer and coupler occurs with fixation of dye in proportion to the amount of silver present in the positive image. His process included the provision of a yellow filter layer to protect the green- and red-sensitive layers from the action of blue light, and also eventual removal of silver by potassium ferricyanide and sodium thiosulphate. Commercial use was not achieved, however, until more than 20 years later when the *Kodachrome* process was established (1935). This differed from Fischer's process chiefly in that the colour coupling reagents were added to the developing solutions instead of to the emulsions. Somewhat complicated operations were required for development of the finished pictures, each layer being treated separately, but good colour reproduction was secured. The *Agfacolor* film, first marketed in 1936, contains colour coupling compounds in the emulsion layers. The molecules of these compounds are prevented from migration by the presence of long alkyl chains or other bulky residues; as these groups do not form part of the chromophoric systems of the dyes formed they do not affect the hues. Colour development can be carried out in all layers simultaneously and processing is therefore comparatively simple.

The early processes have been modified in detail and many systems have been used in commercial practice. Water-soluble couplers anchored by long aliphatic chains are used in *Agfacolor*, *Anscochrome* (GAF), *Gevacolor* (Gevaert) and *Ferraniacolor* (Ferrania SpA). Another system in which couplers containing anchoring residues but no solubilising group are dissolved in droplets of high-boiling non-polar solvents and dispersed in the emulsion is used in *Ektacolor*, *Ektachrome* and Kodacolor film (all products of Eastman Kodak Co.).

Colour Formers. Colour formers have been described in great numbers in the patent literature; only a few of them can be mentioned here.

Yellow Couplers. Benzoylacetanilides are of chief importance as yellow couplers. The derived hue may be varied by introduction of substituents such as alkoxy or halogen.[9] Higher alkyl substituents are usually present in the molecules of couplers to be incorporated in the emulsion. Typical examples of these are [**239**], [**240**]. The

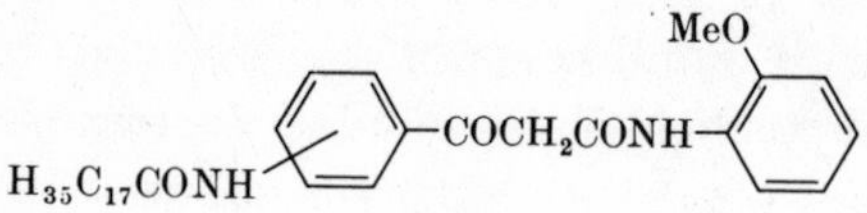

[**239**]

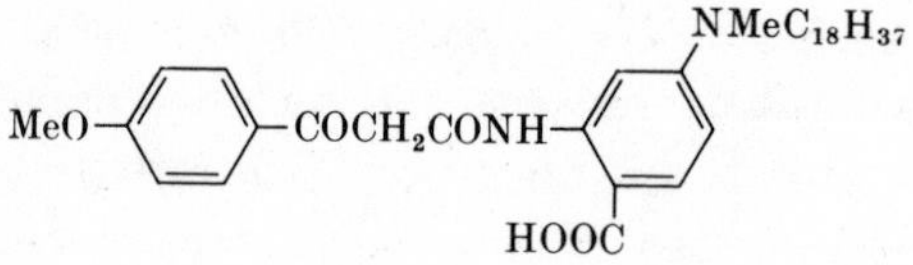

[**240**]

reaction of such couplers with N,N'-dialkyl-p-phenylenediamine in presence of silver ions to give a yellow azamethine dye may be represented as follows:

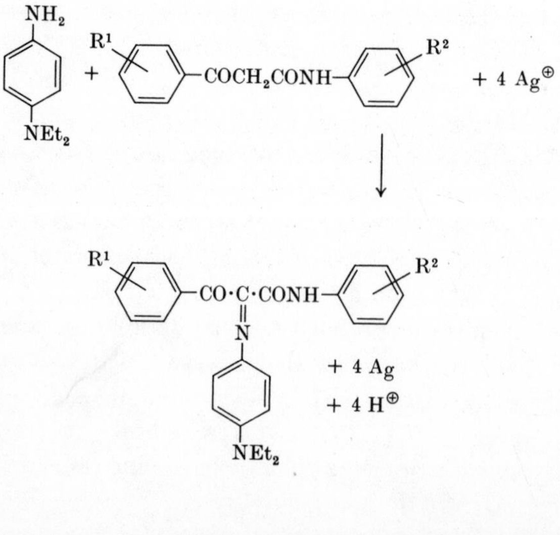

The use of benzoisooxazolones yielding yellow azo dyes on reaction with the developer has been described.[10] In a typical case dye formation takes place as follows:

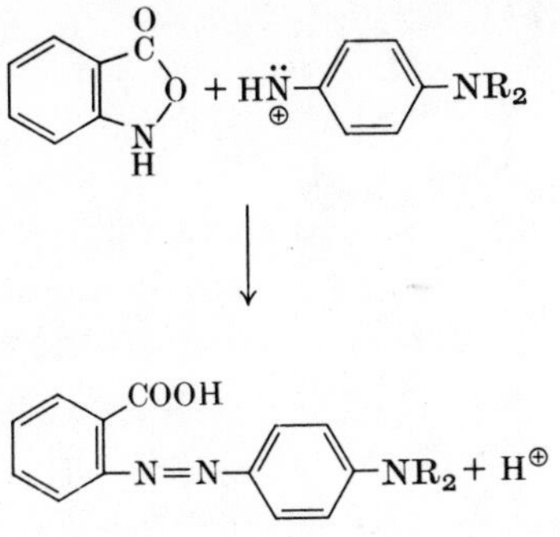

Magenta Couplers. Reactive methylene compounds giving magenta dyes are chiefly cyanoacetyl derivatives or pyrazolones, the latter being especially important. Examples of cyanoacetyl compounds that can be used in this way include ω-cyanoacetophenone, 2-cyanoacetylnaphthalene and cyanoacetylcoumarone [241]. Pyrazolone derivatives of possible value are very numerous and include

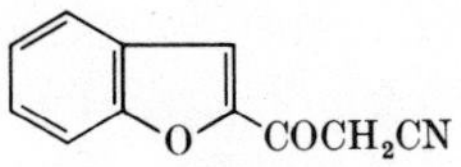

[241]

1,3-dialkyl-, 3-alkyl-1-aryl, 1,3-diaryl-, 3-acylamido-1-arylpyrazol-5-ones and many pyrazolones containing heterocyclic substituents. Long-chain alkyl radicals, solubilising groups or both may be present

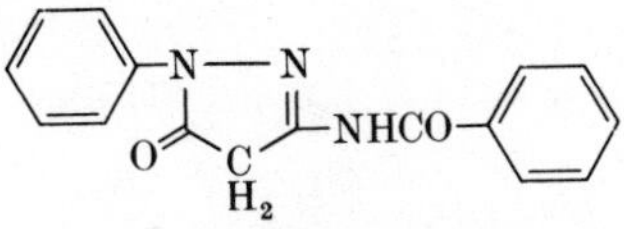

Alkali-soluble, for addition
to colour developer

[242]

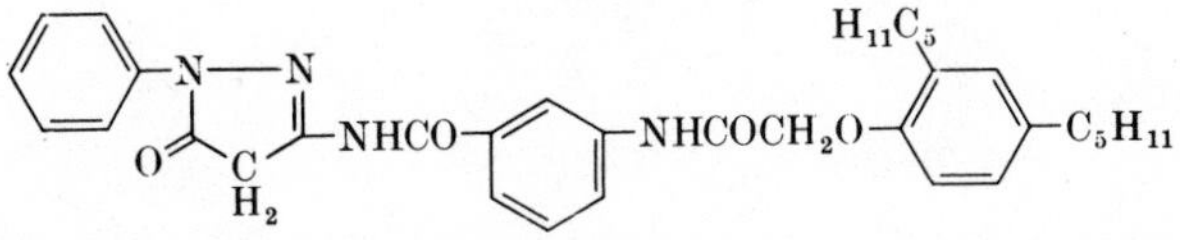

Oil-soluble, for addition
to emulsion

[243]

as substituents in aryl or acylamido groups. Structures [**242**], [**243**] and [**244**] represent pyrazolone derivatives suitable for use as colour formers in processes of various types. The derived dyes are formed by reactions similar to those described above for yellows giving structures of the general type [**245**].

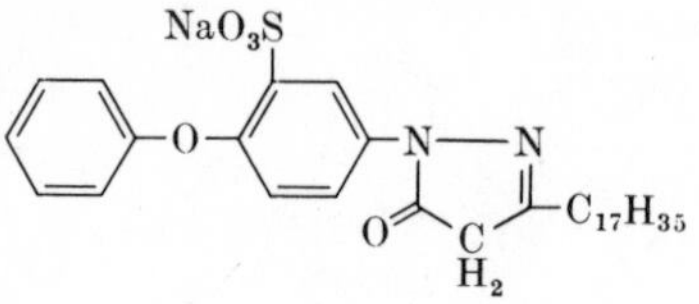

Water-soluble, for
addition to emulsion

[**244**]

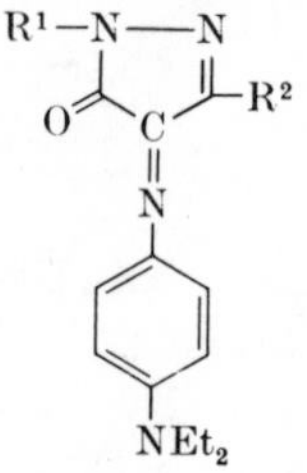

[**245**]

Cyan Couplers. Colour formers for cyan dyes are usually derivatives of phenol or α-naphthol yielding dyes of the indophenol class. The compounds of chief importance are arylamides or alkylamides of 1-hydroxy-2-naphthoic acid. Long-chain alkyl substituents are often present in the molecule and water-solubilising groups are introduced if the coupler is to be added directly to the emulsion. Structures [**246**], [**247**] and [**248**] represent typical examples of couplers giving cyan dyes; the indophenols produced by reaction with

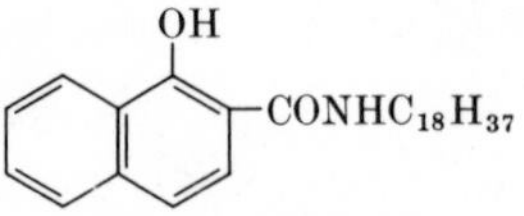

Used in oil phase

[**246**]

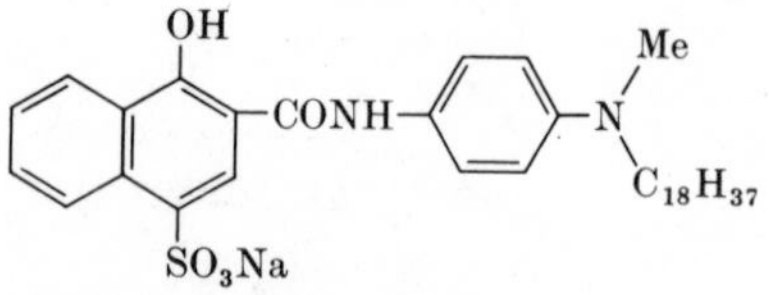

Used in aqueous phase

[**247**]

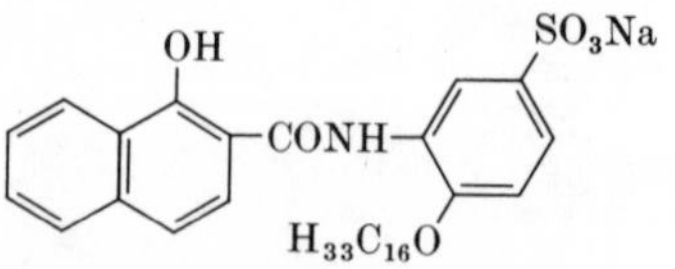

Used in aqueous phase

[**248**]

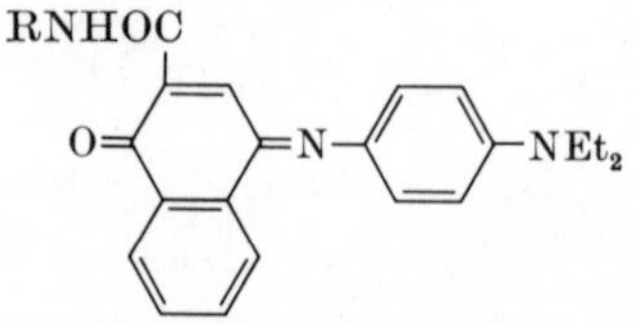

Dye of Indophenol class

[**249**]

N,N'-diethyl-p-phenylenediamine are of the general type represented by [**249**].

Colour developers. All of the examples quoted above are derived from the developer N,N-diethyl-p-phenylenediamine, and this developer is very commonly employed. Other related compounds can also be used, however. Improved solubility may be obtained when necessary by using developers in which one of the ethyl groups in N,N'-diethyl-p-phenylenediamine is replaced by a group such as $-CH_2CH_2OH$, $-CH_2CH_2NHSO_2CH_3$ or $-(CH_2)_nSO_3H$ (where $n = 2$ or more). The rate of development can be increased by introducing electron-donating groups such as alkyl, alkoxy or alkylamino into the benzene ring in a position *ortho* to the amino group.[11] Substituents in the developer molecule naturally also affect the hue of the derived dye.[12]

Colour systems based on dyes of classes other than azamethine and indophenol. The main commercial colour photographic processes are based on dyes of the classes described, but several others have been examined for the purpose. These include azine,[13] amidrazone[14] and azo dyes;[15] the references quoted should be consulted for an account of work in these fields.

Correction of faulty colour reproduction. In order to achieve perfect colour reproduction dyes would be needed absorbing light only in the required regions of the spectrum. A careful selection is made so that this ideal may be approached as closely as possible, but all dyes absorb some light beyond the desired range. In processes in which the final colour print is obtained from a colour negative it is possible to remove the effect of unwanted absorption by a device known as *masking*, which depends on the use of coloured couplers. The method of operation may be illustrated by considering an example in which a magenta dye in the green-sensitive layer absorbs a small proportion of blue light in addition to the green light required. By using a coupler having a yellow colour which absorbs blue light to the same extent as does the magenta dye derived from it the resulting image (varying in green absorption density) will show uniform absorption in the blue region. This constant excess is then corrected by increasing the blue component of light applied in printing. In the same way a reddish coupler can be used to balance unwanted blue and green absorption by a derived cyan dye.[16]

Coloured couplers can be obtained by introducing an azo group into the molecule at the coupling position. It is eliminated by the reaction of the developer so that the hue of the final dye is unaffected. In the case of a pyrazolone coupler giving a magenta dye the reaction may be illustrated as follows:

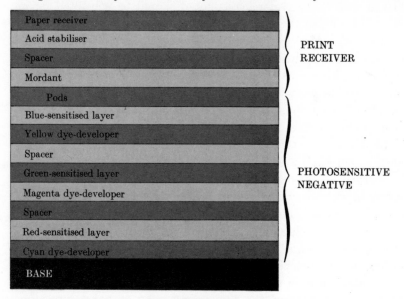

$(R^1, R^2 = \text{alkyl, aryl, etc.}; R^3 = \text{aryl})$
Yellow azo coupler

Developer

Magenta dye NEt_2

$+ N_2 + R^3H$

$+$

$2\,Ag + 2\,HBr$

Polacolor system. In most colour photographic systems process-ing includes many stages and requires about $1\frac{1}{2}$ h for completion. A rapid and fully automatic system has recently been devised,

Paper receiver	
Acid stabiliser	PRINT
Spacer	RECEIVER
Mordant	
Pods	
Blue-sensitised layer	
Yellow dye-developer	
Spacer	
Green-sensitised layer	PHOTOSENSITIVE
Magenta dye-developer	NEGATIVE
Spacer	
Red-sensitised layer	
Cyan dye-developer	
BASE	

Fig. 21-3.

however, by International Polaroid Corporation and is the basis of their *Polacolor film.* After exposure processing is completed within a multilayer pack and a finished print is produced within about 1 min. The system contains a photosensitive negative assembly and a print-receiving assembly which are brought together after the former has been exposed. The structure of the combined pack is represented diagrammatically in Fig. 21-3.

The negative assembly includes the customary blue-, green- and red-sensitised emulsion layers, and immediately below each of these is a layer containing an appropriate *dye-developer*. The molecules of these compounds consist of the residue of a dye (yellow, magenta or cyan) chemically linked with that of hydroquinone or catechol which serves as a developer. The dye-developers are initially present in the acid state and are then non-diffusible. After exposure processing is initiated by bringing together the negative and print assemblies between rollers which exert sufficient pressure to rupture an intermediate container consisting of a series of 'pods' filled with a viscous strongly alkaline activator solution. This solution diffuses rapidly through the film, brings the molecules of the dye-developers into solution and renders them diffusible. Development of exposed areas in each layer of the negative then takes place, and wherever silver is deposited oxidation of the dye-developer occurs, with the result that it is precipitated and prevented from diffusing further. In unexposed regions of the negative the dye-developer molecules remain diffusible and quickly reach the print-receiving assembly where they are fixed by a mordant. Excess alkali is neutralised by the acid stabilising layer. In order to ensure that dye-developers are fully immobilised in the appropriate exposed regions at least one auxiliary developer is incorporated in the alkaline activator solution.

This system depends upon carefully balanced quantities of reagents and adjustment of diffusion rates by means of suitable spacer layers.[17]

21-2-4   Light fastness of colour transparencies and prints

Many of the dyes used in colour photography have fastness properties that would be inadequate for textile applications. In the photographic field conditions are in general much less severe. Paper prints are likely to be exposed to light for longer periods than is usual with transparencies, and colour formers for these must be chosen to give maximum light fastness. Ultra-violet absorbers have been successfully applied to prints either in processing baths or in the form of a lacquer, and provide a measure of protection from fading on exposure to light. Many of these absorbers are fluorescent and have a brightening effect.

Appendix

Constitutions and uses of azo dye intermediates known by trivial names

Trivial name	Constitution	Main uses*
Brönner acid	2-Naphthylamine-6-sulphonic acid	Diazo (A) component
Chromotropic acid	1,8-Dihydroxynaphthalene-3,6-disulphonic acid	Coupling (Z) component
Cleve's acids	1-Naphthylamine-6- + -7-sulphonic acids	Diazo (A) or Middle (M) components. (Used separately or as a mixture)
Crocein acid	2-Naphthol-8-sulphonic acid	Coupling (E) component
Epsilon (ε) acid	1-Naphthol-3,8-disulphonic acid	Coupling (E) component
F acid	2-Naphthol-7-sulphonic acid	Coupling (E) component
Freund acid	1-Naphthylamine-3,6-disulphonic acid	Diazo (A) component
G acid	2-Naphthol-6,8-disulphonic acid	Coupling (E) component
Gamma (γ) acid	7-Amino-1-naphthol-3-sulphonic acid	Middle (M) or Coupling (E) component
GR acid	1-Naphthol-3,6-disulphonic acid	Coupling (E) component
H acid	1-Amino-8-naphthol-3,6-disulphonic acid	Coupling (E or Z) component
J acid	6-Amino-1-naphthol-3-sulphonic acid	Middle (M) or Coupling (E or Z) component
K acid	1-Amino-8-naphthol-4,6-disulphonic acid	Diazo (A), Middle (M) or Coupling (E) component
L (or Oxy-L) acid	1-Naphthol-5-sulphonic acid	Coupling (E) component
Laurent acid	1-Naphthylamine-5-sulphonic acid	Diazo (A) or Coupling (E) component
M acid	1-Amino-5-naphthol-7-sulphonic acid	Diazo (A) or Coupling (E) component
Nevile and Winther's (or NW) acid	1-Naphthol-4-sulphonic acid	Coupling (E) component
Naphthionic acid	1-Naphthylamine-4-sulphonic acid	Diazo (A) or Coupling (E) component
Peri acid	1-Naphthylamine-8-sulphonic acid	Coupling (E) component
R acid	2-Naphthol-3,6-disulphonic acid	Coupling (E) component
2R acid	2-Amino-8-naphthol-3,6-disulphonic acid	Diazo (A), Middle (M) or Coupling (E) component
S acid	1-Amino-8-naphthol-4-sulphonic acid	Diazo (A) or Coupling (E, Z) component
2S acid	1-Amino-8-naphthol-2,4-disulphonic acid	Coupling (E) component
Schäffer acid	2-Naphthol-6-sulphonic acid	Coupling (E) component
Tobias acid	2-Naphthylamine-1-sulphonic acid	Diazo (A) component
1,2,4 acid	1-Amino-2-naphthol-4-sulphonic acid	Diazo (A) component

* The significance of the code letters is explained in Section 3-4.

References

Chapter 1

1. GRAND, Y. LE (*trans.* R. W. G. Hunt, J. W. T. Walsh and F. R. W. Hunt), *Light, Colour and Vision*, 2nd ed., 1968, Chapman and Hall, London.
2. KIERSTEAD, S. P., *Natural Dyes*, 1950, Bruce, Humphries, Boston, USA; E. MAIRET, *Vegetable Dyes*, 1946, Faber and Faber, London; V. THURSTAN, *The Use of Vegetable Dyes*, 1964, Dryad Press, Leicester.
3. *Colour Index*, 2nd ed., 1956, Supplement, 1963, The Society of Dyers and Colourists, Bradford; The American Association of Textile Chemists and Colorists, Lowell, Mass., USA.
4. CLAXTON, G., *Benzoles: Production and Uses*, p. 91, 1961, National Benzole and Allied Products Association, London; G. W. MADARAS, *Dyer*, 1948, **100**, 361.
5. Anon., *Hydrocarbon Processing and Petroleum Refiner*, 1961, **40**, 298.

Chapter 2

1. GRAEBE, C. and C. LIEBERMANN, *Ber.*, 1868, **1**, 106.
2. WITT, O. N., *Ber.*, 1876, **9**, 522.
3. NIETZKI R., *Verhandlungen des Verein zum Beförderung des Gewerbefleisses*, 1879, **58**, 231.
4. ARMSTRONG, H. E., *Proc. Chem. Soc.*, **1888**, 27.
5. BAEYER, A., *Ann.*, 1907, **354**, 152.
6. HEWITT, J. T. and H. V. MITCHELL, *J.C.S.*, 1907, **91**, 1251.
7. WATSON, E. R. and D. MEEK, *J.C.S.*, 1915, **107**, 1567.
8. BROOKER, L. G. S. *et al.*, *J. Phot. Sci.*, 1953, **1**, 173.
9. WATSON, E. R., *Colour in Relation to Chemical Constitution*, p. 89, 1918, Longmans Green, London.
10. ADAMS, E. Q. and L. ROSENSTEIN, *J.A.C.S.*, 1914, **36**, 1472.
11. BURY, C. R., *J.A.C.S.*, 1935, **57**, 2115.
12. PAULING, L., *Proc. Nat. Acad. Sci. U.S.*, 1939, **25**, 577.
13. FORSTER, TH., *Z. Phys. Chem.*, 1940, **47B**, 245; 1941, **48B**, 12; K. F. HERZFELD and A. L. SKLAR, *Rev. Modern Physics*, 1942, 14, 294 (*C.A.*, 1943, **37**, 1653/9).
14. FISHER, N. I. and F. M. HAMER, *Proc. Roy. Soc.*, 1936, **A154**, 703; I. KIPRIANOV and E. S. TIMOSHENKO, *J. Gen. Chem. U.S.S.R.*, 1947, **17**, 1468 (*C.A.*, 1948, **42**, 8475h).
15. KUHN, H., *Helv. Chim. Acta*, 1948, **31**, 1441; *Z. Elektrochem.*, 1949, **53**, 165.

Chapter 3

1. GRIESS, P., *Ann.*, 1858, **106**, 123; *Ann.* 1860, **113**, 201; *Phil Trans.*, 1864, **153**, 679.
2. GRIESS, P., *Ann.*, 1862, **121**, 262; MÈNE, *Wagner's Jahresberichte*, 1861, **7**, 496.

3. MARTIUS, C. and P. GRIESS, *Zeitschrift für Chemie*, 1862, **2**, 132, 689.
4. UK 1074/1884 (P. Griess).
5. UK 4415/1884 (G. W. von Nawrocki).
6. ATHERTON, E. and R. H. PETERS, *Hexagon Digest*, 1956, **23**, 5.
7. ZINCKE, TH. and H. BINDEWALD, *Ber.*, 1884, **17**, 3026.
8. BORSCHE, W., W. MÜLLER and C. A. BODENSTEIN, *Ann.*, 1929, **472**, 201;
   W. M. LAUER and S. E. MILLER, *J.A.C.S.*, 1935, **57**, 520; R. KUHN and
   F. BÄR, *Ann.*, 1935, **516**, 143; K. J. MORGAN, *J.C.S.*, 1961, 2151.
9. MARTYNOFF, M., *Comptes Rendus*, 1953, **236**, 87; G. D. BAGRATISHVILI,
   Doklady Akad. Nauk S.S.S.R., 1954, **96**, 753 (*C.A.*, 1955, **49**, 8161*i*);
   Trudi Inst. Khim. im. P. G. Melikishvili, Akad. Nauk Gruzin S.S.R.,
   1958, **14**, 89 (*C.A.*, 1961, **55**, 7368*e*); G. D. BAGRATISHVILI and N. D.
   SHIGORIN, *Fiz. Sbornik L'vov Univ.*, 1957, No. 3, 190 (*C.A.*, 1961, **55**,
   16148*g*); *Optika i Spektroscopiya*, 1958, **4**, 274 (*C.A.*, 1958, **52**, 15248*d*).
10. PEREKALIN, V. V., *J. Gen. Chem. U.S.S.R.*, 1947, **17**, 1758 (*C.A.*, 1948,
    42, 5868*c*); V. V. PEREKALIN and N. M. SLAVACHEVSKAYA, *Ibid.*, 1951, **21**,
    897 (*C.A.*, 1951, **45**, 8774*f*); V. V. PEREKALIN and L. N. KONONOVA,
    Ibid., 1951, **21**, 1150 (*C.A.*, 1951, **45**, 10589*f*).
11. BAMBERGER, E., *Ber.*, 1895, **28**, 850.
12. STAMM, O. A. and H. ZOLLINGER, *Helv. Chim. Acta*, 1957, **40**, 1955.
13. UK 546,499 (S).
14. PÜTTER, R., *Angew. Chem.*, 1951, **63**, 188; H. ZOLLINGER, *Helv. Chim.
    Acta*, 1955, **38**, 1597.
15. INGOLD, C. K., *Structure and Mechanism in Organic Chemistry*, 1953,
    Bell, London; H. ZOLLINGER (*trans.* H. E. Nursten), *Azo and Diazo
    Chemistry: Aliphatic and Aromatic Compounds*, 1961, Interscience, New
    York; H. ZOLLINGER, *Chem. Rev.*, 1952, **51**, 347; R. WISTAR and P. D.
    BARTLETT, *J.A.C.S.*, 1941, **63**, 413; C. R. HAUSER and D. S. BRESLOW,
    J.A.C.S., 1941, **63**, 418.

Chapter 4

1. *Colour Index*, 2nd ed., p. 1405, 1956, The Society of Dyers and Colourists,
   Bradford; The American Association of Textile Chemists and Colorists,
   Lowell, Mass., USA.
2. BRIGGS, H. and F. L. GOODALL, *J.S.D.C.*, 1939, **55**, 354; F. L. GOODALL
   and R. HULLAH, *J.S.D.C.*, 1940, **56**, 218; F. L. GOODALL and C. HOBDAY,
   J.S.D.C., 1940, **56**, 384.
3. ROWE, F. M., E. RACE and J. B. SPEAKMAN, *J.S.D.C.*, 1946, **62**, 372.
4. GILES, C. H., *J.S.D.C.*, 1944, **60**, 303.
5. SCHWARZENBACH, G. and W. BIEDERMANN, *Helv. Chim. Acta*, 1948, **31**,
   331; J. BJERRUM, *Metal Ammine Formation in Aqueous Solution*, 1941,
   P. Haase and Son, Copenhagen; *Chem. Rev.*, 1950, **46**, 381; J. BJERRUM
   and E. J. NIELSEN, *Acta Chem. Scand.*, 1948, **2**, 297.
6. DREW, H. D. K. and R. E. FAIRBAIRN, *J.C.S.*, 1939, 823.
7. SCHETTY, G., *J.S.D.C.*, 1955, **71**, 705; *Textil-Rundschau*, 1956, **11**, 216;
   G. SCHETTY and H. ACKERMANN, *Angew. Chem.* 1958, **70**, 222;
   UK 667,168; UK 736,034 and US 2,623,871 (Gy).
8. ZOLLINGER, H., (*trans.* H. E. Nursten), *Azo and Diazo Chemistry: Aliphatic
   and Aromatic Compounds*, p. 357, 1961, Interscience, New York.
9. UK 765,355 and Belg. 630,035 (CIBA); UK 851,861 (Gy).
10. SCHETTY, G., *Am. Dyestuff Rep.*, 1965, **54**, P589.
11. GRIEB, R. and A. NIGGLI, *Helv. Chim. Acta*, 1965, **48**, 317.
12. IDELSON, M. and I. R. KARADY, *J.A.C.S.*, 1966, **88**, 186; M. IDELSON
    et al., *Inorg. Chem.*, 1967, **6**, 450.
13. BOWES, J. H. and R. H. KENTEN, *Biochem. J.*, 1948, **43**, 358.

Chapter 5

1. UK 12932/15 (SCI).
2. UK 366,580 (IG).
3. UK 644,883 (CIBA).
4. DRP 571,859, 658,841 and 738,900 (IG).
5. PFITZNER, H. and H. BAUMANN, *Angew. Chem.*, 1958, **70**, 232.
6. UK 209,723 and 466,886 (SCI); H. E. FIERZ-DAVID and A. MATTER, *J.S.D.C.*, 1937, **53**, 433.

Chapter 6

1. GREEN, A. G. and K. H. SAUNDERS, *J.S.D.C.*, 1923, **39**, 10; 1924, **40**, 138.
2. ELLIS, G. H., *J.S.D.C.*, 1924, **40**, 285; UK 219,349 (British Celanese).
3. UK 211,720 (British Dyestuffs Corp.).
4. UK 181,750 and 237,739 (British Dyestuffs Corp.).
5. BOULTON, J., *J.S.D.C.*, 1955, **71**, 451; A. MELLOR and H. C. OLPIN, *J.S.D.C.*, 1955, **71**, 817; F. FORTESS, *Am. Dyestuff Rep.*, 1955, **44**, p524.
6. HALL, A. J., *Textile Recorder*, 1965, **83**, (October), 72; UK 935,125, 966,489, 969,998, 966,488 and 967,393 (ICI); UK 992,561 (Allied Chem.).
7. ROFF, W. J., *Rev. Text. Prog.*, 1962, **14**, 154.
8. WEGMANN, J., *Melliand Textilber.*, 1958, **39**, 408.

Chapter 7

1. UK 2757/80 (Thomas and Robert Holliday).
2. ROWE, F. M., *The Industrial Chemist*, 1926, **2**, 208.
3. DRP 80409, 82456, 83963 and 86937 (MLB).
4. UK 20605/93 (BASF).
5. UK 21227/94 (MLB).
6. UK 15353/97 and 23945/13 (Cassella).
7. SCHÖPFF, M., *Ber.*, 1892, **25**, 2744.
8. UK 6379/12, 13237/13, 23732/13 and 238,704 (Griesheim-Elektron).
9. UK 211,772 (Griesheim-Elektron).
10. UK 365,351 (IG).
11. UK 313,865, 286,274 (IG).
12. DRP 486,190 (IG).
13. UK 374,951 and 376,307 (ICI).
14. UK 367,907 (IG).
15. UK 603,753 (ICI).
16. GUND, F., *J.S.D.C.*, 1960, **76**, 151; Anon., *Dyer*, 1958, **120**, 796.
17. UK 811,221 (FBy).
18. UK 303,901 and 343,164 (IG).
19. JOSHI, B. S., V. N. KAMAT and D. F. RANE, *J.C.S. (C)*, 1969, 1518; K. VENKATARAMAN (unpublished); R. L. M. ALLEN and P. HAMPSON (unpublished).
20. UK 426,564 (IG).
21. DRP 260,998 (Griesheim-Elektron).
22. DRP 392,077 (Griesheim-Elektron).
23. UK 211,752 (Griesheim-Elektron).
24. UK 347,113 (IG).
25. UK 238,676 (BASF).
26. FEER, A., *Farber-Zeitung*, 1890–1, 349; A. FEER, *Bull. Soc. Mulhouse*, 1891, **61**, 220.
27. UK 1645/96 (MLB).
28. UK 269,212 (IG).

29. UK 246,181 (IG).
30. UK 275,245 (IG).
31. UK 273,352 (IG).
32. UK 332,630 (IG).
33. DRP 515,205 (IG).
34. UK 399,753 (IG).
35. Fr. 849,724 (IG).
36. UK 475,942 (IG).
37. UK 414,768 (IG).
38. UK 246,870 (IG).
39. EVEREST, A. E. and J. A. Wallwork, *J.S.D.C.*, 1939, **55**, 477.
40. UK 1,062,776 (FH); GROSS, R., *Textil-Praxis*, 1960, **15**, 1046; W. KIRST, *Melliand Textilber.*, 1960, **41**, 851; W. STAAB, *Melliand Textilber.*, 1963, **44**, 978; R. BAMBERGER and R. GROSS, *Textil-Praxis*, 1961, **16**, 931; 1962, **17**, 485.
41. UK 924,319 (FH).
42. UK 951,452 (FH).
43. UK 963,994 (FH).
44. UK 1,062,776 (FH).
45. UK 806,166 (Fran).
46. UK 443,222 and 1,077,777 (FH).
47. BRASS K. and P. SOMMER, *Ber.*, 1928, **61**, 993.
48. ROWE, F. M., *J.S.D.C.*, 1926, **42**, 207; P. BEAN and F. M. ROWE, *J.S.D.C.*, 1929, **45**, 67.
49. DRP 81791, 83010 (BASF).
50. DRP 291,076 (Griesheim-Elektron).
51. UK 328,383 (IG).
52. UK 329,353, 334,529 and 308,660, DRP 530,396 (IG).
53. UK 448,459 (IG).
54. UK 454,869 (DuP); Anm. F 10315 (FBy).
55. UK Appln. 34786/38 (IG).
56. JOMAIN, B., *J.S.D.C.*, 1953, **69**, 661.
57. SIEGRIST, W., *Teintex*, 1961, **26**, 887.
58. PETITCOLAS, P. and G. THIROT, *Chemie et Industrie*, 1962, **88**, 610.
59. Sw 227,977 (IG).
60. *FIAT* 1313, **3**, 141.
61. UK 762,269, 771,812, 778,689 and 778,928, Fr 1,138,220 (FBy).
62. DRP 950,292 (FBy).
63. UK 821,926 (FBy).
64. UK 377,207 (IG).
65. EVEREST, A. E. and J. A. WALLWORK, *J.S.D.C.*, 1928, **44**, 101; 1929, **45**, 235; 1934, **50**, 37.
66. POKORNÝ, J., *J.S.D.C.*, 1926, **42**, 345; J. A. WALLWORK, *J.S.D.C.*, 1939, **55**, 477.
67. UK 539,195, 712,414 and 730,653 (ICI); UK 874,118 (FBy); UK 833,669 (FH).
68. HADFIELD, H. R. and W. F. LIQUORICE, *J.S.D.C.*, 1959, **75**, 303.
69. UK 872,948 and 824,269 (FH).

Chapter 8

1. GURR, E., *Chemistry in Britain*, 1967, **3**, 301.
2. *FIAT* 1313, **2**, 368.
3. HODGSON, H. H., *J.S.D.C.*, 1946, **62**, 178.
4. *FIAT* 1313, **2**, 329.
5. UK 20678/89 (MLB).

6. *FIAT* 1313, **2**, 317.
7. FIERZ-DAVID, H. E. and H. KOECHLIN, *Helv. Chim. Acta*, 1918, **1**, 210.
8. RUNGE, F. F., *Ann. Phys. Chem.*, 1834, **31**, 65, 70, 513.
9. FISCHER, O. and G. KÖRNER, *Ber.*, 1884, **17**, 203; *Ann.*, 1884, **226**, 175.
10. *FIAT* 1313, **2**, 370.
11. EHRLICH, P. and L. BENDA, *Ber.*, 1913, **46**, 1931; A. ALBERT, *J.C.S.*, 1941, **121**, 484; UK 137,214 (Poulenc Frères, R. Meyer).
12. *BIOS* 1433, 4; *FIAT* 1313, **2**, 376.
13. GREEN, A. G. and A. E. WOODHEAD, *J.C.S.*, 1910, **97**, 2388; A. G. GREEN and W. JOHNSON, *J.S.D.C.*, 1913, **29**, 338; A. G. GREEN and S. WOOLF, *J.S.D.C.*, 1913, **29**, 105; K. H. SAUNDERS, *J.S.D.C.*, 1944, **60**, 85.
14. LANTZ, R., *Teintex*, 1966, **31**, 104, 173; R. LANTZ and J. GASCON, *Bull. Soc. Chim. France*, 1965, 816.
15. ZUBER, C. and B. JOMAIN, *J.S.D.C.*, 1952, **68**, 242.
16. *FIAT* 1313, **2**, 372.
17. *BIOS* MISC 20, Appendix 37.
18. Bayer Technical Literature, *Astrazon Blue GL*.
19. WEGMANN, J., *Melliand Textilber.*, 1958, **39**, 408.
20. UK 846,562 (FH).
21. UK 808,713 (FBy).
22. UK 785,988 (DuP).
23. UK 788,708 (FBy).
24. UK 789,263 (Gy).
25. UK 1,004,284 and 1,048,482 (S).
26. KELLETT, H., *J.S.D.C.*, 1968, **84**, 257.

Chapter 9

1. *FIAT* 1313, **2**, 230; *cf.* DRP 644,408 (IG).
2. UK 449,010 (ICI).
3. GRAEBE, C. and C. LIEBERMANN, *Ber.*, 1868, **1**, 49, 104.
4. UK 1936/1869 (H. Caro, C. Graebe and C. Liebermann).
5. UK 1948/1869 (W. H. Perkin).
6. GEORGIEVICS, G. VON and G. GRANDMOUGIN (*trans.* F. A. Mason). *A Textbook of Dye Chemistry*, p.260, 1920, Scott, Greenwood, London.
7. FIERZ-DAVID, H. E. and M. RUTISHAUSER, *Helv. Chim. Acta*, 1940, **23**, 1298.
8. KIEL, E. G. and P. M. HEERTJES, *J.S.D.C.*, 1963, **79**, 21, 61, 186.
9. ROWE, F. M. and K. A. J. CHAMBERLAIN, *J.S.D.C.*, 1937, **53**, 268; *cf.* MLB, *J.S.D.C.*, 1913, **29**, 128.
10. GILES, C. H., *J. Appl. Chem.*, 1965, **15**, 541.
11. UK 211,720 (British Dyestuffs Corp.).
12. *FIAT* 1313, **2**, 202.
13. UK 268,891 (British Dyestuffs Corp.).
14. *BIOS* 1484, 61.
15. *BIOS* 1484, 53.
16. *BIOS* 1484, 57.
17. *BIOS* 1484, 59.

Chapter 10

1. RODD, E. H. (ed.), *The Chemistry of Carbon Compounds*, Vol. 3, p. 1380 et seq., 1956, Elsevier, Amsterdam; A. GEAKE, *Trans. Faraday Soc.*, 1938, **34**, 1395; 1941, **37**, 68; D. APPLETON and A. GEAKE, *Ibid.*, 1941, **37**, 45, 60; *cf.* H. H. BÜHLER *et al.*, *Helv. Chim. Acta*, 1962, **45**, 1811.
2. SUMNER, H. H., T. VICKERSTAFF and E. WATERS, *J.S.D.C.*, 1953, **69**, 181; R. WEGMANN, *Textil-Rundschau*, 1953, **8**, 157.

3. BAEYER, A., *Ber.*, 1883, **16**, 2204.
4. REIS, A. and W. SCHNEIDER, *Z. Krist.*, 1928, **68**, 543.
5. HELLER, G., *Ber.*, 1939, **72**, 1858.
6. KUHN, R., *Naturwissenschaften*, 1932, **20**, 618.
7. ALPHEN, J. VAN, *Rec. Trav. Chim.*, 1940, **59**, 289; E. B. KNOTT, *J.S.D.C.*, 1951, **67**, 302.
8. DRP 137,955, 141,749 and 180,394 (Deutsche Gold- und Silber-Scheideanstalt).
9. UK 186,057 (Durand and Huguenin).
10. UK 247,787 (Morton Sundour Fabrics); UK 258,626 (Scottish Dyes).
11. FRIEDLÄNDER, P., *Monatsh. Chem.*, 1907, **28**, 991; *Ber.*, 1909, **42**, 765; *Chem. Z.*, 1911, 640.
12. GEORGIEVICS, G. VON and E. GRANDMOUGIN (*trans.* F. A. Mason), *A Textbook of Dye Chemistry*, p. 516, 1920, Scott, Greenwood, London.
13. FRIEDLÄNDER, P., *Ber.*, 1906, **39**, 1060.
14. *FIAT* 1313, **2**, 295; *BIOS* 983, 11.
15. DRP 360,690; *BIOS* 983, 3.
16. *BIOS* 960, 1–8; *BIOS* 1156, 24.
17. *BIOS* 983, 5.
18. *BIOS*, 983, 4, 24.
19. *BIOS* 983, 22.
20. *BIOS* 1493, 33.
21. *BIOS* 1493, 14.
22. *FIAT* 1313, **2**, 131, 123; UK 501,897 (CIBA).
23. *FIAT* 1313, **2**, 113–114.
24. SCHOLEFIELD, F. and C. K. PATEL, *J.S.D.C.*, 1928, **44**, 268; G. M. NABAR, F. SCHOLEFIELD and H. A. TURNER, *J.S.D.C.*, 1935, **51**, 5; 1937, **53**, 5; A. LANDOLT, *J.S.D.C.*, 1949, **65**, 659; C. H. BAMFORD and M. J. S. DEWAR, *J.S.D.C.*, 1949, **65**, 674; K. VENKATARAMAN, *The Chemistry of Synthetic Dyes*, p. 1228, 1952, Academic Press, New York.
25. DRP 194,252 (BASF).
26. DRP 441,748; 443,022 and 448,262 (IG); UK 367,462 (DuP); UK 370,905 (ICI).
27. UK 181,304 (Scottish Dyes); FRASER THOMSON, R., *J.S.D.C.*, 1926, **42**, 124.
28. *BIOS* 987, 70.
29. UK 193,431 and 230,600 (Scottish Dyes).
30. *BIOS* 1493, 29.
31. *BIOS* 1493, 12; *FIAT* 1313, **2**, 106.
32. *BIOS* 1493, 15; *FIAT* 1313, **2**, 119.
33. *FIAT* 1313, **2**, 101.
34. *BIOS* 987, 121–124; *FIAT* 1313, **2**, 181.
35. *BIOS* 1493, 23; *FIAT* 1313, **2**, 129.
36. BRADLEY, W. and P. N. PANDIT, *J.C.S.*, 1957, 819.
37. *BIOS* 987, 128; *FIAT* 1313, **2**, 159.
38. *FIAT* 1313, **2**, 109.
39. *FIAT* 1313, **2**, 152.
40. *FIAT* 1313, **2**, 61.
41. *BIOS* 987, 6, 73.
42. *BIOS* 987, 71.
43. *BIOS* 987, 7, 76; *FIAT* 1313, **2**, 140, 195.
44. *BIOS* 987, 52, 54; *FIAT* 1313, **2**, 73.
45. *FIAT* 1313, **2**, 78–79; R. FRASER THOMSON, *J.S.D.C.*, 1936, **52**, 237.
46. UK 471,743 and 475,913 (IG); *FIAT* 1313, **2**, 96.
47. DRP 138,119.

48. SCHOLL, R., *Ber.*; 1907, **40**, 1691; *cf. Ber.*, 1908, **41**, 2304, *Ber.*, 1910, **43**, 1740.
49. *FIAT* 1313, **2**, 177.
50. MAKI, T. and K. EGUCHI, *J. Soc. Chem. Ind. Japan*, 1941, **44**, 788 (*C.A.*, 1948, **42**, 2105*d*).
51. FRASER THOMSON, R., *J.S.D.C.*, 1936, **52**, 241.
52. *BIOS* 1493, 51.
53. *BIOS* 987, 89, 95, 173.
54. UK 245,587; 247,787; 248,802; 251,491 and 273,399 (Morton Sundour Fabrics); UK 258,626 and 334,902 (Scottish Dyes); UK 630,459 (ICI).
55. *BIOS* 987, 106–107; *FIAT* 1313, **2**, 163, 168.
56. UK 26690/13 (BASF).
57. SCHOPOV, I., *J. Polymer Science B* (*Polymer Letters*), 1966, **4**, 1023.
58. UK 891,794; 892,382; 902,364; 923,740; 925,998; 936,414; 962,353; 966,497; 973,910; 996,244; 999,792; 1,012,316 and 1,027,565 (CIBA).
59. UK 1,023,705 (CIBA).
60. UK 1,003,790; 1,023,705; 1,025,915 and 1,027,565 (CIBA); US 3,238,231 and 3,254,935 (DuP).

Chapter 11

1. UK 1489/73 (Croissant and Bretonnière).
2. UK 23578/93 (St. Denis).
3. *BIOS* 1155, 35–6.
4. *BIOS* 1155, 34.
5. *BIOS* 1155, 27.
6. *BIOS* 1155, 29.
7. *BIOS* 983, 98.
8. *BIOS* 1155, 10.
9. *BIOS* 1155, 38.
10. *BIOS* 983, 61.
11. GNEHM, R. and F. KAUFLER, *Ber.*, 1904, **37**, 2617, 2032; A. v. WEINBERG, *Ber.*, 1930, **63A**, 117; H. E. FIERZ-DAVID, *J.S.D.C.*, 1935, **51**, 50; E. BERNASCONI, *Helv. Chim. Acta*, 1932, **15**, 287; E. KELLER and H. E. FIERZ-DAVID, *Helv. Chim. Acta*, 1933, **16**, 585; W. ZERWECK, H. RITTER and M. SCHUBERT, *Angew. Chem.*, 1948., **60A**, 141.
12. UK 541,146 and 544,953 (ICI).
13. *BIOS* 983, 43, 53–58, 71–74.
14. SHAH, K. H., B. D. TILAK and K. VENKATARAMAN, *Proc. Indian Acad. Sci.*, 1948, **28**, 111 (*abstracted in J.S.D.C.*, 1950, **66**, 333); K. VENKATARAMAN, *The Chemistry of Synthetic Dyes*, p. 1105, 1952, Academic Press, New York.

Chapter 12

1. *BIOS* 1493, 6; *FIAT* 1313, **2**, 198.
2. *BIOS* 987, 141.
3. UK 229,721 (IG).
4. WILLIAMS, C. H. G., *Trans. Roy. Soc. Edinburgh*, 1856, **21**, 377.
5. MILLS, W. H. and R. S. WISHART, *J.C.S.*, 1920, **117**, 579.
6. VOGEL, H., *Ber.*, 1873, **6**, 1302; 1875, **8**, 1635.
7. MIETHE, A. and G. BOOK, *Ber.*, 1904, **37**, 2008.
8. UK 16227/05 (MLB).
9. KÖNIG, W., *Ber.*, 1922, **55**, 3293.
10. HAMER, F. M., *Cyanine Dyes and Related Compounds*, Vol. 18 of *The Chemistry of Heterocyclic Compounds*, ed. A. Weissberger, 1964, Interscience, New York.

11. UK 458,405 (IG).
12. DIEPOLDER, E. et al., J. prakt. Chem. [2], 1923, 106, 41.
13. HAMER, F. M., J.C.S., 1924, 125, 1348.
14. FUCHS, K. and E. GRAUAUG, Ber., 1928, 61, 57.
15. FISHER, N. I. and F. M. HAMER, J.C.S., 1937, 907.
16. UK 447,038 (J.D. Kendall).
17. FIAT 1313, 3, 270.
18. BIOS MISC 20, 30.
19. DAS 1,038,522 (BASF); DAS 1,004,748 (CIBA).
20. VOLTZ, J., Angew. Chem. (Intern. Ed. Engl.), 1962, 1, 532.
21. UK 13672/12 (MLB).
22. US 1,618,415 (G. H. Ellis).
23. FISCHER, P., Ber., 1891, 24, 3794.
24. FUCHS, F., Ber., 1875, 8, 1022.
25. BIOS 1548, 213; BIOS 1661, 148.
26. BIOS 961, 31.
27. BIOS 1482, 28; FIAT 1313, 2, 384.
28. GREEN, A. G., J.C.S., 1904, 85, 1424; A. G. GREEN and P. F. CROSLAND, J.C.S., 1906, 89, 1602; A. G. GREEN and J. BADDILEY, J.C.S., 1908, 93, 1722.
29. GREEN, A. G., J.C.S., 1889, 55, 227; J.S.D.C., 1888, 4, 39; 1889, 5, 81.
30. GREEN, A. G., C. F. CROSS and E. J. BEVAN, J.S.D.C., 1891, 7, 107.
31. DRP 51738 and 55333 (Cassella).
32. UK 1,027,616 (DuP).

Chapter 13

1. STEPHEN, W. E., Chimia, 1965, 19, 261; UK 797,946 and 798,121 (ICI).
2. PRESTON, C. and A. S. FERN, Chimia, 1961, 15, 177.
3. FIERZ-DAVID, H. E. and M. MATTER, J.S.D.C., 1937, 53, 424; E. M. SMOLIN and L. RAPOPORT, The Chemistry of Heterocyclic Compounds: s-Triazines and Derivatives, 1959, Interscience, New York.
4. CĂLIN, C., V. SĂNDULESCU, S. ROSENBERG and E. TIBREA, Coloristica (Buletin Informativ al Laboratorului Central Coloristic), 1968, 4, (No. 11), 179.
5. ZOLLINGER, H., Angew. Chem., 1961, 73, 126.
6. UK 838,340 (ICI).
7. MANABE, O., S. KITAHARA and H. HIYAMA, J. Chem. Soc. Japan Ind. Chem. Section, 1958, 61, 89 (Chem. Zentralblatt, 1961, 132, 12452).
8. STAMM, O. A., H. ZOLLINGER, H. ZÄHNER and E. GÄUMANN, Helv. Chim. Acta, 1961, 44, 1123.
9. UK 874,508 (ICI).
10. UK 878,527 (ICI).
11. PANCHARTEK, J., Z. J. ALLAN and F. MUZÍK, Coll. Czech. Chem. Commun., 1960, 25, 2783.
12. LUKOS, A. and W. ORNAF, Barwniki Reaktywne, 1966, Wydawnictwo Przemyslu Lekkiego i Spozywczego, Warsaw; UK 858,989 (ICI).
13. UK 1,028,811 (ICI).
14. UK 924,599 (ICI).
15. HORROBIN, S., J.C.S., 1963, 4130; UK 838,337 and 842,193 (ICI).
16. KLASON, P., J. prakt. Chem. [2], 1886, 34, 152.
17. UK 849,772 (ICI).
18. UK 1,091,178 (ICI).
19. UK 852,911; 885,059; 885,547; 908,352 and 927,773 (ICI).
20. UK 846,765; 925,994 and 926,039 (ICI).

21. DAWSON, T. L., *J.S.D.C.*, 1964, **80**, 134; W. E. STEPHEN, *Rev. Text. Prog.* 1964, **16**, 209; UK 937,182; 946,998; 950,327 and 974,136 (ICI); UK 977,561 (Koppers Co.).

22. UK 822,047 (ICI).

23. UK 902,618 (Gy).

24. UK 1,051,684 (Gy); UK 1,067,852 (S).

25. KLEB, K. G. and E. SIEGEL, *Angew. Chem.* (*Intern. Ed. Engl.*), 1964, **3**, 408; UK 995,791–6 (FBy).

26. WEGMANN, J., *Melliand Textilber.*, 1968, **49**, 687.

27. DRUEY, J., *Angew. Chem.*, 1958, **70**, 5.

28. HENSEL, H. R. and G. LÜTZEL, *Angew. Chem.* (*Intern. Ed. Engl.*), 1965, **4**, 312.

29. UK 1,120,761 (FBy).

30. SIEGEL, E., *Chimia Supplement*, March, 1968, 107.

31. RATTEE, I. D., *J.S.D.C.*, 1969, **85**, 24.

32. UK 1,002,648 (FBy); *cf.* Fr 1,336,679 (Fran).

33. Fr. 1,379,470 (ACNA); UK 1,032,371 (BASF); UK 1,000,801 (FBy); Fr 1,290,839 and 1,315,233, Fr Addn. 80,225 (Fran); UK 977,807 (CIBA).

34. UK 1,087,033 and 1,097,361 (FH).

35. UK 1,103,422–3 (FH).

36. UK 1,087,033 and 1,103,423 (FH).

37. UK 712,037; 733,471 and 740,533 (FH).

38. HEYNA, J., *Angew. Chem.* (*Intern. Ed. Engl.*), 1963, **2**, 20; E. BOHNERT and R. WEINGARTEN, *Melliand Textilber.*, 1957, **40**, 1036; E. BOHNERT, *J.S.D.C.*, 1959, **75**, 581; H. ZIMMERMANN, *Melliand Textilber.*, 1958, **39**, 1026; H.-U. VON DER ELTZ, *Melliand Textilber.*, 1959, **40**, 69; O. A. STAMM, *J.S.D.C.*, 1964, **80**, 416; H. ZOLLINGER, *Angew. Chem.*, 1961, **73**, 125.

39. STAMM, O. A., *J.S.D.C.*, 1964, **80**, 416.

40. HENSEL, H. R. and G. LÜTZEL, *Angew. Chem.* (*Intern. Ed. Engl.*), 1965, **4**, 312; G. LÜTZEL, *J.S.D.C.*, 1966, **82**, 293; G. MEYER, Melliand Textilber., 1966, **47**, 1296; UK 923,162; 952,810 and 971,358 (BASF).

41. BAUMGARTE, U., *Melliand Textilber.*, 1968, **49**, 1432.

42. UK 846,505 (ICI).

43. FOWLER, J. A., and W. J. MARSHALL, *J.S.D.C.*, 1964, **80**, 358.

44. BENZ, J., *J.S.D.C.*, 1961, **77**, 734.

45. RATTEE, I. D., *J.S.D.C.*, 1969, **85**, 23.

46. VICKERSTAFF, T., *J.S.D.C.*, 1957, **73**, 237; J. WEGMANN, *Melliand Textilber.*, 1958, **39**, 1006; O. A. STAMM, H. ZOLLINGER, H. ZÄHNER and E. GÄUMANN, *Helv. Chim. Acta*, 1961, **44**, 1123; R. C. SENN, O. A. STAMM and H. ZOLLINGER, *Melliand Textilber.*, 1963, **44**, 261; O. A. STAMM, *Helv. Chim. Acta*, 1963, **46**, 3008; J. WEGMANN, *Melliand Textilber.*, 1968, **49**, 687.

47. UK 934,809 (Cassella); UK 1,071,319 and 1,087,474 (CIBA); UK 1,086,996; 1,104,911–5; 1,118,785; 1,119,404; 1,124,132; 1,145,847 and US 3,351,594 (ICI).

48. UK 712,037; 733,471 and 740,533 (FH).

49. UK 899,714 (ICI).

50. UK 880,886 (ICI).

51. UK 895,424 (ICI).

52. ELÖD, E. and U. EINSELE, *Melliand Textilber.*, 1960, **41**, 1377.

53. SCOTT, D. F. and T. VICKERSTAFF, *J.S.D.C.*, 1960, **76**, 104.

Chapter 14

1. MILLIGAN, B. and J. M. SWAN, *Text. Res. J.*, 1961, **31**, 18; *cf.* ref. 4 also;

F. Osterloh, *Melliand Textilber.*, 1963, **44**, 57; G. Kaufmann, *Melliand Textilber.*, 1963, **44**, 1245.

2. Luttringhaus, H., *Am. Dyestuff Rep.*, 1964, **53**, 728.
3. Bunte, H., *Ber.*, 1874, **7**, 646.
4. Schimmelschmidt, K., H. Hoffmann and E. Baier, *Angew. Chem.*, 1962, **74**, 975.
5. Kaufmann, G., *Melliand Textilber.*, 1963, **44**, 1245.
6. UK 927,774; 929,398 and 953,428; US 3,088,790 (FH).
7. UK 1,083,165–6; 1,145,655 and 1,146,002; Belg. 718,861; US 3,325,511, 3,334,084–5; 3,334,116 and 3,367,929 (Martin–Marietta).
8. Weston, C. D. and W. S. Griffith, *Textile Chemist and Colorist*, 1969, **1**, 462; Fr 1,522,275 (Martin–Marietta).
9. UK 1,014,703; 1,016,085; 1,016,850; 1,018,459; 1,020,706 and 1,025,042–3 (Martin–Marietta).
10. McCleary, H. R., A. L. Cate, F. Fordemwalt and F. F. Loffelman, *Am. Dyestuff Rep.*, 1967, **56**, p46.
11. Wegmann, J., *Melliand Textilber.*, 1968, **49**, 687.
12. UK 1,033,778 and 1,052,992 (CIBA).
13. UK 1,046,751 (Asahi Kasei Kogyo Kabushiki Kaisha).
14. UK 1,036,691 (FH).
15. UK 1,012,497 (BASF).
16. UK 1,047,546 (Shell Internat. Res. Maatschappij, NV).
17. UK 1,064,470 (BASF).
18. UK 1,065,961 (Dainichiseika Color and Chem.).

Chapter 15

1. UK 322,169 (ICI).
2. Linstead, R. P., *J.C.S.*, 1934, 1016; G. T. Byrne, R. P. Linstead and A. R. Lowe, *J.C.S.*, 1934, 1017; R. P. Linstead and A. R. Lowe, *J.C.S.*, 1934, 1022; C. E. Dent and R. P. Linstead, *J.C.S.*, 1934, 1027; R. P. Linstead and A. R. Lowe, *J.C.S.*, 1934, 1031; C. E. Dent, R. P. Linstead and A. R. Lowe, *J.C.S.*, 1934, 1033.
3. de Diesbach, H. and E. von der Weid, *Helv. Chim. Acta*, 1927, **10**, 886.
4. Braun, A. and J. Tcherniac, *Ber.*, 1907, **40**, 2709.
5. Robertson, J. M., *J.C.S.*, 1935, 615; 1936, 1195; R. P. Linstead and J. M. Robertson, *J.C.S.*, 1936, 1736; J. M. Robertson and I. Woodward, *J.C.S.*, 1937, 219; 1940, 36.
6. Linstead, R. P., *J.C.S.*, 1934, 1016; UK 389,842 (Scottish Dyes).
7. Dent, C. E. and R. P. Linstead, *J.C.S.*, 1934, 1027.
8. UK 410,814 (ICI).
9. Lecher, H. Z., H. T. Lacey and H. P. Orem, *J.A.C.S.*, 1941, **63**, 1326.
10. UK 457,786 (ICI).
11. UK 464,126 (ICI).
12. UK 464,673 (ICI).
13. UK 476,243 (ICI).
14. Moser, F. H. and A. L. Thomas, *Phthalocyanine Compounds*, 1963, Reinhold Publishing Corp., New York.
15. Wolf, W., E. Degener and S. Peterson, *Angew. Chem.*, 1960, **72**, 963.
16. *BIOS* 960, 33; *FIAT* 1313, **3**, 273.
17. UK 457,526 and 470,079 (IG); UK 569,402 (ICI); US 2,402,167; 2,556,726 and 2,556,728 (DuP).
18. US 2,770,629 (Amer. Cyanamid Co.); UK 912,526 (ICI); F. M. Smith and J. D. Easton, *J.O.C.C.A.*, 1966, **49**, 624.
19. UK 410,814 (ICI).

20. UK 460,594 (ICI); UK 457,526 and 476,168 (IG).
21. BYRNE, G. T., R. P. LINSTEAD and A. R. LOWE, *J.C.S.*, 1934, 1020.
22. US 2,214,454 (ICI).
23. BARRET, P. A., D. A. FRYE and R. P. LINSTEAD, *J.C.S.*, 1938, 1158.
24. BARRETT, P. A., C. E. DENT and R. P. LINSTEAD, *J.C.S.*, 1936, 1719; R. P. LINSTEAD and A. R. LOWE, *J.C.S.*, 1934, 1022; UK 410,814, US 2,116,602 (ICI).
25. DENT, C. E. and R. P. LINSTEAD, *J.C.S.*, 1934, 1027.
26. US 2,163,768 (DuP).
27. SMITH, F. M. and J. D. EASTON, *J.O.C.C.A.*, 1966, **49**, 620; US 2,486,304 and 2,486,351 (Amer. Cyanamid Co.); US 2,556,726; 2,556,728 and 2,556,730 (DuP).
28. BARRETT, P. A., E. F. BRADBROOK, C. E. DENT and R. P. LINSTEAD, *J.C.S.*, 1939, 1820.
29. UK 850,237 (ICI).
30. UK 586,340 and 587,636 (ICI); N. H. HADDOCK, *Research*, 1948, **1**, 685.
31. UK 704,310 (FBy); F. GUND, *Melliand Textilber.*, 1950, **31**, 46; F. GUND, *J.S.D.C.*, 1953, **69**, 671.
32. BAUMANN, F., B. BIENERT, G. RÖSCH, H. VOLLMANN and W. WOLF, *Angew. Chem.*, 1956, **68**, 133 (*cf.* ref. 15); UK 698,039; 698,049 and 698,070 (FBy).
33. BLOOR, J. E. and A. R. THOMPSON, *Rev. Text. Prog.*, 1956, **8**, 307.
34. GUND, F., *J.S.D.C.*, 1960, **76**, 151.
35. UK 711,433 and 731,257 (ICI).
36. US 2,772,283–8; 2,782,207–8 and 2,795,586 (DuP).

Chapter 16

1. FARNSWORTH, M., *J. Chem. Educ.*, 1951, **28**, 72.
2. *Paint Technology Manuals, Part 6: Pigments, Dyestuffs and Lakes*, 1966, (Oil and Colour Chemists' Association and Chapman and Hall, London).
3. KEGGIN, J. K. and F. D. MILES, *Nature*, 1936, **137**, 577; H. HOLTZMAN, *Ind. Eng. Chem.*, 1945, **37**, 855.
4. PRYCE-JONES, J., *Ultramarine* in *Thorpe's Dictionary of Applied Chemistry*, 4th ed., Vol. 11, p. 776, 1954, Longmans Green and Co., London.
5. UK 15951/14 (BASF).
6. UK 216,486 (FBy); UK 292,253 (IG).
7. UK 730,384 (CIBA); H. GAERTNER, *J.O.C.C.A.*, 1963, **46**, 13.
8. US 2,396,327 (DuP).
9. UK 835,459; 839,634 and 861,218 (FH).
10. GAERTNER, H., *J.O.C.C.A.*, 1963, **46**, 13.
11. LIEBERMANN, H. *et al.*, *Ann.*, 1935, **518**, 245.
12. UK 828,051–2 and 851,976 (DuP).
13. UK 387,565 (IG); *BIOS* 960, 75.
14. *BIOS* 1661, 148; *BIOS* 1548, 213.
15. UK 833,548 and 1,093,669 (Gy); PUGIN, A. and J. VON DER CRONE, *Official Digest of Federation of Paint and Varnish Production Clubs*, 1965, 1071.

Chapter 17

1. *BIOS* 960, 60; UK 520,199 (IG).
2. DRP 227,648 (R. Hömberg and K. Jörns).
3. UK 792,210 (ICI); D. A. GARRETT, *J.S.D.C.*, 1957, **73**, 365.
4. UK 1,127,967, 1,128,989 and 1,153,221 (Gy).
5. GANTZ, G. M. and G. SIEGRIST, *Text. Chem. and Colorist*, 1969, **1**, No. 3, 70.

Chapter 18

1. UK 151/63 (J. Lightfoot).
2. UK 498,755 (St. Denis); C. ZUBER and B. JOMAIN, *J.S.D.C.*, 1952, **68**, 241.
3. UK 15062/01 (MLB).
4. DRP 51073 (H. Erdmann).

Chapter 19

1. BIRD, C. L., *The Theory and Practice of Wool Dyeing*, 1963, The Society of Dyers and Colourists, Bradford.
2. MEYER, K. H. and H. MARK, *Ber.*, 1928, **61**, 593.
3. PAINE, C. and F. L. ROSE, Private communications quoted by T. Vickerstaff, *The Physical Chemistry of Dyeing*, 2nd ed., p. 179, 1954, ICI and Oliver and Boyd, London.
4. BOULTON, J., *J.S.D.C.*, 1951, **67**, 522.
5. VICKERSTAFF, T., *The Physical Chemistry of Dyeing*, 2nd ed., pp. 182–3, 1954, ICI and Oliver and Boyd, London.
6. HODGSON, H. H., *J.S.D.C.*, 1933, **49**, 213.
7. SCHIRM, E., *J. prakt. Chem.*, 1935, **144**, 69.
8. VICKERSTAFF, T., *The Physical Chemistry of Dyeing*, 2nd ed., p. 179, 1954, ICI and Oliver and Boyd, London.
9. VICKERSTAFF, T., *The Physical Chemistry of Dyeing*, 2nd ed., p. 186, 1954, ICI and Oliver and Boyd, London.
10. VALKÓ, E., *Kolloidchemische Grundlagen der Textilveredlung*, 1937, Springer, Berlin.
11. COATES, E., *J.S.D.C.*, 1969, **85**, 355.
12. LEAD, W. L., *J.S.D.C.*, 1957, **73**, 464.
13. GILES, C. H. and A. S. A. HASSAN, *J.S.D.C.*, 1958, **74**, 846.
14. LEAD, W. L., *J.S.D.C.*, 1959, **75**, 195.
15. PETERS, R. H. and H. H. SUMNER, *J.S.D.C.*, 1955, **71**, 130.
16. GREEN, A. G. and K. H. SAUNDERS, *J.S.D.C.*, 1923, **39**, 10.
17. VICKERSTAFF, T. and E. WATERS, *J.S.D.C.*, 1942, **58**, 116.
18. BIRD, C. L. and F. MANCHESTER, *J.S.D.C.*, 1955, **71**, 604.
19. DARUWALLA, E. H., S. S. RAO and B. D. TILAK, *J.S.D.C.*, 1960, **76**, 419.
20. VICKERSTAFF, T., *Hexagon Digest*, No. 20 (ICI, Dyestuffs Division, 1954).
21. WATERS, E., *J.S.D.C.*, 1950, **66**, 609; D. BALMFORTH, C. A. BOWERS, J. W. BULLINGTON, T. H. GUION and T. S. ROBERTS, *J.S.D.C.*, 1966, **82**, 405.
22. JONES, F. and J. KRASKA, *J.S.D.C.*, 1966, **82**, 333; F. JONES, *Teintex*, 1969, **34**, 594.

Chapter 20

1. UK 292,393 and 417,488 (Waterlow).
2. UK 442,530 (ICI).
3. KRAIS, P., *Melliand Textilber.*, 1929, **10**, 468.
4. ADAMS, D. A. W., *J.S.D.C.*, 1959, **75**, 22; L. CHALMERS, *Specialities*, 1966, **2**, (4), 35.
5. UK 645,413 (ICI).
6. US 2,526,668 and 2,539,766 (Gy).
7. UK 484,484 (Lever Bros.); US 2,521,665 (Gy); US 2,589,519; 2,581,059 and 2,623,064 (G); US 2,700,046 (DuP).
8. DRP 746,569 (IG).
9. R. ZWEIDLER, *Textilveredlung*, 1969, **4**, 75.
10. UK 666,198 and 668,200 (Gy).
11. US 2,762,802 (Gy).

12. UK 717,889 (Gy).
13. US 2,713,057 (Gy).
14. US 2,972,611 (Gy).
15. UK 774,010 (Gy).
16. UK 917,242 (Gy).
17. US 2,668,777 (FBy).
18. US 2,424,778 (Lever Bros.).
19. US 2,600,375; 2,610,152 and 2,654,713 (S).
20. US 2,881,186, UK 786,234 and 885,847 (Gy).
21. HOFMANN, A. W., *Ber.*, 1880, **13**, 1235; G. G. TAYLOR, *J.S.D.C.*, 1950, **66**, 185.
22. US 2,488,094; 2,488,289 and 2,515,173 (CIBA).
23. US 2,875,089 (CIBA).
24. UK 1,033,385 (Nippon).
25. UK 669,590 (Ilford); UK 808,113 (FBy); UK 883,826 (Unilever); A. WAGNER, C.-W. SCHELHAMMER and S. PETERSEN, *Angew. Chem. (Intern. Ed. Engl.)*, 1966, **5**, 699.
26. UK 741,798 (BASF); Fr 1,344,883 (Mitsubishi).
27. UK 985,484 (ICI).
28. UK 1,141,454 (Unilever).
29. US 2,653,795; 2,573,652 and 2,702,759 (ACY).
30. *FIAT* 1302, 6; *BIOS* 1239, 7.
31. US 3,017,412 (Gy).
32. US 2,620,282 and 2,649,385 (Ilford).
33. UK 813,843 (Gy).
34. US 2,700,043–4; 2,713,054; 2,713,056 and 2,715,632 (DuP).
35. UK 746,046–7 (CIBA).

Chapter 21

1. MAXWELL, CLERK, *Proc. Roy. Inst.*, 1862, **3**, 370.
2. EVANS, R. M., *J. Phot. Sci.*, 1961, **9**, 243.
3. VOGEL, H. W., *Ber.*, 1873, **6**, 1302; 1875, **8**, 1635.
4. VOGEL, H. W., *Ber.*, 1874, **7**, 976.
5. KENDALL, J. D., *Chem. and Ind. (London)*, 1950, 121.
6. HAMER, F. M., *Cyanine Dyes and Related Compounds*, Vol. 18 of *The Chemistry of Heterocyclic Compounds*, ed. A. Weissberger, 1964, Interscience, New York.
7. COLLINS, R. B. and C. H. GILES, *J.S.D.C.*, 1952, **68**, 421.
8. UK 15055/12; 2562/13 and 5602/13 (R. Fischer).
9. DRP 744,265 (AGFA); US 2,407,210 and UK 800,108 (Eastman Kodak).
10. UK 778,089 (ICI).
11. BENT, R. L. *et al.*, *J.A.C.S.*, 1951, **73**, 3100.
12. HÜNIG, S. and P. RICHTERS, *Ann.*, 1958, **612**, 282.
13. SCHMIDT, W. A. *et al.*, *Ind. Eng. Chem.*, 1953, **45**, 1726.
14. HÜNIG, S. *et al.*, *Angew. Chem.*, 1958, **70**, 215; DRP 963,297 (Schleussner Fotowerke).
15. SCHMIDT, W. A., *Wissenschaftliche Photographie*, p. 456, 1958, Helwich, Darmstadt.
16. GANGUIN, K. O. and E. MACDONALD, *J. Phot. Sci.*, 1966, **14**, 260.
17. NEWMAN, A. A., *Brit. J. Phot.*, 1962, **109**, 212; G. W. CRAWLEY, *Brit. J. Phot.*, 1963, **110**, 76; UK 853,481 (Internat. Polaroid Corp.).

Bibliography

The following references are intended to provide supplementary reading. Items included in the foregoing main reference list are usually not repeated here.

General

VENKATARAMAN, K., *The Chemistry of Synthetic Dyes*, 1952, Academic Press, New York.

LUBS, H. A., ed., *The Chemistry of Synthetic Dyes and Pigments*, 1955, Reinhold Publishing Corp., New York.

DONALDSON, N., *The Chemistry and Technology of Naphthalene Compounds*, 1958, Arnold, London.

ZOLLINGER, H. (*trans.* H. E. Nursten), *Azo and Diazo Chemistry: Aliphatic and Aromatic Compounds*, 1961, Interscience, New York.

SCHWEITZER, H. R., *Künstliche Organische Farbstoffe und ihre Zwischenprodukte*, 1964, Springer-Verlag, Berlin.

ABRAHART, E. N., *Dyes and their Intermediates*, 1968, Pergamon, Oxford.

TROTMAN, E. R., *Dyeing and Chemical Technology of Textile Fibres*, 4th ed., 1970, Griffin, London.

VICKERSTAFF, T., *The Physical Chemistry of Dyeing*, 2nd ed., 1954, ICI and Oliver and Boyd, London.

Thorpe's Dictionary of Applied Chemistry, 1937–54, Longmans Green, London.

Kirk–Othmer Encyclopedia of Chemical Technology, 1947, 2nd ed., 1963, Interscience, New York.

Chapter 1

BILLMEYER, F. W. and M. SALTZMAN, *Principles of Color Technology*, 1966, Interscience, New York.

BOUMA, P. J., *Physical Aspects of Colour*, 1947, N. V. Philips Gloilampenfabrieken, Eindhoven.

BOWEN, E. J., *The Chemical Aspects of Light*, 2nd ed., 1946, Clarendon Press, Oxford.

EDISBURY, J. R., *Practical Hints on Absorption Spectrometry (Ultra-violet and Visible)*, 1966, Hilger and Watts, London.

CARTER, G. S., *Eye and Vision*, p. 547, Vol. 5 of *Chambers's Encyclopaedia*, 1959, Newnes, London.

Committee on Colorimetry, The Optical Society of America, *The Science of Color*, 1953, Crowell, New York.

WRIGHT, W. D., *The Measurement of Colour*, 4th Ed., 1969, Hilger and Watts, London.

HARDY, A. C., *Handbook of Colorimetry*, 1963, The Technology Press, Massachusetts Institute of Technology, Cambridge, Mass.

ARENS, H., *Colour Measurement*, 1967, Focal Press, London.

WYSECKI, G. and W. S. STILES, *Color Science; Concepts and Methods, Quantitative Data and Formulas*, 1967, Wiley, New York.

PERKIN, A. G. and A. E. EVEREST, *The Natural Organic Colouring Matters*, 1918, Longmans Green, London.

MEYER, F. (*trans.* and revised A. H. Cook), *The Chemistry of Natural Colouring Matters*, 1943, Reinhold, New York.

BENTLEY, K. W., *The Natural Pigments*, 1960, Interscience, New York.

BAKER, W., *Plant Pigments*, p. 1, Vol. 10 of *Thorpe's Dictionary of Applied Chemistry*, 4th ed., 1950, Longmans Green, London.

GOLDSTEIN, R. F. and A. L. Waddams, *The Petroleum Chemicals Industry*, 3rd ed., 1967, Spon, London.

STEPHENSON, R. M., *Introduction to Chemical Process Industries*, 1966, Reinhold, New York.

Chapter 2

BROOKER, L. G. S. and E. J. VAN LARE, *Color and Constitution of Organic Dyes, Kirk–Othmer Encyclopedia of Chemical Technology*, 1964, Interscience, New York.

JONES, F., *The Colour and Constitution of Organic Molecules*, Chap. 2 of *Pigments: An Introduction to their Physical Chemistry*, ed. D. Patterson, 1967, Elsevier, Amsterdam.

MACCOLL, A., *Colour and Constitution*, (*Quart. Rev.*, 1947, **1**, 16).

BAYLISS, N. S., *The Free-Electron Approximation for Conjugated Compounds*, *Quart. Rev.*, 1952, **6**, 319.

DEWAR, M. J. S., *Modern Theories of Colour*, p. 64, Special Publication No. 4, 1956, The Chemical Society, London.

PLATT, J. R., Wavelength Formulas and Configuration Interaction in Brooker Dyes and Chain Molecules, *J. Chem. Phys.*, 1956, **25**, 80.

MASON, S. F., Molecular Electronic Absorption Spectra, *Quart. Rev.*, 1961, **15**, 287.

COATES, E., Colour and Constitution, *J.S.D.C.*, 1967, **83**, 95.

MASON, S. F., The Electronic Spectroscopy of Dyes, *J.S.D.C.*, 1968, **84**, 604.

FLETT, M. ST. C., *Physical Aids to the Organic Chemist*, 1962, Elsevier, Amsterdam.

Chapter 4

LAPWORTH, M., Dyestuffs, Azo, p. 190, Vol. 4 of 4th ed., *Thorpe's Dictionary of Applied Chemistry*, 1940, Longmans Green, London.

PFITZNER, H., Inner Complex Formation in Dye Chemistry, *Angew. Chem.*, 1950, **62**, 242.

WAHL, H., The Past, Present and Future of Metalliferous Dyes, *Teintex*, 1963, **28**, 257.

McLAUCHLIN, G. D. and E. R. THEIS, *The Chemistry of Leather Manufacture*, 1945, Reinhold, New York.

O'FLAHERTY, F., W. T. RODDIS and R. M. LOLLAR, eds., *The Chemistry and Technology of Leather*, 1956, Reinhold, New York.

PRESTON, J. M., *Fibre Science*, 1953, The Textile Institute, Manchester.

KNIGHT, A. H., Recent Trends in the Search for New Azo Dyes. I. Dyes for Wool, *J.S.D.C.*, 1950, **66**, 34.

Chapter 5

LAPWORTH, M., Dyestuffs, Azo, p. 190, Vol. 4 of 4th ed., *Thorpe's Dictionary of Applied Chemistry*, 1940, Longmans Green, London.

KNIGHT, A. H., Recent Trends in the Search for New Azo Dyes. III. Direct Dyes for Cotton, *J.S.D.C.*, 1950, **66**, 410.

Chapter 6

GREEN, A. G., Acetate Silk Dyes, p. 39, Vol. 1 of 4th ed., *Thorpe's Dictionary of Applied Chemistry*, 1937, Longmans Green, London.

KNIGHT, A. H., Recent Trends in the Search for New Azo Dyes. II. Dyes for Acetate Rayon and Nylon, *J.S.D.C.*, 1950, **66**, 169.

SKELLY, J. K., Colouration of Synthetic Polymer Fibres, *Chemistry and Industry*, 1965, 1525.

Chapter 7

KUNERT, F., Naphthol AS and its Use in Dyeing and Printing, *Rev. Gen. Mat. Color.*, 1912, **16**, 255.

KUNERT, F. and E. ACKER, Naphthol AS and its Application in Dyeing and Calico Printing, *J.S.D.C.*, 1914, **30**, 128.

WILLIAMS, A. F., Recent Improvements in Naphthol AS Dyeings, *J.S.D.C.*, 1934, **50**, 204.

BLACKSHAW, H., Azoic Colours on Cotton: Some Observations on Fastness Properties Relative to Soaping Aftertreatment, *J.S.D.C.*, 1935, **51**, 309.

BLACKSHAW, H., Application of Azoic Dyes to Textiles, *J.S.D.C.*, 1936, **52**, 135.

ROWE, F. M., Colour, Constitution, Properties and Identification of Insoluble Azo Colouring Matters, *J.O.C.C.A.*, 1938, **21**, 189.

YATES, S., The Insoluble Azo (Azoic) Colouring Matters, *The Industrial Chemist*, 1944, **20**, 489, 605, 667.

ADAMS, D. A. W., Recent Trends in the Search for New Azo Dyes. IV. Azoic Dyes, *J.S.D.C.*, 1951, **67**, 223.

OLPIN, H. C. and J. WOOD, Some Observations on the Dyeing of Dicel and Tricel Yarns and Fabrics, *J.S.D.C.*, 1957, **73**, 247.

WIASMITINOV, A., The Application of Insoluble Azo Dyes by Printing, *Textil-Rundschau*, 1958, **13**, 507.

SAUNDERS, K. H., *The Aromatic Diazo Compounds and their Technical Applications*, 1949, Edward Arnold, London.

Chapter 8

HAMER, F. M., The Cyanine Dyes and Related Compounds, Vol. 18 of *The Chemistry of Heterocyclic Compounds*, ed. A. Weissberger, 1964, Interscience, New York.

HAMER, F. M., The Cyanine Dyes, *Quart. Rev.*, 1950, **4**, 327.

LARE, E. J. VAN, Cyanine Dyes, p. 605, Vol. 6 of 2nd ed., *Kirk–Othmer Encyclopedia of Chemical Technology*, 1965, Interscience, New York.

GLENZ, O., Physico-chemical Experiments on the Dyeing of Polyacrylonitrile Fibres with Basic Dyes, *Melliand Textilber.*, 1957, **38**, 1152.

HADFIELD, H. R. and W. M. SOKOL, The Dyeing of Acrilan Acrylic Fibre, *J.S.D.C.*, 1958, **74**, 629.

PETERS, A. T., Some Recent Aspects of the Technology of Acrylic Fibres and their Colouration, *Textile Recorder*, March, 1966, p. 58; April, 1966, p. 66.

RILEY, A., Triarylmethane and Xanthene Dyes, p. 689, Vol. 11 of 4th ed., *Thorpe's Dictionary of Applied Chemistry*, 1954, Longmans Green, London.

Chapter 9

THOMSON, R. FRASER, Anthraquinone Dyes, p. 402, Vol. 1 of 4th ed., *Thorpe's Dictionary of Applied Chemistry*, 1937, Longmans Green, London.

BIRD, C. L., The Dyeing of Acetate Rayon with Disperse Dyes, *J.S.D.C.*, 1954, **70**, 68.

GUNTHARD, J., Recent Advances in the Field of Acid and Substantive Anthraquinone Dyestuffs, *Am. Dyestuff Rep.*, 1957, **46**, 9.
Review of Textile Progress, 1949–67, 1–18: Chapters on Colouring Matters. (Published annually by the Textile Institute, Manchester, The Society of Dyers and Colourists, Bradford and Butterworth and Co., London.)

Chapter 10

RANDALL, D. I., Vat Dyes, p. 664, Vol. 14 of 1st ed., *Kirk–Othmer Encyclopedia of Chemical Technology*, 1955, Interscience, New York.
FOX, M. R., *Vat Dyes and Vat-dyeing*, 1946, Chapman and Hall, London.

Chapter 11

CHAPMAN, E., Sulphur Dyes, p. 245, Vol. 11 of the 4th ed., *Thorpe's Dictionary of Applied Chemistry*, 1954, Longmans Green, London.
GANTZ, G. M. and J. R., ELLIS, eds., Sulfur Dyes, p. 551, Vol. 7 of 2nd ed., *Kirk–Othmer Encyclopedia of Chemical Technology*, 1965, Interscience, New York.
CRIST, J. L. and R. E. RUPP, The Sulfur Dyes, *Am. Dyestuff Rep.*, 1957, **46**, P83.

Chapter 12

HAMER, F. M., Cyanine Dyes, p. 514, Vol. 3 of 4th ed., *Thorpe's Dictionary of Applied Chemistry*, 1939, Longmans Green, London.
VAN LARE, E. J., Cyanine Dyes, p. 605, Vol. 6 of 2nd ed., *Kirk–Othmer Encyclopedia of Chemical Technology*, 1965, Interscience, New York.
BROOKER, L. G. S., Sensitizing and Desensitizing Dyes, Chap. 11 of *The Theory of the Photographic Process*, ed., C. E. K. Mees, 1954, Macmillan, New York.
HAMER, F. M., The Cyanine Dyes, *Quart. Rev.*, 1950, **4**, 346.

Chapter 13

SMOLIN, E. M. and L. RAPOPORT, *The Chemistry of Heterocyclic Compounds: s-Triazines and Derivatives*, 1959, Interscience, New York, London.
Procion Dyes in Textile Dyeing, 1962, ICI.
Procion Dyes in Textile Printing, 1960, ICI.
VICKERSTAFF, T., Reactive Dyes for Textiles, *J.S.D.C.*, 1957, **73**, 237.
VICKERSTAFF, T., The Principles of Dyeing with Reactive Dyes, *Hexagon Digest*, 1958, **27**, 3.
ZOLLINGER, H., Colouring Matters, *Rev. Text. Prog.*, 1959, **11**, 215.
WEGMANN, J., Some Relations between the Chemical Constitution of Cibacron Dyes and their Dyeing Characteristics, *J.S.D.C.*, 1960, **76**, 205.
RATTEE, I. D., Reactive Dyes for Cellulose, *Endeavour*, 1961, **20**, 154.
ACKERMANN, H. and P. DUSSY, Cellulosereaktive Chlorpyrimidylfarbstoffe—Chemische Reaktionsfähigkeit und Fixiervermögen, *Melliand Textilber.*, 1961, **42**, 1167.
REUBEN, B. J. and D. M. HALL, The Chemistry of the Reactive Dyes and their Application to Textile Materials, *Am. Dyestuff Rep.*, 1962, **51**, 811.
STAMM, O. A., Mechanism of the Reaction of Reactive Dyes with Cellulose and Other Fibres, *J.S.D.C.*, 1964, **80**, 416.
OSTERLOH, F., Einwirkung von Reaktionsfarbstoffen mit der Vinylsulfongruppe auf Wolle, *Melliand Textilber.*, 1960, **41**, 1533.
BAUMGARTE, U., Über die Reaktion von Acrylamidfarbstoffen mit Wolle und Aminosäuren, *Melliand Textilber.*, 1962, **43**, 1297.

Chapter 15

HADDOCK, N. H., Phthalocyanine Colouring Matters—Their Chemistry and Uses, *J.S.D.C.*, 1945, **61**, 68.

HADDOCK, N. H. and R. P. LINSTEAD, Phthalocyanines, p. 617, Vol. 9 of 4th ed., *Thorpe's Dictionary of Applied Chemistry*, 1949, Longmans Green, London.

MOSER, F. H., Phthalocyanine Compounds, p. 488, Vol. 15 of 2nd ed., *Kirk–Othmer Encyclopedia of Chemical Technology*, 1968, Interscience, New York.

GUND, F., New Developments in the Application of Phthalocyanines in Textile Printing, *J.S.D.C.*, 1953, **69**, 671.

GUND, F., New Ideas in the Application of Phthalocyanine Derivatives to Textiles, *J.S.D.C.*, 1960, **76**, 151.

MELTZER, Y. L., *Phthalocyanine Technology, 1970 (Chemical Process Review No. 42)*, 1970, Noyes Data Corp., Park Ridge, N.J.

Chapter 16

EHRICH, F. F., Pigments, Organic, p. 555, Vol. 15 of 2nd ed., *Kirk–Othmer Encyclopedia of Chemical Technology*, 1968, Interscience, New York.

GLOGER, W. A., Pigments, Inorganic, p. 465, Vol. 15 of 2nd ed., *Kirk–Othmer Encyclopedia of Chemical Technology*, 1968, Interscience, New York.

KERR, T. D., and H. K. HOWARD, Pigments and Lakes, p. 623, Vol. 9 of 4th ed., *Thorpe's Dictionary of Applied Chemistry*, 1949, Longmans Green, London.

LABANA, S. S. and L. L. LABANA, Quinacridones, *Chem. Rev.*, 1967, **67**, 1.

VESCE, V. C., Vivid Light-fast Organic Pigments, *Official Digest of Federation of Paint and Varnish Production Clubs*, 1956, **28**, No. 377, Part 2, 1.

MORGANS, W. M., *Outlines of Paint Technology*, 1969, Griffin, London.

PATTERSON, D., ed., *Pigments: An Introduction to their Physical Chemistry*, 1967, Elsevier, Amsterdam.

PRATT, L. S., *The Chemistry and Physics of Organic Pigments*, 1947, John Wiley, New York.

REMINGTON, J. S. and W. FRANCIS, *Pigments, their Manufacture and Use*, 3rd ed., 1954, Leonard Hill, London.

HARRISON, A. W. C. (revised J. S. Remington and W. Francis), *The Manufacture of Lakes and Precipitated Pigments*, 1957, Leonard Hill, London.

Chapter 18

ERMEN, W. F. A., Notes on Fur Dyeing, *J.S.D.C.*, 1921, **37**, 168.

LAWRIE, L. G., Fur Dyeing, *J.S.D.C.*, 1923, **39**, 242.

FORSTER, R. B. and C. SOYKA, Fur Dyes: Their Oxidation and Identification on the Fibre, *J.S.D.C.*, 1931, **47**, 99.

PARKIN, T. R. V., Fur Dyeing, *J.S.D.C. Jubilee Issue*, 1934, 203.

Chapter 19

PRESTON, J. M., *Fibre Science*, 1953, The Textile Institute, Manchester.

TROTMAN, E. R., *Dyeing and Chemical Technology of Textile Fibres*, 4th ed., 1970, Griffin, London.

ZOLLINGER, H., The Dye and the Substrate: The Role of Hydrophobic Bonding in Dyeing Processes, *J.S.D.C.*, 1965, **81**, 345.

Chapter 20

ZWEIDLER, R. and H. HÄUSERMANN, Brighteners, Optical, p. 737, Vol. 3 of 2nd ed., *Kirk–Othmer Encyclopedia of Chemical Technology*, 1963, Interscience, New York.

ZWEIDLER, R., Einführung in die Chemie der optischen Aufheller, *Textilveredlung*, 1969, **4**, 75.

BLUME, W., Weisstönen von Polyacrylonitril-Fasern, *Textilveredlung*, 1969, **4**, 88.

HEFTI, H., Optische Aufheller für Polyesterfaserstoffe, *Textilveredlung*, 1969, **4**, 94.

HEUBERGER, H., Echtheitsprüfung optischer Aufheller, *Textilveredlung*, 1969, **4**, 101.

Chapter 21

CORNWELL-CLYNE, A., *Colour Cinematography*, 3rd ed., 1951, Chapman and Hall, London.

GLAFKIDES, P., *Photographic Chemistry*, 1958, Fountain Press, London.

FRIEDMAN, J. S., *History of Color Photography*, 2nd ed., 1968, Focal Press, London.

MEES, C. E. K. and T. H. JAMES, eds., *The Theory of the Photographic Process*, 1966, Macmillan, New York.

THIRTLE, J. R. and D. M. ZWICK, Color Photography, p. 812, Vol. 5 of 2nd ed., *Kirk–Othmer Encyclopedia of Chemical Technology*, 1964, Interscience, New York.

SCHNEIDER, W., The Agfacolor Process, *FIAT* 976, 1947.

VITTUM, P. W. and A. WEISSBERGER, The Chemistry of Dye-forming Development, *J. Phot. Sci.*, 1954, **2**, 81.

BROOKER, L. G. S. and P. W. VITTUM, A Century of Progress in the Synthesis of Dyes for Photography, *J. Phot. Sci.*, 1957, **5**, 71.

VITTUM, P. W., Chemistry and Color Photography, *J. Soc. Motion Picture Television Engrs*, 1962, **71**, 937.

NYS, J., Die Farbenchemie und die moderne Photographie, *Chimia Supplement*, March, 1968, 115.

Author Index

Authors' names quoted only in the Reference list are indexed with page and reference numbers.

Dye Index

This index includes named commercial dyes, pigments, dye precursors and fluorescent brighteners. Some of the products are no longer in use.

Subject Index